# The Life and Twelve-Note Music
of Nikos Skalkottas

EVA MANTZOURANI
*Canterbury Christ Church University, UK*

ASHGATE

© Eva Mantzourani 2011

All rights reserved. No part of this publication may be reproduced, stored in a retrieval system or transmitted in any form or by any means, electronic, mechanical, photocopying, recording or otherwise without the prior permission of the publisher.

Eva Mantzourani has asserted her right under the Copyright, Designs and Patents Act, 1988, to be identified as the author of this work.

Published by
Ashgate Publishing Limited
Wey Court East
Union Road
Farnham
Surrey, GU9 7PT
England

Ashgate Publishing Company
Suite 420
101 Cherry Street
Burlington
VT 05401-4405
USA

www.ashgate.com

**British Library Cataloguing in Publication Data**
Mantzourani, Eva.
  The life and twelve-note music of Nikos Skalkottas.
  1. Skalkottas, Nikos, 1904–1949 – Criticism and interpretation. 2. Twelve-tone system.
  3. Composers – Greece – Biography.
  I. Title
  780.9'2-dc22

**Library of Congress Cataloging-in-Publication Data**
Mantzourani, Eva.
  The life and twelve-note music of Nikos Skalkottas / Eva Mantzourani.
    p. cm.
  Includes bibliographical references and index.
    ISBN 978-0-7546-5310-3 (hardcover : alk. paper) – ISBN 978-1-4094-3403-0 (ebook)
  1. Skalkottas, Nikos, 1904–1949–Criticism and interpretation. 2. Twelve-tone system. 3. Skalkottas, Nikos, 1904–1949. 4. Composers–Greece–Biography. I. Title. II. Title: Life and 12-note music of Nikos Skalkottas.
  ML410.S596M36 2011
  780.92–dc22
  [B]
                                                                                    2011010444
ISBN 9780754653103 (hbk)
ISBN 9781409434030 (ebk)

Bach musicological font developed by © Yo Tomita

Printed and bound in Great Britain by
TJ International Ltd, Padstow, Cornwall.

*To Stephen Cottrell*

> *As you set out for Ithaca*
> *wish your journey to be a long one,*
> *full of adventures, full of knowledge.*
> *Laistrygonas and Cyclops,*
> *the angry Poseidon – don't be afraid of them,*
> *you will never find them in your way,*
> *as long as you keep your thoughts raised high,*
> *as long as an exquisite excitement*
> *touches your spirit and your body.*
> (Konstantinos Kavafis, *Ithaca*)

# THE LIFE AND TWELVE-NOTE MUSIC
OF NIKOS SKALKOTTAS

Nikos Skalkottas (by permission of the Skalkottas Archive)

# Contents

| | |
|---|---|
| *List of Illustrations* | *ix* |
| *List of Tables* | *xi* |
| *List of Music Examples* | *xv* |
| *List of Conventions* | *xxi* |
| *Acknowledgements* | *xxiii* |
| *List of Abbreviations* | *xxv* |
| Introduction | 1 |

## PART I: A BIOGRAPHICAL STUDY

| | | |
|---|---|---|
| 1 | The Early Years in Greece (1904–1921) | 11 |
| 2 | The Berlin Period | 17 |
| 3 | The Greek Period | 53 |

## PART II: TWELVE-NOTE TECHNIQUE

| | | |
|---|---|---|
| | Introduction to Part II | 81 |
| 4 | The Sets and Set-groups | 87 |
| 5 | Manipulation of the Sets | 99 |
| 6 | Derivation Techniques | 115 |
| 7 | Serial Transformations: Transposition, Retrograde, Inversion | 125 |
| 8 | Set Structure and Phrase Structure | 131 |
| 9 | Set Structure and Large-scale Form | 151 |

## PART III: TWELVE-NOTE COMPOSITIONAL DEVELOPMENT: CASE STUDIES

Introduction to Part III                                                                 179

10   Berlin Works                                                                        181

11   Linear Serialism of the Mid-1930s: 'Strict' Twelve-Note
     Technique                                                                           213

12   Expansion of the Mid-1930s 'Strict' Twelve-Note Technique:
     First Symphonic Suite (1935)                                                        245

13   Towards a Free Dodecaphonic Technique                                               275

14   New Directions in the Last Chamber Works: Tonal Serialism                           319

*Epilogue*                                                                               *337*
*Appendix A: List of Sets*                                                               *343*
*Appendix B: Chronological Worklist*                                                     *379*
*Bibliography*                                                                           *389*
*Index*                                                                                  *405*

# List of Illustrations

| | | |
|---|---|---|
| Frontispiece: Nikos Skalkottas (by permission of the Skalkottas Archive) | | ii |
| 1.1 | A youthful Nikos Skalkottas | 16 |
| 2.1 | Nikos Skalkottas performing in a string trio in Berlin | 23 |
| 2.2 | Nikos Skalkottas with Manolis Benakis (Koblenz, 7 May 1928) | 40 |
| 2.3 | Nikos Skalkottas in Seeham (Austria), 1929 | 42 |
| 3.1 | Nikos Skalkottas (c.1938–40) | 60 |
| 3.2 | Nikos Skalkottas on his return to Greece (undated, but probably 1940s) | 62 |
| 3.3 | Nikos Skalkottas (undated, but probably 1940s) | 75 |
| 3.4 | Nikos Skalkottas's signatures | 77 |

# List of Tables

| | | |
|---|---|---|
| II.1 | First Piano Suite, *Preludio*: Concurrent set presentation | 86 |
| 4.1 | Concertino for two pianos, *Allegro*: Set structure and troping technique in Exposition I | 98 |
| 5.1 | Second Sonatina for violin and piano, *Allegro*: Twelve-note thematic set and its trichordal transformations | 105 |
| 5.2 | First Piano Suite, *Preludio*: Second theme (bars 14–17) – segmental permutation of (S1–S2) – (S3–S4) | 105 |
| 5.3 | Fourth Sonatina for violin and piano, *Adagio*: S2 and S3 – correspondences with *Moderato*'s S2 and S3 | 108 |
| 5.4 | Second String Trio, *Moderato*: Associative relationships between the thematic line and the cadence at bar 12 | 110 |
| 6.1a | Third String Quartet, *Allegro vivace (Rondo)*: Derived sets through source segments | 116 |
| 6.1b | Third Sonatina for violin and piano: *Allegro giusto* – derived set S4; *Andante* – derived set S2a; *Allegro giusto* – S2 | 116 |
| 6.2a | Second Sonatina for violin and piano, *Allegro*: Derivation of S2 | 117 |
| 6.2b | Octet, *Presto*: Derivation of S7 | 117 |
| 6.2c | Third String Quartet, *Allegro moderato*: Derivation of S4 and S7 | 118 |
| 6.2d | First Piano Concerto, *Andante cantabile*: Derivation of S1a and S1b | 118 |
| 6.3 | Octet, *Presto*: Derived sets I, II, III | 119 |
| 8.1 | Second String Trio, *Moderato*: Set topography and phrase structure | 133 |
| 8.2 | Second String Trio, *Andante*: Set topography and phrase structure | 134 |
| 8.3 | Second String Trio, *Presto*: Set topography and phrase structure | 134 |
| 8.4 | *Passacaglia* for piano: Right-hand sets | 140 |
| 8.5 | *Passacaglia* for piano: Six harmonic groups within the theme | 141 |
| 8.6 | Duo for violin and cello, *Andante molto espressivo*: Presentations of motive x (bars 1–11) | 148 |
| 9.1 | First Piano Concerto, *Allegro moderato*: Formal structure and set structure | 154 |

| | | |
|---|---|---|
| 9.2 | Concertino for two pianos, *Allegro*: Formal structure and set structure | 155 |
| 9.3 | Second Sonatina for violin and piano, *Allegro*: Formal structure and set structure | 157 |
| 9.4 | First Piano Suite, *Finale (Presto)*: Formal structure and set-group transpositional and retrograde structure | 158 |
| 9.5 | Second Symphonic Suite: Palindromic structure of the *Ouvertüre Concertante* | 160 |
| 9.6 | First Piano Suite, *Preludio*: Set topography and formal structure | 164 |
| 9.7 | First Piano Suite, *Serenade*: Set topography and formal structure | 165 |
| 9.8 | First Piano Suite, *Menuetto–Trio*: Set topography and formal structure | 166 |
| 9.9 | First Piano Suite, *Finale (Presto)*: Set topography and formal structure | 167 |
| 9.10 | Fourth String Quartet, *Allegro molto vivace*: Set structure and formal structure | 171 |
| 9.11 | Fourth String Quartet: Large-scale formal structure and set structure | 175 |
| 10.1 | *15 Little Variations* for piano: Formal structure | 183 |
| 10.2 | First String Quartet, *Allegro giusto*: Formal structure | 186 |
| 10.3 | First String Quartet, *Allegro (ben ritmato) vivace*: Formal structure | 188 |
| 10.4 | First Piano Concerto, *Allegro moderato*: Set structure and set transformation process | 192 |
| 10.5 | First Piano Concerto, *Andante cantabile*: Formal structure and set structure | 194 |
| 10.6 | First Piano Concerto, *Allegro vivace*: Formal structure and set structure | 198 |
| 10.7 | Octet, *Allegro moderato*: Reading of the formal design as a combination of rondo and ternary forms | 200 |
| 10.8 | Octet, *Allegro moderato*: Reading of the formal design as a sonata form | 203 |
| 10.9 | Octet, *Andante cantabile*: Formal structure, texture and set structure | 204 |
| 10.10 | Octet, *Presto*: Formal structure and set structure | 210 |
| 11.1 | Third String Quartet, *Allegro moderato*: Formal structure and set structure | 214 |
| 11.2 | Third String Quartet, *Andante*: Set topography and phrase structure | 222 |
| 11.3 | Third String Quartet, *Andante*: Tonal cadence (bars 106–9) | 225 |
| 11.4 | Third String Quartet, *Allegro vivace (Rondo)*: Formal structure and set structure | 226 |

| | | |
|---|---|---|
| 11.5 | Third String Quartet, *Allegro vivace (Rondo)*: Set topography and phrase structure | 230 |
| 11.6 | Third Sonatina for violin and piano, *Allegro giusto*: Formal structure and set structure | 234 |
| 11.7 | Fourth Sonatina for violin and piano, *Moderato*: Set topography and formal structure | 239 |
| 11.8 | Fourth Sonatina for violin and piano, *Adagio*: Set topography and formal structure | 242 |
| 11.9 | Fourth Sonatina for violin and piano, *Allegro moderato*: Set topography and formal structure | 244 |
| 12.1 | First Symphonic Suite, *Ouvertüre*: Schematic presentation of formal structure and set structure | 247 |
| 12.2 | First Symphonic Suite, *Ouvertüre*: Formal structure and set structure | 248 |
| 12.3 | First Symphonic Suite, *Thema con Variazioni*: Formal structure and set structure | 253 |
| 12.4 | First Symphonic Suite, *Marsch*: Formal structure and set structure | 256 |
| 12.5 | First Symphonic Suite, *Marsch*: Second theme (bars 16–48) – set presentation and instrumentation | 259 |
| 12.6 | First Symphonic Suite, *Romance*: Sections A and B – set structure and phrase structure | 263 |
| 12.7 | First Symphonic Suite, *Siciliano–Barcarole*: Formal structure and set structure | 266 |
| 12.8 | First Symphonic Suite, *Siciliano–Barcarole*: First theme (bars 1–17) – set structure and phrase structure | 268 |
| 12.9 | First Symphonic Suite, *Rondo–Finale*: Formal structure and set structure | 270 |
| 13.1 | Second Piano Concerto, *Allegro molto vivace*: Formal structure | 276 |
| 13.2 | Second Piano Concerto, *Andantino*: Formal structure | 280 |
| 13.3 | Second Piano Concerto, *Allegro moderato*: Formal structure | 281 |
| 13.4 | Violin Concerto, *Molto appassionato*: Formal structure and set structure | 284 |
| 13.5 | Third Piano Concerto, *Moderato*: Formal structure | 288 |
| 13.6 | Third Piano Concerto, *Andante sostenuto*: Formal structure | 292 |
| 13.7 | Third Piano Concerto, *Allegro giocoso*: Formal structure | 295 |
| 13.8 | Second Symphonic Suite, *Largo Sinfonico*: Formal structure and set structure | 299 |
| 13.9 | Second Symphonic Suite, *Largo Sinfonico*: Variation theme (bars 1–16) – phrase structure and set structure | 303 |
| 13.10 | Overture for large orchestra (*The Return of Ulysses*): Formal structure | 310 |

| | | |
|---|---|---|
| 13.11 | Overture for large orchestra (*The Return of Ulysses*): Main themes | 312 |
| 14.1 | Serenata for cello and piano: Formal structure and set structure | 322 |
| 14.2 | Sonatina for cello and piano, *Allegro moderato*: S1, S2 – pairing of tetrachordal segments | 325 |
| 14.3 | Sonatina for cello and piano, *Allegro moderato*: Formal structure and set structure | 328 |
| 14.4 | *Tender Melody* for cello and piano: Formal structure | 331 |

# List of Music Examples

| | | |
|---|---|---|
| II.1 | First Piano Suite, *Preludio*: Opening gesture (bars 1–6) | 85 |
| 4.1 | Second String Trio, *Moderato*: Opening gesture (bars 1–4) | 87 |
| 4.2 | Second String Trio, *Moderato*: Cadence to transition and opening gesture of second theme (bars 19–24) | 87 |
| 4.3 | First Symphonic Suite, *Thema con Variazioni: Thema* – motivic and harmonic relationships in the opening gesture (bars 1–5) | 88 |
| 4.4 | First Symphonic Suite, *Romance*: S3–S6, textural layout of chordal segments within the phrase structure | 90 |
| 4.5 | First Symphonic Suite, *Rondo–Finale*: Superset (S1–S12) and associative relationships between its constituent sets | 92 |
| 4.6 | Concertino for two pianos, *Allegro*: First theme – opening gesture (bars 1–5) | 95 |
| 4.7 | Concertino for two pianos, *Allegro*: Second theme – opening gesture (bars 16–22) | 96 |
| 5.1 | Octet, *Allegro moderato*: Set S2 – reordering, note repetition and interpolation of segments (bars $7^4$–12) | 102 |
| 5.2 | First Piano Concerto, *Andante cantabile*: Second theme – opening gesture (bars 36–42) | 103 |
| 5.3 | Third String Quartet, *Allegro moderato*: Segment repetition within sets | 104 |
| 5.4 | First Piano Concerto, *Allegro vivace*: Opening gesture (bars 1–5), and interpolation of segments (bars 29–32) | 106 |
| 5.5 | Fourth Sonatina for violin and piano, *Adagio*: Interpolation of segments (bars 31–4) | 107 |
| 5.6 | Fourth Sonatina for violin and piano, *Adagio*: Partitioning of the twelve-note sets and free distribution of the notes in the texture (bars 18–20) | 108 |
| 5.7 | Third String Quartet, *Andante*: Simultaneous presentation of set segments (bars $47^6$–$58^1$) | 110 |
| 5.8 | Concertino for two pianos, *Allegro giusto*: Opening gesture (bars 1–9) – free manipulation of the sets | 111 |
| 5.9 | Violin Concerto, *Allegro vivo vivacissimo*: First theme – opening gesture (bars 1–10) | 112 |

| | | |
|---|---|---|
| 5.10 | First Piano Suite, *Menuetto (Moderato assai)*: Opening gesture (bars 1–10¹) | 113 |
| 6.1 | Second String Trio, *Presto*: Derived sets S4, S5, S6 (bars 89⁶–94) | 119 |
| 6.2 | Third Sonatina for violin and piano, *Allegro giusto*: Derivation of S3 | 120 |
| 6.3 | Third Sonatina for violin and piano, *Andante*: Derivation of S3a, S4a | 121 |
| 6.4 | Second String Trio, *Andante* | 122 |
| | (a) Section A – opening gesture (bars 1–6) | 122 |
| | (b) Section B – opening gesture (bars 20–26) | 122 |
| | (c) Section C – opening gesture (bars 48–52) | 122 |
| 7.1 | Concertino for two pianos, *Andante*: Set structure of the first theme (bars 1–14) | 127 |
| 7.2a | Fourth String Quartet, *Allegro molto vivace*: Use of retrograde (bars 124–5) | 127 |
| 7.2b | Fourth String Quartet, *Scherzo (Presto)*: Use of retrograde (bars 170–72) | 128 |
| 7.3a | Second Symphonic Suite, *Ouvertüre Concertante*: Use of retrograde (bars 20, 27) | 128 |
| 7.3b | Second Symphonic Suite, *Toccata*: Use of retrograde (bars 12, 55, 293) | 129 |
| 7.3c | Second Symphonic Suite, *Largo Sinfonico*: Use of retrograde (bars 89–90) | 130 |
| 8.1 | Second String Trio, *Moderato*: Harmonic progression of the bass line | 138 |
| 8.2 | First Symphonic Suite, *Thema con Variazioni: Thema* – schematic pitch-class and harmonic structure | 139 |
| 8.3 | *Passacaglia* for piano: Harmonic structure of the theme | 140 |
| 8.4 | *Passacaglia* for piano: Harmonic structure of Variations II, V, XI, XX | 143 |
| 8.5 | Third Sonatina for violin and piano, *Allegro giusto* | 144 |
| | (a) Segmental rotation of S1 | 144 |
| | (b) Transition – opening gesture (bars 17–21¹) | 144 |
| 8.6a | Third Sonatina for violin and piano, *Maestoso–Vivace: Maestoso* (bars 1–12) | 145 |
| 8.6b | Third Sonatina for violin and piano, *Maestoso–Vivace*: Derivation of the hexachords set-class 6–5 from S2 | 146 |
| 8.7 | Duo for violin and cello, *Andante molto espressivo*: Opening gesture (bars 1–12) | 147 |
| 9.1 | Second Sonatina for violin and piano, *Allegro*: Harmonic structure of the first theme (bars 1–17) | 156 |
| 9.2 | Second Piano Concerto, *Andantino*: Piano cadenza (bars 120–24) | 159 |
| 9.3 | First Piano Suite, *Serenade*: Opening gesture (bars 1–4) | 163 |

*List of Music Examples*  xvii

| | | |
|---|---|---|
| 9.4a | Fourth String Quartet, *Allegro molto vivace*: First theme – opening gesture (bars 1–7) | 169 |
| 9.4b | Fourth String Quartet, *Allegro molto vivace*: Second theme (bars 65–79) | 170 |
| 9.5 | Fourth String Quartet, *Thema con Variazioni* | 172 |
| | (a) *Thema*: Opening gesture (bars 1–4) | 172 |
| | (b) Var.I and Var.III –opening gestures (bars 23–4 and 85–6) | 172 |
| | (c) Var.V (bars 181–6 and 200–06) | 173 |
| 9.6 | Fourth String Quartet, *Scherzo*: Opening gesture (bars 1–6) | 174 |
| 9.7 | Fourth String Quartet, *Allegro giusto*: Opening gesture (bars 1–6) | 174 |
| 10.1 | *15 Little Variations for piano solo: Thema* | 184 |
| 10.2 | First String Quartet, *Allegro giusto*: Opening gesture (bars 1–5) | 185 |
| 10.3 | First String Quartet, *Andante con variazioni*: Opening gesture (bars 1–6) | 187 |
| 10.4 | First String Quartet, *Allegro (ben ritmato) vivace*: Opening gesture (bars 1–4) | 187 |
| 10.5 | First Piano Concerto, *Allegro moderato*: First subject group – opening gestures of first, second and third themes | 189 |
| 10.6 | First Piano Concerto, *Allegro moderato*: First theme of the second subject group – distribution of the pitch-class trichordal segments in the texture (bars 34–45) | 191 |
| 10.7 | First Piano Concerto, *Andante cantabile*: First theme – opening gesture (bars 1–5) | 195 |
| 10.8 | First Piano Concerto, *Andante cantabile*: Piano entry at bars 54–8 | 196 |
| 10.9 | Octet, *Allegro moderato*: Section A – opening gesture (bars 1–4[1]) | 201 |
| 10.10 | Octet, *Allegro moderato*: Large-scale movement in the bass line | 202 |
| 10.11 | Octet, *Andante cantabile*: Section A – opening gesture (bars 1–4) | 205 |
| 10.12 | Octet, *Andante cantabile*: Harmonic structure of section A | 207 |
| 10.13 | Octet, *Andante cantabile*: Section B – opening gesture (bars 23–4) | 207 |
| 10.14 | *Andante cantabile*: Harmonic structure of section B | 208 |
| 10.15 | Octet, *Presto*: Section A – opening gesture (1–10) | 211 |
| 11.1 | Third String Quartet, *Allegro moderato*: Section A – opening gesture (bars 1–14) | 215 |
| 11.2 | Third String Quartet, *Allegro moderato*: Harmonic structure of the opening gesture | 216 |
| 11.3 | Third String Quartet, *Allegro moderato*: Section B – opening gesture (bars 42–52) | 218 |
| 11.4 | Third String Quartet, *Allegro moderato*: Section B (bars 61–8) | 219 |
| 11.5 | Third String Quartet, *Allegro moderato*: Harmonic structure within sections A and B | 220 |
| 11.6 | Third String Quartet, *Andante*: Opening thematic gesture (bars1–12) | 224 |

| | | |
|---|---|---|
| 11.7 | Third String Quartet, *Allegro vivace (Rondo)*: Opening thematic gesture (bars 1–8) | 229 |
| 11.8 | Third String Quartet, *Allegro vivace (Rondo)*: Thematic gesture (bars 8³–19¹) | 229 |
| 11.9 | Third Sonatina for violin and piano, *Allegro giusto*: First theme (bars 1–12) | 233 |
| 11.10 | Third Sonatina for violin and piano, *Allegro giusto*: Second theme – opening gesture (bars 46²–52) | 235 |
| 11.11 | Third Sonatina for violin and piano, *Allegro giusto*: Final cadence (bars 131–41) | 236 |
| 11.12 | Third Sonatina for violin and piano: Large-scale harmonic and formal structure | 238 |
| 11.13 | Fourth Sonatina for violin and piano, *Moderato*: First theme – opening gesture (bars 1–14) | 241 |
| 12.1 | First Symphonic Suite, *Ouvertüre*: First theme – opening gesture (bars 1–7) | 250 |
| 12.2 | First Symphonic Suite, *Ouvertüre*: Subsection **b** – opening gesture (bars 44–7) | 250 |
| 12.3 | First Symphonic Suite, *Ouvertüre*: Second theme – opening gesture (bars 62–6) | 251 |
| 12.4 | First Symphonic Suite, *Ouvertüre*: Schematic presentation of the harmonic structure | 252 |
| 12.5 | First Symphonic Suite, *Thema con Variazioni: Thema* – opening gesture (bars 1–7) | 254 |
| 12.6 | First Symphonic Suite, *Marsch*: First theme – opening gesture (bars 1–12) | 257 |
| 12.7 | First Symphonic Suite, *Marsch*: Second theme – opening gesture (bars 16–31) | 258 |
| 12.8 | First Symphonic Suite, *Marsch*: Cadential gesture to the Scherzo (bars 71–3) | 260 |
| 12.9 | First Symphonic Suite, *Marsch*: Final cadence (bars 160–65) | 260 |
| 12.10 | First Symphonic Suite, *Romance*: Section A – opening gesture (bars 1–10) | 262 |
| 12.11 | First Symphonic Suite, *Siciliano–Barcarole: Siciliano* – first theme (bars 1–17) | 267 |
| 12.12 | First Symphonic Suite, *Rondo–Finale*: Introduction – opening gesture (bars 1–19¹) | 269 |
| 12.13 | First Symphonic Suite, *Rondo–Finale*: First theme (bars 44–72) | 272 |
| 12.14 | First Symphonic Suite, *Rondo–Finale*: Second theme (bars 112–33) | 273 |
| 13.1 | Second Piano Concerto, *Allegro molto vivace*: First theme – opening gesture (bars 1–9) | 277 |

| | | |
|---|---|---|
| 13.2 | Second Piano Concerto, *Allegro molto vivace*: Second theme – opening gesture (bars 15–19) | 278 |
| 13.3 | Second Piano Concerto, *Allegro molto vivace*: Third theme – opening gesture (bars 41–5) | 278 |
| 13.4 | Violin Concerto, *Molto appassionato*: First subject group (bars 1–5 and 8–13) | 283 |
| 13.5 | Violin Concerto, *Molto appassionato*: Second theme (bars 35–50) | 286 |
| 13.6 | Third Piano Concerto, *Moderato*: First theme – opening gesture (bars 1–3$^2$) | 289 |
| 13.7 | Third Piano Concerto, *Moderato*: Second theme – opening gesture (bars 27–8) | 290 |
| 13.8 | Third Piano Concerto, *Andante sostenuto*: First theme – opening gesture (bars 1–2) | 291 |
| 13.9 | Third Piano Concerto, *Andante sostenuto*: Second theme – opening gesture (bars 7–8) | 291 |
| 13.10 | Third Piano Concerto, *Allegro giocoso*: First theme – opening gesture (bars 1–4) | 293 |
| 13.11 | Third Piano Concerto, *Allegro giocoso*: Second theme – opening gesture (bars 42–6) | 294 |
| 13.12 | Second Symphonic Suite, *Largo Sinfonico*: Variation theme – set structure (bars 1–16) | 302 |
| 13.13 | Second Symphonic Suite, *Largo Sinfonico*: Variation I – opening gesture (bars 17–20) | 304 |
| 13.14 | Second Symphonic Suite, *Largo Sinfonico*: Variation II – opening gesture (bars 28–9) | 304 |
| 13.15 | Second Symphonic Suite, *Largo Sinfonico*: Variation V – opening gesture (bars 40–41) | 305 |
| 13.16 | Second Symphonic Suite, *Largo Sinfonico*: Second theme – variation VIII (bars 75–84) | 306 |
| 13.17 | Second Symphonic Suite, *Largo Sinfonico*: Recapitulation – opening gesture of first theme (bars 180–81) | 307 |
| 13.18 | Second Symphonic Suite, *Largo Sinfonico*: Coda (bars 259–65) | 307 |
| 13.19 | Overture for large orchestra (*The Return of Ulysses*): Introduction – opening gesture (bars 1–5) | 311 |
| 13.20 | Overture for large orchestra (*The Return of Ulysses*): *Haupt-Thema* 1 – opening gesture (bars 46–9) | 314 |
| 13.21 | Overture for large orchestra (*The Return of Ulysses*): *Neben-Thema* 1 – opening gesture (bars 71–4) | 315 |
| 13.22 | Overture for large orchestra (*The Return of Ulysses*): *Haupt-Thema* 2 – opening gesture (bars 163–7) | 315 |
| 13.23 | Overture for large orchestra (*The Return of Ulysses*): Coda – opening gestures of Presto and Prestissimo sections (bars 603–5, 655–7) | 316 |

| | | |
|---|---|---|
| 14.1 | Serenata for cello and piano: Opening thematic gesture (bars 1–8) | 321 |
| 14.2 | Serenata for cello and piano: Rondo section B (bars 9–16) | 321 |
| 14.3 | Sonatina for cello and piano, *Allegro moderato*: First theme (bars 1–15) | 326 |
| 14.4 | Sonatina for cello and piano, *Allegro moderato*: Bridge (bars 16–18) | 327 |
| 14.5 | Sonatina for cello and piano, *Allegro moderato*: Second theme (bars $32^2$–42) | 327 |
| 14.6 | *Tender Melody* for cello and piano: Opening thematic gesture (bars 1–3) | 332 |
| 14.7 | *Tender Melody* for cello and piano: Harmonic progression | 332 |
| 14.8 | *Tender Melody* for cello and piano: Second theme – opening gesture (bars 10–13) | 333 |
| 14.9 | *Tender Melody* for cello and piano: End of retransition and beginning of Recapitulation (bars 36–41) | 334 |
| 14.10 | *Tender Melody* for cello and piano: Coda (bars 48–58) | 335 |

# List of Conventions

Throughout the book I have italicized quotations taken from Skalkottas's letters, analytical notes and other writings. This presentation deliberately distinguishes Skalkottas's own voice from those of others in the text.

The translations of Greek texts are my own. Greek words, particularly in the bibliography, have been transliterated and are followed by their English translation. German translations were undertaken in collaboration with Dr Nina-Maria Wanek (neé Jaklitsch).

For the production of all the annotated musical examples I have worked from Skalkottas's manuscript scores, although, where available, I have also consulted the published scores. I have produced my own reductions from orchestral and large ensemble scores, to illustrate clearly the set analysis of each musical extract. In all examples transposing instruments have been written at sounding pitch.

For the description of twelve-note set properties, chords and chordal successions, I use pitch-class set theory and the terminology provided by it. A set-class is identified only with the number assigned to it by Forte in *The Structure of Atonal Music* (1973), that is, the Forte set name 3–3, 4–10, 6–Z10, and not with its prime form, that is, with the number matching its intervallic content measured in semitones (for example, [014], [0235]).

The integers 1 to 12 are used to indicate the order number of a pitch-class within a set; these are represented as 1 (i.e. order number 1 of a set), 2 (order number 2), and so on.

$T_0$ indicates the prime form of a twelve-note set, but also the original, untransposed pitch level of a harmonic region; $T_7$ indicates the transposition of both a set and a harmonic region at the interval of the fifth, and so on.

For the presentation of pitch levels I have used Helmholtz's notation in which:

$B_1$ indicates the note B two octaves and a semitone below middle C.
C = the C two octaves below the middle C.
c = the C one octave below the middle C.
$c^1$ = middle C.
$c^2$ = the C one octave above the middle C.
$c^3$ = the C two octaves above the middle C, and so on.

# Acknowledgements

My interest in Nikos Skalkottas originated during my undergraduate studies in Greece. An aura of secrecy surrounded Skalkottas, and his music was hardly ever performed (apart from a handful of the ubiquitous *Greek Dances*). I was warned of the difficulty of obtaining information, and problems involving access to the Skalkottas Archive. Provoked by the challenge, and wanting to find out for myself what was really going on in Skalkottas's music, I decided to focus my research on this fascinating composer. And this youthful idealism turned into a life-long journey – challenging, often frustrating, but ultimately vindicating and rewarding; my insertion of lines from Kavafis's poem, *Ithaca*, may be read as some indication of this journey.

In the course of this research several individuals and institutions have supported me, and it is my duty and desire to thank all those who have helped me complete this task. I particularly wish to thank my employer, Canterbury Christ Church University, for generously granting me two periods of research leave, and providing financial support towards the production costs of the book; the Arts and Humanities Research Council of Great Britain (AHRC), for supporting a further period of research leave; Universal Edition (Vienna) for supplying me with scores, and Pamela Miller of Margun Music Inc., who also sent me scores and recordings from the USA.

Therese Muxeneder, archivist at the Arnold Schoenberg Centre (Vienna) has repeatedly provided helpful information on the relation between Skalkottas and Schoenberg. Dr Dietmar Schenk of the Hochschule der Künste and Dr Norbert Kampe of the Stiftung Archive der Akademie der Künste both assisted my research into Skalkottas's studies in Berlin. Dr Judit Alsmeier shared her research on Skalkottas and kindly allowed me access to her music archive. Dr Nina-Maria Wanek (neé Jaklitsch) not only shared her research with me and sent me valuable material, but also helped me with the translation of German texts, for all of which I am particularly thankful.

I am grateful to Michel Bichsel, who facilitated my access to the Skalkottas Archive in Athens; the late John Papaioannou, who provided me with copies of a large number of Skalkottas's manuscripts; Costas Mantzoros, of the Contemporary Music Research Centre (KSYME) and the Skalkottas Archive, who granted the necessary permissions to reproduce photographs and allowed me to use Skalkottas's manuscripts as the basis for my own reductions and analyses. The book has benefited from the copy-editing of Marija Duric-Speare, and the excellent work of Andrew Wyver, who typeset my musical examples – his professionalism and patience with my endless requests are gratefully acknowledged.

I am especially indebted to Nikos Skalkottas Jr, Skalkottas's son, for his interest in my work, his permission to use his father's manuscripts, and his support in helping me to complete the production of the manuscript. His involvement in this project meant a great deal to me.

One of the greatest pleasures during my research was meeting Artemis Lindal, Skalkottas's daughter, and her family in Sweden. Her openness, warmth, hospitality, trust with invaluable and at times confidential information, letters and photographs of Skalkottas, gave a new purpose to my project. I am most grateful to her and her family for the help and information they gave me, and for allowing me to use extracts from Skalkottas's letter to Matla Temko.

Finally, I wish especially to thank my husband and dear friend Stephen Cottrell for his unfailing support and encouragement throughout my research and the writing of this book, for giving enormously of his time and talents, and for his insightful comments and criticisms on various drafts of the manuscript. He has been present at every step of this project, accompanying me on my various research trips, rejoicing at the good times and picking up the pieces at the difficult ones. Without his help and support this work would never have finished, and it is gratefully dedicated to him.

# List of Abbreviations

## Skalkottas's letters

| | |
|---|---|
| LetAsk | to Nelly Askitopoulou. |
| LetGN | to George Nazos. |
| LetKon | to Yiannis Konstantinidis. |
| LetMB | to Manolis Benakis. |
| LetMM | to Melpo Merlier. |
| LetMT | to Matla Temko. |

## Skalkottas Archive, Athens

A/K        Archive Catalogue number of Skalkottas's manuscript scores (for example, A/K1).

## Archival Sources

| | |
|---|---|
| AASCV | Archiv des Arnold Schönberg Center, Vienna (Archive of the Arnold Schoenberg Centre, Vienna). |
| AHMB | Archiv der Hochschule für Musik, Berlin. |
| APrAKB | Archiv der Preussischen Akademie der Kunste, Berlin. |
| ASOR | Athens State Orchestra Records. |
| AthConsDM | *Odeio Athinon: Leptomeris Ekthesis 1914–1921* (*Athens Conservatory: Detailed Minutes 1914–1921*). |

## Greek Periodical Sources

| | |
|---|---|
| *ME* | *Musiki Epitheorisis* [*Music Review*] monthly Greek periodical. |
| *ME1* | *Musiki Epitheorisis*, vol.1 (October 1921). |
| *ME2* | *Musiki Epitheorisis*, vol.2 (November 1921). |
| *ME10* | *Musiki Epitheorisis*, vol.10 (July 1922). |

## Musical Abbreviations

| Abbreviation | Explanation | Abbreviation | Explanation |
|---|---|---|---|
| WW | Wood wind | Tbn | Trombone |
| Fl | Flute | Tba | Tuba |
| Ob | Oboe | Hrp | Harp |
| Cl | Clarinet | Pno | Piano (RH = right hand; LH = left hand) |
| Bcl | Bass clarinet | Str | Strings |
| CA | Cor anglais | Vln 1 | First violin |
| Bsn | Bassoon | Vln 2 | Second violin |
| CBsn | Contra bassoon | Vla | Viola |
| Hn | Horn | Vlc | Cello |
| Tpt | Trumpet | DB | Double bass |
| Orch | Orchestra | timp | Timpani |
| pc(s) | Pitch-class(es) | segm interpol | Segment interpolation |
| hex | Hexachord | var/v | Variation |
| accomp | accompaniment | harmon progr | Harmonic progression |
| subj | Subject | recap | Recapitulation |

# Introduction

'In modern Greece Orpheus tunes his lyre atonally. This scordatura was initiated by Nikos Skalkottas'.[1]

Is Nikos Skalkottas the last great 'undiscovered' composer of the twentieth century? Perhaps. Norman Lebrecht's summary of him as 'a pupil of Schoenberg, who returned to Athens with a gospel no-one wanted to hear, played violin for a pittance and died at 45' (1992, 327) encapsulates the thumbnail image most frequently preserved of this often-marginalized Greek composer. But in the 1920s Skalkottas was a promising young composer in Berlin, and a student of Schoenberg between 1927 and 1932. Although Schoenberg lost contact with Skalkottas after 1933, he continued to remember his student's talent and included him among his most gifted pupils:

> The harshness of my requirements is also the reason why, of the hundreds of my pupils, only a few have become composers: Anton Webern, Alban Berg, Hans Eisler, Karl Rankl, Winfried Zillig, Roberto Gerhard, Nikos Skalkottas, Norbert von Hannenheim, Gerald Strang, Adolf Weiss. (Schoenberg, 1984, 386).

It was only after his return to Greece in 1933 that Skalkottas, shunned by his compatriots and confronted by enmity and harsh criticism, became an anonymous and obscure figure. He was a young, iconoclastic composer, who had found his own musical language at a time when art music in Greece was still trying to find its own identity and largely reflected the conservative and deeply nationalistic ideals of the political and cultural environment. Skalkottas, although absorbing and imaginatively using traditional Greek folk elements in his music, did not try to follow or adapt to the prevailing folkloristic musical aesthetics of his compatriots. Until his death in 1949, he composed his 'serious' dodecaphonic works in complete isolation, thus maintaining his high ideals and developing an idiosyncratic musical language. Consequently, nearly all his works remained unpublished and, apart from some tonal compositions, unperformed during his lifetime.[2]

---

[1] Slonimsky, 1966, 225.

[2] The works that were published during Skalkottas's lifetime include the second movement (*Andantino*) of the First Sonatina for violin and piano, issued in the Greek magazine *Musiki Zoë*; the folk-song arrangement 'The Doe', and the first four of the *Greek Dances* (*Tsamikos*, *Kritikos*, *Epirotikos* and *Peloponnisiakos*), published by the

After Skalkottas's death his family entrusted his manuscripts to three of his acquaintances – Minos Dounias, Nelly Askitopoulou-Evelpidi and John G. Papaioannou. They formed the Society of Skalkottas's Friends, and founded the Skalkottas Archive, which gradually accumulated manuscripts acquired from the composer's two Athenian residences, donated by contemporaries, and bought at auction in Berlin (Bichsel, 2008, 482). Thanks to his old friend Walter Goehr, some of Skalkottas's compositions were published by Universal Edition, and others were published by Margun Music (in the United States) – though several of the latter are just photographic reproductions of the manuscripts. Over the years, however, the Society's endeavours declined and gradually ceased. Today the archive, consisting of a number of filing cabinets containing Skalkottas's manuscripts and some of his writings,[3] is housed in a dark room at the Contemporary Music Research Centre in Athens, and is still largely inaccessible.

John G. Papaioannou,[4] notwithstanding his invaluable efforts to sustain the archive and promote Skalkottas's music abroad at a time when the composer was largely unknown even in his own country, somewhat distorted both Skalkottas's image and his legacy. Papaioannou's relationship with his subject was, in Demertzis's words, that of 'the painter and his model', and the bond between the two was so strong that 'it is difficult to distinguish one from the other' (Demertzis, 2004b, 24). But a painter presents to the world an image of his model that is by definition subjective, and Papaioannou's output arguably reveals more about the artist than the model. Thus, almost exclusively through his efforts, a certain mythology built up around Skalkottas. For 50 years after the composer's death, until his own passing, Papaioannou single-handedly created a one-sided image of the composer through anecdotes, second-hand information and unsubstantiated claims that are at times highly subjective and contradictory, while certain inaccuracies also extend to his analyses of Skalkottas's twelve-note music.

Additionally, the hitherto accepted periodization of Skalkottas's compositional output was established by Papaioannou (1976, 322–3). Based only on his understanding of the changes in the composer's twelve-note technique, and without the support of any musical examples, it is divided into four main periods: the pre-Schoenberg years (1925–27), the first period (1928–38), the middle period (1938–45) and the last period (1946–49). For Papaioannou, Skalkottas's 'first

---

French Institute in Athens in 1948. During the 40 years after Skalkottas's death, there were occasional performances of some of his works both in Greece and in Europe; and since the 1990s, recordings of his music have been more widely available, notably through an initiative by BIS records.

[3] Skalkottas's manuscripts are not well preserved. In the past, some individuals were allowed access to them, with several performing directly from them. This resulted in inevitable damage, as fingerings, bar numbers, conducting marks and occasional 'serial analyses' were written directly onto the manuscripts.

[4] John G. Papaioannou (1915–2000) was a younger contemporary of Skalkottas and one of the main sources of information about the composer's life.

compositional period (1928–38) is characterized by a more transparent, sharp, somewhat disconnected style, pronouncedly Schoenbergian and using exclusively his "strict serial technique"' (*ibid.*, 324); in his archive catalogue he calls this 'strict twelve-note' system 12 or 12A. In relation to the later periods he argues that: 'Every serial work of his middle or last period uses its own serial technique, this technique being a [...] new "system" of twelve-note writing. At the same time, in the last two periods, Skalkottas uses what seems to be a non-serial system, where nothing like a tone-row seems to be present' (325); in the catalogue he calls this system 12B.

Demertzis (1998), following Papaioannou's assertions, and perhaps prompted by Skalkottas's undefined use of the terms 'strict' and 'free' in his writings, identifies three, coexisting 'musical systems' and attempts to provide a theoretical framework for their study; this, however, is vague and difficult to understand. He defines these 'musical systems' as follows: (i) the 'serial dodecaphonism' with 'a predetermined number of series', which starts in 1928–29; (ii) the 'free, post-dodecaphonic system 12B', which 'does not employ predetermined series or other dodecaphonic collections although the rule of octave avoidance is observed', and which is associated with the composition of many short works starting at around 1938; and (iii) the 'non-serial dodecaphonism, or serialism of the non-repeated series', which is based on an 'undetermined number of series, or non-repeated (*free*) series'.[5]

Although it is useful to distinguish Skalkottas's compositional approaches to dodecaphonic composition, the terminology used by these musicologists is problematic and confusing. Furthermore, these categorizations and 'systematizations' make Schoenberg the catalyst for Skalkottas's musical orientation and development, and the yardstick by which his stylistic identity and compositional integrity are judged. They ignore the fact that Skalkottas's formal education in Berlin coincided with the early stages of the development of the twelve-note method – at a time when Schoenberg did not teach twelve-note composition, and before the formulation of its theoretical framework and nomenclature. These precepts perpetuate a mythology that seeks to validate Skalkottas the student through his association with the master. Yet Skalkottas, throughout his 25-year compositional career, was in Schoenberg's orbit for only six months each year from 1927 to 1930 and then only sporadically in 1931 and 1932. Although he benefited from Schoenberg's tuition, Skalkottas had already

---

[5] Demertzis defines this last 'system' as follows: 'In non-serial dodecaphonism the series are not repeated because **the absolute avoidance of the repetition of the series leads to the maximum [use] of the available material** [...] **Skalkottas, therefore, with this system, proposes the absolute non-repetition of the series** [instead of] **Schoenberg's absolute repetition**' [original emphasis] (1998, 96 and 355). Garmon Roberts, without further explanation, repeats Papaioannou's and Demertzis's typology of 'three serial systems [...] 12, 12b, and 12r', the latter being 'a serial system [...] invented by Skalkottas, combining Systems 12 and 12b' (1996, 8).

developed the basic principles of his compositional technique before attending Schoenberg's masterclasses. This technique, although inevitably refined and developed over the years, remained conceptually essentially unchanged both during and after his studies with Schoenberg; his adoption and adaptation of the twelve-note method reveal an integrity and unity of conception that remained constant throughout his career.

Furthermore, Skalkottas's compositional style and harmonic language did not evolve progressively through 'phases' from tonality to atonality to dodecaphonism, but instead they are characterized by both stylistic division and stylistic synthesis – tonality and dodecaphonism. Throughout his compositional career following his early experimental works, he often composed twelve-note, atonal and tonal works simultaneously, or alternately, and occasionally he used different harmonic idioms in the same piece. For example, in Berlin in 1931–32 he composed the dodecaphonic Octet and First Piano Concerto alongside his first tonal *Greek Dance, Peloponnisiakos*; and in the mid-1930s he perfected his 'strict' dodecaphonic technique while completing his *36 Greek Dances*.

Overall, Skalkottas's compositional output is characterized by:[6]

1. Serial twelve-note works composed on a small, predetermined number of sets, using his 'strict', idiosyncratic version of the twelve-note method, as found in the chamber music pieces of the mid-1930s.
2. Free twelve-note works of various types, composed on an unspecified number of sets and other pitch-class collections, and based on progressively freer approaches to his twelve-note method, as, for example, in the concertos of the late 1930s and the large-scale orchestral works of the early and mid-1940s.
3. Twelve-note works that are based on or incorporate folk-like elements; for example, *Eight Variations on a Greek Folk Theme* for piano, violin and cello (1938).
4. Atonal works including some dodecaphonic elements, particularly for piano and chamber groups, for example, *32 Piano Pieces* and *Ten Sketches* for strings (both 1940).
5. Tonal works based exclusively on or directly inspired by folk music, such as the *36 Greek Dances* (1931–36).
6. Tonal works of various types, which may feature: modal, folk-style material, for example, *Classical Symphony* (1947) and Sinfonietta in B♭ (1948); popular elements, particularly in works written for ballet, such as the *Little Dance Suite (Four Images)* for orchestra (1948) and *The Sea* (1949); and/or limited or no folkloristic elements, for example Concertino in C major for piano and orchestra (1948–9).

---

[6] For an expanded discussion of these general categories of Skalkottas's stylistic output, see Zervos (2008, 60–66).

Consequently, I suggest that it would be more appropriate to divide Skalkottas's compositional and stylistic development into two major periods: the Berlin period (1921–33) and the Greek period (1933–49). My criteria for such classification include not only the development of Skalkottas's compositional style but also his personal circumstances and the prevailing social and political conditions of the time. The Berlin period can be subdivided as follows:

1. The first student years (1921–24), featuring juvenile attempts at tonal, Greek-influenced composition.
2. The middle, reorientation years (1924–27), with the surviving works of 1925–27 establishing some of his trademark compositional processes.
3. The Schoenberg years (1927 to first half of 1931), during which Skalkottas gradually developed his idiosyncratic twelve-note technique.
4. The last Berlin years (second half of 1931 to 1933). Few manuscripts survive from these years, but Skalkottas probably completed his experimental dodecaphonic First Piano Concerto, and he composed a handful of tonal pieces inspired by the Greek folk tradition.

The Greek period, based more on personal and socio-political factors, rather than exclusively on stylistic compositional evolution, can be subdivided as follows:

1. The first Athenian years (1933–39), featuring the simultaneous development of a large number of stylistically diverse works. The compositions of 1935–39, including pieces for small chamber ensembles, large orchestra and concertos, exhibit developmental stages of both his 'strict serial' and 'free' dodecaphonic compositional techniques. From 1938, parallel with his dodecaphonic works, Skalkottas also composed a series of small-scale atonal pieces (exhibiting similar principles of construction to those of his dodecaphonic compositions), and works that combine tonal, atonal and/or folk material with versions of his dodecaphonism, as for example in the *Eight Variations on a Greek Folk Theme* and the dance suite *The Maiden and Death*.
2. The middle Athenian years (1940–45); 1940 marked Greece's entry into the Second World War, inevitably resulting in a new political and social situation. It also marked a compositional phase in Skalkottas's development in which the piano predominates, either solo or as part of chamber groups. Concurrently, in the large-scale orchestral works, such as the Second Symphonic Suite and *The Return of Ulysses*, Skalkottas reached the limits of development in his free dodecaphonic technique.
3. The final Athenian years (1946–49), which are characterized largely by the composition of a substantial number of tonal works (and this is the only period in which Skalkottas wrote such a quantity of tonal music), including ballets, symphonic works, and reorchestrations and transcriptions of pieces composed at earlier times. During the last year of his life, there is a sudden

reorientation towards another version of his dodecaphonic technique, which might be described as 'tonal serialism'.

Skalkottas has written a prodigious number of large-scale works of enormous complexity.[7] He never abandoned tonal composition, and his *Greek Dances* provided him with some success and posthumous recognition; however, the vast majority of his surviving works use predominantly twelve-note idioms. It is perhaps because of the wide range of his output that the subtleties and evolutionary stages of his dodecaphonic technique have not been widely understood.[8] Yet, deciphering and mapping out the technical parameters of this technique is necessary for any informed future discussion of Skalkottas's dodecaphonic music and its historical and theoretical contextualization.

The present study represents a first step towards this task. It is not intended to be a 'Life and Works', but rather a critical biography of the composer and an introduction to and thorough investigation of his twelve-note compositional processes, since these characterize the majority of his output. A discussion of Skalkottas's use of tonality and his engagement with the Greek folk-song tradition, while interesting and relevant, is beyond the scope of this monograph and must wait for a separate publication.

The book is divided into three parts, each self-standing, although taking Parts II and III together would provide a comprehensive study of the compositional technique used in a particular work. Part I comprises a substantial biographical study, and reappraises the man behind the mythology. Based as much as possible on documentary evidence, it attempts to elucidate his personality, relationships, the motives behind particular decisions he made concerning his career, and the marginalization he experienced on his return to his homeland. These aspects are seen within the political, social and musical contexts in which he worked. Part II presents the structural and technical features of Skalkottas's twelve-note compositional technique, outlining the different types of sets, their properties

---

[7] Skalkottas is predominantly a composer of instrumental music. There are nine (out of eleven) surviving concertos (four for piano, one for two pianos, one for violin, one for violin and viola, one for two violins, and one for double bass), a large corpus of piano solo and chamber music works (including four string quartets, works for violin and piano and cello and piano), and several monumental orchestral compositions.

[8] Thus far there are three comprehensive studies that explore Skalkottas's dodecaphonic compositional technique, albeit each having its limitations. Mantzourani (1999) has offered an introduction to certain compositional elements of Skalkottas's dodecaphonic music and a detailed analysis of several works. Alsmeier (2001, in German) has given an overview of certain compositional aspects of Skalkottas's twelve-note music. Garmon Roberts (2002) has provided analyses of Skalkottas's last three works for cello and piano. Other notable studies on Skalkottas include those by Demertzis (1998, in Greek), Mantzourani (2001, 2004a, 2004b, 2006, 2008), Thornley (2002a, 2002b, 2008a, 2008b), Jaklitsch (2003, in German), Vrondos (ed., 2008 in Greek and English). Various other books and articles, most of them by Papaioannou, are included in the Bibliography.

and their manipulation. It also provides an overview of Skalkottas's approach to musical forms, particularly sonata form, and his methods for achieving integration and functional differentiation at both small- and large-scale levels. Part III contextualizes the development of Skalkottas's twelve-note technique. It comprises a series of analyses of several individual movements and/or entire pieces, which are presented largely in chronological order, thus providing a diachronic framework within which Skalkottas's dodecaphonic compositional development might be more effectively viewed. Each case study considers the twelve-note set, thematic and phrase structures, and the large-scale form of the piece, and where appropriate, the texture, rhythm, orchestration and the incorporation of tonal elements within the twelve-note texture, so that 'the essence of the music will be grasped by way of technical facts' (Adorno, 1994, 39). Each analysis is accompanied by a tabulated formal outline of the movement.

Throughout Parts II and III, I use the terms 'twelve-note music' and 'dodecaphony' interchangeably, understanding them both to 'refer to music based on 12-note sets', notwithstanding that they 'might more logically refer to any post-triadic music in which there is constant circulation of all pitch classes' (Perle and Lansky, 1980/19, 287). In all his writings, Skalkottas consistently used the German term *Reihe*, and the Greek σειρά [*seirá*], to refer to his diverse source pitch-class material. Although the term *Reihe* may mean 'row', 'series' or 'set', in this study I use the term 'twelve-note set' to describe Skalkottas's twelve-note material, and 'set' for any other clearly established pitch-class collection, since the regularity in the pitch-class order (characteristic of the 'row' and 'series', but not of the 'set') is not always observed in his pieces. Skalkottas used more than one set in each section of a piece; such sets are identified as S1, S2, S3, and so on. Occasionally the untransposed inverted and retrograde forms of the sets are used, and these are indicated by IS1, RS2. The transpositional and inversional relationships of sets, segments, and harmonic areas at a level other than the original ($T_0$) are indicated by $T_n$, $I_n$ and $R_n$ for transpositions, inversions and retrogrades respectively; for example, $S1(T_n)$, $I_nS2$, $R_nS3$. For the description of sets, set segments, chords and chord progressions, I use the terminology provided by set theory. In order to keep the presentation of the analyses clear and comprehensible, throughout the book a set-class is identified only with the number assigned to it by Forte (1973); that is, the Forte set name 3–3, 4–10, 6–Z10.[9] For most of the pieces I have provided set analyses, indicating the precise deployment of the various sets within clearly defined formal sections. Where possible this is in conjunction with the textural layout and instrumentation, so that the complicated set structure of each piece is clearly mapped out and easy to follow. A list of the various sets of the pieces discussed in this study is given in Appendix I, and the annotated musical examples should be read in conjunction with it.

---

[9] Sets are said to be 'equivalent' when their normal order forms reduce to the same prime form by transposition, or inversion followed by transposition.

My intention has always been to discover and understand what lies beneath the surface, instead of problematizing music theory for its own sake. I wished to write about Skalkottas the man, as he emerged from those primary sources I have unearthed; to introduce his idiosyncratic twelve-note compositional techniques; and to explain the evolution of these techniques through systematic and in-depth analyses of both the pitch-class set and formal structures of a large number of works. Despite the musical attitudes he adopted and adapted from Schoenberg, Skalkottas is a significant figure in his own right, a fully independent composer with a distinct artistic personality whose compositional approach can now be seen to have added another dimension to the early development of the twelve-note method – a method thus far associated with the aesthetic of Schoenberg and his better-known students – and who deserves a more significant position within the Western art music canon than that which he has previously held.

It has always been my desire to share my discoveries with the wider academic community, and I hope that my research will provide the springboard for further systematic studies of Nikos Skalkottas and his music.

# PART I
# A Biographical Study

*Laistrygones, Cyclops,*
*the wild Poseidon – you will not encounter them,*
*unless you bring them along inside your soul,*
*unless your soul sets them up in front of you.*
(Konstantinos Kavafis, *Ithaca*)

# Chapter 1
# The Early Years in Greece (1904–1921)

'But are there such violinists in Greece?'[1]

Following its recognition as an independent state in 1830 (after almost 400 years of Ottoman rule), mainland Greece was greatly afflicted by political upheavals and wars in the Balkans and Asia Minor in the late nineteenth and early twentieth centuries. This political, economic and social instability, whereby the last traces of feudalism gave way to an emerging middle class, coupled with religious objections towards musical innovation, delayed the growth of an indigenous art music. The Ionian islands, which were never under Ottoman domination, had enjoyed a rich musical life as a result of cultural contact with Italy.[2] In contrast, Western art music was almost unknown in continental Greece until the end of Ottoman rule. Only in 1834 was modern European music, played by a Bavarian band imported by Greece's first king, Otto, heard in the new capital, Athens (Leotsakos, 2001, 350). Gradually, mainland Greeks became exposed to polyphonically structured Western art music through such touring bands, which gave concerts in Athens and other provincial towns, performing popular dances and excerpts from symphonies by Beethoven, Mozart and Rossini. Their impact was profound, and by the end of the nineteenth century most Greek cities had their own municipal band, called *Philharmonikes*, which in turn generated a need for music schools (Trotter, 1995, 20). Nevertheless, art music in mainland Greece appealed only to a small minority of the upper classes, and serious students tended to emigrate to Italy, France or Germany for their musical training.

Formal musical education essentially started with the foundation in 1871 of the Athens Conservatory. Following two decades of parochial activities, it was subsequently reorganized and developed under the directorship of George Nazos (1891–1924), whose appointment led to an abrupt 'Germanization' of the curriculum, with the championing of French and particularly German music at

---

[1] As Willy Hess, the violin teacher at the Berlin Hochschule für Musik, reportedly exclaimed when he first heard the 17-year-old Skalkottas playing the violin in 1921 (Fimios, *ME10*, 14).

[2] The Ionian islands were occupied successively by the Venetians (1386–1797), the French (1797–1814) and the English (1814–64). The composers from these islands, who belonged to the so-called Ionian (Eptanisian) Music School, wrote operas to Italian librettos usually performed by Italian companies, and became the first Greek composers following the integration of the Ionian islands with mainland Greece in 1864.

the expense of Italian-trained Greek composers. It also led to the establishment of the Athens Conservatory Orchestra in 1903 (Romanou, 2006, 131–2).[3] The orchestra's concerts, under the leadership of Filoktitis Economidis, José de Bustinduy and Jean Boutnikoff, exposed the Athenian public to western European orchestral and chamber music. Although the conservatory was organized according to European educational principles, teaching standards remained low, and the orchestra's performances steadily deteriorated because of insufficient rehearsal time and the musicians' parallel engagements in opera and operetta companies (Leotsakos, 2001, 350). The conservatory primarily served the musical education of the upper social classes, thus preserving privileges and social inequalities (Motsenigos, 1958, 328), and this exclusivity and social snobbery on the part of the musical establishment would later encumber Skalkottas's career to a significant degree.

The turn of the twentieth century saw an intellectual revival, resulting from a cultural and artistic influx from western Europe and the rise of national self-awareness, and for the first time mainland Greek composers consciously attempted to establish a national musical identity. They were influenced by the linguistic struggle between advocates of the artificial *katharevousa* as the language of the upper classes, and supporters of the vernacular, *demotiki*, spoken by the majority of the population. This struggle was played out in the works of poets such as Kostis Palamas (1859–1943) and Angelos Sikelianos (1884–1951), who fought for the dominance of the *demotiki* Greek language, and by literary journals such as *Noumas* and *Eleftheri Skini*. Similarly, the composer George Lambelet (1875–1945), in his essay 'The National Music' (1901, 82–90), invited Greek composers to be inspired by folk-song, while Manolis Kalomiris (1883–1962), the doyen of the Greek National School and a powerful cultural figure,[4] set the 'manifesto' of this school in the programme notes of his first concert in Greece (11 June 1908), arguing that 'Greek music should find its roots, on the one hand, in the music of our pure folk songs, and, on the other, it [should be] decorated with all the technical means which we were granted through the constant work of the musically developed nations, and first of all the Germans, French, Russians and Norwegians' (Anoyianakis, 1960, 581). Kalomiris and his followers were vehemently opposed both to earlier Greek – mostly Ionian – composers, whom they rejected as 'Italianate', and to modernist composers such as Dimitris Mitropoulos (1896–1960) and Skalkottas.

It was at this time of considerable political, social and cultural change that Nikos Skalkottas was born into a working-class family, albeit a musical one. His great-grandfather Alekos was a folk singer and violinist from the Cycladian island of Tinos. His grandfather Nikos, while still young, moved to the island of Evia, where he married local girl Marigo Konstandara (Papaioannou, 1997, vol. 1, 54).

---

[3] The Athens Conservatory Orchestra became the Athens State Orchestra in 1942. See also, Drosinis (1938, 223–35).

[4] For a comprehensive survey of the Greek National School and its composers, see Leotsakos (1980, 673; and 2001, 351) and Fragou–Psychopaidi (1990, 46–69).

Skalkottas's father, Alexandros (Alekos), was a self-taught flautist who played in the Philharmonic Band in Chalkis, the capital of Evia, together with his (also self-taught) violinist older brother Kostas, who became director of the city's Philharmonic Society in 1896 (Jaklitsch, 2003, 136–7). Skalkottas's mother, Ioanna Papaioannou,[5] was a domestic servant for a rich household in Chalkis, where his father also worked as a gardener. It was in a room in this wealthy employer's house that Nikos was born on 21 March 1904.[6] His sister Angeliki (Kiki) was a later addition to the family. At the age of five, Nikos started violin lessons with his father, who allegedly helped him to build a small violin (Papaioannou, 1997, vol. 1, 62); he later continued lessons with his uncle Kostas. A few years later the family moved to Athens, although the reasons for this and the exact date are uncertain.[7] They appear to have had a difficult time in the capital, and until 1916 they frequently moved house around Metaxourgio, a lower working-class neighbourhood of Athens.[8]

On 17 September 1914, aged 10, Skalkottas passed the Athens Conservatory violin entrance exam, and he was immediately placed in the intermediary grade in the violin class of the German professor Tony Schultze.[9] Coming from a rather poor family of unschooled musicians, he received free tuition, with funds from the Averof scholarship.[10] His progress was impressive, and only two years later (1916–17)

---

[5] There is no familial connection between Skalkottas's mother and his biographer John Papaioannou.

[6] This information was provided by Dalmati (1988–89, 208). In 1904, Greece still followed the old Julian calendar, according to which Skalkottas was born on 8 March. The modern, Gregorian calendar was adopted in January 1923.

[7] While in Chalkis, the young family lived in the house of Skalkottas's grandmother at 9 Androutsou Street, in the 'Kastro' neighbourhood, behind the church of St Paraskevi (Papaioannou, 1997, vol. 1, 56). Papaioannou suggests that the family moved in 1909, because of Nikos's exceptional musical ability, so that he might receive a better musical education (1969a, 122; 1976, 321; 1997, vol. 1, 62). Octave Merlier in the preface of the edition by the French Institute of Skalkottas's *Four Greek Dances* (1948) puts the move in 1906, which Thornley adopts (2001, 464). The reason for the move is more likely to be the result of political intrigue within the musical scene in Chalkis and the capital's potentially better work prospects (Jaklitsch, 2003, 137).

[8] Eventually the family settled at 43 Thermopilon Street, where they stayed until 1938; finally, they moved to 34a Iasonos Street, in the centre of the city, where Skalkottas lived until 1946, then he moved to his wife's house at 41 Kallidromiou Street, where he stayed until his death (Papaioannou, 1955, 4-5; 1997, vol. 1, 62).

[9] Skalkottas also studied the compulsory subjects of music history, theory and harmony, choral singing, sight-reading, chamber music, ensemble studies and piano. His studies at the Athens Conservatory are chronicled in *Athens Conservatory: Detailed Minutes 1914–1921* (Ωδείο Αθηνών: Λεπτομερής Έκθεσις), kept in the conservatory's archive; henceforth (AthConsDM); (AthConsDM, 1914–15, 29); (AthConsDM, 1912–17, 7).

[10] This could be inferred from his letter to George Nazos from Berlin (1 March 1923) (Kostios, 2008, 222). Georgios Averof's endowment was intended for the postgraduate studies of the best students, and for prizes to composers of works with a 'Greek content'.

he advanced to the higher grade in his violin class and for the first time played second violin in the Conservatory Orchestra, appearing at several evening student concerts; in 1918–19 he moved to the viola section, and finally to the back desks of the first violins.[11] His talents were soon to be further rewarded in a series of competition prizes,[12] culminating in his final year with a monthly stipend of 500 drachmas from the Averof fund, given on account of his 'unusual musical talent', and in addition to his free tuition (AthConsDM, 1919–20, 12). Skalkottas graduated in 1920, aged 16, having excelled in his final exams and being awarded the gold medal of Andreas and Iphigenia Syngros (AthConsDM, 1919–20, 128). His graduation performance took place at the Athens Municipal Theatre on 25 May 1920 during the Athens Conservatory Orchestra's last concert of the season; the programme included, among other pieces, the first movement of Beethoven's Violin Concerto. On the recommendation of Nazos, Skalkottas was awarded a further Averof scholarship for the continuation of his studies abroad, which started the following academic year, 1921–22, after the return from Berlin of another scholarship holder, Antigoni Kopsida (AthConsDM, 1920–21, 10; *ME10*, 14).

Although the conservatory's funding was vitally important to Skalkottas because of his family's difficult financial situation, it had the unintended consequence of emphasizing his disadvantaged position and his low social status, thus reinforcing difference and discrimination within the institution. It also influenced his future within Athenian professional musical circles, by assigning him to the class of 'the proletariat of the music players' (Kostios, 2008, 198).[13] Despite Skalkottas's apparently exceptional talent, he was not promoted as a soloist (as other students were, for example Mitropoulos);[14] he appears not to have been given recital opportunities in the conservatory's concert hall in Athens, unlike other privileged but less talented graduates,[15] and was only allowed to play in the back desks of the orchestra. The adolescent Skalkottas felt excluded and disappointed, and he revealed his dissatisfaction with the musical establishment in a letter to the

---

Nazos, however, was using some of these funds to finance the studies of a substantial number of amateurs (mainly lady pianists), professional musicians in financial difficulties, and others who were in some way socially disadvantaged (*ibid.*, 196).

[11]   Skalkottas performed in concerts on 22 April 1917 (AthConsDM, 1916–17, 67); on 13 January and 10 February 1918; on 6 March 1919 and 10 April 1919; and on 2 March 1920 (AthConsDM, 1918–19 and 1919–20). The printed list of players for 1919–20 of the Athens Conservatory Orchestra indicates their sitting position rather than being given in alphabetical order, 'Nikos Skalkottas' appears as the penultimate name in the column of the first violins (14 out of 15) (Kostios, 2008, 200).

[12]   For details of Skalkottas's competition prizes, see Jaklitsch (2003, 139–40).

[13]   For a discussion of the social outlook of the Athens Conservatory and Skalkottas's treatment compared to that of the upper-class Mitropoulos, see Kostios (2008, 194–225).

[14]   For biographical details on Mitropoulos, see Kostios (1985) and Trotter (1995).

[15]   The only exception was a 'memorable' concert Skalkottas gave at the 'Roi Georges' theatre in Thessaloniki on 27 September 1920 (Kalogeropoulos, 1998, 413).

composer and conservatory professor Marios Varvoglis, whom he considered *'the most musical, the most unspoiled person inside this villainous clique of our conservatory'*;[16] perhaps unwisely he advised Varvoglis that he should *'for God's sake be aware of the others'*. On his graduation, and in order to survive financially, the talented but poor Skalkottas had little choice but to earn a living playing the violin at a variety of functions and in cafés in Athens and elsewhere,[17] where he received enthusiastic reviews for his performances (*ME2*, 14). Painfully aware of his situation, in a letter to the correspondent of *Musiki Epitheorisis* he wrote: '*I don't want to be and I'm not one of those people who feel flattered in the courtyard of the cafenion* [coffee house] *and are getting lost in the idea of wealth.*' (*ME10*, 14). His perennially difficult financial circumstances would become a lifelong concern and a recurring theme in all his correspondence.

---

[16] The extract from the letter to Varvoglis, dated Volos, 5 June 1921, is cited in Romanou (1985, 21–2). Varvoglis, an important member of the establishment and the Greek National School of composers, never helped Skalkottas, not even when he later returned a broken man from Berlin. However, he posthumously dedicated a string quartet to him, 'Tribute to Nikos Skalkottas', which remained unfinished (Symeonidou, 1995, 62–5).

[17] Photographic and other documentary evidence prove such activities, for example newspaper articles (*Tachydromos*, dated 21 July 1921), concert reviews (*Musiki Epitheorisis*), and letters to Varvoglis and to his conservatory friend Nelly Askitopoulou.

Illustration 1.1   A youthful Nikos Skalkottas

# Chapter 2
# The Berlin Period

*God save me from any disappointment!*[1]

**The Years 1921–1927: Early Studies**

In October 1921, Skalkottas travelled to Berlin to further his musical education. In the early 1920s Greece was in political turmoil, and within a year of his departure this resulted in devastating political and financial chaos and the influx of 1.5 million refugees into the country from Asia Minor, profoundly changing its sociocultural balance.[2] In contrast, Berlin at this time was the cultural and spiritual centre not only of the Weimar Republic but also of Europe. Skalkottas would stay there for the next 12 years, living through the depression and economic chaos that followed the hyperinflation of 1922–23, the economic prosperity and stabilization during the Republic's middle years (1924–29), and the rapid decay (1929–33) after the collapse of the American stock exchange in 1929, the last ultimately resulting in political and economic unrest, mass unemployment and the rise of National Socialism. But in the early 1920s, Berlin enjoyed a rich, stimulating and varied musical life.[3] The 17-year-old Skalkottas found a world of arts and music of which he could barely have dreamed in the culturally provincial Athens. Berlin had three permanent opera houses – Athens had none. Celebrated conductors, such as Furtwängler, Walter, Klemperer and Kleiber worked in the city. Several of the most prominent composers of the age also worked and taught there, including Busoni, Schoenberg, Schreker and Hindemith; Kurt Weill, Hans Eisler and Paul Dessau sought their own successes in the capital. Berlin had become not only the centre of music but more importantly the centre for new music, and young composers had many opportunities to hear their works performed. There were also new and unfamiliar popular music styles that he experienced, such as jazz.

Skalkottas settled in the Lankwitz neighbourhood of Berlin and registered at the Hochschule für Musik, in Willy Hess's violin class, for three years until

---

[1] LetAsk, Berlin 16 June 1925.

[2] For details about the sociopolitical changes in Greece during the 1920s, see Campbell and Sherrard (1968, 123–38); Tsoucalas (1981, 24–6); and Mazower (1991, 63–5).

[3] For a discussion of the changes in Weimar culture and musical life, see Gay (1981) and Hinton (1989). For details about the musical life in Berlin, see Gerhard (1975) and Taylor (1977).

30 September 1924.[4] Hess was immediately impressed by his Greek student and wrote in the admission report: 'Good, musical, technically very good, admission doubtless' (AHMB–1, 634). The writer of an article in the Greek periodical *Musiki Epitheorisis*, recycling information perhaps given to him by Mr Koutsimanis (a Greek student at the Hochschule), portrayed Skalkottas's first contact with Hess as follows: 'Mr. Hess immediately said that Skalkottas had an extraordinary talent in his left hand; its technique was brilliant […] he still lacked musical feeling but in two years he would be able to give concerts in Berlin, because he had never seen another person so naturally made for the violin. What startled Mr. Hess […] was Skalkottas's musical ear.' (Fimios, *ME10*, 14). Skalkottas's progress was apparently impressive and his technique and expression improved dramatically under Hess's instruction (*ibid.*, 15). His close friend at the time, the composer Yiannis Konstantinidis, even in old age, could still remember how impressed he was with Skalkottas's playing, commenting on his sight-reading ability, his exactitude in pitching, the quality of his sound, lack of vibrato, amazing rhythm and 'the way he knew how to interpret every composition and composer of every era' (Sakalieros, 2005, 19).[5] There is some confusion about Skalkottas's compositional activities at this time, and it is often asserted that he also studied composition with Robert Kahn and Paul Juon.[6] Kahn and Juon both taught composition at the Hochschule and both were head of a chamber music class. However, Skalkottas only attended Kahn's chamber music and counterpoint classes (AHMB–2, 40–48),[7] although it remains possible that he may have shown him some of his early attempts at composition.

The first two years in Berlin, financed by the Averof scholarship, appear to have been untroubled. In 1923, however, Skalkottas had the first in a series of financial problems, and in the following few years he experienced several hardships and disappointments. The scholarship money, seriously eroded by German inflation and by the gradual devaluation of the drachma during 1922, became enough to support only his living costs, and he found it difficult to pay his Hochschule fees,

---

[4] Because Skalkottas missed the entrance exam on 1 October, he had private lessons with Hess until 1 April 1922, when he passed the official entrance exam to the Hochschule (AHMB–1, 634).

[5] Apart from his violin lessons, Skalkottas also had to take piano lessons, music theory and music history, instrumental and ensemble studies (Jaklitsch, 2003, 174), and from 1922 to 1924 he participated in several student concerts, both as a member of a chamber group and as a soloist in orchestral performances (AHMB–2, 36, 46, 48, 50).

[6] Papaioannou (1976, 321), (1997, vol. 1, 68), and in all his Greek articles. In such writings Papaioannou mistakenly refers to Robert Kahn as Paul Kahn. This mistake, probably emanating from the biographical note written by Octave Merlier in the preface to Skalkottas's *Four Greek Dances* published by the French Institute in 1948, is repeated in most of Skalkottas's biographical studies. See for example, Thornley (1980, 361, and 2001, 464); Demertzis (1991, 26, and 1998, 375); and Symeonidou (1995, 379).

[7] In a letter to George Nazos, Skalkottas confirmed: '*I also progress at the Kontra Punkt, which I do with professor Kahn.*' (LetGN, Berlin 1 March 1923).

which were double those paid by German nationals. His written request to the board of directors for a reduction in fees was refused (Jaklitsch, 2003, 178). In March 1923 he wrote to Nazos, describing rather tragically his difficult situation and pleading for an increase to his scholarship:

> *My respected Director, [...] in Germany chauvinism has grown with increased intensity [...] Non-Germans are not permitted to work [...] my* [violin] *professor is very pleased with me. [...] I am sure that at this critical moment of my life you will prove again to be my good protector as you have always been and act promptly so that I come out of the Tragic situation I am in [...] I never forget the sacred purpose of my stay here and I hope one day I will prove worthy of your expectations and of the kindness you have always showed me.* (LetGN, Berlin, 1 March 1923)

Skalkottas succeeded in getting an extension to his scholarship beyond the end of the academic year 1922–23.[8] But his financial problems were now coupled with health concerns, a pattern that would recur throughout his life. He appears to have developed tendonitis, and in June 1923, in a letter to Hess, he expressed his distress and regret at not being able to attend lessons during the summer semester, because of the worsening pain in his hand.[9] Struggling with these financial and health difficulties he eventually resolved to give up his violin studies and turn to composition.

Because of the lack of documentary evidence, there is confusion about the exact dates and nature of Skalkottas's studies during this transitional period. Papaioannou put forward a neat but rather subjective and often contradictory account of Skalkottas's compositional activities,[10] and given these contradictions

---

[8] He was awarded a generously increased grant of 13,200 drachma for 1923–24, but the following year's grant was only 3000 drachma (AthConsDM, 1920–21, 10; 1921–22, 18; 1922–23, 13; 1923–24, 14). Papaioannou erroneously claims that the scholarship ended in the summer of 1922 (1997, vol. 1, 66).

[9] In this letter, dated 13 June 1923, Skalkottas wrote: '*I go repeatedly to the doctor, but he always says: tendonitis. He has forbidden me to practise for two months, and if it gets no better I must let him operate. You can imagine, professor, how distressed I am and how sorry that I must again stop my studies. I must stop for two months so it doesn't get any worse.*' (AHMB 3, 159 61).

[10] According to Papaioannou (1997, vol. 1, 66–81), Skalkottas 'ended brilliantly' his violin studies with Hess in the Hochschule in 'May–June 1923' (69). After some thought during the summer, and 'prompted by his friend Yiannis Konstantinidis', he started composition lessons with Kurt Weill 'probably at the beginning of the autumn (September, October?) of 1923' (69), or 'from the end of 1923 until the summer of 1925' (71), or 'from the beginning of '24 until mid-'25' (90), or 'for a short period in 1931' (1976, 321). Weill, 'after the end of his studies with him in 'May 1925' (1997, vol. 1, 70), 'sent Skalkottas to Philipp Jarnach', with whom he studied 'from September 1925 until the summer of 1927' (71–2, 80–81). Thus Skalkottas's pre-Schoenberg life in Berlin has been neatly compartmentalized into successive academic years with the requisite summer break, notwithstanding the nature

and some factual errors contained in his account, some re-evaluation is in order. Skalkottas's friend and colleague Konstantinidis recalled that when he first met him in 1923 Skalkottas had already started losing interest in the violin and was studying the piano instead, because it was through playing this instrument that he would be able to learn a significant amount of music. Yet Skalkottas's last concert appearance representing Hess's class was on 4 June 1924 (AHMB–2, 50), and in September that year he left the Hochschule without taking his final violin diploma exam. We can only speculate on the reasons for such a decision. Possibly he gave up practising the violin to the level required due to tendonitis and/or his pressing financial problems; or perhaps he wasn't allowed to take the exam because he did not finish the compulsory theoretical course in counterpoint, since '*in order to be allowed to take the diploma exams one must have done the entire Kontra Punkt*' (LetGN, Berlin, 1 March 1923).

Some time in the mid-1920s Skalkottas had lessons with Kurt Weill. Weill, in the early 1920s, had complemented his own studies with Busoni at the Akademie der Künste with counterpoint lessons from Philipp Jarnach; from 1923 until 1926 he supplemented his income by teaching privately.[11] In 1926 Skalkottas studied orchestration and perhaps composition with Weill, although it is possible that he started his lessons some time earlier. According to Konstantinidis's much later reminiscences, 'following the trend of the times', the two friends 'decided simultaneously [...] to go to Kurt Weill', which Konstantinidis did at the beginning of 1926 (Sakalieros, 2005, 24). But they were both 'a little disappointed' with Weill's instructions, as 'he had nothing to teach us – on the contrary he seemed to admire us [...] He was giving us piano pieces to orchestrate and they were always empty. He didn't correct them' (24–5).[12] Skalkottas wrote to his close friend Nelly Askitopoulou asking her to help him with a funding application to the University

---

of the composer's private studies. Papaioannou's different accounts of Skalkottas's studies with Weill have been variously used by other authors. For example, Demertzis adopts the first dates (1998, 282), while Orga (1969, 36) prefers the year 1931. Dounias affirms that 'parallel with his commitments in the Hochschule he studied composition first with Kurt Weill and later with Paul Jarnach [sic]' (1963, 65). Thornley in his 1980 *New Grove* article claims that 'he also took some lessons with Weill (1928–29)' (1980, 361), while in his 2001 revised version mentions that 'he took orchestration lessons from Weill in 1926' (2001, 464).

[11] For a discussion of Weill's activities during this time, see Farneth (1986, 346), Taylor (1991, 49–50) and Mercado (1987, 56–8).

[12] In a handwritten letter from Berlin, dated 3 June 1926, Weill confirmed that Konstantinidis 'studied composition with me for the past six months' (Sakalieros, 2005, 24–5). In 1927 Skalkottas helped Konstantinidis with the orchestration of his operetta *Das Lieberbazillus*, which was performed under the pseudonym 'Costa Dorres' on 10, 11, 15 March and 9 April 1927 at the Stadttheater Stralsund (*ibid.*, 27). Despite his own financial problems, in 1929 Skalkottas also sent Konstantinidis 100 DM in order to help him financially and facilitate the latter's trip to Greece. The accompanying letter, offering practical advice about this trip and written in German (17 August 1929), is the last documented communication between the two friends (*ibid.*, 30–31).

of Athens, reminding her to mention that '*I study composition with Jarnach and Weill*' and confirming that he had already sent her a reference from the latter in support of his application.[13] Skalkottas had private composition lessons with Jarnach from 1925 to 1927,[14] but it is not clear if these were academic or calendar years. In November 1925 he wrote to Nelly, '*This year – with luck – I will finish composition (I still miss Instrumentation and a little Fugue) with my teacher Jarnach*' (LetAsk, 11 November 1925), and nine months later he was still on the same subject, '*I will finish my studies this year (Fugue and Instrumentation)*' (LetAsk, 18 August 1926). From the surviving fragments of Skalkottas's own writings and Konstantinidis's reminiscences it is tempting to infer that Skalkottas did not finish '*the entire Kontra Punkt*' at the Hochschule, but had counterpoint (including fugue) and composition lessons with Jarnach, and studied orchestration with Weill. But the exact dates and nature of Skalkottas's lessons with both Weill and Jarnach remain at present conjectural.

During these formative years Skalkottas composed a number of works, most of which are now lost but mentioned in his correspondence. Konstantinidis indicated that Skalkottas played his first works to him: some Greek songs based on the folksong collection of Nikos Politis and piano pieces in the style of Milhaud, Poulenc and Stravinsky (Sakalieros, 2005, 19–21). Other works, mentioned in Skalkottas's correspondence with Nelly Askitopoulou but now lost include a Sonatina for piano (1925), which he sent to Mitropoulos, an orchestration of Veracini's Violin Sonata in A major, a suite for violin and piano, a string quartet and a string trio (1926);[15] the last two he hoped would be performed '*in Berlin and in other German cities*' (LetAsk, 18 August 1926), although it is not clear if these performances in fact took place. Apart from the orchestration of Mitropoulos's *Cretan Feast*,[16] the surviving works of this period are mainly for piano, and include the juvenile, simple, tonal *Greek Suite* for piano solo (inscribed 'Berlin' – probably 1924), and two suites for two pianos, one of which is dedicated to Mitropoulos.[17] Other surviving

---

[13] Although the letter is undated, judging by its context and its relation to a previous letter dated 18 August 1926, it is likely that it was written some time in September 1926.

[14] In the programme of a concert by Schoenberg's masterclass students on 19 June 1929 at the Prussian Academy of Arts, next to Skalkottas's name there is the inscription '1925 27 student of Ph. Jarnack [*sic*]' (AASCV, 57/8).

[15] In the Archive Catalogue (compiled by Papaioannou) the date of composition for both this String Quartet (A/K31a) and the String Trio (A/K40b) is given as 1923–24 (Papaioannou, 1969a, 149–50). However, Skalkottas mentioned composing these pieces in his 1926 correspondence with Nelly Askitopoulou.

[16] Mitropoulos composed the *Cretan Feast* for piano in 1919. Although there is no date for the orchestration, Demertzis speculates that 'most likely' Skalkottas orchestrated it some time during 1922–24, when both composers lived in Berlin, and revised it in 1933–37, when both lived in Athens (1998, 9, 72, 73).

[17] In 1936 Skalkottas composed another piano suite, which he entitled First Suite for piano solo (thereafter, First Piano Suite). It is thus likely that he did not consider these early

compositions include the Sonata for solo violin (1925), dedicated to his friend Nelly, and the Sonatina for piano solo (6 March 1927); the *15 Little Variations* for piano dates from 24–26 July 1927, and is dedicated to the pianist Spyros Farandatos, at one time Skalkottas's room-mate in Berlin (Demertzis, 1991, 79).

**Life in Berlin: Personality and Relationships**

*My isolation is immense!*[18]

Forty years after their first meeting the Greek musicologist Minos Dounias remembered the young Skalkottas of the first Berlin period:

> He was a good-hearted, carefree child, who loved passionately life and sweets […] His deep gaze, however, revealed the power of a born artist. I never heard him boasting. From strangers I found out that he played the violin excellently. His teacher at Berlin's Hochschule, Willy Hess, often spoke with admiration about the excellent 'Athenian violinist' […] Despite his success, Skalkottas always remained affable, an enemy of ostentation and vanity, the way we knew him all his life. (Dounias, 1963, 64–5)

In his early years in Berlin, Skalkottas immersed himself in Lankwitz's Greek community of musicians and artists. Acquaintances included Anthonis Skokos, Katina Paraskeva (later to marry Skokos), Spyros Farandatos, Polyxeni Rousopoulou-Mathéy, Katina Paxinou, Margarita Perra, Titos Xirelis, George Likoudis, the composers Antiochos Evangelatos and Yiannis Konstantinidis, and the composer–conductor Dimitris Mitropoulos. Skalkottas often played second violin in a string quartet led by Likoudis, with Dounias playing the viola (Kostios, 1999, 146). His relationships with Mitropoulos and his violinist friend Nelly Askitopoulou are particularly revealing and worthy of further consideration.

Mitropoulos arrived in Berlin in 1921 after a year's study in Brussels, supported by both the Averof and Emanuel Benakis scholarships. He studied informally with Busoni, and from 1922 to 1924 he was assistant director at the opera 'Unter den Linden', returning to Greece in 1924.[19] Skalkottas knew Mitropoulos from the Athens Conservatory, and his admiration for his older compatriot is evident from his correspondence with Nelly.[20] He considered Mitropoulos to be '*a great musician*

---

youthful attempts at composition as sufficiently important to be catalogued.

[18] LetAsk, 25 August 1925.

[19] For further information about Mitropoulos's activities in Berlin, see Kostios (1985, 30–31) and Trotter (1995, 33–5).

[20] In his biography of Mitropoulos, Trotter, misinformed about Skalkottas's time in Berlin, writes that Skalkottas 'went to Berlin in 1924 [*sic*] to study with Weill, Schoenberg and Philipp Jarnach. He and Mitropoulos just missed each other in Berlin, and Skalkottas

Illustration 2.1    Nikos Skalkottas performing in a string trio in Berlin

*for Greece and the first great figure that has emerged to this day!*' (LetAsk, 25 August 1925), '*a wonderful person and possibly more simple in his manners than I am*' (12 September 1925), '*modest more than any other Greek musician and* [...] *the only great figure of Greece!*' (9 January 1926). Skalkottas's decision to turn to composition, as well as his fascination with contemporary music, might possibly have been influenced by his association with Mitropoulos. As already noted, Skalkottas orchestrated Mitropoulos's *Cretan Feast*; he also dedicated to him the Suite for two pianos (A/K79z), and in 1936 one of the two manuscripts of his *36 Greek Dances* (the dedication reads: '*To our great Greek musician with great friendship and gratitude.*

confessed somewhat enigmatically to a mutual friend – pianist John Papaioannou – that "it was probably just as well the meeting hadn't come off"' (Trotter, 1995, 74). He reproduces Papaioannou's allegation that Skalkottas was prejudiced against Mitropoulos, but he doubts that this was because of the latter's homosexuality, due to 'the ambivalence of Skalkottas's own sexual preferences' (*ibid.*). These remarks about Skalkottas's sexuality and his apparent prejudice against Mitropoulos are highly questionable and not substantiated elsewhere. On the contrary, in one of his letters to Nelly, Skalkottas, showing rather more open-mindedness, expressed once again his admiration for Mitropoulos: '*Is it about moral degradation, or the collapse of his health? If it is the first I'm not interested, because this belongs to his private life and sure enough it is proof of Athenian stupidity.* [...] *But if it is the second then it is the misfortune or tragedy of wretched Greece*' (LetAsk, 15 December 1925).

*N. Skalkottas*'). They continued to correspond after Mitropoulos's return to Greece, and initially the older composer was supportive of Skalkottas and his early compositions – or so Skalkottas believed.[21] He had sent Mitropoulos three of his compositions, hoping that he would play his Sonatina for piano in one of his recitals, and that Nelly would play in the same concert his Sonata for solo violin. The pieces were not played, and even though Skalkottas was disappointed with Mitropoulos, he still looked up to him and eagerly sought '*the impressions of the great one of Greece*' in relation to his Sonata for solo violin (LetAsk, 8 November 1925). Their paths would cross later in life, but Mitropoulos's attitude towards Skalkottas and his music would be ambivalent, if not discouraging, and he would not meaningfully support him in the future. Even later, after Mitropoulos had left Greece, in 1947, despite expressing interest in receiving some of Skalkottas's scores, and notwithstanding the efforts of his friend Katy Katsoyani to persuade him to conduct some of Skalkottas's dodecaphonic works, he did not promote the latter's 'serious' music, performing instead only a handful of the *Greek Dances*.[22] Mitropoulos's justification was: 'If Skalkottas's music has any value, there will be no need for fights either this year or next year or in ten years from today. Every good music that has vital elements will be presented in time, and this is particularly right for this type of music, which, in some ways, is ahead of its time.' (Kostios, 1985, 295–6).

At the end of May 1925 Skalkottas travelled to Brussels to visit Nelly, who was studying the violin there. On his return to Berlin he entered into an intense period of correspondence with her,[23] which lasted until the beginning of 1926 and then diminished. For a while he was uncharacteristically open and clearly emotionally attached to her.[24] Indeed, the very personal nature of his writing suggests that for some time he might have been in love with her,[25] and his euphoric emotional state resulted in a rush of creativity. Within a few weeks, or perhaps just days, in the

---

[21] Skalkottas had sent Mitropoulos his Suite for piano, which '*he must have liked very much* [as] *he has lately written to me a very enthusiastic letter about me*' (LetAsk, 25 August 1925). He was also planning to meet him '*in a place close to Germany* [and] *stay with him for a few days*' (*ibid.*), but the meeting did not take place.

[22] Mitropoulos's reluctance to promote Skalkottas's dodecaphonic music can be seen in his correspondence with Katy Katsoyani (Kostios, 1985, 294–7).

[23] In his letters to Nelly (most dating from 1925) Skalkottas capitalizes, perhaps for emphasis, the first letter of the words 'You', 'Life', 'Music', 'Silence' and 'Tragic'.

[24] '*By writing to You I can relieve all my sorrows of this cursed Life, and if I didn't know that a letter was waiting for me with a good word, full of sympathy, this summer of my Life would be awful as well*' (LetAsk, 16 June 1925). And elsewhere, '*You know how much strength your letters give to me*' (LetAsk, 1 October 1925) […] *My dear, I'm again with you* […] *I breathe again and I relax by writing to you. Soul-saving and breathing again. Thus my beloved, I forget, even for a short time, the miseries and ugliness of my Life around me. And I become reborn*' (LetAsk, 24 June 1925).

[25] '*My wonderful person my letter is only for You! Your letter: the sky with the stars would say a romantic poet. The sky with the stars I say, me, the poor antiromantic devil. I have it opposite, facing me. I had it yesterday throughout the evening with me in the upper*

summer of 1925, he composed the (now lost) Suite for violin and piano,[26] and his Sonata for solo violin, which he dedicated to her. The intensity of his feelings could not be more clearly expressed:

> *Today [...] I expressed myself by playing Bach at the piano. I took the violin in my hands with love. And I took with yearning the pencil in my hand to compose. To add something in the sonata that belongs to You. [...] And another piece of news: I started for you a new Suite for violin and piano. I'm drowned with zest and inclination to finish as soon as possible something for You. Something coming out of my blood, a child of mine.* (LetAsk, 24 June 1925)

He used such emotionally charged writing in his letters of June and July 1925; thereafter, although he still depended on their communication and her support, he became more detached, self-absorbed and avoided such personal references, clarifying that, '*from Nelly I seek more a friendship than, for God's sake, a girlfriend*' (LetAsk 25 August 1925).[27]

Apart from revealing something of the nature of Skalkottas's relationship with Nelly, these letters allow a glimpse into his life at that time in Berlin, and give a fascinating insight into his studies, decisions, character and outlook. He expresses his hopes, plans and disappointments, family pressures, his sense of betrayal by his fellow human beings, his frustration, depression and, above all, his feelings of loneliness and immense isolation. His letters also reveal a fragile emotional and mental state, with frequent mood swings oscillating between short bursts of optimism and high spirits accompanied by concentrated compositional activity, and long depressive periods with dark moods and inactivity. His sensitivity to rejection – real or imaginary – and the unstable shifts from intense attachment and admiration to anger and depression, might suggest a person suffering from bipolar personality disorder. Yet, with only a handful of his own letters surviving, and some often questionable second-hand information about his life, it cannot be unequivocally asserted that he was battling with a mental illness, particularly one that would not have been diagnosed as such at the time.

---

*left pocket of my jacket. I read it and re-read it, I caressed it* [...] [you] *wonderful person*' (LetAsk, Berlin-Lankwitz, 16 June 1925).

[26] In the Archive Catalogue this Suite for violin and piano is included in the unspecified 'conjectural' works, A/K100 (Papaioannou, 1969a, 155).

[27] In October 1933 in Athens Nelly married Chrissos Evelpidis, a professor of agricultural economy and later a government finance minister. After his return to Greece, around 1934–35, Skalkottas and Nelly played together in a string quartet and he also accompanied her on the piano. She was very supportive of his artistic goals and helped him materially during the German Occupation and the difficult years of famine. According to Skalkottas's sister, Nelly was 'the only person [to whom] the composer really opened his soul.' (Thornley, 2004, 18).

With no further financial help from the Averof scholarship, from 1924 (and perhaps even earlier) until 1928 Skalkottas supported himself with occasional work as a musician in cafés and silent film cinemas, playing the violin, piano or directing small ensembles, jobs that he disliked and found difficult to keep. In his letters he makes frequent references to these unsatisfactory jobs: '*I just came home. It's past 1:30 at night.* […] *I play in a Hotel from 8–12:30* […] *the payment is wonderful, but the job is horrific.* […] *And every night seems to be like a year, and this year* [is] *endless and Skalkottas* [is] *in the middle looking ridiculous either conducting or playing; I have nothing else but to send this nightmare away, to send my thoughts full of hope to the future and to endure it*' (LetAsk, 23 June 1925). And a month later: '*My new job lasts long: 5–7 and 8:30–12* […] *Thank God however that this time I don't have to play the first violin. I work in a Russian café with a Russian colleague of mine*' (LetAsk, 17(18) July 1925). As an immigrant, Skalkottas's difficult financial situation was often made worse: '*I had a good engagement in a cinema. In my absence my enemies found the opportunity, in a disgraceful manner, to pass over one disagreeable foreigner for another foreigner, but* [one] *less troublesome and of course cheaper.* […] *My enemies are good and honourable because they give me the opportunity to study people and Life: this is the thousandth time this has happened to me*' (LetAsk, 16 June 1925).

His financial problems, the hard work at the cafés and cinemas, and his disappointments had taken their toll on his well-being, and so his health deteriorated. He described his suffering and the raw emotions and thoughts that overwhelmed him: '*I'm in my house alone. In my room. It's the time that I tear papers up, I throw books, I beat chairs, I mumble, chew, swear, smoke, it's the time that a weariness and a laziness overcome me*' (LetAsk, 13 June 1925). And four days later: '*At this moment I have the need to start screaming and wake up the entire house. I vented* [my frustration] *on* [writing] *letters. Me, the knight of the dark fog and of the grand ideas I can't but have frequent similar moments during which I feel that my entire nervous system and my head are being fractured!* […] *God is great, but he has forsaken me tonight*' (LetAsk, 17 June 1925). And elsewhere: '*This time I'm hard pressed by my health; it would be impossible to continue this Life, the café, etc.; of course, I would fast become bed-ridden.* […] *I was really in a desperate situation and many times in the evenings, apart from the fact that I couldn't close my eyes, I waited from moment to moment for my heart to break*' (LetAsk, 25August 1925).

He was morbidly aware of his capacity for self-destruction: '*I never got wasted and never despaired.* […] [I wish that] *God just takes away any disappointment! I am capable, with a scratched wound, to demolish every foundation that I have so quietly, patiently and solidly built!*' (LetAsk, 16 June 1925). A few months later, depressed by Mitropoulos's refusal to play his pieces in Athens, he even found it difficult '*to make the long trip from the table to the paper!*' and he was '*seized with nervousness*', which resulted in lethargy: '*until the last few weeks I did nothing and I didn't work*' (LetAsk, 8 November 1925). By the summer of 1926 he had even stopped writing so frequently to Nelly, blaming his health problems for his silence: '*I haven't written to you for so long because I was terribly nervous and distressed* [...] *I have this illness twice a year – but particularly my jobs – musical of course – don't happen as I would have liked them to* [...] *I must rest, and for a while get rid of my worries and nerves. Yes, Nelly I'm still desperately nervous* [...] *My nerves and my worries are culpable for my Silence*' (LetAsk, 20 July 1926).

Loneliness and solitude are ever-present themes in all his letters. He was self-absorbed, often longing for his '*absolute loneliness and incomparable company*' (LetAsk, 21 June 1925). His introversion was compounded by his social ineptitude and deep mistrust of people: '*The dogs and the bitches that surround me, I know well, they show me love and interest only out of habit or to take advantage*' (LetAsk, 6 July 1925). He had suffered this misanthropic disposition from a young age:[28]

> *The voluntary subjection to disappointments sometimes is not only the distillation of misfortunes but also something that tortures my brain and thought. I had this in my young age, I have it now in my present age: the almost romantic* [...] *mistrust of other people! I don't know why. I was always a friend of good books and of loneliness* [...]. *Until recently, with the events of the last year above all, with the unfulfilled big promises of acquaintances whom I considered close friends, and* [for] *many other reasons, I had formed a solid and positive opinion that only Nikos is my most sincere friend!* (LetAsk, 17(18) July 1925)

Jarnach described Skalkottas as distant and reticent, someone who did not participate in jokes and games with the other students (Papaioannou, 1997, vol. 1, 75). Yet Papaioannou claims that when Skalkottas was with his Greek friends he was more open, free, extrovert and 'naughty' (*ibid.*). Skalkottas's own descriptions of his character and lifestyle in his letters, and his general demeanour in later life, however, cast some doubt on these assertions. He wrote:

> *I'm thinking: how do other young people live in my years!* [...] *apart from my work, from my Music, my books and my thoughts, nothing else interests me. I never envied the friendships, the strolls. All those which can be labelled with one word: time-wasting! I don't know what current pushed me so far away from the world and what urge still pushes me, but anyway the way I have built my Life, a change is impossible!* (LetAsk, 23 June 1925)

His abrupt mood swings are reflected in his unstable plans and decisions, and his shifting attitudes towards people. Although in the summer of 1925 Mitropoulos apparently offered him a conducting job at the Athens Conservatory, '*to replace

---

[28] From a young age Skalkottas appears to have had difficulty relating to other people. In his letter to Marios Varvoglis from Volos (5 June 1921), the 17-year-old Skalkottas gave a beautiful and romantic description of the town, but he found '*the people of Volos* [to be] *wild animals, the society vile* [with] *regressive ideas. Even the cultured and educated are* [...] *repulsive in their conversation*' (Romanou, 1985, 21–2).

*next year – 1926 – Boutnikoff* (LetAsk, 25 July 1925), he turned it down. Yet only a month later his situation was so bad, both financially and in terms of his deteriorating health, that he considered the possibility of returning to Greece in exchange for some financial support from a Greek benefactor, Mrs Negroponte (LetAsk, 25 August 1925), which never materialized. Skalkottas's misanthropic tendencies clearly made it difficult for him to judge the true intentions of other people, particularly in relation to financial or other support he expected from them. Time and again such hopes were crushed, and this pushed him into further disillusionment and depression. Following this latest disappointment, and despite his dire financial circumstances, a few months later he was again demonstrating his resolve not to return to Greece. Now he thought of finishing his composition studies with Jarnach, studying '*more seriously Bach's oeuvre for solo violin*', preparing for orchestral work by learning '*a repertoire that is enough for a concertino violin* [leader or concertmaster] *in a symphony orchestra*', studying literature at the university and emigrating to America.[29] Naturally, he proceeded with none of these plans. A month later his mood changed completely, and he appeared to be '*content and very happy*', while his '*new mania is to learn the Japanese language*' (LetAsk, 15 December 1925). Even his disappointment with Mitropoulos appears to have been forgotten, as he continued to express his deep admiration for him (LetAsk, 9 January 1926).

The one unchanging aspect of Skalkottas's character, and one that continually provided him with a focus for his inner reality, was his conviction that he wanted to compose. His decision to dedicate himself to composition and to stay in Germany to accomplish his dream was difficult and challenging: he had to overcome both pressure from his family, who wanted him to return to Greece, and mounting personal, financial and health problems. His letters to Nelly graphically portray not only the young student's determination to become a composer but also, in stark contrast to the rest of his thoughts and emotions, the lucid and logical arguments he used to support his choice. He observed that:

> *I came here and I found a flood of letters, from my home, from friends, the majority of my acquaintances. It seems they all have one topic to communicate to me: my return to Greece. My sister calls me different names, the most important 'destroyer of my home'* […] [another acquaintance] *says that I made my mother 'a martyr of life' and that 'first comes the family, the mother, and then the studies'* […] *My friends have all thrown a hook with poisoned bait* […] *They heap upon me social positions, material rewards, laurels, wreaths, glories, and the like!* (LetAsk, 16 June 1925)

---

[29] '*In spite of my efforts, my return to my country is impossible to happen under such circumstances and particularly after all the <u>interest</u> of all my acquaintances.* […] *Recently the idea of America revolves over in my head again and today, I don't know how, as I found myself so disappointed I wrote to a doctor friend to ask him if there was a way to take me with him.* […] *I begged him if he could do something for me for the coming summer or autumn. Let's see.*' [original emphasis] (LetAsk, 11 November 1925).

But he ignored them, justifying his decision:

> *And now listen to how I am thinking! For my home: I love it, but the path I have chosen comes first!* [...] *For my mother: she has my entire thought, and my life is hers. What does it matter if I am not with her? For my friends who love and care for me: I thank them* [...] *but my return to Greece now would be worse than death. I need to learn so much more.* [16 June 1925]. [...] *How many times have I tried to explain to them that it would be wrong for me to return to Greece yet. That for me, a development is possible only in the musical centres of Europe.* (LetAsk, 23 June 1925)

Skalkottas often vehemently expressed his antipathy towards the musical life of Athens; he considered that returning '*to Greece so soon to ply the profession of musician in that cemetery*' would be not only '*so annoying, so unbearable, so ludicrous*' but also '*signing at just 21 years of age my spiritual and musical death warrant*' (LetAsk, 6 July 1925). When Nelly returned to Greece, following the end of her studies in Brussels, he pleaded with her not to stay there: '*It would be a shame if you as well go downhill, which, besides, is natural for all of those who return to the homeland.* [...] *for God's sake, don't stay there, at any cost you must leave*' (LetAsk, 8 November 1925). A year later, despite his difficult financial position, he had not changed his mind, and for the second time he turned down a job offer in Greece:

> *I had a proposition from the Athens Conservatory to become a teacher of the first class and 'concertino' in the orchestra with 5000 drachma salary – that's a joke for me the way I am today. Not from an egoistic viewpoint, or a financial one, but from a clearly artistic one: today I am not a violinist* [...] *Composition is my only occupation and my only ideal, because* [...] *I find that in composition I have more flair and a brighter future.* [...] [And he concluded prophetically] *My homecoming to my country would bring me disappointments – bitterness – laziness, apathy, while the break in my studies, now that I'm so busy, would be very destructive.* (LetAsk, 18 August 1926)

When he left the Hochschule without taking his violin diploma exam, and turned to composition, he kept his decision secret from both his family and the Athens Conservatory, as there was a clear expectation that he would return to contribute to Greece's musical life as a violinist or teacher. Now, sure about his future, he was at last ready to announce his decision. In the process he was openly dismissive about his compatriot Greek composers:

> *I would be grateful if you could say this to all my compatriots: Composition is my only ideal and my only ideal is to learn to compose. Not like the Greek composers, for God's sake, who are all good amateurs! Yes, Nelly, believe me*

*that I don't say this last thing out of wickedness, or egoism – it is the bitter truth!*
(LetAsk, 18 August 1926)

Having rejected the security that a job in Greece would have afforded, Skalkottas turned to certain influential Greeks requesting further financial support to continue his studies in Germany. He hoped that his friends and family would try to get him a scholarship from the University of Athens, '*so that I can live and work* [i.e. compose], *without having this sentence of* [working at] *the cinema*' (LetAsk, 18 August 1926). But his application was unsuccessful, and he would get no other financial assistance until 1928, when the Greek benefactor Manolis Benakis offered to help.

Skalkottas often portrays himself as a driven artist, ready to sacrifice the social and financial rewards offered by a return home in favour of his studies and the intellectual riches of culturally progressive Germany. The only purpose in his life was composition, and he considered all else to be a waste of time (LetAsk, 23 June 1925). His preoccupation with composing was inextricably connected with his personality. As he confessed to Nelly, '*It is true Nelly, you can't imagine that I have lost any connection with the external world. Always immersed in my study, in Music I forget even my most dear persons*' (LetAsk, 30 March 1927). Such self-absorption inevitably made him difficult to get to know, yet he did form at least one close relationship in Germany during this period – with a woman who would become the mother of two of his children.

Matla (Mathilde) Temko, a half-Jewish Latvian violinist, was one of Skalkottas's fellow students in the Hochschule.[30] The notion that she was his 'first wife', as mentioned in most biographies, derives from Papaioannou's version of events.[31]

---

[30] Matla Temko studied the violin from April 1921 to March 1922 and again from October 1922 to March 1925. Her first teacher was Gustav Havemann, and in 1924 she had lessons with Willy Hess. The interruption in the flow of correspondence between Skalkottas and Nelly suggests that his relationship with Matla might have started some time during winter 1925–26, after his intense emotional attachment to Nelly of the previous summer. Also, in June 1925 his denial and protestations against his family's accusations that the reason he stayed in Berlin instead of returning to Greece was because he was married ('*they are fantasizing - i.e. that I am married and other such nonsense*' (LetAsk, 24 June 1925)) could be considered genuine.

[31] Papaioannou's version of Skalkottas's relationship with Matla is questionable, if not extensively fabricated, given the contradictions it includes and the facts that emerge from Skalkottas's correspondence. In his various writings Papaioannou refers to Matla as his 'first wife' (1997, vol. 1, 10), whereas later in the same document he contradicts himself, claiming that 'they were living together as husband and wife (although this relationship was never made official)' (74). He states that 'their relationship, which was particularly warm and mutual, lasted until the beginning of 1931' (1997, vol. 2, 96), but elsewhere he suggests that during the years 1927–31 Skalkottas's 'relationship with Temko was continuing normally and warmly, although he himself, as we know, was considerably "naughty" in his conquests' (1997, vol. 1, 86). These statements are doubtful considering Skalkottas's character and lifestyle as revealed in his letters and confirmed by other sources. Gradenwitz,

They shared a house in Lankwitz, probably from 1925 to 1928;[32] they never married, although Skalkottas was considering it just before he left Germany (Thornley, 2002a, 209); and their relationship, according to Matla's family, was quite open and unconventional, reflecting the liberal attitudes of bohemian Berlin at the time. It was also a difficult relationship and they had many arguments; yet this did not prevent Skalkottas later writing to Matla from Greece that '*Despite all the arguments we had in the past I regret that we are separated and so far apart*' (LetMT, 27 November 1935). Both Matla and Skalkottas appear to have been heavily involved with their studies and career ambitions. Skalkottas in particular was self-absorbed and antisocial, even towards those who were close to him. As he observed to Nelly, '*There must be something sudden or unexpected to remind me of all my acquaintances, loved ones and my people*' (LetAsk, 30 March 1927) – a statement that is given particular resonance in light of the fact that Matla had given birth to his twins just a month earlier. They were born on 27 February 1927: a girl named Artemis Temko-Skalkottas and a boy, Yiorgos, who died a few days after birth. Skalkottas appears to have had little time for his new 'family', and it is notable that he never mentioned his daughter in his letters to Nelly. Neither parent took responsibility for Artemis, and she ended up being put into care.[33]

There are only two passing references to Matla in Skalkottas's surviving correspondence with Nelly and Benakis. Skalkottas's Greek Orthodox family disapproved of his relationship with a half-Jewish foreigner, and, according to Artemis, when his sister Kiki visited him in Berlin she made clear her dislike of Matla. Some years later, in one of his letters from Greece, Skalkottas asked Matla to send him a photograph of herself, because his sister '*has hidden the big one*' (LetMT, 27 November 1935). They kept in touch and sent long letters to each other. He also sent her manuscripts of his music, which, unfortunately, do not survive. Eventually, according to Matla's family, she became tired and hurt by his attitude and his permanent avoidance of his responsibilities towards their daughter, so she stopped writing after 1937. There is little further information about this relationship. A certain amount of secrecy surrounds the whole affair, and it was a topic avoided within Skalkottas's family in Greece, to the extent of being

---

using Papaioannou as his main source, mistakenly suggests that 'his first marriage in Germany ended in divorce' (1998, 175), that Skalkottas 'didn't keep any contact with his first wife, their daughter and her children', and that after his flight from Berlin 'Temko sold his manuscripts' (179). Actually Skalkottas died shortly after their daughter Artemis's wedding to Kurt Lindal, and Matla destroyed some of his manuscripts (Artemis Lindal, personal communication).

[32] Thornley suggests that by the summer of 1928 Skalkottas and Matla had split up (2002a, 186), although this remains uncertain.

[33] Artemis was visited by her father occasionally, and even taken to Schoenberg's house. When both her parents left Berlin in 1933 she was left in care, alone, until 1940, when she emigrated to Sweden to join her mother; but even there she was put into care. (Artemis Lindal, personal communication).

kept secret from his other children, born later, for more than 20 years. All that has survived are Matla's occasional comments, passed on to her family, that 'she liked Skalkottas, but she was very hurt by him'. The picture she gave of him appears to be that of a generally depressed, self-absorbed, somewhat uncaring person obsessed entirely with composition – the same picture that can be drawn from his letters to Nelly. Matla summarized Skalkottas's behaviour on several occasions to both Artemis and her granddaughter Anna Lindal: 'He was an impossible man to live with. He cared only about composing.'[34]

**Studies with Schoenberg**

In 1927, Jarnach was appointed Professor of Composition at the Cologne Musikhochschule; so he left Berlin and inevitably Skalkottas's lessons with him ended. In autumn of that year, Skalkottas joined Schoenberg's masterclass at the Prussian Academy of Fine Arts.[35] Following Busoni's death in June 1924, Schoenberg had been invited to replace him, and he took up the position in January 1926. He was expected to be in Berlin for six months of the year and to teach classes to those students who seemed to him qualified. Prospective students were required to submit three to five compositions, including: 'a) where possible, a solid contrapuntal student composition for the evaluation of his knowledge in this area; b) one or two works written as a student under the guidance of the teacher from which it should be possible to gather the success of the instruction; c) one or two recently written works that he regards as his most mature' (Auner, 2003, 193; AASCV, 286).

It is not known which compositions Skalkottas submitted, but following his entrance exam he was registered for three years from 1 October 1927 until 30 September 1930 (APrAcKB, 1123/51; AASCV, 161),[36] although he continued attending Schoenberg's masterclasses until the summer semester of 1932 (APrAKB, 128).

---

[34] Artemis Lindal, personal communication.

[35] Thornley claims that Skalkottas was prompted to join Schoenberg's masterclass by Walter and Rudi Goehr (2002b, 104). According to Hadjinikos, every time they visited Israel, Walter Goehr and his wife stopped in Athens, and Skalkottas was waiting for them at the airport. When once he didn't turn up they went to his house, arriving at the moment his coffin was taken to his funeral (Hadjinikos, 2006, 181–2). After Skalkottas's death, Goehr conducted several of his works, and helped with the publication of some of his compositions by Universal Edition.

[36] Skalkottas's admission form was signed by Schoenberg on 8 November 1927 (AASCV, 161). Apart from Skalkottas, Schoenberg's masterclass in the Academy of Fine Arts included Josef Rufer, Walter Goehr, Walter Gronostay, Adolf Weiss, Winfried Zillig, Roberto Gerhard, Alfred Keller, Hansjörg Dammert, Peter Schacht, Erich Schmid, Norbert von Hannenheim, Joseph Zmigrod, Natalie Prawossudowitsch, Max Walter, Johannes Moenck and the Greek Charilaos Perpessas (AASCV, 152).

These classes probably started shortly after Schoenberg arrived in Berlin from Vienna on 6 or 7 October (Stuckenschmidt, 1977, 319); they took place at Schoenberg's home once a week and were structured as discussion groups.[37]

Schoenberg's teaching was founded upon a thorough knowledge of the Classical repertory; he was concerned not only with the study of composition but also with matters of performance and interpretation. Compositions from the Classical repertory (such as Beethoven's string quartets) as well as students' own works were performed at the piano, sometimes with four hands. This greatly influenced Skalkottas's own approach to musical study for the rest of his life. Every point was 'abundantly illustrated and exemplified with passages or entire works taken from the repertoire ranging roughly from Bach to Brahms' (Gerhard, 1975, 64). Only very occasionally would a modern work be chosen for analysis, including some of Schoenberg's own compositions. Skalkottas found Schoenberg's '*analyses of classical works, Beethoven, Brahms, Mozart etc.* [...] *very interesting*' (LetMB, 24 September 1932; in Thornley 2002b, 116), possibly because Schoenberg did not refer to these Classical and Romantic pieces as models to be imitated, but used them instead as examples of possible explanations to compositional problems. What mattered to him was 'the search itself' (Schoenberg, 1983, 1).

Some of Schoenberg's pupils were interested in the twelve-note method, including Skalkottas, who had already developed the early stages of his own version. But although Schoenberg scrutinized his students' dodecaphonic works and made helpful suggestions, supporting his comments with references to works by Beethoven, Mozart and Brahms, he did not lecture on the subject. For him 'it was all the same [...] whether his pupil[s] wrote tonally, atonally or used the 12-tone method' (Stuckenschmidt, 1977, 333); instead he encouraged them to develop their own identity and individual style. As Gerhard recalled:

> Everyone could use his own idiom (if he had any of his own) or adopt whatever manner he chose. Matters of idiom would hardly ever be the subject of criticism with him [...] Least of all would he expect us to write in his own style or try to imitate him [...] He was the least dogmatic of Schoenbergians and he warned [his pupils] repeatedly of the dangers of orthodoxy [...] Above all he taught one to be true to oneself. (Gerhard, 1975, 64)

Although he 'was an intimidating person to meet', as a teacher 'he was unique' (Gerhard, *ibid.*). One original touch was that he would let his pupils discuss and even argue about their compositions among themselves first, before making his own observations; and these arguments 'greatly encouraged the remorseless

---

[37] Josef Rufer was Schoenberg's assistant; he provided the more elementary tuition to the majority of Schoenberg's composition pupils and familiarized them with the master's methods and theoretical views (Stuckenschmidt, 1977, 310). For a discussion of Schoenberg's teaching methods and masterclasses in Berlin, see among others Reich (1971), Gerhard (1975), Smith (1979–80), Walton (2001), Auner (2003) and Holtmeier (2008).

honesty which Schoenberg himself practiced, and which he absolutely demanded of his pupils' (Reich, 1971, 156). But he was also considerate, perhaps even paternalistic, towards his talented students, among whom he considered Skalkottas.[38] Schoenberg's aim in teaching was 'to lead the pupil to knowledge of himself, to make him express every phrase [...] And even to chase up the pupil in his own conflict. Quite unintentionally one learns an enormous amount, one sharpens one's feeling about other works and about oneself' (Stuckenschmidt, 1977, 333).

Skalkottas was influenced by Schoenberg not only in his musical training and compositional thinking but also in his overall personal development, since Schoenberg used to discuss in his classes painting, architecture, literature, philosophy and politics (Smith, 1986, 231–3). Schoenberg appears to have been impressed by his Greek student. From his own handwritten reports – in which he also enumerated Skalkottas's compositions – it is clear that he was satisfied with his pupil's diligence, attendance and progress (which was 'very good' in the first semester 1927–28, and 'excellent' thereafter, until the summer semester 1932). He considered him 'very independent and purposeful', and somebody who could 'really do very much' (APrAKB, 128). During the first semester in Schoenberg's masterclass (winter 1927/28) Skalkottas presented or worked further on his violin sonata and a string quartet (probably the one mentioned in his correspondence with Nelly). In his progress report of the summer semester of 1928 there is reference to a Violin Concerto and a Symphony for Winds, neither of which survives. On 11 March 1928 his orchestration of Mitropoulos's *Cretan Feast*, conducted by the composer, was performed in Athens by the Athens Conservatory Orchestra, and it was received positively by both the Greek public and the musical press (Kostios, 1996, 48).

Despite his continuing financial problems, and falling behind with his fees payment at the academy (AASCV, 152), the years 1929 and, initially at least, 1930, appeared to be artistically promising for Skalkottas. In addition, Schoenberg helped him (as he also did for other students) pay his fees by arranging receipt of an academy grant (AASCV, 174; Stuckenschmidt, 1977, 332). During this time Skalkottas composed two sonatinas for violin and piano, his Second String Quartet, a Concerto for wind orchestra, a *Little Suite* for violin and orchestra, a Concerto for violin and piano and an 'orchestral piece'.[39] In a letter to Benakis in

---

[38] In his unfinished, handwritten autobiography Schoenberg explained how he taught composition to 'talented pupils like: Webern, Berg, Eisler, Zillig, Hannenheim, Skalkottas, Schacht [...] 1) I had to read (I can not play the piano) the works they had written [...] 2) I had to find out if and what was wrong and why. 3) I had to find out how it should be corrected. After having fulfilled these three tasks, it was only (!) necessary to find a way to explain all this to the pupils and (!) to explain how I thought it could be improved' (Auner, 2003, 303).

[39] This orchestral piece was perhaps an early version of the First Symphonic Suite for large orchestra, which he completed or recomposed in 1935. In a letter to Manolis

late December 1929 he also mentioned that he had composed an Octet for piano, flute, clarinet, bassoon, trumpet, trombone, violin and cello (now lost), and 'three fine songs' for the Greek soprano Margarita Perra.[40] He was also already working on his First Piano Concerto, and wanted to write a three-act dramatic epic opera on a libretto by Rolf Stein.[41]

In 1929 Skalkottas experienced his first public success in Berlin. On 19 June his First String Quartet and the First and Second sonatinas for violin and piano were performed at the Prussian Academy of Arts, as part of Schoenberg's masterclass concert that year (AASCV, 57/58).[42] They were favourably received by the Berlin music critics: Fritz Zweig in the *Deutsche Allgemeine Zeitung* praised his string quartet as 'the most mature work' of the programme, with 'all three movements attesting to the inner logic of somebody who has been brought up to think musically. The force of his invention is inexhaustible and the form is very clear' (Zweig, 21 June 1929; AASCV, 53). The conservative critic Heinz Pringsheim in the *Allgemeine Musikzeitung* was similarly impressed, and described the two sonatinas as 'not in the least Schoenbergian in flavour – [they] could hail from the polytonal districts of Milhaud' (cited in Thornley, 2002a, 191).

In late 1929 and the first half of 1930 Skalkottas assisted Schoenberg with the musical preparation of *Erwartung* and a radio production of the new opera *Von Heute auf Morgen*; later he helped him with *Gurrelieder*,[43] in which he shared the conducting of the orchestral rehearsals with Schoenberg himself and one of the Goehr brothers (AASCV, T 77.14). In a letter to Manolis Benakis he boasted that:

---

Benakis from late October 1931, Skalkottas mentioned that he was composing an orchestral overture, but he wasn't sure whether he would finish it, because of his health problems (Thornley, 2002a, 200). Such a piece from this period does not exist.

[40] These songs might have been, although it cannot be confirmed, 'I Lafina' (The Doe) (A/K86), 'Ali Pasas' (A/K87), and 'Astrapse i Anatoli' (Lightning in the East) (A/K88). Margarita Perra studied in Berlin and became a member of the ensemble of the Berlin State Opera. Thornley suggests that Skalkottas considered her a loyal friend and colleague (2002a, 205).

[41] In an interview with the newspaper *Vradini* (30 October 1930), Skalkottas mentioned Rolf Stein as the librettist of his choral work the 'Tomb of the Unknown Soldier'. There is no further reference to this choral work in any other document; perhaps Skalkottas had planned it but never finished it (Thornley, 2002a, 188–9; and 2002b, 113)

[42] In the 1929 programme and in Skalkottas's manuscript the quartet is entitled 'Streichquartett', without a number, whereas in the Archive Catalogue it is listed as First String Quartet. His sonatinas were performed by Anatol Knorre (violin) and Else C. Kraus (piano), and in the String Quartet Skalkottas played second violin.

[43] Schoenberg's *Erwartung* was performed on 7 June 1930 in the Berlin Krolloper, under the direction of Zemlinsky (Stuckenschmidt, 1977, 334–5); *Gurrelieder* was performed on 5 June 1931 at the Hochschule für Musik, under the direction of Franz Schreker (*ibid,* 343); and the radio production of his opera *Von Heute auf Morgen* was first performed in Frankfurt on 1 February 1930, while on 27 February 1930 Schoenberg himself conducted the piece on the Berlin Radio (*ibid.,* 330–31).

'*As you know, I am now Schoenberg's right hand, he entrusts me with all his tasks, the preparation of his works* [for performance]' (LetMB, end of December 1929 or beginning of January 1930; in Thornley, 2002a, 189; and 2002b, 113).[44]

In February 1930 Skalkottas met Mitropoulos, who had come to Berlin to conduct the Berlin Philharmonic Orchestra, and introduced him to Schoenberg (Auner, 2003, 285–6). Two concerts of Skalkottas's new works were given in April and May in the Singakademie, Berlin. The first was on 6 April, sponsored by the Greek Embassy in Berlin, and featured the premieres of both his Concerto for violin, piano and chamber orchestra – played by the violinist Anatol Knorre and the Greek pianist Polyxene Mathéy – and the *Little Suite* for violin and orchestra (Ramou, 2008, 420; Thornley, 2002a, 191). In the second concert, on 20 May, which featured works by Schoenberg's students (AASCV, 39), Skalkottas conducted the Berlin Symphony Orchestra. On 23 May Skalkottas and Hannenheim wrote together to Schoenberg to express their gratitude for his support in facilitating the concert (AASCV, 41), but the negative observations made in the Berlin press doubtless tainted their enjoyment of the experience. An anonymous reviewer in the Berlin *Tempo* could not find 'any essential quality' in the works heard in the concert, which exhibited 'poor imagination' (Z.V., 22 May 1930; AASCV, 35). W. Sachse thought that Skalkottas's composition, with its 'use of provocative jazz rhythms', was 'more vertical' and showed 'grotesque characteristics' (Sachse, 22 May 1930; AASCV, 33). In *Allgemeine Musikzeitung*, Pringsheim dismissed Skalkottas's Concerto, not only because 'it sound[ed] hideous' but also because of the treatment of the twelve-note harmony and the instrumentation (Pringsheim, 6 June 1930). Only the critic of the *Berliner Dienst* was less critical of Skalkottas's work and felt that it was 'formed relatively clearly' in comparison to the other pieces (anonymous, 27 May 1930; AASCV, 34).

Skalkottas's lessons with Schoenberg at the Academy officially ended in June 1930, and in a letter to Marika Papaioannou, on 19 June, he wrote: '*Today I said goodbye to Schoenberg for good! All other is secondary*' (cited in Thornley 2002b, 111). He went to Athens, where he stayed until January 1931, but on his return to Berlin he again attended Schoenberg's masterclasses at the Academy, this time as a guest student during the winter semester 1930–31 (APrAKB, 128).[45]

---

[44] According to Thornley, Skalkottas wrote 56 letters to Benakis (2002a, 179). These letters are untraceable today, but in June 1973 Benakis apparently showed them only to Thornley, who took extensive notes. In the present study, all the references to these letters have been taken from Thornley's published articles 2002a and 2002b, which, to my knowledge, are the only sources referring to this episode of Skalkottas's life. Unless otherwise indicated, all reference to these letters in the present chapter will be cited with the letter date, and the page number from Thornley's 2002a publication; for example, (LetMB, date [of the letter], page [of Thornley's 2002a article]).

[45] In the report of the winter semester 1930–31 Schoenberg wrote that Skalkottas had taken 'time off' from his studies for a few weeks, but he was now 'taking part in the

Skalkottas's *Little Suite* for violin and orchestra was broadcast by the Frankfurt Radio Station on 22 January 1931 as part of a concert that also featured Schoenberg's Eight Songs op.6 and Zillig's Serenade. The work was favourably received by none other than Theodor Adorno, who introduced the concert, and whose analysis of the piece reinforced the fact that Skalkottas was not using Schoenberg's strict twelve-note technique but his own variation of it, as is clearly seen in other works surviving from this period (Adorno, 1984, 570; Jaklitsch, 2003, 198). In the same year Skalkottas completed his First Piano Concerto; he also composed an Octet for four woodwinds and string quartet, which was performed on 2 June at a concert of music by Schoenberg's pupils at the Academy, conducted by Erich Schmid and with Skalkottas playing the second violin (AASCV, 4). This was his last public appearance as both composer and performer in Berlin. Schoenberg was not present, and the concert overall was not well received (Brust, 1931, 519).

Perhaps as a consequence of the negative reception of his music, compounded with his perennial financial and health problems and also Schoenberg's absence from Berlin for a year, Skalkottas's compositional output had waned by the end of 1931. However, during this time away from Schoenberg and his circle, Skalkottas became interested in traditional Greek music (for reasons that will become clearer below). On 15 December 1931 there was a Berlin Radio broadcast of a programme on Greek folk music presented by the ethnomusicologist Kurt Sachs, in which Skalkottas accompanied the soprano Margarita Perra and the tenor Konstantinos Milonas in his own arrangements for voice and piano of four Greek folk-songs. As he wrote to Benakis, '*It did me much good, because something stirred in my soul as I listened to our folk songs*' (LetMB, 17 December 1931, 205). As a consequence, he began conceiving and sketching some of his *Greek Dances*, and in March 1932 he sent to Benakis his first composed *Greek Dance* (*Peloponnisiakos*), which '*turned out quite well: tonal*' (LetMB, 23 March 1932, 207).[46]

Following Schoenberg's return to Berlin in June 1932, Skalkottas spent the summer semester attending his masterclasses, again as a guest student (APrAcKB, 128)[47] – and his interest in Greek folk music subsided. In July he played to Schoenberg a two-piano arrangement of his First Piano Concerto at the Bechstein studios in Berlin, which Schoenberg must himself have hired since Skalkottas could not have afforded this at the time (Thornley, 2002a, 208). It seems that Schoenberg offered some constructive criticism, which was always a sign of

---

exercises with diligence', and he praised him for having 'achieved quite a lot' and for being 'very independent and purposeful' (APrAKB, 128).

[46] He sketched a *Kleftikos*, a *Syrtos*, a *Kritikos* and the *Dance of Zalongo*, and made plans to write another three or four dances. On the score of the completed *36 Greek Dances* that Skalkottas gave to Benakis in December 1936, he wrote the date 'January 1931' against the dance *Peloponnisiakos* (No.4 of Series/Set I; Skalkottas Archive).

[47] Schoenberg was reprimanded by the assistant secretary of the Prussian Academy of Arts, Prof. Alexander Amersdorffer, because Skalkottas was not at the time officially registered and apparently had not paid any fees since 1930 (Gradenwitz, 1998, 21–2).

distinction;[48] however, Skalkottas, perhaps in something of a fragile emotional state, appears to have been unwilling to accept his teacher's feedback. He wrote to Benakis: '*He is not in agreement with many things* [in the score]. *From his point of view he's right, just as I'm right from my point of view. But I've no intention of changing anything, just* [as] *I've never changed anything in my works. That's not egoism: I just don't like making minor repairs, altering the clothes after getting dressed up, then dressing up all over again!*' He went on to describe a complex attitude towards Schoenberg:

> *I wrote to you once that I am not nor was I his disciple, because my music is primitive in comparison with the music of Schoenberg. In time, I shall end up taking a different path, my own path, an independent one, insofar as that is possible, of course. This doesn't mean that I am ungrateful towards Schoenberg. I feel great gratitude and love* [for him]*, but he believes the opposite because I showed my gratitude and my love in the clumsiest way. I'm not responsible for that.* (LetMB, 12 July 1932, 208)

Skalkottas only intermittently attended Schoenberg's classes during the following summer semester, and apart from the sketches and orchestrations of a few *Greek Dances*, none of his other 1932–33 Berlin compositions (if indeed he composed any) have survived. In 1932, together with Norbert von Hannenheim and Peter Schacht, he entered the competition for the Felix Mendelssohn-Bartholdy composition scholarship (Staats-Stipendium für Komponisten 1932). The work he submitted was his Octet. Schoenberg, who was a member of the jury, praised Skalkottas's talent and put him in joint first place with Hannenheim, observing that: 'One can see the systematic way with which he builds his themes and sentences, the elaboration of the motivic work, qualities with which I judge my students' works. This is an outstanding work' (AASCV, 'Zum Mendelssohn Preis', T22.13). Nonetheless, the first prize was given to Hannenheim alone, and Skalkottas's hopes for further recognition and an improvement in his precarious financial situation were crushed.

Although they lost contact with each other after their departure from Berlin in 1933, Schoenberg always remembered Skalkottas as one of 'the best of my "Meisterklasse an der Akademie der Künste zu Berlin"', and wrote about him in

---

[48] We don't know the exact suggestions Schoenberg made about the concerto, nor the particular details for this encounter. It has been claimed that Schoenberg criticized Skalkottas's First Piano Concerto as having 'too many notes', to which Skalkottas replied '*it has as many as are needed*' (Hadjinikos, 1966, 148). This anecdote, originating with George Hadjinikos, has become an established 'fact' in the mythology surrounding Skalkottas, and the deliberate allusion to the anecdotal dialogue between Mozart and Emperor Joseph II, after the premiere of *The Marriage of Figaro*, is unmistakable here. Although Hadjinikos never knew Skalkottas personally, Demertzis claims that 'it is possible' Hadjinikos might have talked to some of Skalkottas's colleagues (Demertzis, 1998, 286, and 376–7).

glowing terms: 'Nicolas Skalkottas is a highly gifted composer, an excellent violinist and good pianist. He was in my "Meisterklasse" but returned to his native country, Greece, in 1932 [sic]' (Auner, 2003, 285–6). Years later, Skalkottas recalled his teacher's influence, writing in a letter to Matla that: *'With every word and with every work I'm about to do, I feel his strong influence. His instructions to young people and young musicians to progress were always right. I would like to have carried on studying composition with him*' (LetMT, Athens, 27 November 1935).

**The Benakis Affair**

A few months after he started lessons with Schoenberg, in the spring of 1928, Skalkottas met Manolis Benakis, a member of one of the wealthiest and most influential families in Greece and a patron of the arts. Benakis visited Berlin in February 1928, and on the advice of pianist Spyros Farandatos (a former fellow student of Skalkottas at the Hochschule für Musik) he met Skalkottas and agreed to provide him with a scholarship for the next three years, until 1931.[49] In return, Skalkottas had to oversee Benakis's dealings with various Berlin booksellers and auction houses, buying and selling music manuscripts, luxuriously bound published scores, gramophone records, books on music and high-quality editions of poetry (Thornley 2002a, 183–5). Skalkottas entered into correspondence with Benakis, an exchange that sheds further light on the composer's psychological development during his last five years in Berlin. In these letters, written in a vein similar to that demonstrated in his earlier correspondence with Nelly, Skalkottas showed similar signs of extreme emotional attachment, and appeared now to emphasize an exclusive friendship with Benakis, as demonstrated in a letter from late December 1929: '*You're the only Greek outside my family, the only Greek friend with whom I can write and speak as if to my brother*'. And elsewhere: '*You're **the only human being** whom I consider as a friend, you gave me the possibility of going ahead with my work, with my art. I don't have any other friends, in fact these days I probably have enemies – to you I've entrusted almost my entire life, almost all my secrets. Don't let that go unnoticed [...] I'm nobler and better than I appear to be!*' [original emphasis] (LetMB, 4 May 1931, 187). Skalkottas's letters reveal his ongoing depression, and possibly some artistic tension between the composer and his benefactor. Benakis loved the late Romantic music of Wagner, Strauss and Bruckner, and had probably never heard Skalkottas's music prior to supporting

---

[49] Papaioannou variously suggests that Skalkottas was given the 'famous "personal Benakis scholarship"' during the years: 1924–27 (1955, 6); from '1923 onwards, which enabled him to study independently' (1976, 321); '1927?' (with a question mark) (1997, vol. 1, 67). However, it is clear from Skalkottas's correspondence with Manolis Benakis, Nelly Askitopoulou and Matla Temko that he received what he called a 'hypotrofia' (scholarship) in 1928. Thornley accepts this year as the beginning of Benakis's financial support in the form of a monthly grant (2002a, 184).

him financially.[50] When he later expressed his dislike of Skalkottas's work, the composer reproached him rather angrily, writing: '*My Concerto for Winds is not horrible and dreadful, nor is any other of my compositions. All the works I've written since 1928 up to today are OK and I maintain that to the death*' (LetMB, 12 July 1932, 204).

Illustration 2.2    Nikos Skalkottas with Manolis Benakis (Koblenz, 7 May 1928)

During his visits to Berlin in the spring of 1928, 1929 and 1930, Benakis took Skalkottas to the opera, to prestigious concerts at the Philharmonic, and to nightclubs. He also took him to Vienna several times, and in 1928 gave him money both to visit his family and to try to release himself from national service (Thornley, 2002a, 182, 185, 186). This two-month return to Greece in 1928 was Skalkottas's first since he left in 1921. He felt disappointed with his country, and his negative stance towards his compatriots showed no change, despite the positive response shown to his orchestration of Mitropoulos's *Cretan Feast*, performed a few months previously. On his return to Berlin in autumn 1928 he set about buying the manuscripts and gramophone records that Benakis had ordered. However, he was hardly the best-qualified person for such business transactions; he was so absorbed in his composing that he had difficulty in dealing with practical matters of his own, let alone those of a distant benefactor. Although he took the responsibility seriously and conscientiously, he found it difficult to combine his own work with

---

[50]   Skalkottas observed in one of his letters that, '*You love and adore Romantic music and yet you're almost entirely a man of the twentieth century. I love, and am more interested in, the music of the twentieth century, and* [yet] *I'm a man of the Middle Ages*' (LetMB, 4 May 1931, 187).

Benakis's affairs, and he was often late fulfilling his promises. As he admitted some time later: '*In matters of* [practical] *life I'm the most incapable person you can imagine. Apart from notes and musical combinations I can't think clearly. In everything else I make mistakes and blunders*' (LetMB, mid-January 1932, 185).

Benakis's financial support allowed Skalkottas in late October 1928 to move from his house in Kaiser-Wilhelm str. 80, in the suburb of Lankwitz (where Matla lived, as well as most of his Greek friends), to Nürnberger str. 19 in the fashionable west end of Berlin (APrAKB, 128; also Thornley 2002a, 186). For a while he also reduced his evening freelance work at cafés and cinema orchestras, at Benakis's insistence. Skalkottas's relief was clear, and during his first visit to Vienna (late April and early May 1928) he wrote to Nelly that, '*This journey raised my morale inconceivably. A great joy fills my heart that I shall now be free in the evenings*' (LetAsk, 8 May 1928). However, the scholarship wasn't enough to allow him to give up his freelance work completely, and by the end of 1928 his previous optimism was replaced by the usual pessimism, as he bemoaned: '*Life is difficult isn't it, Manoli, but I'm being patient, and I shan't lose my courage*' (LetMB, 10–12 December 1928, 188). His hopes that the Havemann Quartet would perform his String Quartet came to nothing, and he consequently castigated himself and his inability to deal with life: '*I am rather irritated with myself that I'm so clumsy about* [promoting] *my own works, that I haven't up to now been able to be a better craftsman in the art of living. I often reflect,* [but] *perhaps I'm wrong, that there should be brashness at the core of one's idealism, otherwise one becomes a witness to life*' (*ibid.*). Undoubtedly, Skalkottas lacked this brashness.

Encouraged by the success of the concert on 19 June 1929 at the Prussian Academy of Arts, and perhaps trying to impress Benakis with his fame in Berlin, he wrote to him that he was about to receive two commissions for the 1930 festivals of Munich and Baden-Baden, and he hoped that a 'special article' on his work, complete with musical examples, would appear in *Melos* (Thornley 2002a, 190). But nothing came of all this, and his hopes were once again dashed. To make matters worse, Benakis reduced his financial support, perhaps because of the Wall Street crash of October 1929 and the ensuing economic depression. Skalkottas rather tartly observed that Benakis had compounded his difficulties: '*Independently of the reduction in the grant you give me, I'm in a difficult financial position. Following your advice last year, I rather lost contact with the musical circles through which I'd been earning my living*' (LetMB, late December 1929, 191). Despite the reduced scholarship, he was still expected to take care of Benakis's complicated affairs, by which he felt overburdened (*ibid.*, 192).

In the summer of 1930, following the completion of his studies with Schoenberg and after the final concert at the Academy, Skalkottas travelled twice to Vienna with Benakis, and in August he returned to Athens (via Salzburg), where he stayed until January 1931. Just before Skalkottas left Athens to return to Berlin, Benakis indicated that because of 'financial reasons' he could provide no further support beyond the end of March 1931. Nevertheless, he asked Skalkottas to continue buying and selling manuscripts on his behalf in Berlin, a task to which the composer agreed, but

Illustration 2.3   Nikos Skalkottas in Seeham (Austria), 1929

which he continued to have problems accomplishing (*ibid.*, 195–6). Only a month after returning to Berlin, Skalkottas persisted in asking Benakis for another grant for a further two years. Benakis would not commit himself, apart from promising a 'present' if Skalkottas managed to complete his tasks.

### '*My homecoming to my country would bring me disappointments*'[51]

The events that took place during Skalkottas's trip to Athens (August 1930 to January 1931), and his reactions to them, marked a turning point both in his career and his psychological development. Musical life in Athens had evolved noticeably since Skalkottas's departure from Greece as a 17 year old, but the Greek capital was some way from reaching the cultural standards to which he had become accustomed during his nine-year stay in Berlin. There was fierce rivalry (with respect to national prestige and levels of financial support) between the three

---

[51]   LetAsk, 18 August 1926.

conservatories – Athens, Hellenic and National;[52] and this rivalry was inextricably connected with the ownership of the country's Symphony Orchestra, with dire consequences for musical life generally. Years later Mitropoulos, who had been appointed chief conductor of the Athens Conservatory Orchestra in 1927, referred to the Athenian musical scene as 'an awful nest of intrigue' (Trotter, 1995, 56–7). In a letter to the Prime Minister, Eleftherios Venizelos, dated 19 October 1928, he wrote:

> In Athens at this moment, for better or worse (worse according to my opinion), there are three Conservatories [...] this situation is seriously fragmenting the pool of native Greek talent [...] These Conservatories fight each other for which one will get the allowance from the state, to enable it to constitute the orchestra [...] They kill each other to determine in which Conservatory the orchestra will belong, whose the title will bear [...] This injurious rivalry is not confined only to claiming the state allowance; while each orchestra tries to obtain for itself the best musicians, parallel capable performers are excluded because they belong to the 'rival side', splintering off and weakening the artistic manpower. (Kostios, 1985, 38–9).

Most of the players had to perform on poor-quality instruments that were in need of repair or replacement, for which the orchestra's budget did not allow (Trotter, 1995, 54–5). Despite all these problems, by 1929 the Athens Conservatory Orchestra had considerably improved, due predominantly to Mitropoulos's efforts (*ibid.*, 65).

Audiences, too, were relatively unsophisticated, at least by the standards that Skalkottas had been used to in Berlin. In the late 1920s and early 1930s, Greek audiences were unwilling to appreciate music that did not conform to the ideals and aesthetics of Greek nationalism. Several of the wealthy upper-class patrons of the orchestra influenced programming and the choice of soloists, and could threaten to withdraw their financial support if all was not to their liking (Kostios, 1985, 42). Mitropoulos tried to educate audiences by introducing more modern compositions among works from the established classical repertory, as well as premieres of works by Greek composers. However, he was met not only with the indifference of these audiences, who sought the comfortable familiarity of recognizable pieces, but also with the fierce reaction of many critics, who frequently replaced critical judgement and objective appreciation with dogmatic aphorisms and arbitrary subjectivity. Some sense of the prevailing cultural climate can be gained from the tone of surviving reviews. For Greek critics, works by Debussy, Schoenberg, Milhaud and Stravinsky represented the 'communist and subversive tendencies of

---

[52] The Hellenic Conservatory (1919) and the National Conservatory (1926) were both established by the nationalist composer Manolis Kalomiris as the result of infighting and personality clashes within the Athens Conservatory; they were in direct competition with the latter and their appearance contributed to the fracturing and instability of the musical scene in the capital.

the time', 'decay' and 'moral degradation'; they found Wagner 'hard to digest'; Brahms was 'boring'; Bruckner 'long-winded'; Schumann 'impoverished in his ideas'; even Beethoven's 'Pastoral' Symphony was dismissed as 'over-long and exhausting to listen to'; while the 'Eroica' was described, intriguingly, as 'full of wrinkles' (*ibid.,* 41–2). Even Mitropoulos did not escape this harsh criticism when his own compositions were performed at the Athens Conservatory in 1927 and 1929 (*ibid.,* 86). During the 1927 concert in particular, a large part of the audience walked out of the hall, and the critical response ranged from mild indignation to revulsion. Mitropoulos was accused of 'aesthetic degeneracy', of having been 'seduced by aesthetic psychopathy' and having 'no sense of cultural roots in his music' (Trotter, 1995, 62–3).[53] Such negative outpourings were not only based on bigotry and subservience to particular patrons and their agendas, they were also motivated by the rivalry between the three conservatories to which the critics themselves belonged as teachers or members.

Into this musical environment Skalkottas introduced, in two concerts, his uncompromisingly modern works. On 23 November 1930, at the first concert of the 'Popular Concert' series of the Athens Conservatory Orchestra winter season at the Olympia Theatre, Skalkottas appeared as both conductor and composer, directing the first Greek performance of his Concerto for wind orchestra. The programme also included Schubert's Seventh Symphony, Liszt's Second Piano Concerto in A major, with soloist Polyxeni Mathéy, and Wagner's Overture from the *Meistersingers of Nuremberg*. A few days later, on 27 November, a concert consisting exclusively of his own chamber works was given in the prestigious main concert hall of the Athens Conservatory. The event included his friends Nelly Askitopoulou on the violin and Spyros Farandatos on the piano, and the programme comprised five of Skalkottas's compositions – the First and Second sonatinas for violin and piano, and the *Easy*, First and Second string quartets. These concerts were important events not only in the Athenian concert calendar but also in Skalkottas's burgeoning career. A few weeks previously, the newspaper *Vradini* featured an article on Skalkottas. The anonymous journalist was impressed with the young composer's enthusiasm for all the arts, including cinema, theatre, radio, recording, painting and music, but was cautious about the inevitable comparisons that would be drawn between him and the established Mitropoulos, and with an uncanny foreboding he prophesized, 'if unsuccessful, the young man will destroy his future' (*Vradini*, 30 October 1930).

Whereas Skalkottas was generally praised as a conductor, and was in fact encouraged to devote himself to conducting instead of composition,[54] the

---

[53] A similarly negative attack on Berg's *Wozzeck* was launched in 1928 by George Lambelet, who wrote that Berg was 'one of those extreme modernist [composers], whose controversial melodrama Wozzeck represents the most cruel sentence to death of the tradition' (Lambelet, 1928, 68).

[54] The 'Musician' (pen name of an anonymous reviewer) advised: 'It is beyond doubt that Mr. Skalkottas has talent as a composer, but I think that he can more safely reach the

critical and public reception of his music was overwhelmingly negative, and the newspaper reviews were harsh and scornful.[55] For the critic Ioannis Psaroudas, the Concerto for wind orchestra was 'a provocation to the intelligence of the audience, and to any kind of aesthetic judgment and common sense'. He found it 'difficult to hear anything uglier' and hard to believe that Skalkottas 'wanted to amuse himself at the expense of the respectful audience' (Psaroudas, *Eleftheron Vima*, 24 November 1930). Although Psaroudas did not attend the chamber music concert of 27 November, he was 'informed' that Skalkottas's works 'caused the audience to feel discomforted and disappointed'; and he wondered how it was possible 'to find pleasure writing not only incomprehensible but ugly music?' (*Eleftheron Vima*, 30 November 1930). An unsigned article in the newspaper *Kathimerini* described Skalkottas's work as 'the invasion of the barbarians' and a 'monstrosity' (30 November 1930). The much feared and influential critic Sofia Spanoudi was similarly scathing; she observed the 'non-value' of Skalkottas's works, asserting that they were representative of 'the complete musical derailment and negative levelling of art', and that Skalkottas was 'a heretic for the sake of heresy, and particularly for the sake of rejecting musical orthodoxy' (Spanoudi, *Proia*, 29 December 1930). Not everybody was entirely negative towards Skalkottas. A few critics recognized his talent even if they found the musical language incomprehensible. Kalomiris, for example, while admitting that he 'didn't understand a thing of Mr. Skalkottas's composition', felt that he should not condemn it, because he believed Skalkottas was 'not an ordinary musician. He seems to be a master of all the secrets of his technique and it is a pity that Greek musical art should lose a brilliant musician so that Germany would acquire one more imitator of the exterior types of art of Schoenberg or Hindemith' (Kalomiris, *Ethnos*, 24 November 1930).

Skalkottas would not have expected to find much sympathy for his music in such a conservative environment, but faced with the reality of this reaction in Greece he felt devastated and humiliated. By way of some small revenge he did something he lived to regret. On his return to Berlin he wrote a stinging and ironic attack on the main institutions of Greek musical life, which was published in the Athenian periodical *Musiki Zoë* in March 1931.[56] This was the only time that the otherwise withdrawn Skalkottas publicly retaliated with such strong language. Although he was aware of the probable consequences, admitting that '*with this step I won't win the favour of the Athenian music critics*', he lashed out not only at his critics but also at the orchestra and the Athens Conservatory – the latter for what he saw as its poor standards of teaching. Directly attacking the music critics, he wrote:

---

highest rank as a conductor' (*Vradini*, 24 November 1930).

[55] For more on the reception of Skalkottas's music by the Greek public, see Belonis (2002, 29–48) and (2004, 18–20).

[56] Skalkottas was the Berlin correspondent for *Musiki Zoë* from February to July 1931.

*The majority of Greek music criticism (that is, Athenian) is represented by amateurs or non-musicians [...] And it is difficult for me to decide whether this amateurism is the result of our Conservatories, or whether it stems from the various opportunities and influence that critics often have at their disposal. But of one thing I'm sure: what happens in our capital city wouldn't even happen in a tribe of negroes [...] Our music criticism is still at the stage of provincial correspondence and of cheap philology [...] Most of our capital's music critics are incapable of reading even an easy page of a score of my work, of analysing systematically its form – to prove with musical arguments (and not only with the power of the press) that it is imperfectly written. [...] None of our music critics read, nor even saw closely, any of my pieces. And there is the question: how is it possible for so and so lady or so and so ignorant critic to follow infallibly at first hearing a complicated modern work, and form a decisive opinion about it? [...] They all rushed to criticize me, many without listening to my works, to attack me – for what reason? Simply: their acknowledged musical ability stopped once and for all at the borders of 18$^{th}$-century music.* (1931/33, 124–6)

His criticism of the Conservatory Orchestra was equally scathing:

*The winds of our symphonic orchestra frequently play half a tone lower than the strings. The social position of our musicians is becoming daily unbearable, our orchestra cannot develop into a presentable entity as long as it lacks the following: organizational homogeneity, interest, and a sense of duty (unfortunately the salary level of our musicians is pitiful).* (Ibid.)

Ironically, within three years he would join this very orchestra and stay in its ranks for the rest of his life. But in the mean time, by insulting the influential Athenian critics, conservatory teachers, musicians, orchestral management and audiences he made life considerably more difficult for himself. On 21 January 1931, realizing that he could not establish himself in Athens, Skalkottas left for Berlin, intending to remain there. The hostile reception of the Athenian critics gave him a lasting feeling of bitterness, sadness and disappointment, which he found difficult to come to terms with. As he wrote to Benakis: '*When I last visited Athens, it was as anything but a compatriot that my compatriots received me. You are the one big exception; I hope and wish that you will always be so (even if we don't agree about my musical outloook) [...] They can insult me as much as they want: let them. But they mustn't call me a slave to foreign fashions or unpatriotic, because that would be the biggest lie and the only thing that would seriously wound me*' (LetMB, 17 December 1931, 204). A few months later, still traumatized from the critics' personal attacks, but putting on a brave face, he wrote of his still-painful feelings: '*It wasn't the bad reviews that affected me, nor the fact that they didn't like my music or couldn't understand it [...] What hurt me was the nasty manner, the extreme position in matters that don't have anything at all to do with my music*' (LetMB, 16 February 1932, 193). And only a day later, in a more combative mood, he exploded: '*In connection with last year's rows, I feel like going down to Athens to beat up Economou* [the editor of *Musiki Zoë*]. *Who gave him the idea of annihilating me with his acts of malevolence and his nasty remarks?*' (LetMB, 17 February 1932, 195). Again the act of composing provided him with an emotional release, and he would '*let off steam in some new work*', a '*venting of steam* [that was] *very left-wing from a musical point of view, i.e. very modern*' (LetMB, 17 September 1931, 104).

**The Last Berlin Years: Deception and Desperation**

On his return to Berlin, Skalkottas's precarious finances and emotional instability deteriorated further. He was unable to find work as a freelance violinist or pianist at cafés and cinemas because of the recession; instead he was reduced to earning a living as a music copyist, one of the lowest-paid jobs available to him (Thornley 2002a, 198). Schoenberg tried to help him by offering him a job as a coach at the Berlin State Opera, but despite his bleak prospects Skalkottas refused the position on grounds of low salary (120 RM per month, '*a sum on which it's impossible to live here*'), and because the long hours involved would have prevented him from composing and from earning the extra money he needed for basic living costs (LetMB, 10 March 1931, 184–5). His decision to decline Schoenberg's offer (meagre though it may have been), which would have allowed him to follow Mitropoulos's early steps as an opera coach in Berlin, is in many ways difficult to comprehend, and perhaps indicates once again Skalkottas's generally confused state.

Skalkottas's attitude towards Schoenberg at this time was contradictory. In his last report to *Musiki Zoë* (as its Berlin correspondent, June–July 1931) he wrote about the first concert of the International Society for New Music, observing that Schoenberg's Suite op.29 should be considered '*a masterpiece of contemporary chamber music*' (1931/35, 113). In July he changed tack, writing of his relationship with Schoenberg in a letter to Benakis: '*I'm not in his good books. He's learnt of the change in my musical ideas, and that he's lost a disciple he never had!*' (LetMB, 25 July 1931, 208). Skalkottas's motives in seeking to suggest some distance between himself and Schoenberg are questionable. Either he was suffering a state of emotional unrest, or he was deliberately embroidering or inventing a disagreement with his teacher in order to ingratiate himself with Benakis, since he knew that Benakis disliked Schoenberg and his music. Angling for further financial support from Benakis he boasted of his Octet that, '*it was performed* [...] *with great success. The moral result = the best to date. The practical result = 0000000!!!!!*' (LetMB, May–June 1931, 200).[57] He also wrote of his desire to compose more music for the sake of his country, possibly in an attempt to appeal

---

[57] Skalkottas endeavoured further to ingratiate himself with Benakis by writing of the Octet that '*it's my most recent work and not at all modern*' (LetMB, 26 May 1931), which was far from the truth considering its avowedly dodecaphonic language.

to Benakis's nationalist instincts and thus elicit further financial support: '*I don't care about my own life so much as about my work. I'd like very much to have written between ten and twenty more works, so that my country would have its first composer. And I hope to manage it in spite of all these setbacks*' (LetMB, 26 October 1931, 203).

Skalkottas's deteriorating health was causing him considerable distress. He complained of a swollen face, a skin irritation, an eye infection, and of becoming more susceptible to colds and bronchitis. He blamed Benakis for the decline of his health, which he claimed was brought on by those '*overnight stays in the cabarets*' during Benakis's annual visits to Berlin.[58] By October 1931 he was convinced he was seriously ill, and he begged Benakis to help him pay for any medical care that might be necessary; but Benakis was writing less frequently and did not reply to his pleas for further support. Meanwhile, the composer's family pressured him to return to Athens, causing him further anguish. As he began to sink into poverty, and in order to be able to send money to his parents, he started using some of the funds that Benakis had provided for buying manuscripts – but without telling his erstwhile benefactor (*ibid.*, 199). It is unclear how much Skalkottas spent of Benakis's funds, and only from other sources did Benakis later discover that Skalkottas had misappropriated the money. Eventually Skalkottas admitted his misdeed: '*I owe it to tell you that I certainly have spent some of those enormous amounts of money that you sent me, both something on myself and something for my parents who are suffering financially. I had no right to do so, but I counted on your friendship with me, on your interest in me* […] *So, please don't be so very angry with me*' (LetMB, 23 January 1932, 199). Although he promised that he would copy out '*thousands of pages of score*' to repay his debt, Benakis was furious and demanded full repayment immediately. Skalkottas was unable to repay the debt, yet continued unperturbedly to write to Benakis, in the process demonstrating an unusual degree of emotional attachment and an increasing need for financial and emotional support.

The version of Skalkottas's life put forward by Papaioannou suggests that in May–June 1931 Skalkottas entered a period of depression that continued until 1934; apparently, without explanation he cut himself off completely from the world, stopped seeing his friends, including Konstantinidis and Matla, and ceased writing progressive music.[59] Documentary evidence proves that Skalkottas

---

[58] Thornley suggests that Skalkottas had contracted some form of venereal disease in the summer of 1930 (2002a, 198). However, he does not provide any evidence to justify this claim.

[59] Papaioannou relates an anecdote from the composer Konstantinidis, who 'one day found him completely changed. Skalkottas told him: "I will ask you not to come to my house again […] neither you nor any of my friends, and please let them know. It's my final decision."' Papaioannou also alleges that Skalkottas broke off abruptly from Matla, who 'went mad' when he told her that 'he never wanted to see her again' (Papaioannou, 1997, vol. 1, 88). She kept sending him letters during his last two years in Berlin, which

continued to correspond with Matla until the late 1930s. Moreover, years later Konstantinidis refused to give the details of his relationship with Skalkottas during this period, blaming Papaioannou for 'clouding the issue'; he mentioned only that Skalkottas 'was not well [...] After 1929–30 he wasn't the Skalkottas that I knew. You couldn't be close to and socialize with him'; and even after Skalkottas's return to Greece in 1933, although Konstantinidis tried to contact him a couple of times, he 'couldn't do anything', and they became estranged (Sakalieros, 2005, 31–2). Papaioannou also claimed that Skalkottas's crisis 'arose from [his] conflict with Schoenberg's twelve-tone system, which [Skalkottas] transformed radically to suit his own views' and which led him to 'stop composing advanced works' (1997, vol. 1, 89). Although this comment is perennially reiterated, it does not accord with the facts, as will be discussed later in this book. Schoenberg himself not only approved of Skalkottas's music but praised it and promoted it, notwithstanding his suggestions for improvement. The depressive episode that occurred during late 1931 and 1932, and which coincided with Schoenberg's absence from Berlin, one in a series of such episodes, is more likely attributed to other reasons. Skalkottas's financial and health problems, his immense frustration and disappointment at his compatriots' rejection not only of his music but of him personally, and perhaps his sense of guilt and shame at mismanaging Benakis's affairs and misusing his money, are all likely to have destabilized him.

Despite – or perhaps because of – his previous attack on the Greek musical establishment, Skalkottas now began to show an increased passion for Greek folk music and Greek affairs, and concern for his own identity as a Greek composer. Although he had previously expressed occasional interest in traditional Greek music,[60] it was only after the traumatic Athenian episode and Benakis's withdrawal of funds that 'the Greek theme', combined with constant requests for further financial support, was continuously reiterated in his correspondence with Benakis during 1931 and 1932. He became increasingly preoccupied with composing with Greek folk material and developed the idea of returning to Greece for a while, supported by a scholarship either from Benakis or the Greek government, in order to '*study the Greek language, Greek music, and to discover the combination that I've been seeking for such a long time, of a strict technique* [applied to] *our folk songs, but with a new content*' (LetMB, 17 December 1931, 205).[61] Skalkottas

---

Skalkottas supposedly threw away unopened, an attitude that continued after his return to Greece (*ibid.*). However, much of this appears to be contradicted by the facts.

[60] In 1929 Skalkottas had already asked Benakis to bring him '*Greek folk songs*' (Thornley, 2002a, 201), perhaps to respond to Benakis's conservative tastes in the hope of attracting further financial support.

[61] In early 1932 Skalkottas wrote the following: '*For the past two years I've been secretly contemplating the problem of Greek music* [...] *why don't you see to it that I'm given a state commission to arrange a large number of folk songs?* [...] *You think I wouldn't want to? Do you want me to spell out the moral benefit – a vibrant relationship with my country, with my compatriots* [...] *Apart from that, I want to make some people shut their*

considered the composition of the first of his *Greek Dances* to *'be more or less the "Solemn Reconciliation"'* (LetMB, 23 March 1932, 207). This musical 'reconciliation' was accompanied by an uncharacteristically chauvinistic, if not outright hypocritical, outpouring of patriotic emotions, clearly aimed to further appease Benakis:

> *Wouldn't it be better for me to work close to our wealth of folk-songs? Wouldn't it be better for me to live in Greece?? But how shall I come and what shall I do?? I'm more homesick than you can imagine for my native country* […] *Instead of drinking foreign poison it's better to be in the place where one belongs. And the place where I belong is the Great Idea.*[62] *I was slow in realizing this, but I've finally understood it.* (LetMB, 23 March 1932, 207)

However, these tonal peace-offerings to both Benakis and Greece failed to provide Skalkottas with either the material or emotional succour for which he had hoped. Although his relationship with Benakis rapidly deteriorated during 1932, paradoxically, Skalkottas became even more emotionally dependent on him. He continued writing to him, pleading for financial help, blaming Benakis for his increasing poverty and confiding in him about his personal life. He oscillated between asking Benakis for advice about his future on the one hand, and accusing him of exploiting him for his business affairs, instead of seeing him as a friend, on the other (Thornley 2002a, 209–10). By June, Benakis had cut off his relations with Skalkottas, refusing to write to him or support him in any way, and demanding the return of his letters (*ibid.,* 180). Skalkottas replied prophetically: '*I beg you to tear up my own* [letters], *so they don't appear in some piece of musical criticism or as the plot of some novel or film*' (LetMB, 11 June 1932, 209).

The autumn brought further difficulties for Skalkottas. In September his uncle Kostas, with whom he learnt the violin as a child, died. Depressed but less polemical towards Benakis, who continued to ignore him, Skalkottas was still agonizing over his future and considering the alternatives: whether to return to Greece and look for financial support there, or to find a scholarship in order to stay in Berlin, work on composition and conducting, and write a book on orchestration.

---

*mouths, the ones that make out I'm not capable of writing tonal music*' (LetMB, undated, mid-Jan? 1932, 206).

[62] The Great Idea (Megali Idea) implies the Greek Nation. It is an intellectual as well as a political concept of Greek nationalism, expressing the goal of re-establishing a Greek state that encompasses all ethnic Greeks of the Mediterranean and the Balkans. Eleftherios Venizelos was a major advocate of the idea, but following the Asia Minor disaster and the loss of Anatolia in 1922, its legacy poisoned Greek politics, and by 1932 the phrase had become the slogan of nationalists. It is difficult to associate the musically rebellious Skalkottas with this inflated chauvinism. It rather appears to be desperate opportunism on his behalf, invoking the nationalistic ideals of Venizelos (a personal friend of the Benakis family), to persuade Benakis that he was now, or wanted to be, a 'Greek' composer.

His plans were again haphazard and confused. He now intended to teach music, to revise some of his old works (thus changing his mind and contradicting his recent claim that he '*never changed anything in* [his] *works*') and '*above all, to write something nice, something you* [Benakis] *will like*', suggesting that he might write an opera on a Greek folk subject (LetMB, 30 September 1932, 210). But, struggling with poverty and depression, Skalkottas found it almost impossible to compose. In a terrible state, and having been evicted by his landlady, in early 1933 he sent his last letter to Benakis from Berlin:

> *Dear Manoli, Yesterday I left my room for one night and came here* [the Pension Steinplatz] […] *My room at Frau Fischer's house is very small, and* […] *without heating. I hope 1933 will bring me great happiness and finally a little peace of mind* […] *I don't have any news of my own.* [.] *What are you doing then? Now with the new year you'll have to change your life a little, to write to me. I'll be very happy when we start to correspond [again]. I'm sorry for the financial mistakes, we should meet quickly to get to know one another better, so I can talk about everything with you personally. You'll see that there is a place for justice and for forgiveness. I hope you understand what I mean?* […] *I'm expecting your letter with infinite amounts of news and lots of friendship.* […] *for God's sake, please write to me!* (LetMB, 2 January 1933, 211)

But Benakis never replied, and he never forgave Skalkottas, who in due course became increasingly conscious of the damage he had caused to their relationship. Two years later he wrote to Matla, outlining his side of the story:

> *I meet Benakis from time to time; he became really upset about the autograph manuscripts; for me that was, and still is very shattering, because he has the impression and the certainty that I abused his friendship with the carelessness of youth.* […] *Weighing up the rights on both sides, in my opinion I owe him money, and quite a large sum* […] *That's very bad, and perhaps because of that my departure from here is a matter of course: one cannot be looking forever for a false reconciliation.* (LetMT, 27 November 1935)

When he finished his *36 Greek Dances*, Skalkottas dedicated to Benakis one of the two manuscripts – a leather-bound orchestral score. Still unable to repay his debt, he took the manuscript himself to Benakis's house on Christmas Eve 1936 as an act of reconciliation, but Benakis refused to receive him. (Thornley, 2002a, 215). This marked the end of Skalkottas's relationship with Benakis.

The political and cultural situation in Germany had quickly deteriorated in the early 1930s, and on 30 January 1933, Adolf Hitler became chancellor of the German Reich. The anti-intellectual and anti-artistic attitudes of the National Socialists, together with their brutal anti-Semitic policy, had a fatal impact upon the country's cultural life, with anything innovatory being abruptly stifled and frequently banned by the new regime as 'degenerate' (Morgan, 1991, 221).

Many of the leading artistic figures fled, Jewish and non-Jewish alike, and most of Skalkottas's friends left Berlin. The half-Jewish Matla, no doubt worried about her prospects in Germany and seeking a better life for herself elsewhere, left Berlin in early 1933 for a job as a violinist in Sweden, leaving behind her daughter.[63] She and Skalkottas never met again. Schoenberg left Berlin for Vienna in February 1933, and it wasn't until months later that Skalkottas learnt of his teacher's enforced emigration to France. By now Skalkottas was unable to find work, and, according to his colleague Peter Schacht, 'he became so run down that he couldn't work any more [and] he lived only on debts' (Schmid, 1974, 203). He owed money to many people, including his ex-landlady, who had impounded his belongings (Thornley, 2002a, 212). Emotionally and physically run down, and exhausted by poverty, his only option was to return to Greece for a few months to find financial support; he hoped later to return to Berlin – to pay off his debts and carry on composing. In March 1933, with Schacht's help, he turned to the staff of the Greek Embassy in Berlin for help, and they put him on a train to Athens; but because of his debts, and to ensure he repaid the costs of his repatriation, his passport was confiscated by the Greek Foreign Ministry (*ibid.,* 212; 2008a, 335–6).

Skalkottas's daughter Artemis claims that her father visited her for the last time before leaving Berlin. He also gave a chest containing some of his composition manuscripts to Ortmann, a music dealer in Charlottenburg, for safekeeping until his return. Ortmann later tried to give this chest 'full of the manuscripts of this poor Greek composer' to Thanos Bourlos, an opera singer who had lived in Berlin during the war, so that it could be returned to Skalkottas. But Bourlos did not think much of it and left it with Ortmann (Bourlos, 1981, 127–8). Ortmann's shop was bombed, and in 1955 only four of the pieces were recovered by the pianist George Hadjinikos: the Octet, the First and Second string quartets and the First Piano Concerto.

---

[63] Artemis Lindal, personal communication.

# Chapter 3
# The Greek Period

*Everything is a big disappointment.*[1]

**A Bitter Homecoming**

Skalkottas left Berlin in the throes of National Socialism and unwillingly returned to his native Greece. There, however, the political situation had been unstable for much of the 1920s into the 1930s. Following the Asia Minor disaster in the early 1920s, and the destruction of the 'Great Idea', the country suffered continuous political wrangling between monarchists and Venizelist liberals. The political scene was dominated by a quick succession of governments, rigged elections and military coups, and after 1931 Greece faced a serious economic crisis that eventually pushed the country off the gold standard and resulted in the devaluation of the drachma (Mazower, 1991, 143–202). Around the time that Skalkottas returned to Greece, the liberal government of Venizelos fell at the general election of 5 March 1933, leading to further political unrest. In 1936 the dictator Ioannis Metaxas, with the king's assent, abolished the constitution and parliament, and imposed a police state. Metaxas, showing his deep ideological affiliation with fascism, declared that Greece had become 'an anti-communist, anti-parliamentary, totalitarian state. […] If Hitler and Mussolini were really fighting for the ideology they preached, they should be supporting Greece' (Campbell and Sherrard, 1968, 155–66). Metaxas abolished political freedoms, incarcerated communists in concentration camps, and systematically persecuted and imprisoned everyone opposed to his policies. Greece sank into obscurantism, with severe censorship being imposed in the press and books being destroyed in organized bonfires.

Given this political situation, it is unsurprising that the conservative Greek National School of composers, and the promotion of nationalist orthodoxy – rather than more modern, internationalist pluralism – predominated within Greece's musical scene in the 1930s. Academic and artistic communities mirrored the political world, with political interference, nepotism and petty treachery ever-present facts of life. Those artists or institutions who were not part of the more influential circles found themselves obstructed and sidelined. Even Mitropoulos was not exempt. When in February 1933 he was elected to a chair in the Academy of Athens (an honorary and ceremonial organization patterned after the French Academy), there was bitter reaction from the conservative, right-wing members

---

[1] LetMT, 27 November 1935.

of the National School (Trotter, 1995, 73). On 6 April 1933, a few days after Skalkottas had arrived in Athens, six members of the Greek Composers' Union – Kalomiris, Varvoglis, Lavrangas, Lambelet, Spathis and Prokopiou – protested in the Athenian newspaper *The People's Voice* against the Academy's decision, on the grounds that as a composer Mitropoulos 'has nothing of any value to offer, neither as to the quantity nor to the quality of the music that he has produced' (Kostios, 1985, 51–2). Several years later Mitropoulos continued to be accused by Athenian critics of suffering from 'a lack of self-criticism […] incessant narcissism' and of simply 'making a poor copy of hyper-modern international composers' (M.K., *Ethnos*, 5 October 1936). Frustrated by the cultural stagnation in Athens, and hurt by the malicious critical reviews, he decided to pursue his conducting career abroad. In 1937 he left Greece permanently to become principal conductor of the Minneapolis Symphony Orchestra (*ibid.*, 61–2).

It was to this bleak economic, political and artistic environment that Skalkottas returned. The pianist Antonis Skokos, a colleague from Berlin, years later recalled: 'He arrived in Athens in a state of moral shock, with a wounded soul […] a melancholy sorrow written forever on his ascetic face […] His only passion in life was composition' (Skokos, 1950, 599). The ex-gold medallist and promising violin virtuoso, the budding composer of avant-garde music, accepted and praised in Schoenberg's Berlin circle, now returned home broken, dogged by misfortune, and unsuccessful by Greek standards. On his return to the family home he had a complete nervous breakdown and for several months remained confined to his room. When the pianist Spyros Farandatos, his former colleague and flatmate in Berlin, now an increasingly influential Professor of Piano at the Athens Conservatory, invited him to examine some diploma candidates in the summer exams, he refused (Thornley, 2008a, 336). This hardly helped his precarious relationship with the musical establishment, and Farandatos, who became Deputy Director and then, from 1939 until 1962, Director of the Conservatory, would never help him again.

Skalkottas's lack of political party involvement meant he was not immediately affected by the broader political situation. But in the musical world he faced enmity and oppression in place of the recognition and encouragement he had received in Berlin. Many influential figures were aware of his talents but ignored him or in some way obstructed his career.[2] In particular Filoktitis Economidis[3] and

---

[2] Papaioannou called the influential figures of the musical establishment who 'fought' against Skalkottas 'the Big Collusion', on the grounds that they were afraid of his talents and capabilities, and he includes among them Economidis, Kalomiris, Farandatos, Poniridis, Petridis and Mitropoulos (1997, vol. 1, 96–104). Mitropoulos, in a radio interview broadcast by the 'Voice of America', lashed out with bitterness at the Greek intellectual establishment for its treatment of Skalkottas by saying: 'They killed him, you know, Skalkottas, they killed him. And if I hadn't left, they would have killed me, too' (Trotter, 1995, 75).

[3] Filoktitis Economidis (1889–1957) was a conservative and controlling musical politician, a prominent orchestral, choral and opera conductor in Athens and a powerful educational administrator from the early 1920s. After 1930, during Mitropoulos's prolonged

Manolis Kalomiris,[4] the leading figures of the Athenian musical establishment during Skalkottas's lifetime, both of whom he had managed to insult in his earlier public attacks, showed a personal antipathy towards him, in addition to their aversion to his musical aesthetic. Although Economidis had been one of Skalkottas's teachers at the Athens Conservatory, he did not support him after his return in 1933. His opposition towards the younger composer – whom he may have seen as a rival for his conducting position – meant that Skalkottas was never allowed to conduct the Athens Conservatory Orchestra, even in his own *Greek Dances*. Following Skalkottas's death, Economidis conducted three of these dances at a concert on 30 October 1949, making a brief speech in which he described Skalkottas as a 'colleague, who, among other things, also wrote music'; by all accounts he considered Skalkottas to be an 'odd specimen' (Chamoudopoulos, 2 November 1949). Similarly, although in 1931 Kalomiris reacted to Skalkottas's music with patronizing tolerance, now his antipathy towards the young composer became legendary in Athenian musical circles. Acquaintances of Skalkottas recalled in later life that as a conductor Kalomiris refused to shake Skalkottas's hand when the latter was leading the orchestra, and he never properly acknowledged him as a composer. When Skalkottas applied for membership of the Greek Composers' Union (of which Kalomiris was president) in around 1940, his application was marked that he 'has a different profession' (Thornley, 2008a, 350).[5]

Skalkottas's nervous breakdown lasted for most of 1933, during which time he managed to complete only his first four *Greek Dances*.[6] These were first

---

absences abroad, he gradually took over the Athens Conservatory Orchestra, becoming its director after Mitropoulos's emigration to America. Two years before Skalkottas's return to Greece, in 1931, he was appointed Deputy Director of the Athens Conservatory, becoming its Director in 1935, and although he retired from this post in 1939 he remained influential in the Athenian musical life until his death in 1957 (Leotsakos, 1987, 424–5).

[4] Manolis Kalomiris (1883–1962) was an influential and controlling figure, the embodiment of the musical establishment in Greece. Composer, teacher, administrator, writer and music critic, and a leading opera conductor from 1930 onwards, Kalomiris promoted his nationalistic ideology. He created the first large-scale symphonic and operatic compositions in Greece, and wrote a substantial amount of chamber music and songs, combining Greek folk melodies with a predominantly Wagnerian orchestral and harmonic language. He taught at the Athens Conservatory from 1911 until 1919, when, after a rift with Nazos, he resigned to found the Hellenic Conservatory; he left the latter in 1926 to establish the National Conservatory. In 1936 he became president of the Greek Composers' Union that he had helped to found, and held several other posts throughout his life (Symeonidou, 1995, 164–9; Romanou, 2006, 133–7, 169–82).

[5] Thornley presumes this to mean that Skalkottas was viewed as 'an amateur composer', but it is also possible that the union wished to indicate its view of Skalkottas as a violinist rather than a composer.

[6] These four dances are *Tsamikos* – '*An Eagle*', *Kritikos*, *Epirotikos* and the *Peloponnisiakos I*. Papaioannou alleges that during his 'crisis' Skalkottas 'stopped composing completely'; but, while still bedridden, when his father Alekos suggested that

performed in Athens on 21 January 1934 by the Athens Conservatory Orchestra, conducted by Mitropoulos, with Skalkottas present. They were warmly applauded by the audience but received rather more patronizingly by the critics. Psaroudas, for example, wrote: 'When a few years ago Mr Skalkottas was presented as a composer at the symphony concerts, he was judged quite severely and rightly in my view. [...] Today I am happy to confirm that, when he wants to, this musician can compose in a delightful way' (*Eleftheron Vima*, January 1934). In the same year Skalkottas was asked by Melpo Merlier, the director of the Kendro Mikrasiatikon Spoudon (KMS) (Musical Folklore Archive of the Centre of Asia Minor Studies), to transcribe several folk-song recordings for the archive.[7] He was handed 15 78 rpm records, and transcribed 32 songs from Crete, five from Sifnos, two from Vourla (Ionia) and two from Rhodes; 15 of these transcriptions were accompanied by extensive comments. He spent several months, from 15 June 1934 to 30 January 1935, transcribing these 41 folk songs, a job he often found challenging. In an apologetic letter to Merlier he explained his difficulties:

> *The work of the songs is not ready* [...] *The transcription from the gramophone is quite difficult, each instrument is not heard very clearly. Maybe it is the fault of the gramophone I have, but maybe* [it is] *that I work for the first time in transcribing Greek folk songs from a gramophone.* [...] *In many of these songs it's not at all easy to discern the accompanying instrument, lute or santuri. I leave many bars harmonically empty, I don't add any harmony before I consult you* [...] *The song is heard mainly clearly, but in records without accompaniment and in songs with free rhythm I find many difficulties in their transcription* [...] *I hope, despite all the technical difficulties, that you will be satisfied with my work.*
> (LetMM, 16 August 1934, in Dragoumis, 1978–79, 31–2)

Despite these problems and the extremely low rate of pay, he found the work '*very interesting, especially dictating from a gramophone record. It is very interesting for a musician to transcribe on paper all 42* [sic] *songs and dances and deliver them*' (LetMT, 27 November 1935). In addition, this collaboration with the KMS was important because it gave Skalkottas the impulse to complete within the next two years all his *36 Greek Dances* for orchestra.

---

he 'write a few Greek Dances for orchestra [...] he gave in: he sat down and started (1934) writing the well-known group of Dances' (1991, 38). This frequently quoted anecdote appears improbable if only because Skalkottas composed the first version of the *Peloponnisiakos I*, and sketched several of the others, in Berlin. The complete set of the *36 Greek Dances* for large orchestra is dated by Skalkottas himself '1934–36'.

[7] Melpo Merlier's folk-song recording project, supported by the Venizelos government, had begun in Athens on 23 October 1930. Other composers who also worked on this project, transcribing the recorded folk-songs, were Kalomiris, Petridis, Sklavos, Lavrangas, Poniridis, Riadis and the ethnomusicologist Samuel Baud-Bovy.

In 1934 Skalkottas also undertook a substantial, but again poorly remunerated, job for the Greek National Theatre, arranging and orchestrating a Stravinsky-like ballet, *Cyclops*, by Manolis Skouloudis. Apart from his '*joy that there is a theatre here*', he complained about the theatre conditions in Athens, and that he had '*lost quite useful days for myself* […] *and have been taken quite ill*' (LetMT, 27 November 1935) because of the amount of work he had to do, which included playing the piano and copying out all the orchestral parts for the performance.

**Working in the Athenian 'Nest of Intrigue'**

Skalkottas's minor success with the *Greek Dances* neither helped his financial situation nor raised his spirits, and he was obliged to continue seeking financial support from wealthy Greek families. But he failed – not only because of the economic turmoil, but also because of his widely known financial dealings and subsequent rift with Benakis, which alienated potential patrons. Consequently, he joined the Athens Conservatory Orchestra, having no other option through which he might generate a steady income. In 1938 he also joined the newly formed Athens Radio Orchestra, and in 1940 the orchestra of the *Lyriki Skini* (National Opera Orchestra). Nevertheless, his financial situation did not improve substantially. In 1934 he entered the Conservatory Orchestra on the first desk of the first violins, but over the course of a few years he was moved to the back desks, where he stayed until the end of his life.[8] Although he had little choice but to accept his predicament and this gradual demotion, he felt humiliated and embittered by being treated this way in a professional environment he had detested since he was a student. He still suffered from nerves and various unspecified illnesses, and he despaired for his life, the underlying reasons for his ongoing depression having shifted from his Berlin problems to his aversion to working in Athens. He felt frustrated, undervalued, underpaid and trapped inside a country in which he no longer wished to live.

To make matters worse, his isolation and continuing depression gave rise – within the orchestra and other Athenian musical circles – to the rumour that he was psychologically disturbed (Papaioannou, 1997, vol. 1, 106). Minos Dounias, on his own return to Athens from Berlin in 1936, was shocked at seeing the change in Skalkottas:

---

[8] The orchestral records show Skalkottas's position movement in the orchestra. His name first appears in the orchestral register on 19 March 1934. He was second player on the first desk in the first violins, where he remained during the 1934–35 season. In 1935–36 he appears as the first player on the third desk; in 1936–37 second player on the second desk. In 1937–38 he was moved to the back desk of the first violins, where he remained until his death (AthConsDM 1935–41, and ASOR 1943–49). Thornley suggests that Skalkottas either moved to the back desk of his own volition, to avoid orchestral politics, or that he was moved back to make way for younger and more ambitious players (2002a, 214; 2008a, 336).

> When I met him again here in Athens, after a three-year separation, I found myself in front of a man irretrievably psychologically wounded, forced to live under the shadow of lesser talents and the pressure of the difficult and inexorable struggle to make a living. One could appreciate how this artist, who gained so many honours in maybe the biggest centre in Europe, here, in the small land which gave him birth, found himself suddenly in the margin [...] It remains surprising, the fact that the musical leaders and artistic institutions of our land were so disinterested in offering spiritual support, positive, substantial help to a talent so idiosyncratic, maybe the rarest our country has produced so far. (Dounias, 1963, 66)

Perhaps the rumour was not so far from the truth. In a long, repetitive, and often incoherent letter to Matla Temko, dated 27 November 1935, Skalkottas obsessively reiterated his disgust, depression and disappointment with life in Athens:[9]

> *You don't know how bad I am here in my own country, with regard to my health as well as my finances. I am hoping with all my heart that things will get better. [...] Everything is a great disappointment and* [there is] *no improvement to my present difficult existence. This terrible nervousness has changed me a lot, the dismal and above all irregular family life is simply driving me crazy – one doesn't find a way out* [...] *It is a bitter and immensely bad time, I am getting this indescribable revulsion with regard to all the earthly and celestial things. [...] This is not a nice and happy state for me. A terrible, almost mean and disgustingly great disappointment, depressions from one minute to the next and from one second to the next. Everything, dear Temko, that you are going to hear from me is very depressing – almost all the impressions that I have made during the last years, from 1933 onward until today, are bad and not good evidence for my surroundings, the milieu, where one finds oneself and from which one doesn't see the right way out.* [...] *It is impossible to write down on paper my horror, my disgust, my moroseness* [...] *It's almost a crime!* [...] *The most terrible disgust overcomes me* [...] *a dangerous repulsion.* [...] *It is bad, dear Temko, very bad compared to earlier times.*

The letter continues for 15 pages in a torrent of discontent:

> *Everywhere people throw stones at you. One is hindered with his own work. It is all a terrible disappointment and it makes you sick* [...] *The worst of it is that people have made up their minds* [...] *I feel disgusted and it makes me feel sick* [...] *It is a cruel state indeed to be in for a young person who wants to progress,*

---

[9] The original German in this letter does not translate easily into English. However, I have given, as much as possible, a literal translation to convey Skalkottas's writing style and psychological condition. The extracts used in the following discussion have all been taken from his letter (LetMT, 27 November 1935).

*who is able to progress. One does not find a way out and one thinks the exit is closed. It is a really poisoned air that is not easy to breath; […] I cannot find here a stronger will, or a way out for myself, neither from the country, nor the people, and not to mention the unpleasant conflicts, which happen in daily life […] Here unfortunately everything has been stolen from me, I've been well and truly robbed, if not covered in dirt from head to foot, perhaps both. […] in truth everything is certainly dirtier than I can describe it to you […] There are few open doors to young people with a good education in theatres, academies, orchestras and so on. And what small payment, and what dirt and what other losses too one can suffer here – it simply makes you scream and throw up – well, it's simply horrible. […] Neither the country nor the people are the right and proper thing for me at this moment in my life […] Those in charge are playing too many games with people.*

For some time during 1934–35 he played the second violin in a quartet led by his old friend Nelly (now Nelly Evelpidi), but he found the experience frustrating and unrewarding, both musically and financially. Matters of technique and interpretation in particular, which were instilled in him during his student years with both Hess and Schoenberg, were not considered to be as important in his Greek artistic environment.[10] They played quartets by Haydn, Beethoven, Dvořák and Debussy, but despite their practice '*the result was nought […] the pieces sounded rather unrecogniz*[ably] *wrong and jumbled*'. Not being the leader of his own quartet Skalkottas felt frustrated that he couldn't '*instruct, lead or rehearse a quartet in a really modern way, in today's sense* [;] *there could be a completely different result*'. He also complained bitterly about his life in the orchestra, the working conditions of which hadn't improved since the time he wrote his caustic attack on it in 1931:

*I am currently working in the orchestra […] I play the violin […] and earning just as much that it isn't enough […] A more thankless, more indescribably difficult concert life doesn't exist, there isn't even a feeling, not even some contact – which might take place between the audience, the conductor and the musicians. […] It simply makes you want to commit suicide. Nothing good about the Athens symphony orchestra. My income for the whole season amounts to 10000–12000 drachmas, which is approximately 250 marks. […] So, this is [my] homecoming, my moral and financial reward after the long hardship and the attentive studies, which I have done abroad. Depressed and depressed again.*[11]

---

[10]  He complained that, '*Here they play music in the wrong way, only falsely, only horribly […] What will come of it though, when four people play music in the wrong way and are successful?*'

[11]  He emphasized his difficult financial situation perhaps because he wanted to avoid contributing towards Artemis's upbringing in Berlin; and he repeatedly used his meagre

He was disappointed at the lack of performances of his '*serious*' twelve-note music, taking little notice of performances of his tonal *Greek Dances*, which were the only pieces that provided him with some success among Greek audiences: '*All these years I have been here nothing of my work has been performed, nobody has such a hard time as I have. The four Greek Dances have been performed three times with me as violinist in the orchestra. The scores go from one place to another, but unfortunately, I only get rejections with performances.*' Given what he saw as the bleakness of his situation, he set aside memories of the depression and difficulties he had experienced in Berlin and instead became painfully nostalgic about the good times he had had among Schoenberg's circle, where he felt his creative voice had been recognized:

> *It would have been better for me if I had stayed in Germany and kept working with Schoenberg. […] with the parting from Schoenberg's students, from my friends, with my return I've lost almost everything that belongs to a normal human being; it's very strange, but abroad I found love and a normal life more natural than here, and love to almost everyone without exception!*

As a result Skalkottas became withdrawn and uncommunicative. He seldom talked and did not discuss music or his work, even with friends and family. He was overtaken by a melancholy – more so than in Berlin – that he never managed to lose. The change in his character and his ongoing depression were reflected in his physical appearance. He developed short-sightedness and wore thick glasses, his hair receded, he had skin problems, and he looked prematurely aged.

Illustration 3.1    Nikos Skalkottas (c.1938–40)

---

income as an excuse: '*Pray dear Temko to Moses that my financial situation will improve; that might do you and myself a lot of good.*'

Athens dance school director Dora Vlastou, for whom Skalkottas worked for a while as accompanist, vividly described her impression of him:

> The silhouette of a very thin man with discoloured trousers, old rubber shoes, and, thrown over his bent shoulders, a very worn-out coat. His face was almost hidden by a deeply tucked hat. I couldn't imagine he was the visitor we had expected. But when I approached him to shake his hand, I saw behind his thick glasses two large black eyes with an unforgettable expression of gentleness and melancholy. We didn't say much – it was as if he had a difficulty with verbal expression […] He immediately sat at the piano and, looking at us, he played a melody, and then another, endless variations on the same idea. How easily, how spontaneously the melodies welled out from his beautiful fingers on the piano. (Vlastou, 1961, 51)

Similarly, the composer George Kazasoglou later conjured up a romanticized image of the 'hidden, silent man':

> My friendship with Skalkottas made me […] respect and love the 'hidden man', whose delicate and sensitive soul would be closed, quiet and silently contemplating for some time before […] [he let] his 'sacred' silence fall. Then, sometimes slowly and sometimes immediately, the hidden, but so beautiful, introvert Nikos would ascend and reveal himself! (1978–79, 15–16).

Skalkottas appeared reluctant to contact people, even those he respected, such as Schoenberg, whom he knew was in Boston at the time: '*It is a shame that I have not written a few words to him; I have often meant to, but in the end I haven't done it. Hopefully I'll soon find the time for it, for I haven't left him.*' But he never wrote to Schoenberg, or to his old friend Rudi Goehr: '*I have received two cards from Rudolf Goehr from Corsica […] I have also received a letter from him right after my arrival […] Unfortunately I did not have the time to write to him.*' He did not even contact the Kolisch Quartet: '*I thought about a Greek tour, but I don't know how the people in high authority will take it. It is my moral duty to accomplish this; I think the quartet players will be very pleased to go on tour in Greece. […] Perhaps there is a possibility to send Kolisch and his assistants this good news. Everything depends on the right time. For me this would mean something good, if I succeeded with this intention.*' But he never contacted them because of his lack of motivation and his incompetence in practical matters. This was an attitude he had already exhibited earlier in his life, when he prophetically wrote to Nelly from Berlin, '*It was never convenient, or Fate* [prevents me from] *bringing to completion what I promise and plan*' (LetAsk, 8 November 1925).

Skalkottas's constant battle with his weak body, and the psychological impact of what he perceived as life's injustices, exacerbated his apathetic and generally defeatist attitude. He abandoned any fight with the Greek musical establishment and, disheartened, retreated into an inner self-exile, isolating himself from his

Illustration 3.2    Nikos Skalkottas on his return to Greece (undated, but probably 1940s)

surroundings. Although he was outwardly polite, he lived the rest of his life *in absentia*. He wrote to Matla of this abandonment: '*It is depressing, terrible to lead this lonely life. I don't have any motivation to do anything, to take any new and healthy action* […] *It is very sad for me.*' Despite all his problems, or perhaps because of them, Skalkottas channelled his anger, frustration and creative energy into writing and composition. Curiously, in stark contrast to his inner anguish, his writings display a different, more passionate and forceful individual. In his essay 'The School of Modern Composers' he declared that '*Every composer can have his own school. To conquer this, he should excel spiritually, and if he is very revolutionary he should fight with every means*' (MS essay). Composition continued to absorb him entirely. By day he would play the violin in the orchestra, but at night he would compose tirelessly, often until dawn; this passion for composition, in near isolation, continued until his death.[12]

The year 1935 marked the beginning of a ten-year period of prolific compositional activity. As he wrote to Matla (27 November 1935): '*Despite the difficulties and many disappointments I have suffered, my strength and stamina for my work have not been affected. I have composed a lot, especially pieces which apparently cannot be heard* [performed] *here*'; and he went on to enumerate his compositions:

> *A large orchestral piece in six movements – duration 3/4 of an hour,* [this was the First Symphonic Suite]*, which I had already composed – sketched thematically alone – beside Schoenberg in Berlin; a good String Trio* [the Second String Trio] [;] *8 new Greek Dances!, making 12 overall; two new Sonatinas* [the Sonatinas for violin and piano Nos 3 and 4] [;] *a Third String Quartet, a short Concertino for two pianos and orchestra*[;][13] *and* [a] *private work consisting of transcribing Greek songs from records* [the Merlier project].

This is an enormous amount of music for any composer to write in one year, indicating perhaps the intensity with which Skalkottas composed. However, as will be shown later in this book, these large-scale works exhibit developmental stages in his twelve-note compositional technique, suggesting that he must have been working on them in some way during the previous years, notwithstanding his apparent depression.

By the end of 1936 he had completed his *36 Greek Dances*.[14] A few were performed several times during his lifetime, and were always enthusiastically

---

[12]  Dounias recalled: 'Skalkottas's grieving widow tells me about her husband's big passion: composition. He would return at midnight, tired from duty at the orchestra, and immediately set himself to work. Often, dawn found him bent over the music manuscript' (1963, 67).

[13]  In 1935 Skalkottas composed the Concertino for two pianos (A/K20) for his friends from Berlin Antonis Skokos and his wife Katina Paraskeva, who were the leading piano duo in Greece in the 1930s and 1940s. However, they never performed the piece.

[14]  The *36 Greek Dances* (probably Skalkottas's most well-known work) were originally organized in three sets of twelve. Nos 1–4 of Set I were composed 1931–33, and Nos 5–12 were composed in 1935. The remaining twenty-four dances (included in Sets II and III) were composed by the end of 1936 (according to the flyleaf of the full score now in the Benakis Archive). At least seven of the *36 Greek Dances* for orchestra were inspired by the songs he transcribed for KMS (*Sifneikos I–II*, *Kritikos II–V*, and *Nisiotikos*). The song 'Mother, Don't Beat Me' for voice and piano was also inspired by a song of the same title from the island of Rhodes. Some of the *Greek Dances* also exist in other instrumental combinations, for string orchestra (five dances), violin and piano, and piano solo. Skalkottas during 1940–43 transcribed nine of these dances for wind orchestra, and he re-orchestrated them all in 1948–49 (see Appendix A: Chronological Worklist). For a detailed discussion of the *36 Greek Dances*, see Christodoulou (2008, 144–69).

received by Athenian audiences – which may be seen as evidence of a certain rehabilitation among conservative Greek nationalists. George Kazasoglou remembered the reception of such a performance of the *Four Greek Dances* in Athens: 'During the last bar of the fourth dance an enthusiastically frenzied applause erupted together with endless cheering from the audience. […] The conductor [Economidis] indicated Skalkottas, who stood up in front of the last desk of the first violins, and with a bitter smile, he nervously bowed a couple of times to the audience, who in turn intensified their cheering and applauded with unrestrained enthusiasm' (Kazasoglou, 1978–79, 17). Even the conservative critics were positive in their judgements. Dounias believed the *Greek Dances* were 'written with exceptional talent, with deep knowledge of the folk rhythms and scales, but most of all with genuine and unfeigned musical feeling' (12 December 1936); and he praised Skalkottas for having been able 'not to make Greek music, but to give the impression of Greek music' (18 March 1939, in Dounias, 1963, 34–5). Psaroudas, who was so cruel in his review of Skalkottas's 1931 concerts, now exclaimed that the dances were 'one of the most successful Greek works of the last few years' (9 December 1936), and later observed that these 'musical pages of the first order […] unreservedly rate among the very best of the whole Greek musical output' (2 February 1941). Similarly, Theodoropoulou proclaimed that 'there is no doubt that this young man has rare possibilities' (1939, 502) and considered the dances to be 'true musical gems' (1941, 117).[15]

Having finished the tonal *Greek Dances*, Skalkottas also composed in 1936 several dodecaphonic works – including the Piano Trio, the Scherzo for quartet with piano, and the First Piano Suite – and he started the Ten Canons for piano, which he completed in 1937. The next few years saw the development of two separate strands in Skalkottas's output. In parallel with his uncompromising large-scale dodecaphonic works he began to write shorter chamber music works in a freer, atonal idiom. By 1939 he had composed atonal pieces for violin and piano (*March of the Little Soldiers*, Rondo, Nocturne, *Small Chorale and Fugue*, Gavotte and *Scherzo and Menuetto cantato* for violin and piano,[16] and the Duo for violin and viola) and a series of large-scale instrumental concertos (the Second Piano Concerto, the Violin Concerto, the Third Concerto for piano, ten winds and percussion, and the Concerto for violin, viola and wind orchestra). In certain works he combined twelve-note, tonal and folk elements, such as in the *Eight Variations on a Greek Folk Theme* for trio with piano, and the orchestral ballet suite *The Maiden and Death*. The latter was written in 1938 and first performed by the Athens Conservatory Orchestra on 10 May 1940, with Skalkottas present. In several of the lighter pieces

---

[15] Mitropoulos conducted three of the *Greek Dances* for the first time in America on 14 April 1939 to positive reviews (Kostios, 1985, 285).

[16] In January 1939 Rudi Goehr visited Athens briefly. He met Skalkottas and brought him news about Schoenberg. Before he returned to Paris, Skalkottas gave him the Gavotte and the *Scherzo and Menuetto cantato* for violin and piano (Papaioannou, 1997, vol. 2, 77; Thornley, 2002b, 120).

there are nostalgic references to the Berlin world that Skalkottas had left behind, with its jazz music, music for silent movies and the ad hoc ensembles in which he used to play.

In 1939 he collaborated with Koula Pratsika, the director of the Pratsika Dance School, in the production of *The Gnomes* (*Ta Paganá*). He produced a ballet suite based on his orchestration of small piano pieces, predominantly by Bartók, together with three small original pieces by himself. Apart from his work in the orchestra and his collaboration with a few ballet companies in Athens, which he considered as private work, his prolific compositional output – away from the public eye – continued unabated. By early 1940 he had completed his Second sonata for violin and piano, and the *Ten Sketches* for strings. During summer 1940, as the German army overran western Europe, and Greece moved closer to war with Italy, in three separate weeks between mid-June and mid-August Skalkottas composed his *32 Piano Pieces*. These were followed by seven large-scale, solo piano pieces (the Second, Third and Fourth piano suites, and Four Studies for piano),[17] the Fourth String Quartet and the Double Bass Concerto.

## The Second World War and the Occupation Years

On 28 October 1940, Greece entered the war. Paradoxically it was the fascist dictator Ioannis Metaxas who rejected Italy's ultimatum, demanding the right to occupy certain strategic positions in Greek territory. Mussolini's troops crossed the Albanian border into Greece but failed to invade the country, due to the resistance offered by the Greek army. Following Italy's withdrawal, Hitler ordered German troops to attack; Greek bravery alone was no match for the German invasion that began in April 1941, and on 27 April the Wehrmacht entered Athens. In May, the Allied troops who had retreated to Crete were defeated, and the entire country suffered triple occupation, by Italy (in the Ionian islands), Bulgaria (in eastern Macedonia and Thrace) and Germany (the rest of Greece).[18] The occupying forces frequently resorted to plundering, and a shocked Minos Dounias exclaimed: 'Where is the traditional German sense of honour? I lived in Germany thirteen years and no one cheated me. Now suddenly with the New Order they have all become thieves' (Delopoulos, 1987, 50; cited in Mazower, 1993, 23–4). The combination of military requisition and inflation led to food shortages. The winter of 1941–42 proved to be one of the most severe in Greek history, and with the bitter cold came famine, resulting in the deaths of around 300,000 people (Mazower, 1993, 32–64).

---

[17] These piano works are undated. Apart from the Second Piano Suite, the Archive Catalogue places them in 1941. However, the handwriting of the Four Studies, in particular, suggests that they were all written in 1940. A lack of evidence prevents us from knowing whether Skalkottas composed these solo piano pieces successively, or whether they were interrupted by the composition of other chamber or orchestral works.

[18] For further details see, Tsoucalas (1981) and Campbell and Sherrard (1968).

Skalkottas's dissociation from his surroundings was most apparent during these years of German occupation, and during the later civil war. Being exempt from the army, probably due to his ill health, he did not fight during the Albanian campaign against the Italians, nor was he involved in the resistance movement in Athens. He remained detached from the struggle and the fighting around him, and the years 1940–45 represent one of his most prolific compositional periods. During the early months of the war he composed the two light-hearted, jazz-influenced quartets for oboe, trumpet, bassoon and piano, and the Concertino for trumpet and piano. In 1939 he had already been asked to compose a Concertino for oboe and piano for an oboist colleague in the orchestra, to which, in 1943, he added the *Sonata Concertante* for bassoon and piano.[19] He was thus led to conceive of a 'cycle-concert' involving these three wind instruments and piano, but no performance of this cycle took place in his lifetime. In the spring of 1941, during the early days of the occupation of Athens, in a period of six weeks from the end of April to the beginning of June, he composed his song cycle '16 Tragoudia (Songs)' for mezzo-soprano and piano. These were based on poems by Christos Esperas, the pseudonym of Chrissos Evelpidis, the husband of his friend Nelly. The poems come from the book *Opos Oli* ('Like Everybody'), which Skalkottas first saw at Nelly's house in spring 1941; when, a year later, he discovered the identity of the book's author, he dedicated his songs to Evelpidis (Thornley, 2004, 18).[20]

During this time Skalkottas wrote a number of essays about music, and he also produced the manuscript (in Greek) of a *Treatise on Orchestration*.[21] The essays are frequently illegible and incoherent, although they allow glimpses into Skalkottas's mindset and his ideas about music. In some of them, as if short of paper, he wrote in the margins of previous pages portions of text that should have appeared later, thus making these writings a confusing and often fragmented sequence of unrelated ideas. Skalkottas seems to have had little interest in polishing these

---

[19] At the end of the first movement in the draft score there is the date 28 July 1943.

[20] In the fair copy of the manuscript there is Skalkottas's handwritten dedication to Evelpidis: 'With much admiration and friendship, to Mr. Chrissos Evelpidis these sixteen songs are dedicated "28 May 1942"' (Skalkottas Archive).

[21] In the Skalkottas Archive there are twenty-three handwritten and undated essays, dealing with the following topics: 'Orchestration', 'New Cinema Music', 'Folk Song', 'Originality and Imitation', 'Theory and Practice of the Musical Rules', 'New Musical Literature', 'The Musical Search', 'Development of Musical Themes', 'The Symphony', 'Harmony and Counterpoint', 'Musical Influences', 'The School of Modern Composers', 'Style', 'Musical Anecdotes', 'Collection of Thoughts', 'How we will Write for the Theatre', 'Piano Technique', 'Musical Accompaniments', 'Compositional Details', 'Dance Music', 'Violin Technique', 'Chamber Music for Wind Instruments and Piano', and 'The Power of Symphonic Concerts'. Demertzis (1998) invariably dates these articles from 1934 to 1942. Similarly, although Skalkottas's *Treatise on Orchestration* is also undated, Demertzis proposes the hypothetical dates from 1939 to 1943. None of these was ever published.

works, leaving them in an unpublishable state.[22] There is an obvious difference in writing style from the letters of the Berlin years, which were better articulated and more clearly presented, the earliest ones often being written in calligraphic style. The letters to Matla from the mid-1930s already show a change in both his writing and his thinking. Although they are still clearly presented on the page, they are written in an idiomatic, occasionally unintelligible German, with disparate ideas strung together and certain words and phrases obsessively reiterated at seemingly irrelevant points. In the writings of the early to mid-1940s the often incoherent language and untidy presentation suggest a change in Skalkottas's personality and perhaps also his mental state.

During the last two darkest years of the German occupation (1942–44) Skalkottas suffered from deprivation, like most other poor and working-class Greeks, notwithstanding that he obtained food from the artists' 'soup kitchen' and benefited from the hospitality of his wealthy friend Nelly. To make ends meet, in addition to his orchestral commitments, he continued to undertake whatever other musical work was available, such as chamber music coaching, private music classes, piano accompaniment and collaborative work in dance schools.[23] Yet despite the difficult times, playing in three orchestras and working privately, he managed to compose several major large-scale works. With blithe indifference to the prevailing inadequacy of orchestral resources and performance standards in Athens, he completed the orchestration of the Double Bass Concerto, which he had already composed in 1940. He offered it to D. Tzoumanis, the principal bass player of the Athens State Orchestra, presumably expecting him to perform it; but Skalkottas should have realized that such a difficult, atonal work demanding an extremely large orchestra and soloistic competence of the highest standards was unlikely to receive a performance from this ill-equipped Athenian orchestra during a time of occupation and famine. Skalkottas, seemingly unconstrained by

---

[22] A typical example of such writing is Skalkottas's attempt to assess the various modern schools of composition in the essay 'The School of Modern Composers': '*One who has an interest could ask how many modern music schools there are. They are innumerable, they are three-four and there are so many that they convey as a necessity their formative naming, [...] The modern expressionistic school, the impressionistic, the modern-classical, the music for use* [i.e. Gebrauchsmusik], *the school of the passing modes, the revolutionary music school of the theatre, have made us understand approximately at which point multi-directional musical evolution is found today*' (MS, 3).

[23] In 1943 Skalkottas composed *Island Images*, 'a ballet suite made up of six pieces – for *corps de ballet* and solo dancing' for the dance diploma exam of Aleka Mazaraki-Katseli, a student at the Koula Pratsika Dance School (and later a celebrated Greek actress). In the Archive Catalogue this work is assigned the title *Ballet Suite* for small orchestra (A/K15). Similarly in 1946, in collaboration with Koula Pratsika, Skalkottas produced *The Beauty with the Rose (Fairy Tale)* (A/K111). The short dance piece for piano, *Echo*, although dated 1946 in the Archive Catalogue was most likely composed in 1942–43 for the dance school of Dora Vlastou, who, according to her testimony, participated in its first performance (Samprovalakis, 2006, 8).

the practical limitations imposed by the real world around him, blindly continued to follow his instincts and kept composing for an ideal medium and an ideal, understanding and appreciative audience. Other such works are the *Little Suite* for strings (1942) and the Overture for large orchestra (*The Return of Ulysses*) (1942–44), an introduction to an unwritten opera of the same title.[24]

In 1943–44 he composed the piano score of the incidental music to the folk tale *Mayday Spell – A fairy drama in five pictures*, by Christos Evelpidis (the brother of Chrissos Evelpidis), with a view to a future stage or radio production. Skalkottas had seen the play at a private performance at Nelly's house around November 1943, shortly after its first publication, and he immediately offered to set it to music (Thornley, 2004, 21).[25] He composed the work with characteristic intensity, and although he had finished most of the numbers by February 1944 and had showed them to Evelpidis, it wasn't until September that he handed over the completed fair score (Thornley, 2008b, 372); this was because of traumatic events that took place during spring and summer.

The first half of 1944 was one of the most difficult periods in Skalkottas's life. On 8 February his father died, and in April he collapsed with pneumonic fever in the orchestra pit of the *Lyriki Skini* during a performance; he was taken to the Red Cross Hospital, where he stayed until the end of the month (Thornley, *ibid.*). From the end of May or beginning of June until mid-July, having been falsely suspected of being a member of the Greek resistance, he was imprisoned for one-and-a-half months at the notorious SS-run concentration camp of Haidari on the outskirts of Athens (Flountzis, 1986, 330). Haidari, in part a transit camp, also housed prisoners awaiting interrogation at the SS headquarters in central Athens, as well as hundreds of hostages who tended not to be members of resistance groups or political prisoners but simply innocent citizens caught in 'blocos' (round-ups). Conditions in the camp were atrocious, with very poor hygiene and scarce food. Its

---

[24] According to Papaioannou, in 1939 the violist John Papadopoulos suggested to Skalkottas that he might look into Homer's *Odyssey* for ideas for writing an opera; Skalkottas found this idea interesting and in 1944–45 [*sic*] composed an overture to the proposed opera, but in 1949 he was still waiting for the libretto (Papaioannou, 1969b, 615). This story, however, is not corroborated by any evidence elsewhere. In the accompanying notes to the manuscript score Skalkottas explained that this was an overture to a planned opera called *Die Rückkehr Odysseus in seiner Heimat*. The opera was never written. In the manuscript of the orchestral score the title, written in both Greek and German, is 'Overture for orchestra', whereas on the manuscript of the two-piano reduction (1949) the title is 'Ouvertüre für grosses Orchester'. Since Skalkottas's death the descriptive name *The Return of Ulysses* has been used for the Overture, rather than its original title.

[25] In this work Skalkottas brought together the two strands of the double musical life that he had been living since his return to Athens – by incorporating long tonal passages representing the real world and 'the folk' within an overall dodecaphonic and atonal context that represents the supernatural world of the fairies. In 1949 he transcribed the piece for orchestra, singer, choir and recitative, and also incorporated folk dance and ballet. On 2 July 1949, two months before his sudden death, he brought it to Evelpidis.

reputation was fearsome – the use of terror there was refined and exploited to the full, with brutal and sadistic guards putting the prisoners in constant fear of their lives. Inmates were liable to be shot, even the innocent ones; those selected for execution had their name called out at the dreaded morning roll-call and were then taken to the execution grounds at Kaisariani (Mazower, 1993, 226–8). Although Skalkottas was never interrogated and was later released without any explanation, the constant fear, the uncertainty and the harsh living conditions must have made this a harrowing experience for the composer, with his ailing body, nervous disposition and history of depression.

While at Haidari, Skalkottas met an old acquaintance, Dimitris Efthimiopoulos, who several years after the composer's death would recall that they were frequently together during the morning roll-call and that he could see Skalkottas's agony and pain as they witnessed what was happening around them (Flountzis, 1986, 330). During imprisonment Skalkottas found refuge in composing, and Efthimiopoulos managed to supply him with around a hundred sheets of music paper. He would compose whenever he had the chance, and many of the pieces were given programmatic titles relating to events in the camp. One piece was called *First of May '44*, in tribute to the 200 hostages from the Akronafplia who on that date were taken from Haidari to the execution grounds at Kaisariani (Flountzis, 1986, 451–511); another was *Klouves* ('Police Vans'), denoting the trucks taking the prisoners to execution; others were entitled the *Roll-call*, the *Glazier*, and *6 June* – in response to the Normandy Landings and the Allied invasion (*ibid.*). Always fearful of the German guards, Skalkottas and Efthimiopoulos hid around fifty of these manuscript papers in boxes in the glassworks storeroom. They were left in the concentration camp after Skalkottas's release and were taken back to Germany by the retreating occupation forces. Thus for the second time in his life a selection of Skalkottas's manuscripts were to be lost in Germany. According to Efthimiopoulos, the rest were smuggled out of the camp and taken to a relative in Piraeus, but it is not certain whether Skalkottas ever recovered this music (*ibid.*, 330). None of these pieces was found among his compositions after his death.

Following his release from Haidari in mid-July, and as the occupation was drawing to a close, Skalkottas applied himself intensively to composition again. He completed the *Mayday Spell*, and a draft of the gigantic Second Symphonic Suite for large orchestra. On 12 October 1944 the war in Greece officially ended and the Germans evacuated the country; three days later, the entry of the British troops in Athens was greeted with ecstasy. But the euphoria of the liberation was short lived, as a new period of political and social upheaval began. In December 1944 the battle between the nationalists (the armed forces of the Greek government) supported by their British allies, against the socialists and the forces of the biggest anti-Nazi resistance organization EAM/ELAS (controlled by the Greek Communist Party

(KKE)), kept Greece in a state of turmoil, leading to the ferocious civil war of 1944–49.[26]

During the first period of the civil war, from 3 December 1944 to 15 January 1945, known as 'ta Dekemvriana' (the December events), Skalkottas composed the Concerto for two violins and orchestra.[27] Remaining detached from the world and undisturbed by the street fighting raging outside his house, and with bombs exploding nearby, he would 'draw staves on cigarette-paper when his supply of manuscript paper ran out' (Thornley, 2001, 465). His desire to escape his immediate surroundings and the traumatic experiences of recent months appears reflected in the second movement (theme with variations) of this concerto, the main thematic idea of which is based on the popular *rebetiko* song by Vasilis Tsitsanis, 'I Magissa tis Arapias' ('The Witch of Arabia'), first released in 1938 but which became very popular after 1944–45 (Petropoulos, 1991, 171). The song's escapist lyrics are infused with the spirit of *rebetiko*, which represents and is a means of expression for those displaced people who feel unable to cope with the problems of their new environment; perhaps all this resonated with Skalkottas's own long-standing desire to escape from his Greek reality, a desire he never gave up on. A few months later, in a letter to Rudi Goehr, who was in Hollywood at the time, he wrote with forlorn hope, '*I would have liked very much to be coming there, maybe later if I manage and with your Protektion* [sic] *and help*' (11 October 1945; in Thornley, 2004, 26); but as usual his reliance on somebody else to be proactive on his behalf meant that his dreams for an escape to America remained unfulfilled.

**The Last Years (1946–49): Changing Directions**

Following the liberation from the German occupation and the short, first phase of the civil war, the communists accepted defeat and agreed to disarm. However, political polarization led to a dramatic and brutal second phase of the civil war,

---

[26] For more information about the Greek civil war, see Tsoucalas (1981, 73–89); Mazower (1993, 340–77).

[27] This concerto, with catalogue number A/K24, survives only with the piano accompaniment. However, in the Concise Catalogue of Skalkottas's works of 1969 it is entered as A/K25. This must be an error because A/K25 is the Concerto for violin and viola. In March 1945, Skalkottas arranged, or possibly composed, what appear to be two rebel marching songs, 'Wake Up' and 'For a New Greece' (Skalkottas Archive Athens, Appendix File 3f). Although the songs are clearly written in his hand and were found among his compositions, the composer's name on the title page is given as Morellos; this may have been an amateur composer whose music Skalkottas arranged and orchestrated, as he often did with many of his colleagues' compositions. The author of the lyrics is not mentioned. As Thornley speculates, it is not clear whether these songs were the result of his imprisonment in Haidari, or a covert attempt secretly to express his sympathy for the communist rebels' cause (Thornley, 2008b, 382–4) – notwithstanding that he took no overt part in their struggle.

which lasted until the early autumn of 1949, and inflicted more damage on Greece than had the Second World War itself.[28] Notwithstanding the chaos enveloping Greek society, however, Skalkottas's personal life entered a new and more promising phase following the traumatic experiences of the previous years. On 15 September 1946 he married the pianist Maria Pangali and moved into her house at 41 Kallidromiou Street. They had met around 1944 at the chamber music classes of the violoncellist Maria Pisti, classes in which Skalkottas assisted and where Maria was a piano student (Papaioannou, 1997, vol.2, 13–14, 83). Their first son, Alekos (named after Skalkottas's father, as dictated by Greek custom), was born a year later on 2 November 1947. For a while Skalkottas appeared to be happier, gradually becoming less misanthropic and more optimistic, and he enjoyed performing with his wife both publicly and at private gatherings (Vlastou, 1961, 55). The euphoria of this early period of his married life recalled feelings expressed to Benakis 14 years earlier, when, in a disillusioned state and seemingly completely divorced from reality, he had fantasized about getting married to Matla Temko and about the happiness this would bring to him: '*I have a feeling that I shall marry the woman I love very quickly. My health is better, if I get married I shall become completely well* […] *what I am thinking of* [now] *is happiness, the joy of an energetic life, big-heartedness, work and fun* […] *It would be wonderful if I could get married quickly. I hope it will happen quickly. If it happens, I'll begin a new life and work*' (LetMB, 2 January 1933). Two weeks before his wedding to Maria he wrote to Walter Goehr in London, soliciting a performance of his First Symphonic Suite and asking for news of their former colleagues in Berlin; he reflected that he should write to Schoenberg and expressed a desire, '*if everything goes well*', to travel to England (30 August 1946; in Thornley, 2002b, 121). As ever, this plan remained unaccomplished. He also wrote to Mitropoulos offering to send him his new works. Mitropoulos, however, showed little interest in his serious atonal and dodecaphonic pieces and only wanted the '3–4 *Greek Dances* for orchestra' (Demertzis, 2004a, 24).

This sudden and uncharacteristic *joie de vivre* did not last, and Skalkottas continued to harbour plans to leave Greece. He considered going to Germany 'to see what was happening in music [there]' (Papaioannou, 1999, vol. 2, 14–15). Just a few days after his son's birth he wrote to Rudi Goehr in New York about his regrets

---

[28] A general election was held in March 1946, which the communists and their followers boycotted. During that year a full-scale guerrilla war was reignited between the Greek Communist Party (KKE) and the nationalists. With British and particularly American intervention, the Greek army successfully defeated the communist guerrillas and pushed them beyond the borders; the war was officially ended on 16 October 1949, when the KKE announced the end of open hostilities (Tsoucalas, 1981, 90–101). This savage and destructive civil war resulted in catastrophic economic disruption and a lasting legacy of bitterness and political division in Greek society that created wounds still not entirely healed even in the late 1990s.

at not having gone to America when he had the chance in 1925, and complaining about his professional and financial difficulties in Greece since his return from Berlin:

> *I think it would have been better for me if I had gone to America back then. I could not bring myself to undertake such a long journey, and sometimes it has seemed so funny that I had made the long journey to Germany. I've been working* [in Athens] *since 1934, without a pause, day and night. Just imagine, I haven't managed to save even a little money* [...] *the reason is surely the bad tempo of these times.* (10 November 1947; in Thornley, 2002a, 213)

Apart from the changes in Skalkottas's personal life, these years also marked a change in musical direction and creative output. Skalkottas now appeared to be writing music intended for public consumption rather than in response to some inner creative need. He transcribed earlier tonal pieces and Greek tunes for different occasions, orchestrated and re-orchestrated earlier works,[29] and composed a large number of mainly tonal works for friends and acquaintances. Perhaps his marriage, and the consequent need to earn more money for his new family, reinforced his interest in more popular, and therefore more commercially viable, tonal music. Tonality predominated in the works he composed from 1947 until mid-1949, and this is in fact the only period during which he wrote a large quantity of tonal music. In 1947 came the *Ancient Greek March* for chamber orchestra, and the *Classical Symphony*, whose middle movements (*Andante molto espressivo (Rondo)* and *Allegro molto vivace (Scherzo)*) were performed in 1947. In 1948 Skalkottas's tonal output reached a peak, and the French Institute in Athens published his four *Greek Dances* (*Tsamikos, Kritikos, Epirotikos, Peloponnisiakos*) with an introduction by Octave Merlier. He composed *Procession towards Acherondas*, which survives in a piano version but with notes for possible orchestration, the Sinfonietta in B♭, the incidental music for the radio play *Henry V*, and the Concertino in C major for piano, requested by Marika Papaioannou. There is also a cluster of ballet music, including what is described in the Archive Catalogue as a Dance Suite for small orchestra, written for the dance group of the Lykion ton Ellinidon. In late 1947 Skalkottas received a commission from Polyxeni Mathéy to write a piano work for her dance school on the subject of *The Land and the Sea of Greece*, and he completed its six ballet dances – *Harvest, Sowing, The Vintage, The Grape Stomping, The Trawler, Dance of the Waves* – the following year.[30] Skalkottas also

---

[29] For example, he transcribed the *Five Greek Dances* for string orchestra (*Epirotikos, Kritikos, Tsamikos, Arkadikos, Kleftikos*). In 1949 he orchestrated the fifth movement of the Second Symphonic Suite, and re-orchestrated the *Maiden and Death*, which was performed on 23 March 1946 (Demertzis, 1998, 296).

[30] There is no mention of this piece in the Archive Catalogue, Skalkottas's manuscript, found in Mathéy's archive, does not have a title page (written in his own hand) with the title *The Land and Sea of Greece*. For a detailed discussion of the provenance and performance and reception history of this ballet suite, see Ramou (2008, 422–39). On 12 June 1948

separated the two themes of this work (the land and the sea) into two independent ballet compositions. In 1948, he orchestrated the four dances related to the 'Land' under the title *Little Dance Suite (Four Images)* for orchestra.

The first half of 1949 was very prolific and devoted predominantly to the orchestration and re-orchestration of earlier works. In addition to composing shorter pieces (such as the *Characteristic Piece* for xylophone and orchestra), he transcribed *The Return of Ulysses* for two pianos, and orchestrated the fifth movement of the Second Symphonic Suite, the Concertino in C major for piano, the *Mayday Spell*, and re-orchestrated his *36 Greek Dances*. He also orchestrated the two 'Sea' piano dances, the *Trawler* and the *Dance of the Waves*, and incorporated them into the folk-ballet *The Sea,* which he expanded into ten 'images' with an introduction (dated on the fair manuscript 29 June 1949). This heightened creativity was coupled with an increased number of performances of his music. After his return to Greece in 1933 none of Skalkottas's major orchestral, 'serious' dodecaphonic works had been performed. The only performances of his music he had heard were a handful of the *Greek Dances,* some of his ballet music and a few small-scale chamber pieces, such as the Fourth Sonatina for violin and piano, that were played privately with acquaintances. Ironically, this state of affairs changed during the last year of his life, when he had the chance to hear three of his orchestral compositions performed by the Athens State Orchestra, albeit without Skalkottas himself on the podium. The *Ten Sketches* for strings, conducted by A. Parisis, were performed on 13 April 1949, and the premiere of the *Little Dance Suite (Four Images)*, conducted by Th. Vavayiannis, was given at the Olympia Theatre on 2 May.[31] In the same month *Trawler* and *Dance of the Waves* from *The Sea* were performed twice (on 22 and 23 May) at the Rex (Kotopouli) Theatre, and again during the Naval Festival in Aegina on 31 July (Ramou, 9 September 2004, 30).

In the last few months of his life Skalkottas changed direction again, returning to a strict twelve-note technique similar to that of his mid-1930s works. Within a very short period he composed several works for cello and piano (*Bolero*, Largo, Serenata, Sonatina and *Tender Melody*) and the *Second Little Suite* for violin and piano. There are many unanswered questions regarding Skalkottas's two changes of stylistic direction after 1945, and in the absence of documentary evidence we can only speculate about the reasons for such changes. Perhaps the financial necessity to

---

Mathéy's dance group presented the *Harvest* dance (choreographed by Robert Saragas) at the Psychiko open-air theatre (Ramou, 2004, 30; 2008, 426).

[31] The reviews of the *Four Images* were mixed. Avra Theodoropoulou could see 'the outstanding genius of Skalkottas, in the rhythm and in the orchestration', and, with a patronizing though forgiving tone, she continued by saying that the composer of this work contrasted with the 'music rebel Skalkottas, authentic pupil of Schoenberg, atonalist, polytonalist, who tortured us many times' (Theodoropoulou, 1949, 799). Georgios Vokos was not convinced by the work. He could not understand Skalkottas's style or harmonic language and, although he considered the orchestration to be 'imaginative', he found the melodic and rhythmic ideas stereotypical and outdated (Vokos, 6 May 1949).

boost his meagre income and provide for his young family prompted him to compose more tonal and popular pieces, thus softening his previous uncompromising stance. However, he must have felt frustrated by – even unsatisfied with – the success of these easy pieces, since the works he wanted to be played by the Greek orchestras, and to be acknowledged for as a composer, were his serious dodecaphonic and atonal compositions, which the Greeks, even the musically educated ones, could not understand and were unwilling to accept; for them Skalkottas's major contribution to Greek music remained his imaginative use of folk material in the *Greek Dances*.[32] And just as he appeared to be getting some success with the Greek public, he turned suddenly to serial composition, as though he wanted to escape from a compromising musical situation and be true to himself. His extreme mood swings and change of direction in life were again being reflected in his work.

Photographs taken towards the end of his life show Skalkottas looking aged, disappointed and tired, and with a bitter smile that perhaps reflects the struggles of his life. Vlastou remembered her horror at seeing him at a concert a few days before his death: he was 'more thin and pale than any time before; and his gaze was totally lost inside the corners of his eyes' (Vlastou, 1961, 56). Two days before his second son, Nikos, was born, on the night of 19 September 1949, Skalkottas died of a strangulated hernia he had neglected to treat. Earlier in the day he had patiently queued to see a doctor for free treatment at the Municipal Hospital, but owing to time restrictions he was sent away. Eventually, later that night, he was rushed back to hospital to undergo an operation, but the poisoning had spread and his life could not be saved. The official date of death at the Athens registry office is given as 20 September, although the family and most of the literature on Skalkottas gives it as 19 September.[33] He was buried in the prestigious section of the Third Cemetery of the city, in a grave made available by the municipal council. Skalkottas's death, like so much of his life, was the product of his absurd neglect of and indifference

---

[32] A few months before Skalkottas's death Dounias wrote: 'This excellent pupil of Schönberg writes truly contemporary music, even if some of his works, with their problematic cerebralism, probably inspire more admiration than emotion' (11 January 1949; in 1963, 42–4). Similarly, Avra Theodoropoulou wrote about the lack of comprehension of Skalkottas's modern language: 'To us this modern idiom is so foreign that it is difficult to understand the real substance of the work and enjoy it. But his mastery of orchestration [...] made the *Greek Dances*, with their characteristic rhythm, particularly loved' (Theodoropoulou, 1961, 48–9).

[33] Death certificate (Lixiarhiki Praxi Thanatou), No.41/KE/49 or 112/KE/49. One of Papaioannou's most frequently repeated (but again highly subjective) anecdotes about Skalkottas's death pictures the composer with a towel in his mouth to muffle his cries from pain so as to avoid disturbing his wife, who had gone into labour with their second child (Papaioannou 1997, vol. 2, 88). Similarly, Antiochos Evangelatos, in his obituary a few days later, relayed another populist anecdote according to which Skalkottas was composing until midnight just a day before he died, despite suffering from great pain; the last 'words he whispered before he passed away were a musical motive of five notes: ta – ta – ta ta ta –.' (Evangelatos, 1949, 6).

Illustration 3.3   Nikos Skalkottas (undated, but probably 1940s)

to practical matters. It went unnoticed by the world, and was a sad conclusion to what had largely been a lonely, depressing, difficult and ultimately tragic life.

Shortly after his death there was an unprecedented outpouring of emotion. Colleagues and acquaintances, few of whom did anything to help him during his lifetime (and perhaps prompted by feelings of guilt), wrote insincere obituaries and flattering articles about him and his music, even though they were either unacquainted with it or had previously expressed their dislike of it. They presented to the world a portrait of a very important musical personality who had been unjustly treated by the Greek musical establishment. Dounias, in his memorial tribute, rebuked Greek musical authorities and organizations for their total lack of support of 'maybe the most extraordinary creative talent our country has known' (1963, 78). In a similar vein, Psaroudas, who had been hitherto negative about Skalkottas's music, now blamed the Greek establishment – of which, ironically, he was an influential member – for 'that cruel lack of appreciation, if not abandonment [of Skalkottas]' (*To Vima*, 11 April 1950). Chamoudopoulos similarly observed that 'unfortunately, our land did not put his genius to good use. He remained almost unrecognized in the margin, with sorrow and disillusionment filling his soul [...] indifference trampled heavily on him' (*Eleftheria*, 2 November 1949). Skalkottas was now viewed as a tragic but warm-hearted human being, an unlucky and unassertive musician, but also an individual who offered his kindness and support to colleagues when they needed him. Dounias remembered the 'unpretending, quiet artist, withdrawn from life without bitterness, without hatred for anybody [...] He offered affection to everybody, the affection that this cruel land had denied him so much' (1963, 64–6). Vlastou, touching on the religious sensitivities of her audiences, painted a hagiographic image of Skalkottas as being 'plain, simple, unaffected, gentle, sensitive, full of silent stoicism, Christian forgiveness, natural politeness and deepest [...] human gloriousness' (1961, 51). Similarly, Vokos described Skalkottas as 'a quiet, modest and tireless worker in the service of Art [...] A natural talent [...] with the flame of the inspired artist. Unaffected, simple, affable, with a deep faith and the highest artistic ideals' (*Acropolis*, 8 November 1949). Even Kalomiris, who had previously despised Skalkottas and who never recognized him as a composer, posthumously praised him: 'Greek music lost in Skalkottas one of its finest exponents, a real musician, a musician to the last drop of his blood and a composer who knew maybe like nobody else orchestral technique and the secrets of the harmonic and contrapuntal avant-garde' (Kalomiris, *Ethnos*, 23 September 1949).[34]

These obituaries would surely have put an ironic smile on Skalkottas's face. They present a very different portrait of him from the one we find expressed in his own words and deeds, in which he appears more the architect of his own misfortune than one who has suffered unreasonably from life's vicissitudes. His general indifference and his defeatist attitude led him constantly to postpone actions and avoid responsibilities, while also provoking behaviour in others that exacerbated the feelings of rejection that hurt him so badly in the first place. On the surface he remained silent, stoical and introvert, but inside he burned with rage against his compatriots, and he poured much of his anger and disappointment into his letters to Nelly Askitopoulou and Matla Temko.

Perhaps his frustration with the external world explains the intensity with which he threw himself into composition. Publicly he was recognized as the composer of the nationalistic, tonal *Greek Dances* – the only pieces his compatriots understood and accepted. But away from this public persona he composed, at neck-breaking speed, an extensive series of atonal and dodecaphonic works, almost as an act of daily resistance to the vulgarity and constraints of the despised environment that he felt surrounded him. Alone in the present, and torn between the world of his past and an ideal imaginary world of the future, where his music would be understood and appreciated, he harboured an intense nostalgic yearning to escape the reality of his Greek existence. But instead of acting, he withdrew in silence and lived the rest of his life in an inner exile. His position on his return to his native country is perhaps most appropriately captured by Edward Said in *Representations of the*

---

[34] For further information about the attitude of Greek newspapers and periodicals towards Skalkottas, see Belonis (2002, 29–48; and 2008, 444–79).

*Intellectual*, where he observes that the exile is someone who exists 'in a median state, neither completely at one with the new setting nor fully disencumbered of the old, beset with half-involvements and half-detachments, nostalgic and sentimental on one level, an adept mimic or a secret outcast on another' (1994, 36). Skalkottas's continuous creativity and obsession with composition allowed him to eliminate the external world, and it is tempting to speculate that the passion and energy that seemed so obviously lacking in his everyday persona was transmuted into the ceaseless vitality and intensity of the music itself. Irrepressible activity, constant forward motion, and an agitated, agonized quest for something unattainable are the characteristic elements that govern his music; exactly those characteristics, in fact, that he had exorcised from his external self. As he once wrote to Nelly, '*It is the habit of my Life: I was always missing something!*' (LetAsk, 30 April 1928).

Illustration 3.4    Nikos Skalkottas's signatures

# PART II
# Twelve-Note Technique

*Hope your journey is a long one.*
*May there be many summer mornings when,*
*with what pleasure, what joy*
*you enter harbours you're seeing for the first time.*
(Konstantinos Kavafis, *Ithaca*)

# Introduction to Part II

> Every one [of my students] has his own manner of obeying rules derived from the treatment of twelve tones.[1]

Skalkottas's idiosyncratic compositional technique, although inevitably refined and developed over the years, remained 'conceptually' unchanged both during and after his studies with Schoenberg and his adoption of the twelve-note method. Schoenberg, when still formulating his theory of composition, wrote to Edgar Prinzhorn from Barcelona in 1932: 'I have published nothing about "composition with twelve tones related only to one another" and do not wish to do so until the principal part of my theory is ready: the "Study of Musical Logic" [...] [A]nd that is also the reason why I do not teach my students "twelve-tone composition", but "composition", in the sense of musical logic' (17 April 1932, in Goehr, 1974, 85–6; and 1977, 4). Skalkottas, who at the time of this assertion was attending Schoenberg's masterclasses in Berlin, did not study 'twelve-tone composition' (in the sense of a prescriptive compositional system replete with an underlying theory, strict rules and appropriate terminology, as it developed later in the twentieth century), but simply 'composition'. His reluctance to discuss the details of his technique, and the complete lack of any sketches for his music, leave us in some doubt as to the precise extent of his knowledge of Schoenberg's twelve-note and serial procedures at that time. Although Schoenberg carefully scrutinized his students' twelve-note works when they were presented to him, he did not lecture on the subject, and he warned against a generalized perception of a compositional school:

> All my pupils differ from one another extremely and though perhaps the majority compose twelve-tone music, one could not speak of a school. They all had to find their way alone, for themselves. And this is exactly what they did; every one has his own manner of obeying rules derived from the treatment of twelve tones. (Schoenberg, 1984, 386)

Skalkottas thus developed his own version of the twelve-note method at an early stage, and although his approach derives from Schoenberg's concept of twelve-note composition (as employed in his early, pre-1933 works), it differs from that of his teacher. To borrow Straus's observation about Stravinsky, Skalkottas 'from the very outset simultaneously invokes and remakes Schoenberg' (Straus, 2001, 11).

---

[1] Schoenberg, 1984, 386.

Many of his compositional processes are idiomatic and deviate from the accepted conventions of serial handling. Skalkottas never abandoned the organizational principles of tonality and the integration of tonal elements in his dodecaphonic works; his harmonic language is inclusive, incorporating tonal, post-tonal and twelve-note elements, while the fusion of tonality and serialism is an important aspect of his compositional style. Overt or disguised tonal harmonic relationships are deliberately used within the twelve-note structure as recognizable sonorities to highlight certain structural points, or to allude to a key, and to achieve the all-important audibility of his music and perceptibility of the thematic and harmonic shifts within a piece. Skalkottas's earliest written testimony in relation to twelve-note composition was published in the Greek periodical *Musiki Zoë* in 1931:

> With the twelve-note system, its inventor does not mean of course, as many wrongly believe, the 'pedantic' continuous repetition of the twelve notes in primary and secondary voices of a piece, but a law similar to that of the seven-note system: the law-making, the restriction, the gathering together of the modern musical material in a solid modern system. The main points of this system are a) the avoidance (as far as possible) of octaves, b) the transparency of the writing, and c) the vast horizon of exploitation of the voices and the harmony. (vol. 6, 1931/33, 138)

In his German writings he consistently used the term '*siebenton harmonik*' to refer to the tonal system and its seven-note scales, thus suggesting a conceptual analogy between the twelve-note and tonal systems that regards the sets as equivalent to scales; each set is identifiable regardless of the ordering of its constituent notes, direction or segmentation, and it may be used freely in the manner of a scale, which retains its tonal definition irrespective of the order of its notes. For Skalkottas the adoption and adaptation of the twelve-note method was simply a codification of some of the techniques and formal organizational procedures that had been a feature of his music from the first Berlin period onwards.

In Schoenberg's twelve-note method all the note relations that govern the musical context of a piece are referable to the specific linear ordering of the 12 notes of the chromatic scale.[2] It is a convention of twelve-note composition that only one twelve-note set should be used in a work, as indicated by Schoenberg's statement that: 'it does not seem right to me to use more than one series' (Rufer, 1961, 106). Webern's works conform to this 'rule', but it does not adequately represent either Berg's practice or, indeed, that of Schoenberg himself, who departed from this principle in several works, including his *Ode to Napoleon* op.41 and the String Trio op.45 (Haimo, 1992; Milstein, 1992). Berg's twelve-note technique has always been

---

[2] In *Structural Functions of Harmony* Schoenberg states what has become the fundamental principle of his twelve-note method: 'For the sake of a more profound logic, the method of Composing with Twelve Tones derives all configurations [elements of a work] from a basic set (*Grundgestalt*) [tone-row or note-series]' (Schoenberg, 1969, 193–4).

recognized as different from that of Schoenberg or Webern, and although it features characteristics of both Schoenberg's and Hauer's approaches, none of his works employs either method exclusively (Jarman, 1979, 81).

A cursory look at Skalkottas's twelve-note works might suggest affinities with Berg's freer interpretation of the method, notwithstanding that the two composers had no direct contact and Skalkottas was unaware of Berg's later compositional techniques. In his dodecaphonic works he does not deal exclusively with a single basic set as the binding element between melody and accompaniment, but uses several independent but closely connected twelve-note sets of various types, which he consistently refers to in his writings as *Reihen*, without making any distinction between the diverse nature of his source material. These types of sets include the following:

1. Linearly ordered sets, defined by their pitch-class order (although Skalkottas manipulates them differently from Schoenberg).
2. Chordal sets: sets partitioned into chordal segments, trichords or tetrachords and used in this harmonic form throughout the piece.
3. Supersets: twelve-note sets in which the single pitch-class is replaced by an entire twelve-note set.
4. Tonal sets: sets that include tonal elements in their internal structure (minor and major trichords, dominant and diminished seventh tetrachords).
5. Sets defined by their segmental content instead of their strict pitch-class order, comparable to Hauer's tropes.
6. Incomplete and irregular twelve-note sets.

Skalkottas presents his referential twelve-note material in groups, and usually with a different set-group for each major section of a piece. In his dodecaphonic works, a theme is a complex basic shape, encompassing the entire texture and consisting of several independent sets of any of the above types. However, with a few exceptions that will be discussed in Part III, none of the sets employed possesses the required hierarchical relationship with the others to be considered the 'basic set' of the movement. Skalkottas derives all the material for his development from the thematic twelve-note set-group, which becomes the generative source of a large formal section or a whole movement (and frequently an entire multi-movement piece), thus functioning as a *Grundgestalt*.[3] This type of thematic generation derives directly from Schoenberg's postulate: 'Whatever happens in a piece

---

[3] There are only a few references to *Grundgestalt* in Schoenberg's writings. He appears to use the term as a synonym for basic set, tone-row or note-series in twelve-note music (Schoenberg, 1952, 527; and 1969, 193–4). However, Joseph Rufer and Erwin Stein, based upon their studies with Schoenberg in the early 1920s, assert that he used the term as a broad musical concept, applying it to all types of music, as 'the musical shape which is the basis of a work and is "its first creative thought" (to use Schoenberg's words). Everything else is derived from this – in music of all kinds, not only twelve-note music'; in twelve-note

of music is nothing but the endless reshaping of a basic shape [...] there is nothing in a piece of music but what comes from the theme, springs from it and can be traced back to it; [...] all the shapes appearing in a piece of music are foreseen in the "theme"' (Schoenberg, 'Linear Counterpoint (1931)', 1984, 290); except that in Skalkottas's case we may substitute the term 'theme' for 'thematic set-group'.

All the sets of a set-group are closely associated through numerous common and transpositionally or inversionally related segments, usually dyads, trichords and tetrachords. Most of the sets include in their internal structure trichordal segments consisting of a semitone plus a minor third (set-class 3–3), a major third (set-class 3–4) or a perfect fourth (set-class 3–5). These recurring semitone-containing cells, used extensively in melodic and chordal forms, provide a substantial element of unity and are distinctive features of his musical language – particularly the omnipresent trichord set-class 3–3. His most common approach is linear, with the different sets employed simultaneously, superimposed as independent lines in a traditional part-writing fashion within a predominantly contrapuntal texture;[4] however, a family of instruments, or groups of instruments sharing similar textures, frequently contribute to the articulation of a set. In the large-scale orchestral works the sets are usually (but not exclusively) presented sequentially, with each statement of a set encompassing the entire texture of the music.[5] Harmonies, or simultaneities, the result of '*the vast horizon of exploitation of the voices*' (Skalkottas, 1931/33, 138) are formed either through the verticalization of a segment of an individual set, or through the part-writing of several discrete sets of the set-group. As with Berg and Webern, Skalkottas does not exploit the combinatorial properties of his twelve-note sets, and, with the exception of a couple of incidental and inconclusive attempts, he does not use hexachordal inversional combinatoriality to control and determine the large-scale harmonic organization in his twelve-note pieces – perhaps because he wasn't familiar with the subtleties of the method, which was only fully developed after his time with Schoenberg in Berlin. Instead, he uses segmental association to connect logically the presentation of the different closely related sets within a group.[6] Unlike Schoenberg, however, who in his earlier twelve-note

---

works, in particular, the *Grundreihe* (basic set) is derived from the *Grundgestalt*; see, Rufer (1961, vi–viii); Stein (1953, 62); Epstein (1987, 17–33).

[4] The use of this polyphonic method to construct his music resembles – but is not identical to – what Bailey, in her set examination of Webern's twelve-note compositions, describes as 'linear topography, in which the fabric is the product of several rows progressing simultaneously in as many voices' (Bailey, 1991, 31). In Skalkottas's treatment the fabric is the product of the simultaneous presentation of independent twelve-note sets.

[5] This handling of twelve-note sets resembles what Bailey describes as 'block topography, in which the rows are set one after the other, with all the notes sounding in the order prescribed by this succession of rows, regardless of texture' (1991, 31).

[6] Segmental association refers to the use of segments common to two or more forms of a twelve-note set (set forms) which can provide a basis for connecting systematically

works also relies on segmental association to connect two or more forms of the basic set, at the local level Skalkottas uses unordered segments common to two or more different sets of the thematic set-group, and he exploits the association of the invariant relations between these different sets as a method of providing coherent relationships and organizing the harmonic structure between successive and simultaneous sets within the phrases and formal sections of a piece. Certain harmonic relationships are generated from the calculated superimposition of sets (and their segments), which are subsequently continuously repeated as a unit. For example, the first movement, *Preludio (Andante)*, of the Suite for Piano No.1 (1936) (henceforth First Piano Suite) is built on four independent sets (S1, S2, S3, S4) and their unordered transpositions at the minor sixth ($T_8$), represented as S5 (instead of S1($T_8$)), S6 (S2($T_8$)), S7 (S3($T_8$)) and S8 (S4($T_8$)) (see Appendix A).

Sets are constantly presented in pairs (S1–S2) – (S3–S4) – (S5–S6) – (S7–S8), as shown in Example II.1. They are partitioned into tetrachords, with each tetrachordal segment of one set generally superimposed on (or appearing near) a segment of its paired set, resulting in particular harmonic formations from their combination. For example, the first tetrachord of S1 (F–A–B–C♯) is always paired with either the entire first tetrachord of S2 (G♭–D–B♭–A) or with one of its dyads (G♭–D)–(B♭–A); similarly, the second tetrachord of S1 (E♭–A♭–G–E) is paired with the second tetrachord of S2 (C–B–F–E♭) or with one of its dyads (C–B)–(F–E♭), and so on (see Table II.1). This adherence to fixed concurrent set presentation preserves pitch-class and harmonic relationships among the paired sets and allows certain harmonic configurations to be constantly reiterated.

Example II.1 First Piano Suite, *Preludio*: Opening gesture (bars 1–6)

---

the musical presentations of these set forms. The set segments are generally unordered, thus emphasizing the 'harmonic' aspect of any associative exploitation of the relationships between the set forms; see, Lewin (1962, 89–116, particularly 95–6); and Milstein (1992, 173).

Table II.1    First Piano Suite, *Preludio*: Concurrent set presentation

| S1 | F–A–B–C♯ | E♭–A♭–G–E | D–F♯–C–B♭ |
|---|---|---|---|
| S2 | (G♭–D)–(B♭–A) | (C–B)–(F–E♭) | (E–G)–(D♭–A♭) |
| S3 | G–B–E♭ [D] | [D] C–C♯–B♭ [A] | [A]F♯–G♯–E♯–E |
| S4 | (C–E)–(D–C♯) | (F–A♭)–( E♭–G♭) | (B–A)–(G–B♭) |
| S5 | D♭–F–G–A | B–E–E♭–C | B♭–D–A♭–G♭ |
| S6 | (B♭–D)–(G♭–F) | (A♭–G)–(D♭–B) | (E♭–C)–( E–A) |
| S7 | E♭–G–B [A] | [A] B♭–A♭–G♭[F] | F–D–E–C♯–C |
| S8 | (A♭–B♭)–(A–C) | (C♯–E)–(G–B–D–F) | (E♭–G♭) |

The character of Skalkottas's twelve-note harmony, conceptually similar to Berg's dodecaphonic music, distinguishes it from the twelve-note music of Schoenberg. In particular, contrary to the total unification of twelve-note harmony that Schoenberg endeavours to achieve (due to the derivation of all melodic and harmonic features from one basic set), Skalkottas's twelve-note harmony, which arises from the simultaneous unfolding of several discrete sets, is not inclusive and homogeneous, but results in frequent pitch-class repetitions and pitch duplications between chords. Skalkottas appears more interested in the linear presentation and the preservation of the audibility of the sets in each contrapuntal voice than the moment-to-moment vertical consequences of set combination.[7] In terms of strict twelve-note technique, he compensates for this disorder with a high degree of internal, linear invariance in the structure of each of his sets.

---

[7]   Skalkottas's freer attitude towards the treatment of vertical, harmonic events may perhaps be influenced by one of Schoenberg's early polemic ideas about the 'new music', as given in an unfinished article dated 29 September 1923. He argued that the composer should not 'look for harmonies, since there are no rules for those, no values, no laws of construction, no assessment. Rather, [he should] write parts. From the way these sound, harmonies will later be abstracted' (von Blumröder, 1982, 97).

# Chapter 4
# The Sets and Set-groups

**Set-groups Consisting of Several Discrete, Closely Related Twelve-note Sets in Polyphonic Combinations**

The first movement, *Moderato*, of the Second String Trio (1935) illustrates Skalkottas's simultaneous use of several, linear, ordered twelve-note sets in polyphonic combinations. The three sets are introduced together at the opening gesture of the first theme (bars 1–4), in a three-part contrapuntal texture, as shown in Example 4.1, and are used throughout in their prime form only.

Example 4.1  Second String Trio, *Moderato*: Opening gesture (bars 1–4)

The second, 'lyrical' theme, played by the viola (bars 20–24), is based on S2, with S1 and S3 providing the contrapuntal accompaniment (see Example 4.2).

Example 4.2  Second String Trio, *Moderato*: Cadence to transition and opening gesture of second theme (bars 19–24)

The sets are closely connected through invariant segments, which Skalkottas exploits in the organization of the motivic and harmonic structure of the movement.

For example, sets S1 and S3 share their first pitch-class, G, while their last transpositionally equivalent trichords – (D–B♭–C) (C♯–A–B ($T_{11}$)) – are usually played together or in quick succession, punctuating cadences. S1 and S2 share the invariant dyad A♭–D♭, which is used as a connective between the two sets. At important structural points when S1 linearly follows S2 it appears as a varied repetition of the retrograde of S2, as for example in the bass line of the transition's cadential gesture and the introduction of the second theme (bar 20).

The second movement (*Thema con Variazioni*) from the First Symphonic Suite (1935) also demonstrates this approach. In particular, the *Thema* is built on a group of four twelve-note sets, which are presented simultaneously superimposed in four textural layers. Skalkottas describes its twelve-note structure as follows: '*Four distinct Reihen* [sets], *in double counterpoint, closely connected harmonically* […] *constitute the theme, its counterpoint, the accompaniment and the basses*' (MS Notes to the Suite). Sets S1, S2 and S3, played linearly by the clarinet, bass clarinet and contrabassoon respectively, furnish the theme, its countertheme and the contrapuntal accompaniment. S4, played by the horns and trombones and providing the harmonic accompaniment, is presented as a block of four three-note chords; the pitch-class order of the set is established in bars 6–10. The four sets are closely connected through transpositionally or inversionally related segments, and Skalkottas relies on segmental association to organize the movement's harmonic structure.

Example 4.3 First Symphonic Suite, *Thema con Variazioni: Thema* – motivic and harmonic relationships in the opening gesture (bars 1–5)

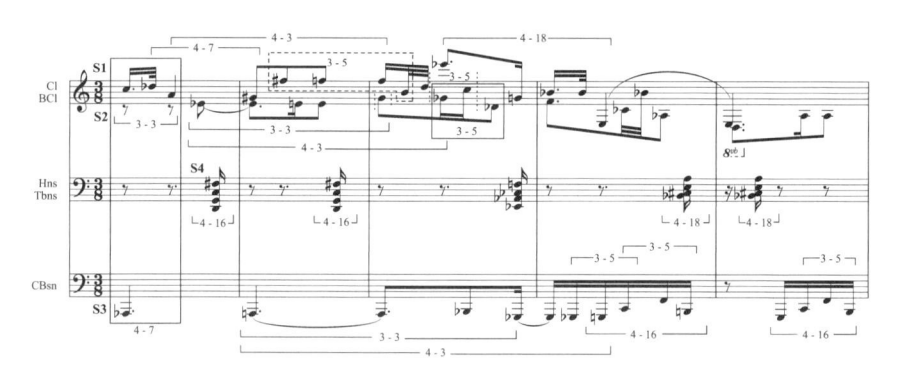

As shown in Example 4.3, the initial simultaneity between the clarinet playing the first trichord of S1 (set-class 3–3) and the contrabassoon playing A♭$_1$ of S3 is the tetrachord set-class 4–7, which is the same as the opening tetrachord of S1, in bars 1–2¹. The first trichord (e♭¹–e¹–g¹; set-class 3–3) of the countertheme, heard in the bass clarinet, is inversionally equivalent ($I_4$) to the first trichord of S1, while its opening four-note motive (e♭¹–e¹–g¹–g♭¹; set-class 4–3) is played contrapuntally at $T_{10}$ with the clarinet motive (a¹–g♯¹–f♯²–f²) in bars 1²–2. The opening three-note thematic motive (c²–d♭²–a¹) is answered by the contrabassoon

($A_1$–$B\flat_1$–$G\flat_1$), rhythmically augmented and transposed at $T_9$, and in bars 2–4² the four-note motive $A_1$–$B\flat_1$–$G\flat_1$–$G_1$ (set-class 4–3, a semitone transposition ($T_1$) of the clarinet motive, $a^1$–$g\sharp^1$–$f\sharp^2$–$f^2$) accompanies contrapuntally both of the upper voices. The trichord set-class 3–5, being a segment of all four sets, saturates the texture and creates a closely-knit web of affinities within the motivic structure. Further motivic and harmonic relationships within this first phrase are established at its cadence in bars 4–5. The contrabassoon, playing S3, supports the melodic cadence of the clarinet with the tetrachord $G_1$–C–F–$B_1$ (set-class 4–16) played twice; this has a perfect fourth transpositional relationship ($T_5$) with the first chordal tetrachord (D–G–c–f♯) of S4, inviting tonal-like associations within the harmonic structure of the passage. This cadence is also punctuated by a double statement of the tetrachord B♭–c♯–e–a (set-class 4–18); this is one of Skalkottas's signature sounds and is often used to indicate points of arrival and resolution. This harmonic tetrachord is a tritone transposition ($T_6$) of the clarinet's final melodic motive (e♭³–g¹–b♭¹–e). In the context of the contrapuntal structure of the passage, this cadential tritonal harmonic relationship between the upper melodic line and the chordal accompaniment both mirrors and neutralizes the tonally suggestive overtones of the tetrachord set-class 4–16, which frames the harmonic movement between the chordal accompaniment (bar 1) and the bass cadential melodic line (bar 5).

## Chordal Sets

In large-scale works, Skalkottas frequently uses chordal sets,[1] which are partitioned into segments and used throughout the piece as three- or four-note chords. Such sets are defined by the initial vertical ordering of each segment, and their identity is determined by their constant reiteration as a group of ordered chords. They are used in many pieces, for example in the *Marsch*, *Romance*, *Siciliano-Barcarolle* and *Rondo–Finale* of the First Symphonic Suite and the *Largo Sinfonico* of the Second Symphonic Suite (1942–44). In particular, the First Symphonic Suite's fourth movement, *Romance*, is based on six closely associated twelve-note sets, two of which, S1 and S2 (sharing the first note E♭), are used linearly throughout. The other four sets, S3, S4, S5 and S6, are chordal sets, presented as three-note chords all sharing the note E♭ in their last trichord; their succession is continuously reiterated throughout the piece, and remains largely unchanged within each phrase. These three-note chords predominantly retain the vertical pitch class ordering of their original statement, whereas occasionally, to avoid monotony and shape the voice-leading movement in the bass line, the inner and lower parts

---

[1] These types of sets are also encountered in Berg's opera *Lulu*; Perle describes them as 'harmonic tropes' (1991, 75); see also Perle (1985, 85–207). However, it is unlikely that Skalkottas was aware of them or had been influenced by the compositional techniques Berg used in this particular opera, as he never had the chance to see or hear it in Greece.

Example 4.4 First Symphonic Suite, *Romance*: S3–S6, textural layout of chordal segments within the phrase structure

*The Sets and Set-groups* 91

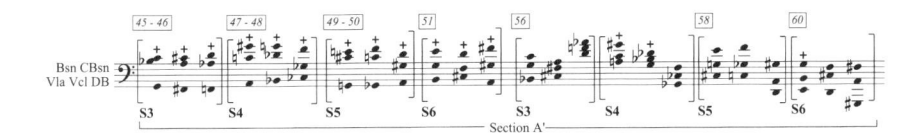

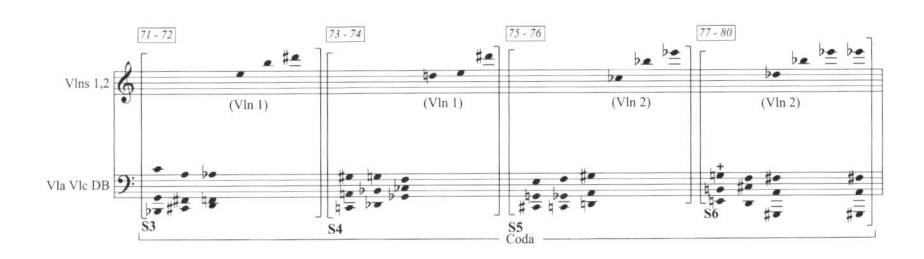

## Supersets

Skalkottas's increasingly expansive use of material in his large-scale symphonic works resulted in the use of supersets, in which a single pitch-class is replaced by an entire twelve-note set. The individual sets are constantly partitioned into segments, which are most frequently presented as three- or four-note chords, or melodic motives encompassing the entire texture. Orchestration, articulation, textural disposition and rhythm largely contribute to the definition of the individual sets, by outlining and grouping together their constituent segments. The twelve-note process involves the strict, sequential presentation of the entire set block, in a manner equivalent to the ordered rotation of individual pitch-classes of a single set. A single set is played again when all the other sets of the superset have been played. The *Rondo–Finale* of the First Symphonic Suite illustrates the use of such a superset, in that it consists of twelve, closely connected twelve-note sets, shown in Example 4.5.

Throughout the movement the twelve twelve-note sets are used in their prime form only, and are presented sequentially from S1 to S12 (with very few exceptions), in the manner of the ordered pitch-classes within a single set. The twelve sets are regularly partitioned into four trichords, whose pitch-class order is not fixed, while the segments can be rearranged and/or superimposed, with the most frequent appearance of the trichords as ABCD, or ACBD.

Example 4.5  First Symphonic Suite, *Rondo–Finale*: Superset (S1–S12) and associative relationships between its constituent sets

[Musical examples for S9, S10, S11, S12 with set-class labels]

## Tonal Sets

Skalkottas frequently employs sets that include in their pitch-class structure major and minor triads, seventh and ninth tetrachords, and/or successions of perfect-fifth dyads, as well as tonally mixed tetrachords (for example, set-classes 4–17, 4–18, incorporating major–minor and/or major–diminished elements), which he manipulates to emphasize their traditional associations. For example, in the *Romance* of the First Symphonic Suite, the melodic set S1 features several tonal elements, particularly two diminished trichords (F D B and G B♭ E), a dominant seventh (C–G–B♭–E) and a diminished seventh (G–B♭–E–D♭) (see set in Appendix A). Furthermore, in most of his compositions Skalkottas uses extensively the E♭ major/minor triad. As with all tonally reminiscent structures in twelve-note music these triads and tetrachords are of purely local significance and do not produce harmonic progressions that create form. Although they allude to a key and retain a sense of familiarity and stability that tonal music affords, they do not carry all the implications of the tonal system. They are segments of a twelve-note set, and they relate to each other not as functional harmonies within a traditional tonal progression, but through their intervallic associations (for example, they may be members of a single set-class, 3–11 or 4–27) constrained by twelve-note relations.[2] The source of musical coherence remains the twelve-note system, a point Schoenberg himself emphasizes: 'As regards hints of a tonality and intermixing of consonant triads one must remember that the main purpose of twelve-tone composition is: production of coherence through the use of a unifying succession of tones which should function at least like a motive' (in Stein, 1964, 248).

**Sets Defined by their Segmental Content**

Skalkottas often composed with sets defined by their segmental content instead of their strict pitch-class order. Such sets are systematically partitioned into segments, particularly trichords and tetrachords, which become the primary building blocks of the piece, as for example in the Concertino for two pianos (1935), the Second Symphonic Suite, and the Sonatina for cello and piano (1949). Each set's predetermined segments are customarily preserved, and are ordered at thematic statements, but unordered thereafter; in the latter case, there is permutation of both their internal pitch-class order and of the segments themselves. Such a set could be conceived as both a collection of pitch-class segments as well as a linear statement of pitch-classes. Sets characterized by the pitch content of their segments may be comparable to Hauer's tropes,[3] though they are not hexachordal in structure, since Skalkottas composes with trichords and tetrachords. However, there is no evidence that Skalkottas knew Hauer or was influenced by him.[4]

In his accompanying notes to the first movement, *Allegro*, of the Concertino for two pianos, Skalkottas states that, '*its compositional work [...] is technically very strict*' and '*the twelve-note harmony predominates in the entire movement*'. However, the piece is based on two sets, S1 and S2, that are not strictly ordered, but defined by their segmental content. Skalkottas preserves each set's identity by grouping together the pitch-classes within its constituent segments, while the identity of each segment is further reinforced by the instrumentation, rhythmic

---

[2] For a discussion of the function and interpretation of triads and other tonal elements in twelve-note music, particularly in works by Berg, Schoenberg, Stravinsky and Webern, see, Straus (1990a, 74–95), and Milstein (1992, 3).

[3] Hauer's twelve-note method does not require an unchanging serial succession; instead, the twelve-note set, which Hauer calls a 'trope', is defined only in terms of the total content of its two constituent hexachords. The note succession within each hexachord can be changed at will and has no referential importance, other than that which the composer chooses to invest in it during the course of the composition; see, Hauer (1962a and 1962b); also, Lichtenfeld (1964 and 1980); Szmolyan (1965); Sengstschmid (1980); Covach (1992).

[4] Here I avoid describing such sets as tropes, since Skalkottas himself describes them as *Reihen* (the same as his other set types), and to prevent comparisons and associations with Berg's troping technique (in *Lulu* in particular); to employ such a term might suggest unfounded connections between the two composers' methods.

pattern and textural disposition. The segments are rotated and used as independent harmonies or melodic motives in the traditional sense. Their manipulation is strict in that they are constantly used in close proximity, maintaining the harmonic formations resulting from their pairing. The tonal set S1 is partitioned into three tetrachords (a B major-diminished, set-class 4–18; an A♭ with added major seventh, set-class 4–20; and an F♯ minor seventh, set-class 4–26), indicated as A, B and C in Example 4.6, which are rotated as ABC, BCA, ACB and are used as unordered segments throughout the movement. Set S2 is partitioned into four trichords (set-classes 3–3, 3–5, 3–9, 3–9(T$_1$)), indicated as A, B, C and D in Example 4.7, which are also distributed in the texture and used independently as chords or melodic motives in the traditional sense.

Example 4.6   Concertino for two pianos, *Allegro*: First theme – opening gesture (bars 1–5)

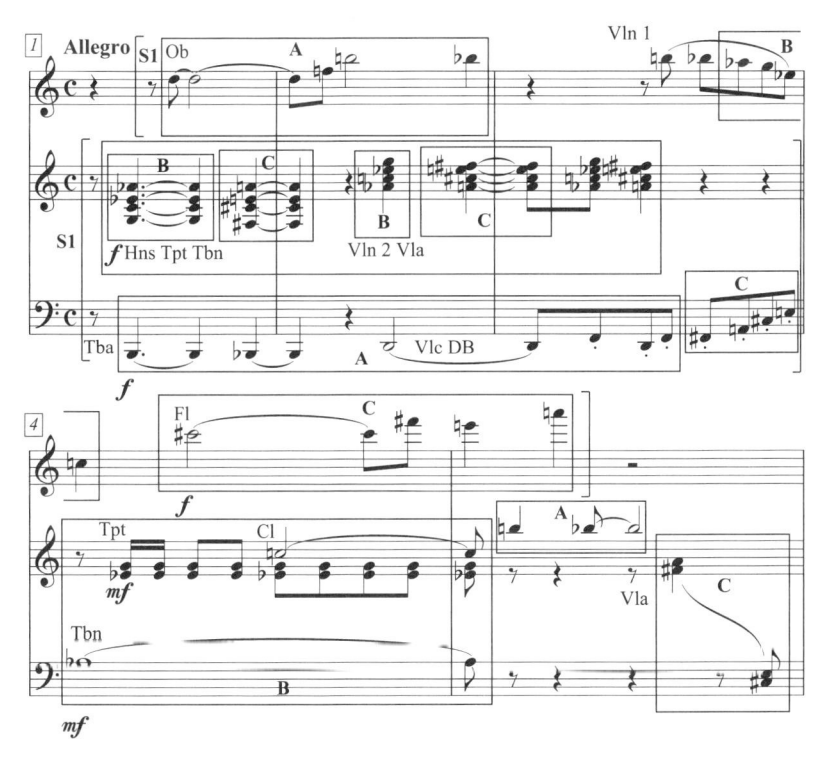

In Exposition I (bars 1–29) the opening gesture of the first theme, played melodically in bars 1–5, is divided between the oboe playing segment A of S1, the violin playing segment B, and the flute playing segment C. This is accompanied by chords in the horns, trumpets and trombone, who play segments B and C sequentially, while the tuba, cellos and basses play linearly a varied version of S1, with unordered segments ACB (see Example 4.6).

Example 4.7  Concertino for two pianos, *Allegro*: Second theme – opening gesture (bars 16–22)

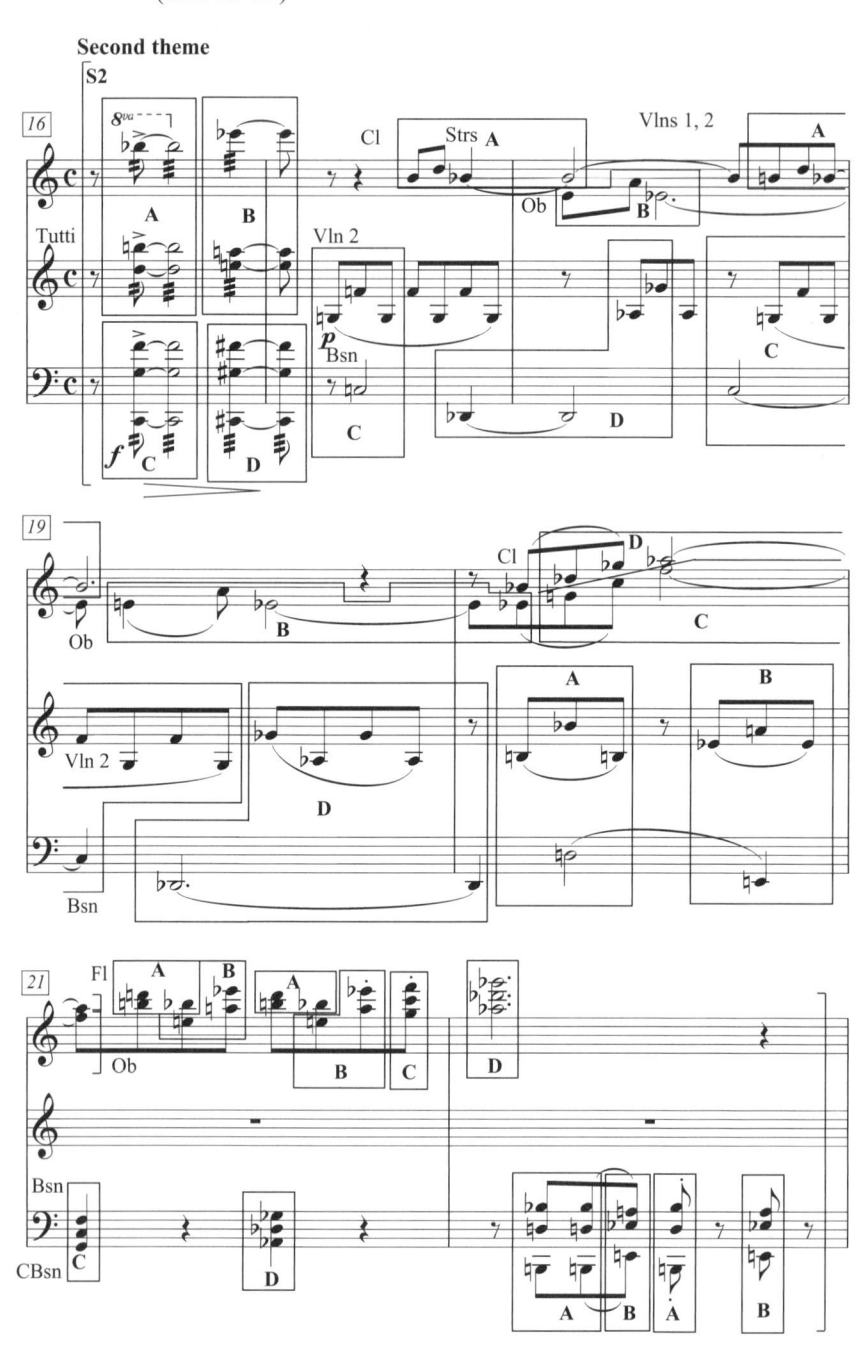

At the opening gesture of the second theme (bar 16), S2 first appears as four superimposed chordal trichords: A over C, and B over D; and the following bars present the realization of this material (see Example 4.7). Segments A and B are played melodically, with the same rhythmic motive, by the clarinet and oboe respectively, and they are accompanied by segments C and D, with their pitch-classes distributed in the second violins and the bassoon. Table 4.1 shows schematically the set structure within each phrase in Exposition I. In the right-hand column, headed 'segmental set structure', each horizontal line represents a different textural layer.

**Incomplete and Irregular Sets**

Skalkottas occasionally includes in a set-group sets that have fewer than twelve notes – particularly eleven-note sets – as for example set S6 in the first movement, *Allegro moderato*, of the Third String Quartet. In large-scale works based on a large amount of pitch-class material there are frequent occurrences of longer sets that include note and/or segment repetitions, as for example in the Overture for large orchestra (*The Return of Ulysses*). The most frequent deviation from the normative twelve-note sets includes twelve-note sets with at least one note missing and another doubled. For example, in the first movement, *Allegro moderato*, of the Octet, set S3 consists of two successive hexachords whose aggregate does not give all the twelve notes of the chromatic scale (F–E–D–C♯–D♯–C–B♭–A–B–C–E–E♭); in the second movement, *Andante cantabile*, the twelve-note set S4 contains the pitch-classes C♯ and A twice, while the pitch-classes E and G♯ are missing; and in the third movement, *Presto*, S3 includes the note B♭ twice and F♯ is missing. Similarly, in the Fourth Sonatina for violin and piano, set S1 has the note B repeated and C♯ missing. Other examples of these set types will occur in the discussions of other works below.

Table 4.1  Concertino for two pianos, *Allegro*: Set structure and troping technique in Exposition I

| Bars | Phrase structure | Sets | Segmental set structure ||||
|---|---|---|---|---|---|---|
| | Exposition I ||||||
| 1–15 | First subject group | S1 | | | | |
| 1–5 | First theme | | A (pcs 1, 2, 3, 4) (ob melodic) | B (vln1 melodic) | C (fl melodic) | |
| | | | B C (hn, tpt, tbn chords) | B C (strings chords) | | |
| | | | A (3, 4, 1, 2) (tba) | C (vlc, db) | B (tpt, tbn) | C (vla) |
| 6–11 | Continuation | | | Note c³ from segment B (vln 1) ||||
| | | | B | C | A | B | C |
| | | | A | | C | | A B |
| 12–15 | Transition | | A | | A | A | |
| | | | B C | | B C | B C | |
| | | | | Minor third dyads ||||
| 16–29 | Second subject group | S2 | | | | |
| 16–20¹ | Second theme | | A | B | A | B |
| | | | C | D | C | D |
| 20²–2 | Continuation | | D/C | A B | D | |
| | | | A B | C D | A B | |
| 23–5 | Secondary theme | | hex.1 | hex.2 | | |
| | | | hex.2 | hex.1 | | |
| 26–7 | | | C | D | | |
| | | | | A ||||
| | | | | B ||||
| 28–9 | Cadence | | hex.2 | hex.1 | | |

# Chapter 5
# Manipulation of the Sets

In the early stages of establishing his new compositional method Schoenberg postulated that the order of the basic set and its three derivatives is 'obligatory for the whole piece', and that 'deviation from this order of tones should normally not occur, in contrast to the treatment of the motive, where variation is indispensable' (Schoenberg, 1969, 193). However, strict adherence to a single set ordering is not characteristic of all twelve-note music, either by Berg, Stravinsky or even Schoenberg; the latter, particularly, viewed a twelve-note set in part as a motivic construction, and 'worked on the basis of an interaction between ordered and unordered pitch collections' (Whittall, 2008, 25). According to Gerhard (who, like Skalkottas, studied with Schoenberg in Berlin), Schoenberg's reorderings, resulting from permutation of the two hexachords of the set, are acceptable on the basis that beyond the set there is an abstract archetype of which the individual set represents only one possible permutation. Regardless of the partitioning of the set into hexachords, tetrachords, trichords or other unequal groups, 'the identity of the series will be maintained in spite of permutation, provided that this takes place exclusively within the constituent units (hexachord, tetrachord, etc.), in other words, as long as these constituent units maintain *their* identity and place' (Gerhard, 1952, 33–4).

Skalkottas's twelve-note compositional technique is largely a manifestation of this permutation principle. He does not necessarily adhere to Schoenberg's order principle; instead, he reflects his teacher's influence regarding motivic treatment and development by partitioning the sets into segments and frequently changing their pitch-class order, thus emphasizing his treatment of them as motives in the traditional sense. Indeed, segmentation and reordering of trichords, tetrachords and, less frequently, hexachords are essential to his compositional style; they are part of his developmental motivic technique, similar to Schoenberg's developing variation.[1] Although Schoenberg's frequent references to developing variation

---

[1] Although Schoenberg's various definitions of 'developing variation' (and its related terms: theme, motive and *Grundgestalt*) were subject to changes of emphasis and nuance during his career, his essential interpretation as given in his unfinished theoretical treatise *Zusammenhang, Kontrapunkt, Instrumentation, Formenlehre* remained constant, defining developing variation as 'the method of varying a motive', according to which 'the changes proceed more or less directly toward the goal of allowing new ideas to arise' (Schoenberg, 1994, 38–9). For Schoenberg, developing variation was predominantly a motivic process through which a theme was constructed by the continuous modification of intervallic and/ or rhythmic components of an initial idea. Later or contrasting events in a piece, which he describes in his 1950 essay on Bach in *Style and Idea* as 'thematic formulations', could be

are found in essays written after his time in Berlin, there seems little doubt that Skalkottas would have been aware of his teacher's thoughts on the subject. Skalkottas's approach, however, is not identical to Schoenberg's, since the latter regarded developing variation as a process evolving primarily within a given melodic line – although Frisch (1990, 17) has shown that the accompaniment was occasionally involved in the process. By contrast, Skalkottas's developmental motivic process involves the interaction between lines. He does not deal exclusively with one basic motive, one melody, or one basic set from which other motive-forms are derived and subsequently developed. Instead, he derives all the elements for his development from both the linear and vertical dimensions of the thematic twelve-note set-group. Each of the contrapuntal lines, based on an independent set, is developed individually during the course of a movement, acquiring thematic status at some point and becoming a source of new motivic material and ideas.

Skalkottas uses the sets predominantly in their prime form, and presents them in a strict, sequential fashion throughout a section and often an entire piece. The original pitch-class order of the sets, as given in their first appearance and/or as adopted after adjustments in the course of the piece, acquires thematic significance. However, since variation is not dependent on serial transformational techniques, following the establishment of the sets, the possibilities of motivic, thematic and harmonic development are increased by their gradual modification through '*the vast horizon of exploitation of the voices and the harmony*' (Skalkottas, 1931/33, 138). Skalkottas's set-modification techniques are largely an extension of his free treatment of the twelve-note material and include the following:

1. Pitch-class doubling and repetition of pitch-classes and/or segments within single set forms.
2. Permutation of the internal pitch-class order of fixed, clearly defined segments.
3. Segmental rotation; reordering of both segments and their pitch-class order.
4. Interpolation of segments from different sets.
5. Free manipulation of the pitch-class content of the sets, including:
   - partitioning of the twelve-note sets and free distribution of the notes in the texture;
   - simultaneous presentation of segments in polyphonic combinations such that new aggregates are generated;

---

understood to be generated from a 'basic unit' (397), that is, from changes that were made in the repetitions of earlier musical thematic elements. There are several important studies dealing with Schoenberg's ideas of developing variation, including those by Frisch (1990), Epstein (1987), Dahlhaus (1990, 128–33) and Haimo (1997). Schoenberg's own valuable thoughts on motive and developing variation can be found in the *Gedanke* manuscript (Goehr, 1977), in *Fundamentals of Musical Composition* (1970/1990), in several essays in *Style and Idea* (1984), in *Zusammenhang, Kontrapunkt, Instrumentation, Formenlehre* (1994) and in *The Musical Idea and the Logic* (1995).

- the use of such segments independently from each other as independent subsets.
6. Derivation of new sets through various manipulations of a source set.

The variant sets that result from these rearrangements are not independent, apart from the derived ones, which are treated as discrete sets of the set-group, as will become clearer below. Rather, Skalkottas appears more interested in the motivic possibilities that arise from the neighbourhood relationships within the segments, and the opportunities for developing variation that his various segmental techniques provide, than in maintaining the pitch-class order of the sets. Extending Schoenberg's principle that 'the two-or-more-dimensional space in which musical ideas are presented is a unit' (1984, 220), for Skalkottas such reorderings and manipulations do not alter the identity of a source set, provided that the set as a whole has referential importance.

## Pitch-class Doubling and Repetition of Pitch-classes and/or Segments within Single Set Forms

Pitch-class doubling and repetition results in the preservation and often intensification of the identity of a specific segment or motive based on a particular set. These repetitions have quite specific harmonic functions, and they frequently serve to generate motives equivalent to a linear segment of one of the twelve-note sets of the set-group. Some of the sets also include insertions and repetitions of segments, which temporarily interrupt the linear presentation of the pitch-class order; and although this disrupts the continuity and logic of a set's intervallic structure, it establishes particular motivic configurations. Such segment interpolation usually underlines the presence of certain motives, which will subsequently predominate in the motivic structure of the movement, and/or establish the predominance of a particular harmonic environment. Set manipulation of this type is strikingly used in the first movement, *Allegro moderato*, of the Octet (1931). As shown in Example 5.1, at bar 10, the exposition of S2 is interrupted at order number 9 (F♯) by the insertion of an ornamental motive based on pitch-class order numbers 8, 7, 9, 4, 2, 1, before proceeding to the last trichord (B–C♯–E). This insertion outlines a series of trichords, set-class 3–2 (A–G♮–F♮, G♮–F♯–F, F♯–F–E♭, F–E♭–D), reinforcing the structural importance of this motivic cell in the construction not only of this section, but also across the entire piece. The ornamental motive is played as a sequence by the flute in bar 11, and clarinet in bar 12. The viola line, accompanying canonically with a countermelody, is based on a permutation of the first nine pitch-classes of the set; this results from the reordering of segments with note repetitions within each varied segment. The insertion of the motive E♭–F–E♭–D reinforces the motivic relationships between the two lines.

Example 5.1  Octet, *Allegro moderato*: Set S2 – reordering, note repetition and interpolation of segments (bars 7[4]–12)

In the second movement, *Andante cantabile*, of the First Piano Concerto (1931), the second theme (bars 36–48) is constructed from five superimposed linear sets, S3, S4, S5, S6 and RS6, as shown in Example 5.2. There is extensive note and segment repetition and interpolation in the exposition of a set, and free distribution of segments in the texture. The frequent repetition of the trichord G–A–B and its variant B–G–A, which are part of the repeated, ascending hexachord G–A–B–C–D–E (of S3), suggests a C major harmonic area in the inner voice at the opening gesture of the theme. Also the repeated and interpolated trichords C–D–E (of S3) and E♭–A♭–G (of S4), played by the oboes in bars 37–8, apart from locally emphasizing a C major chord, result in a new hexachord (set-class 6–16), which is widely used as an independent segment throughout the movement.

In section B of the first movement (*Allegro moderato*) of the Third String Quartet (1935), all four sets S5, S5(T$_3$), S6 and S7 include in their first appearance insertions and repetitions of segments, as shown in Example 5.3. In S5, the insertion and continuous repetition of the tetrachord C–B–A–G (set-class 4–11) during the exposition of the set accentuates the C major context of the thematic

Example 5.2  First Piano Concerto, *Andante cantabile*: Second theme – opening gesture (bars 36–42)

line. Its contrapuntal accompaniment in the second violin, based on its minor-third transposed form (S5($T_3$)), inserts and reiterates the tetrachord E♭–D–C–B♭, while the cello, based on the eleven-note set S6, reiterates the trichord D♭–E♭–E (set-class 3–2), which further reinforces the C major/minor context of the section's opening gesture. The structural significance of this segmental repetition will be discussed in detail in Part III (pp. 217–21).

## Permutation of the Internal Pitch-class Order of Fixed Segments

In certain works, particularly those in which the sets are initially presented chordally, although the order of trichordal or tetrachordal segments remains unchanged, the order of single pitch-classes within each segment may vary ((1, 2, 3), (1, 3, 2),

Example 5.3  Third String Quartet, *Allegro moderato*: Segment repetition within sets

(2, 3, 1), (2, 1, 3), (3, 1, 2) or (3, 2, 1)), albeit without changing the identity of the source twelve-note set as a frame of reference. For example, in the first movement, *Allegro*, of the early Second Sonatina for violin and piano (1929), the first theme (bars 1–17) is based on a twelve-note set; this is partitioned into four trichords, whose succession remains unchanged (ABCD). However, following the initial, protracted exposition of the set, the pitch-class order within each segment varies, while the segments are presented both linearly, as melodic motives, and as chords. As shown in Table 5.1, the thematic set is used four times throughout the movement at important structural points. It provides the opening thematic statement (bars 1–17) as an ordered twelve-note melody; in bars 18–27, furnishing the secondary idea in the upper voice of the piano right-hand texture, it is based on a pitch-class reordering within each trichordal segment; in the opening section of the development (bars 52–64) it appears with each trichord presented as a three-note chord in the piano right hand; and it is recycled in the varied recapitulation of the first theme in the violin (bars 95–102), with each trichordal segment played chordally, and interpolated with the opening theme's accompanimental piano right-hand appoggiatura-like motive.

The accompanimental material, based on a series of fixed hexachordal pitch-class collections, is similarly segmented, but at developmental passages the segments do not always maintain their identity.

**Segmental Rotation: Reordering of Both Segments and their Pitch-class Order**

As a consequence of the permutation of the pitch-class order within segments, Skalkottas also occasionally employs the technique of segmental rotation, with the segments either maintaining their original pitch-class order or being reordered.

Table 5.1  Second Sonatina for violin and piano, *Allegro*: Twelve-note thematic set and its trichordal transformations

| Bars | | Set-class 6–1 (T$_0$) | | | Set-class 6–1 (T$_6$) | | |
|---|---|---|---|---|---|---|---|
| 1–17 | vln | e³–f♯³–a³ | | a♭³–g³–f³ | b♭²–c³–e♭³ | | d³–c♯³–b² |
| 18–27 | pno RH (upper voice) | a²–e²–f♯² | | f²–g²–a♭² | b♭–c¹–e♭¹ | | B–c♯–d |
| 52–64 | pno RH | e² a¹ f♯¹ | | g² f² a♭¹ | b♭¹ e♭¹ c¹ | | c♯² b¹ d¹ |
| 95–102 | vln | c♯¹–d¹ | e²–a¹ f♯¹ | b♭–a   f² a♭¹–g | g¹–g♯¹ | b♭² c²–eb¹ | e¹–d♯¹   b² c♯²–d¹ |

Table 5.2  First Piano Suite, *Preludio*: Second theme (bars 14–17) – segmental permutation of (S1–S2) – (S3–S4)

| Bars | Pno | Sets | Segments | Segmental pitch-class content | | |
|---|---|---|---|---|---|---|
| 14 | RH | S1 | B C A | E♭–E–G–A♭ | D–C–F♯–B♭ | F–A–B–C♯ |
| | LH | S2 | B C A (pc order 4,3,5,6)– (8,7,10,9)– (12,11,1,2) | A–B♭–C–B | E♭–F–G–E | A♭–D♭–G♭–D |
| 15 | RH | S3 | B C A | C♯–D–C–B♭ | F♯–A–E♯–G♯ | E–G–B–E♭ |
| | LH | S4 | B C A | F–A♭–G♭–E♭ | C–E–B–A | G–B♭–C♯D |
| 16 | RH | S2 | C B A | E♭–G–D♭–A♭ | F–A–C–B | B♭–A–D–F♯ |
| | LH | S1 | C A B | D–F♯–B♭–C | C♯–F–A–B | A♭–E–G–E♭ |
| 17–18 | RH | S3 | C A B | C♯–A F♯–G♯–F–E | E♭–B–G–D | C–B♭ |
| | LH | S4 | C B A | G–B♭–B–A | F–A♭–E♭–G♭ | E–D–C♯–C |

The segmental content of all the resulting sets can be seen as variants of a single precompositional formation. An example of set segmentation, reordering, and rotation of the segments is found in the first movement, *Preludio (Andante)*, of the First Piano Suite. As shown in Example II.1, the first theme is built on four sets and their T$_8$ transpositions (S1, S2, S3, S4, S5, S6, S7, S8). The opening gesture of the second theme (bars 14–17) is established through the segmental rotation of the four superimposed paired sets (S1–S2) – (S3–S4), as shown on Table 5.2.

This rotation, however, applied within the segments of each individual set, although resulting in a new thematic–motivic surface, never endangers the integrity and unity of the referential thematic set-group. The relationships of the harmonic groups between corresponding paired set segments are maintained, with rotated harmonic formations remaining constant and recognizable, occurring as related tetrachords or as a tetrachord with a consistent dyad.

**Interpolation of Segments from Different Sets**

In several pieces Skalkottas interpolates segments from the different sets of the set-group to generate new melodic and harmonic material, thus establishing a new harmonic region. For example, in the third movement, *Allegro vivace*, of the First Piano Concerto (1931), the passage at bars 29–32, which is a varied repetition of the opening gesture, is introduced by the piano right hand playing a new melody; this is formed by the amalgamation of two twelve-note sets, S1 and S2, initially presented superimposed in bars 1–5, as shown in Example 5.4. The harmonic accompaniment in the left hand, initially based on S1a (a retrograde variation of S1), at bars 29–32 results from the interpolation of segments from S1a and S5, with each trichord of S1a played as a three-note chord (identified as trichords ABCD in the example), followed by two dyads of S5 (identified as tetrachords ABC).

Example 5.4  First Piano Concerto, *Allegro vivace*: Opening gesture (bars 1–5), and interpolation of segments (bars 29–32)

Similarly, in the *Adagio* from the Fourth Sonatina for violin and piano (1935), the closing cadential passage (bars 31–4) is structured from the sequential interpolation of tetrachordal segments from sets S4, S5 and S6, identified as A, B and C in Example 5.5. Skalkottas exploits the invariant properties of the three sets by arranging the segments in a way that invokes traditional modes of construction, so that they appear as sequences with common notes between the consecutive chords. The note repetition and surface disorder created through the free permutation and interpolation of segments is counteracted by the unifying power of the invariant elements between the sets, and a smooth, chorale-type voice-leading in the piano accompaniment. The violin plays a new cadential melody, including several note repetitions, the product of the sequential presentation of reordered segments from the three sets.

Example 5.5  Fourth Sonatina for violin and piano, *Adagio*: Interpolation of segments (bars 31–4)

## Partitioning of the Twelve-note Sets and Free Distribution of the Notes in the Texture

Following its ordered exposition and establishment, a set may be treated freely in subsequent appearances, with its segments 'splitting up' (Rufer, 1961, 124) and distributed in the texture in order to produce a new motivic surface and establish a new harmonic area. For example, the second movement, *Adagio*, of the Fourth Sonatina for violin and piano is built on the same three sets of the first movement's (*Moderato*) section A and their retrogrades (S1, S2, S3, RS1, RS2, RS3). The sets and their constituent segments have already been aurally established throughout the *Moderato*. In the *Adagio*, Skalkottas composes with the largely unordered segments of the different sets, which are here used as independent motives. In particular, S2 and S3 are used in a varied form, which results from a reordering of the notes within the trichords, shown in Table 5.3.

Table 5.3    Fourth Sonatina for violin and piano, *Adagio*: S2 and S3 – correspondences with *Moderato*'s S2 and S3

| S1 | A–E–D♯–B–C–G | F♯–D–B♭–B–G♯–F |
|---|---|---|
| S2 (*Moderato*) | F–B♭–A–C♯–C–A♭ | B–G–F♯–D–E–E♭ |
| S2 (*Adagio*) | B♭–F–A–C♯–C–A♭ | G–B–D–F♯–D♯–E |
| | | |
| S3 (*Moderato*) | D–C♯–G–E♭–A–E | F♯–G♯–C–F–B–B♭ |
| S3 (*Adagio*) | D–G–C♯–E♭–A–E | F♯–G♯–C–F–B–B♭ |

As shown in Example 5.6, at bars 18–20, the segmentation of the sets, and the rearrangement and distribution of the notes in the texture, result in new thematic–melodic gestures and a new harmonic accompaniment. The passage is based on the sequential presentation of S1, S2 and S3, each set lasting the equivalent of three quavers within the 9/8 metre of the bar.

Example 5.6  Fourth Sonatina for violin and piano, *Adagio*: Partitioning of the twelve-note sets and free distribution of the notes in the texture (bars 18–20)

The violin melody is accompanied contrapuntally by a semiquaver countermelody in the piano left hand, while the right hand provides chordal accompaniment. Set S1 is distributed between the three parts: the violin playing pitch-classes with order number 1, 4, 5, 8, the piano left hand playing melodically pitch-classes 2, 3, 6, 7, and the right hand accompanying chordally with the last tetrachord of the set. Set S2 follows with pitch-classes 5, 7, 10, 12, played by the violin and accompanied melodically by 6, 8, 9, 11, while the first tetrachord makes up the chords in the right hand. The third gesture of the violin melody, based on pitch-classes 8, 5, 4, 1 of S3, is accompanied by the piano left hand playing 7, 6, 2, 3 melodically and 9, 10, 11, 12 chordally. This partitioning of the sets and the distribution of the notes in the texture results in new melodic gestures, with the violin now playing a *dolce* melody with several motivic repetitions and a closely knit intervallic structure ($\boxed{A}$–$\boxed{B-C-D}$$\boxed{C-B-D-E♭}$–G♯–$\boxed{A}$–$\boxed{E♭-D}$), while the harmonic accompaniment establishes a new harmonic region with the fifth B♭–F featuring as a constant, repetitive, pedal-like interval in all three chords. The reordering also produces a new left-hand countermelody that starts with the motive E–D♯–G (set-class 3–3, one of Skalkottas's signature sounds), and ends with the descending diminished triad E–C♯–$G_1$ (set-class 3–10), sharing two pitch-classes with the opening motive and rounding off the opening gesture. Furthermore, the final $G_1$ functions as a link for the continuation phrase, which also starts with $G_1$.

Frequently, Skalkottas exploits the association of non-adjacent elements of a set to create local harmonies that are equivalent to segments of one or more sets of the group. For example, in the first movement, *Moderato*, of the Second String Trio, the chordal cadence of the opening passage (bar 12) is punctuated by three four-note chords resulting from the verticalization of each tetrachord of S1. The distribution of the notes in each voice produces superimposed three-note motives that, although resulting from non-consecutive order numbers of the sets, are all equivalent to segments of the opening thematic line based on S1. Table 5.4 represents the associative relationships between the thematic line and the cadence of the first theme.

## Simultaneous Presentation of Set Segments in Polyphonic Combinations

The simultaneous, polyphonic presentation of a set's segments often generates specific harmonic events that are taken up in the ensuing developmental process. For example, section D (bars 33–64³) of the second movement, *Andante*, of the Third String Quartet, is built on two twelve-note sets S3 and S4 and their various transpositions: $S3(T_5)$, indicated as S3a, S3b [$S3(T_{10})$], S3c [$S3(T_3)$], S4a [$S4(T_3)$], S4b [$S4(T_2)$]). Throughout the developmental passage (bars 47⁶–58¹), S4 and its transpositions S4a and S4b are played melodically. The tonal set S3 and its transpositions S3a, S3b and S3c are partitioned into trichords with the segments distributed among the four instruments, as shown in Example 5.7. This distribution of segments in the texture, together with the sequential use of the

Table 5.4    Second String Trio, *Moderato*: Associative relationships between the thematic line and the cadence at bar 12

| S1 | G | A♭ | C♯ | F | G♭ | E♭ | A | E | B | D | B♭ | C |
|---|---|---|---|---|---|---|---|---|---|---|---|---|
|  |  | 3–5 |  |  |  |  |  |  |  | 3–3 |  |  |
|  |  |  | 3–11 |  |  |  |  |  |  |  |  |  |

| Chordal cadence at bar 12 ||||| 
|---|---|---|---|---|
| vln | F | F♯ | C | set-class 3–5 ($I_{11}$ of S1) |
| vla | C♯<br>G♯ | A<br>E♭ | B♭<br>D | 3–3 ($I_{11}$ of S1)<br>3–5 ($T_7$ of S1) |
| vlc | G | E | B | 3–11 ($I_{10}$ of S1) |
| order number | 4<br>3<br>2<br>1 | 5<br>7<br>6<br>8 | 12<br>11<br>10<br>9 |  |

Example 5.7 Third String Quartet, *Andante*: Simultaneous presentation of set segments (bars $47^6$–$58^1$)

transposed forms of S3, not only affects the melodic organization of this passage, it also results in a 'modulatory' sequential movement of alternating major and minor triads, which define the harmonic structure. In bars $47^6$–$8^3$ each trichord of S3 is played chordally by the second violin and divided cellos, resulting in a progression of triads (B major – G minor – D♭ major – A minor). To counteract this overtly tonal movement, Skalkottas distributes the notes of the sets in each part in such a way that the texture consists of the superimposition of three linear, chromatic tetrachords (set-class 4–1); with the second violin playing order numbers 2, 5, 8, 11, the cello upper part 3, 6, 9, 12, and the cello lower part 1, 4, 7, 10. This harmonic and melodic gesture is repeated sequentially at the perfect fourth ($T_5$), thus outlining a harmonic progression associated with traditional developmental passages by emulating sequences in the circle of fifths.

**Free Manipulation of the Pitch-class Content of the Sets**

Some of Skalkottas's works exhibit a freer approach to twelve-note composition, such as the third movement of the Concertino for two pianos, the third movement of the Concerto for Violin – commonly known as Violin Concerto – (1938), the last three movements of the Second Symphonic Suite (particularly the *Largo Sinfonico*), and *The Return of Ulysses* (1942–44). In these, Skalkottas composes with sets partitioned in unordered segments, similar to twelve-note collections. These are presented sequentially, with each set statement encompassing the entire texture. For example, in the *Allegro giusto* of the Concertino for two pianos, the first theme is built on three such sets (S1, S2, S3), as shown in Example 5.8.

Example 5.8  Concertino for two pianos, *Allegro giusto*: Opening gesture (bars 1–9) – free manipulation of the sets

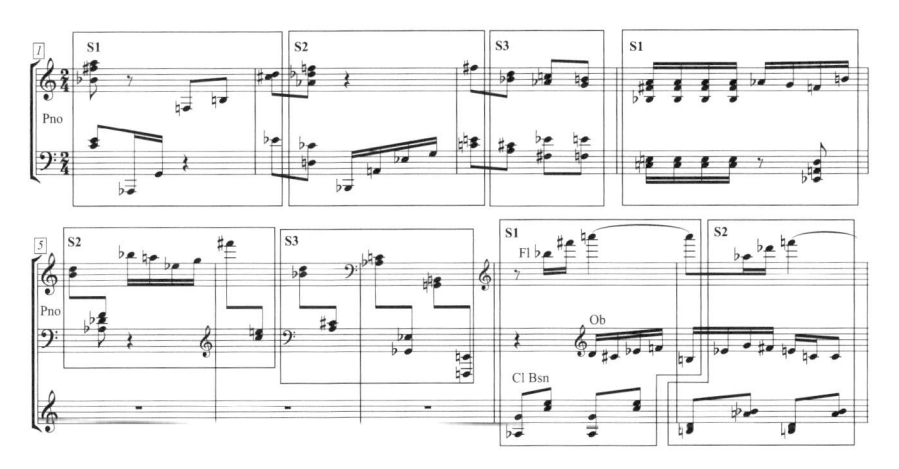

The sets are repeated sequentially four times as a group in the first 13 bars. Although the overall pitch-class order cannot be established, there is a neighbourhood relationship, with certain intervals, dyads or larger segments always brought together, so that certain harmonic groups are established through their consistent reiteration.

In works based on a large number of sets, following the establishment of a set-group Skalkottas frequently treats subsequent appearances of the sets freely.

The opening theme (bars 1–19) of the third movement, *Allegro vivo vivacissimo*, of the Violin Concerto is built on the eleven twelve-note sets (S1–S11) of the first movement's (*Molto appassionato*) opening passage (see Example 5.9).

Example 5.9   Violin Concerto, *Allegro vivo vivacissimo*: First theme – opening gesture (bars 1–10)

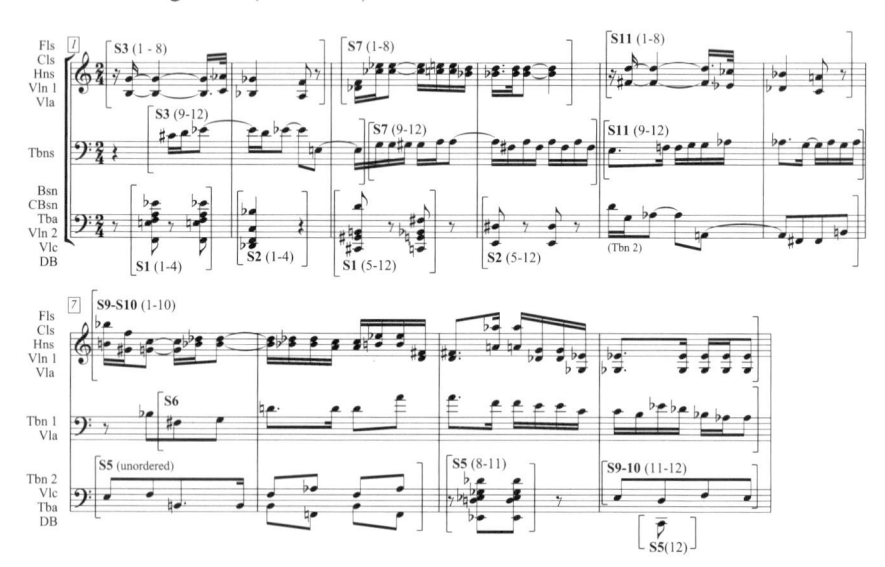

The theme is divided into two sections (bars 1–10 and 11–19), the second a varied repetition of the first. These are further divided into shorter phrases, established by set content, rhythm, articulation and textural homogeneity. In the first phrase (bars 1–4) the predominant thematic idea, played by the trombones, is based on successive segments (pitch-classes 9–12) of S3 and S7, sets that furnish the harmonic accompaniment in the first movement. This thematic gesture is accompanied contrapuntally by the flutes, clarinets, horns, the first violin and viola, playing in unison a melodic line in minor sixths (bars 1–2) and major thirds (bars 3–4), based on the pitch-classes 1–8 of S3 and S7. The melodies are accompanied by chords based on the interpolation of segments from S1 and S2, with order number 1…4 in bars 1–2, and order number 5…12 in bars 3–4. In the second phrase (bars 5–6) the predominant thematic lines are based on segments of S11. In bars 7–10, the dyadic thematic/melodic gesture in the textural layer comprising woodwinds, horns and upper strings is based on the superimposition of pitch-classes 1–10 of S9 and S10; the trombone melodic line is based on S6, and is accompanied by an unordered version of S5 and interpolations of set segments.[2]

---

[2]   The varied repetition of the opening phrase is marked by an abrupt textural and timbral change, although the rhythmic gestures remain the same. The upper strings play chords based on the interpolation of segments from S1 and S2, while the cellos and double

*Manipulation of the Sets* 113

Skalkottas also partitions the twelve-note sets and distributes their segments in the texture in such a way that new aggregates and/or sets (not necessarily dodecaphonic) are generated. For example, the third movement, *Menuetto (Moderato assai)*, of the First Piano Suite is built on the same eight source-sets of the first movement, *Preludio* (discussed above). Here, Skalkottas abandons the previously established paired presentation of the sets, and instead presents them sequentially, partitioned into unequal segments that are distributed in the two-part texture. This set treatment results in new melodic and harmonic material, which in turn is used by Skalkottas in a serial manner. The compositional properties of the *Menuetto* are presented in bars 1–10$^1$ (section A). As shown in Example 5.10, their distribution in the two piano hands results in four non-dodecaphonic sets, played in pairs.

Example 5.10  First Piano Suite, *Menuetto (Moderato assai)*: Opening gesture (bars 1–10$^1$)

In bars 1–5, the ten-note set IIIa results from the linear arrangement in the right hand of certain pitch-classes from both S1 and S3. This is accompanied in the left hand by the fourteen-note set IIIb, which derives from the arrangement of the remaining pitch-classes of S1 and S3. In bars 6–10$^1$ these are followed by two derived sets played in pairs, IIIc in the right hand, resulting from the arrangement of pitch-classes from both S2 and S4, and IIId in the left hand, derived from the remaining pitch-classes of the two source sets; the first trichord of IIId (B♭–D–F♯) always appears as a three-note chord, punctuating the opening and closing gestures of phrases. These are also used in exact retrograde form in section B. Although the resulting sets are of various lengths and include several note repetitions within

---

basses play S3. The phrase continues (bars 15–16) with segments of S5, played chordally by the upper strings, and S11, played by the lower strings. The cadence is established by yet another abrupt timbral and textural change, with the upper woodwind playing chordal trichords of S6 and the contra-bassoon and tuba the remaining notes of S11.

their internal structure, Skalkottas uses them in a strict serial manner, and their exact repetition and reiteration throughout the *Menuetto* reinforces their identity as distinct sets. In the first phrase of section B (bars $10^2$–17) the opening gesture is repeated in strict retrograde form, RS4, RS2, RS3, RS1; the melodies maintain their pitch-class order, although in bars 15–17 they exchange parts. The second developmental phrase of the section (bars 18–25) is based on the juxtaposition of sets RIIIc, IIIb, RIIIa, IIId. The motivic–melodic connections with section A are maintained, with the left hand part being a repetition of bars 1–$10^1$. In terms of pitch-class set, melodic and harmonic structure, bars 26–35 (section A') are an exact repetition of bars 1–$10^1$, albeit with textural and rhythmic changes. A schematic presentation of the phrase and set structure of the *Menuetto* is given in Table 9.8 (p. 166).

# Chapter 6
# Derivation Techniques

For composers of the Second Viennese School, especially Webern, a '*derived series* is a twelve-note series composed of several forms (transpositions, inversions or retrograde inversions) of a single trichord or tetrachord' (Lester, 1989, 219); and in twelve-note theory, 'a derived set is *not* a new set in the composition', but 'it can be thought of as resulting from the juxtaposition of segments from the fundamental forms' (Babbitt, 1955, 59). Similarly, Skalkottas uses several techniques to derive one set from another, or from segments of a number of different sets. Some of these derivational techniques include:

1. The derivation of new sets through source trichords and tetrachords.
2. The unordered presentation of the pitch-classes within hexachordal segments of the transposed, retrograde and inverted forms of a set.
3. The pairing of notes and interpolation of segments from different sets.
4. The interchange of one pitch-class in each hexachord.
5. Cyclic rotation of the pitch-classes within a set.

Although these techniques are similar, indeed often identical, to those used in Skalkottas's manipulation of the sets discussed above, the derived sets are not regarded as variants of the original, but are treated as independent sets. During the course of the movement they establish their own identity; they are presented simultaneously with the other sets of the group at the opening gesture of a section; they may provide the accompaniment or furnish the predominant motivic/thematic idea of a phrase; and Skalkottas uses them to reinforce motivic and harmonic relationships and similarities within the pitch-class content of the twelve-note set-group. Therefore, when describing such a set, although I shall explain its derivational nature, I will consider it as another, discrete set of the set-group.

**Derived Sets through Source Trichords and Tetrachords**

There are only a few instances where Skalkottas produces derived sets from the sequential presentation of several forms of a single segment, dyad, trichord or tetrachord, suggesting that he was perhaps only experimenting with this technique. Such derived sets are found in the Third String Quartet and the Third Sonatina for violin and piano. For example, in the *Andante* of the Third String Quartet, the tonal set S3 consists of four trichords, set-class 3–11, which are presented sequentially at $T_0$, $I_3$, $T_2$, and $I_5$ and produce alternating major and minor triads (B major,

G minor, D♭ major and A minor). In the third movement, *Allegro vivace (Rondo)*, set S2 is built on three equivalent chromatic tetrachords, set-class 4–1 ($T_0$, $T_8$, and $I_1$), as shown in Table 6.1a. Set S5 is structured from four equivalent trichords, set-class 3–8 ($T_0$, $I_2$, $T_5$, $I_7$), and S7 also from four equivalent trichords, set-class 3–3 ($T_0$, $I_9$, $T_2$, $I_{11}$). Set S3 is not entirely 'derived', but is constructed from three equivalent trichords, set-class 3–2 ($T_0$, $I_5$, $T_4$), and a C major trichord (set-class 3–11).

Table 6.1a  Third String Quartet, *Allegro vivace (Rondo)*: Derived sets through source segments

| S2 | F–E♭–D–E | C–D♭–C♭–B♭ | G–G♯–A–F♯ |  |
|---|---|---|---|---|
|  | 4–1 ($T_0$) | 4–1 ($T_8$) | 4–1 ($I_1$) |  |
| S5 | F–A–B | E♭–D♭–G | B♭–D–E | A♭–G♭–C |
|  | 3–8 ($T_0$) | 3–8 ($I_2$) | 3–8 ($T_5$) | 3–8 ($I_7$) |
| S7 | C–D♭–E | F–A–G♯ | D–E♭–F♯ | G–B–A♯ |
|  | 3–3 ($T_0$) | 3–3 ($I_9$) | 3–3 ($T_2$) | 3–3 ($I_{11}$) |
| S3 | D♭–C♭–B♭ | A–A♭–G♭ | F–E♭–D | C–G–E |
|  | 3–2 ($T_0$) | 3–2 ($I_5$) | 3–2 ($T_4$) | 3–11 |

Similarly, in the first movement, *Allegro giusto*, of the Third Sonatina for violin and piano, S4 is a derived set from four exact transpositions of the whole-tone trichord set-class 3–6 ($T_0$, $T_6$, $T_1$, $T_7$) (see Table 6.1b). In the second movement, *Andante*, S2a is built from three chromatic tetrachords. However, these chromatic tetrachords result from a rearrangement of the pitch-class order within the source set S2 of the first movement, *Allegro giusto*. As shown in Table 6.1b, S2 is originally presented as four chordal dyads and a melodic tetrachord. S2a is formed by the melodic presentation of the upper notes, followed by the lower notes of the chordal dyads of S2 plus its final tetrachord.

Table 6.1b  Third Sonatina for violin and piano: *Allegro giusto* – derived set S4; *Andante* – derived set S2a; *Allegro giusto* – S2

| S4 | F♯ E D | C B♭ A♭ | G F E♭ | D♭ B A |
|---|---|---|---|---|
|  | 3–6 ($T_0$) | 3–6 ($T_6$) | 3–6 ($T_1$) | 3–6 ($T_7$) |
| S2a | G–F–F♯–E | E♭–D♭–C–D | B♭–A–B–G♯ |  |
|  | 4–1 ($T_0$) | 4–1 ($T_8$) | 4–1 ($T_4$) |  |
| S2 | G   F | F♯   E | B♭–A–B–G♯ |  |
|  | E♭  D♭ | D    C |  |  |

## Unordered Presentation of the Pitch-classes within Hexachordal Segments of the Transposed, Retrograde and Inverted Forms of a Set

This is Skalkottas's most frequent type of derivation. The resulting sets are repeatedly and deliberately used as new, ordered sets, even though they are all members of the same set-class of the $T_0$ form. The reordering within each hexachord of a source set does not undermine the serial principles of twelve-note set handling because the resulting set is not regarded as a different form of the basic set, but as a new set, albeit one closely connected with the original, and which during the course of the piece establishes its own identity. This derivational technique is first used in the first movement, *Allegro*, of the Second Sonatina for violin and piano. Set S2, which includes several note repetitions, is derived from a rearrangement of the pitch-classes within each hexachord of the perfect-fourth transposed form of S1 ($T_5$), as shown in Table 6.2a.

Table 6.2a   Second Sonatina for violin and piano, *Allegro*: Derivation of S2

| S1($T_0$) | E–F♯–A–A♭–G–F | B♭–C–E♭–D–C♯–B |
|---|---|---|
| S1($T_5$) | A–B–D–C♯–C–A♯ | D♯–F–G♯–G–F♯–E |
| S2 | D–C♯–B♭–A–B–C (D) | E♭–(A)–G–F♯–E–F–(G)–A♭ |

This technique is also widely used in the third movement, *Presto*, of the Octet. For instance, in section B, built on a group of six twelve-note sets (S4–S9), S7 derives from the unordered presentation of the pitch-classes within each hexachord of S6 transposed at $T_8$ (see Table 6.2b).

Table 6.2b   Octet, *Presto*: Derivation of S7

| S6 | D–E♭–C–F–E–B | B♭–G♯–A–C♯–G–F♯ |
|---|---|---|
| S6($T_8$) | B♭–C♭–A♭–D♭–C–G | G♭–F–A–E♭–D |
| S7 | D♭–B♭–C–B–G–A♭ | F♯–A–E♭–D–F–E |

The transpositional relationship between the two sets offers maximum pitch-class similarity, with each hexachord of S7 sharing two pitch-classes with the corresponding hexachord of S6, and four pitch-classes with each of the corresponding hexachords of the retrograde form of S6; the invariant dyads E–F and D–E♭, the most prominent motivic cells of the section, maintain their intervallic identity in both sets, and are used as common elements that provide connection and coherence.

In section A of the *Allegro moderato* of the Third String Quartet, built on four sets (S1–S4), S4 derives from S3. As shown in Table 6.2c, each hexachord of S4, played by the cello and consistently providing the bass line of the four-part texture in this section, is an unordered inversion transposed at I₁₁ of each hexachord of S3, and also shares four pitch-classes with each hexachord of RS3. Skalkottas constantly presents these two sets linearly in their prime form, and uses them as ordered, independent sets. Similarly in section B (built on four sets S5, S5(T₃), S6, S7), S7 derives from RS5 by interchanging the pitch-classes F♯ and G♯(A♭) in each unordered hexachord; it too constantly supports the bass line of the four-part texture in this section.

Table 6.2c  Third String Quartet, *Allegro moderato*: Derivation of S4 and S7

| S3 (I₁₁) | E–B♭–G–G♯–A–B | C–C♯–D–F♯–D♯–F |
|---|---|---|
| S4 | E–A–B–A♯–G♯–G | D–F–G♭–C♯–C–D♯ |
| RS5 | D–A♭–E–F–B♭–C♯ | E♭–F♯–G–A–B–C |
| S7 | D–B♭–E–C♯–F♯–F | E♭–G–C–B–A–G♯ |

Skalkottas occasionally derives new sets by using partial retrograde within each hexachord of a set, or through partial reordering of the notes within each trichord and/or hexachord of the retrograde form of a set. For example in the second movement, *Andante cantabile*, of the First Piano Concerto set S1a derives from a pitch-class reordering within each trichord of the retrograde form of S1, as shown in Table 6.2d. More rarely, he derives sets from the reordering of segments of the retrograde inversion of a set; for instance, in the same movement, set S1b derives from a reordering within each trichord of the retrograde inversion of S1 (RIS1).

Table 6.2d  First Piano Concerto, *Andante cantabile*: Derivation of S1a and S1b

| S1 | G–A♭–D♭–F–A–D | F♯–C–B–E–E♭–B♭ |
|---|---|---|
| S1a (RS1) | D♯–A♯–E–B–F♯–C | A–F–D–G–D♭–A♭ |
| IS1 | G–F♯–C♯–A–F–C | A♭–D–E♭–B♭–B–E |
| S1b (RIS1) | E–B–B♭–A♭–D–E♭ | F–A–C–G–F♯–C♯ |

## Pairing of Notes and Interpolation of Segments from Different Sets

A derived set may result from the pairing of the same order number of segments from different sets. For example, the opening thematic gesture (bars 1–10) of the *Presto* of the Octet is built on three source sets (S1, S2, S3) and three derived ones (I, II, III). The six-note set I results from the pairing of the same order number (1, 2, 3) of the first trichords of S2 and S3. Similarly, the six-note set II is formed by the pairing of the second trichords of S2 and S3; and the twelve-note set III (with the pitch-class D doubled) is formed by the combination of the second hexachords of the above sets, with a displacement of order numbers – 9 placed before 7, and 12 placed before 11 – as shown in Table 6.3. The grouping and pitch-class presentation of each set is used to reinforce the motivic and phrase structure of the thematic ideas that precede and follow them. As will be discussed further in Part III, the three derived sets, used continuously as a group, establish their identity as distinct serial and harmonic units, apart from the passage in section A' (bars 137–45), where, transposed at the fifth ($T_7$), they are played melodically by the clarinet.

Table 6.3   Octet, *Presto*: Derived sets I, II, III

| S2  | G–A–F♯         | C–E–B           | D–G♯–C♯         | B♭–E♭–F         |
|-----|----------------|-----------------|-----------------|-----------------|
| S3  | E♭–F–B♭        | G♯–A–C♯         | B♭–C–D          | G–E–B           |
| I   | G–E♭–A–F–B♭–G♭ |                 |                 |                 |
| II  |                | C–G♯–E–A–B–C♯   |                 |                 |
| III |                |                 | D–C♯–B♭–D–C–G♯  | G–B♭–B–F–E–E♭   |

An example of the interpolation of set segments with the same order number to produce derived sets is found in the third movement, *Presto*, of the Second String Trio, which is built on the same three twelve-note sets (S1, S2, S3) of the first movement. Following the continuous reiteration of the ordered source sets over a long span of the piece, Skalkottas develops his material by introducing three new twelve-note sets (S4, S5, S6) in the development section (bars 89⁶–113). These sets derive from the pairing and interpolation of dyads with the same order number from the three source sets, as shown in Example 6.1.

Example 6.1   Second String Trio, *Presto*: Derived sets S4, S5, S6 (bars 89⁶–94)

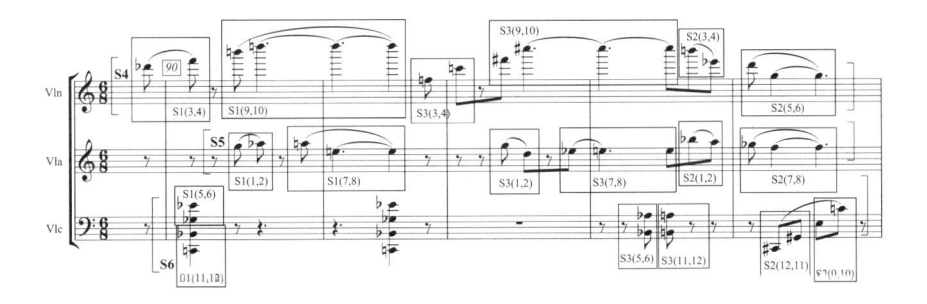

Set S4, played by the violin in bars 89⁶–94, results from the interpolation of dyads with order number 3, 4, 9, 10 from S1 and S3, and order number 3, 4, 5, 6 from S2; S5 results from the interpolation of dyads with order number 1, 2, 7, 8 from S1, S3 and S2; S6 arises from the pairing of the dyads with order number 5, 6, 11, 12 from S1 and S3 and order number 12, 11, 9, 10 from S2. Each of the last tetrachords of S4 and S6 deviates from the established dyadic order and is built on consecutive dyads from S2, so that each gesture in the phrase structure ends with two inversionally equivalent statements of the movement's signature tetrachord, set-class 4–19. The resulting sets feature pitch-class repetitions and do not include all the 12 notes of the chromatic scale. However, they are used in the same linear, serial manner as the source sets of the piece, and establish their identity as independent sets through their continuous sequential presentation as ordered sets. Their dyadic motivic structure is emphasized through phrasing and the framing of the motives by rests, articulation marks, rhythm and register.

**Interchanging One Pitch-class in each Hexachord**

Examples of this derivation technique can be found in the Third Sonatina for violin and piano (1935). The first movement, *Allegro giusto*, is built on two set-groups, each containing two closely connected twelve-note sets (S1, S2 and S3, S4). The first melodic theme, played by the violin, is based on S1, while the second theme is based on S3. The latter derives from S1 by interchanging the pitch-classes F and G in each hexachord of S1 and the order positions 1, 2, 7, which become order positions 2, 1, 8 in S3 (see Example 6.2). This reordering not only results in a new set for the second theme but also ensures a close motivic and harmonic similarity between the two main themes of the movement.

Example 6.2   Third Sonatina for violin and piano, *Allegro giusto*: Derivation of S3

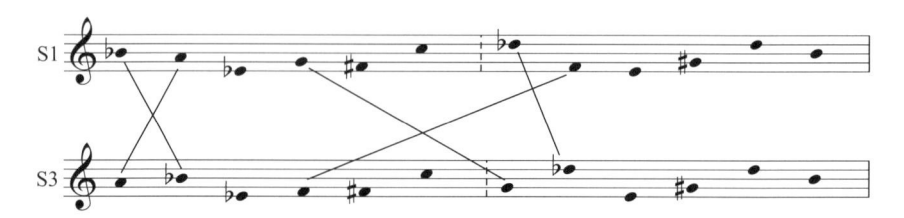

The second movement, *Andante*, is built on the four sets S1a, S2a, S3a, S4a. S3a derives from S3 by interchanging pitch-classes C and G in each hexachord of S3 and order position 1, which becomes order position 5 in S3a. Similarly, S4a derives from S4 by interchanging the pitch-class G, as shown in Example 6.3.

**Cyclic Rotation**

A rare type of derivation occurs in the Second String Trio, and involves the technique of cyclic rotation,[1] whereby a set is internally manipulated so that a note

---

[1]   It is generally asserted that Ernst Krenek was the first composer to apply the technique of rotation in his *Lamentio Jeremiae Prophetae* written in 1940–41; see Krenek

Example 6.3 Third Sonatina for violin and piano, *Andante*: Derivation of S3a, S4a

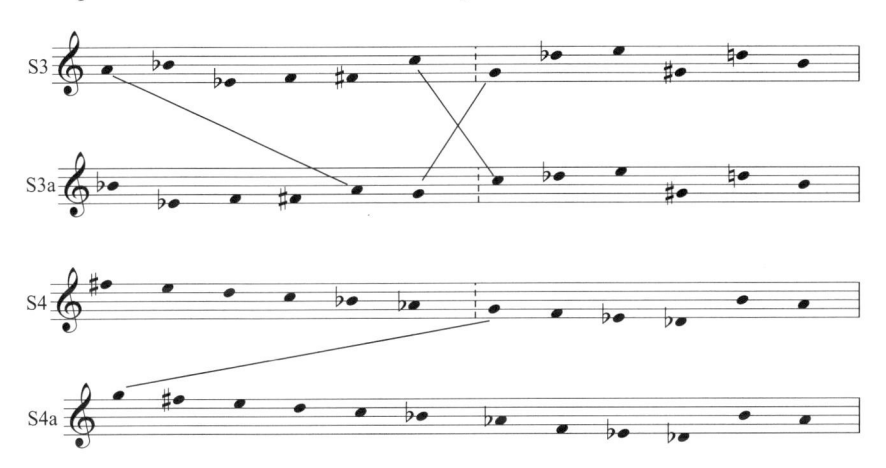

other than order number 1 is in first position. The first movement, *Moderato*, is built on three sets (S1, S2, S3) that are introduced simultaneously at the opening of the movement and are used throughout (see Example 4.1 above). The second movement, *Andante*, in rondo form, is built on three different groups of three twelve-note sets, one for each of the main sections (A, B and C). Two of the sets of the *Moderato* become the source material for the construction of the *Andante*, through tetrachordal cyclic rotation. This type of rotation retains the identity of the original set through the continuous reiteration of its tetrachordal segments over short time spans, and ensures the audibility of the set. For example, as shown in Example 6.4a, in bars 1–6 of section A of the *Andante*, S1a is played by the violin; the viola plays S1b, which is a cyclic rotation of S1, starting at order number 5 and ending at order number 4, with the source tetrachords rotating as B, C, A. The cello plays a rotation of the same set (S1c), starting at order number 9 and ending at order number 8, with the source tetrachords rotating as C, A, B. Significantly, a pre-compositional plan appears to determine this type of derivation. Each rotation is arranged so that the vertical alignment of the same order position of all three sets (1–1–1 ... 12–12–12) gives the four trichords (played three times) of S1 of the first movement, *Moderato* (see p. 354).

Similarly, section B of the *Andante* is built on set S2 of the first movement, which here, to avoid confusion, is designated as S2a and its two cyclic rotations (S2b and S2c). As shown in Example 6.4b, S2b starts at order position 5, with the tetrachords rotating as B, C, A, while S2c starts at order position 9, with the tetrachords as C, A, B. Finally, the developmental section C (bars 48–64[1]) is built

---

(1960, 210–32) and (1966, 84). With this technique Krenek tried to solve the problem of integrating certain principles of the twelve-note technique with those of ancient modality (Hogan, 1982, 28). However, Skalkottas, working in isolation in Greece, systematically used tetrachordal segmental rotation in his Second String Trio five years before Krenek's *Lamentio*.

Example 6.4  Second String Trio, *Andante*

(a) Section A – opening gesture (bars 1–6)

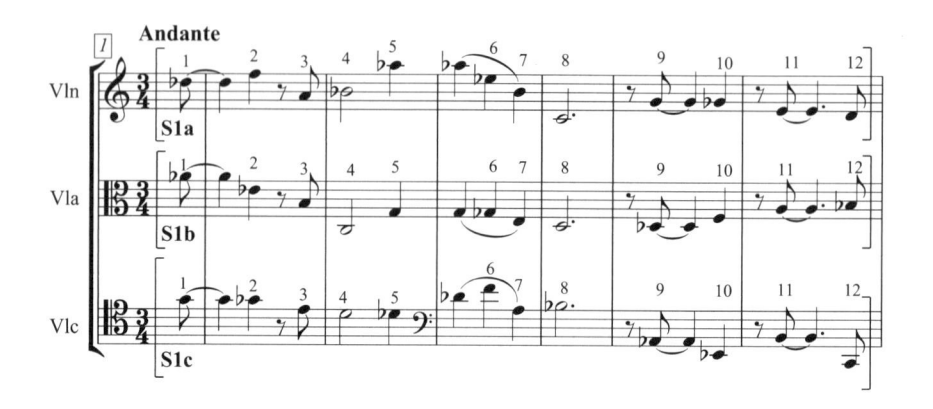

(b) Section B – opening gesture (bars 20–26)

(c) Section C – opening gesture (bars 48–52)

on S3a and its two rotations, in a manner similar to that of section A;[2] S3b starts at order position 5, and S3c at order position 9, as shown in Example 6.4c.

---

[2] Set S3a derives from S1c of the *Andante*; its first hexachord is an unordered inversion transposed at the minor third ($I_3$) of the second hexachord of S1c, while its second hexachord is an unordered inversion transposed at the minor third ($I_3$) of the first hexachord of S1c.

# Chapter 7
# Serial Transformations: Transposition, Retrograde, Inversion

Papaioannou asserts that in Skalkottas's twelve-note music '[t]he rows are usually presented in the original position. Inversion and especially transposition are usually avoided, in order, as Skalkottas said, "to keep rows more easily recognizable". They are used only in exceptional cases for special reasons; retrograde forms of rows are used more frequently' (1976, 325). Both Orga (1969, 39–40) and Thornley (1980, 362–3, 2001, 467) reiterate this view. Such observations on the avoidance of transpositions are inaccurate, and Skalkottas's alleged affirmation of this is, to say the least, curious. It is highly improbable that Skalkottas made such an erroneous statement, and these generalizations about transpositions more likely arise from a mistaken interpretation of his writings in the Foreword to the Notes to the dodecaphonic First Symphonic Suite, where he states that: '*In this Suite, unlike works using diatonic harmony*[,] *harmonic transpositions are avoided.*' It appears that this sentence, taken out of context, has been misinterpreted and expanded to cover his entire compositional output. A careful study of Skalkottas's music reveals that sets are indeed usually presented in their prime form. He does, however, employ transpositions and retrograde forms of the sets both for their local (for the purposes of developing variation) and their large-scale (as a means of formal construction) consequences. Inversions of sets appear occasionally in his early and late twelve-note works only.

**The Use of Transposition**

In a set-group consisting of several superimposed sets, Skalkottas only infrequently combines set-forms of a set at different transpositional levels; this technique is primarily observed in the chamber works of 1935–36, which are built on a limited number of predominantly linear, ordered twelve-note sets. For example, the simultaneous use of both the prime and a transposed form of a set occurs in the *Allegro moderato* of the Third String Quartet; set S5 and its minor third transposed form $S5(T_3)$ are superimposed and played simultaneously throughout section B (see Example 5.3, and Appendix A). Apart from the immediate tonal relationships created by the simultaneous unfolding of the two sets, each of their two hexachords share four pitch-classes, and Skalkottas exploits the common content of these hexachords as part of his developmental motivic technique. He also occasionally uses the source sets in their prime form, immediately followed by certain transposed forms. For instance, the *Preludio* of the First Piano Suite is built on four independent sets (S1, S2, S3, S4) and their transpositions at the minor sixth ($T_8$), identified as S5, S6, S7, S8, which alternate to define the phrase structure (see Example II.1).

Apart from this local and limited use of transposition of independent sets within a set-group, Skalkottas widely employs the technique of transposing the entire texture of a phrase or passage, *en bloc* to define the harmonic and formal structure of a movement. In such cases the pitch-class content of entire sections is transposed, predominantly at the fifth ($T_7$) or perfect fourth ($T_5$), although transpositions at the minor and major third are also used. The consequences of the use of transpositions can be observed in many of his large-scale works, as will be discussed below.

## The Use of Retrograde

Skalkottas uses both the retrograde forms of individual sets, and palindromes that embrace the entire texture. Single sets in retrograde form are usually presented simultaneously or in alternation with their prime form. Apart from the occasional use of the retrograde form of S6 (RS6) employed in the *Andante cantabile* of the First Piano Concerto, retrograde forms of single sets are frequently employed in the chamber music works of the mid-1930s,[1] and occasionally in the large-scale works of the late 1930s and early 1940s. In particular, in the second movement (*Andante*) of the Concertino for two pianos, the theme (bars 1–14), outlining a ternary phrase structure, is built on three sets S1, S2, S3 and their retrogrades.[2] As shown in Example 7.1, in bars 2–5 the thematic melody, played by the viola, is based on S2; the flutes and clarinets accompany with S1 as a series of dyads, while S3 is divided between the basses, brass and upper strings. The second phrase (bars 6–9) is built on the retrograde forms of the three sets, and the closing phrase on the original forms.

In the Fourth String Quartet Skalkottas simultaneously uses prime and retrograde forms of both single sets and twelve-note melodic gestures. For example, in the first movement, *Allegro molto vivace*, at bars 124–5 the twelve-note melody played by the first violin is accompanied by the second violin homorhythmically playing its retrograde, while the viola plays a transpositional variation of the first violin's melody, with the cello accompanying with its retrograde, as shown in Example 7.2a.

---

[1] For example, retrograde forms of sets are used in the second movement of the Third String Quartet, the third movement of the Third Sonatina for violin and piano, in all movements of the Fourth Sonatina for violin and piano and the First Piano Suite, and in the second movement of the Concertino for two pianos.

[2] S3 derives from S1 by interchanging pitch-classes A and B in each hexachord of the set.

Serial Transformations: Transposition, Retrograde, Inversion    127

Example 7.1  Concertino for two pianos, *Andante*: Set structure of the first theme (bars 1–14)

Example 7.2a  Fourth String Quartet, *Allegro molto vivace*: Use of retrograde (bars 124–5)

Similarly, in the third movement, *Scherzo (Presto)*, at bars 170–72 the twelve-note melodies played by the first violin and viola are accompanied homorhythmically by their retrogrades played by the second violin and cello respectively (see Example 7.2b).

Example 7.2b  Fourth String Quartet, *Scherzo (Presto)*: Use of retrograde (bars 170–72)

In the Second Symphonic Suite, Skalkottas extensively uses both prime and retrograde forms of melodies and other gestures simultaneously. In the first movement, *Ouvertüre Concertante*, the thematic statement of the second phrase (initiated at bar 20) is played by the solo first violin, with a descending forward movement of continuous triplet major thirds, accompanied by the solo second violin playing the ascending retrograde form of the same melody. This gesture is repeated transposed in bar 27 (see Example 7.3a).

Example 7.3a  Second Symphonic Suite, *Ouvertüre Concertante*: Use of retrograde (bars 20, 27)

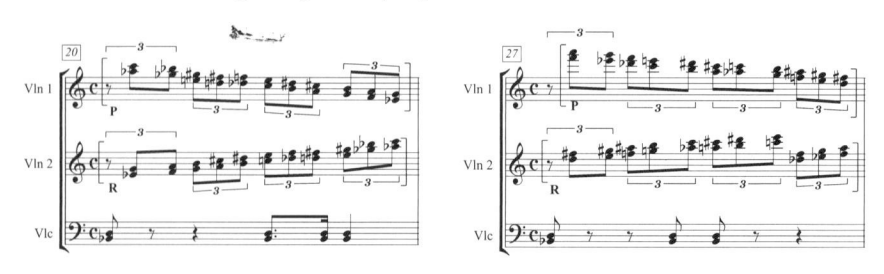

Likewise, in the second movement, *Toccata*, there are several passages in which the prime form of a melody or a set is played simultaneously with its retrograde, as shown in Example 7.3b.

Example 7.3b   Second Symphonic Suite, *Toccata*: Use of retrograde (bars 12, 55, 293)

A more complicated simultaneous presentation of prime and retrograde melodic gestures can be found in the fourth movement, *Largo Sinfonico*. In bar 89 the melody, played in unison by the horns and violas, is based on S5 and is divided into two four-note motivic segments, A and B, separated by semiquaver rests. It is accompanied contrapuntally by the bassoons and cellos playing in unison an unordered version of each motive in retrograde motion. This gesture is repeated in bar 90, with the segments now based on set S6, as shown in Example 7.3c.

**The Use of Inversion**

In contrast to his relatively extensive use of the operations of transposition and retrograde, Skalkottas only sparingly uses inversions of single sets. As already noted, the identity of Skalkottas's sets is largely determined by the neighbourhood relationships between the notes of their segments, rather than by their strict pitch-class order and intervallic structure. In such a system, inversion does not have the same transformational importance as in works based on a single basic set. The first casual use of inversions of single sets and melodies is explored in the experimental First Piano Concerto, a piece built on a profusion of diverse pitch-class material; here, in the Development section (bars 138–47) of the *Allegro moderato*,

Example 7.3c  Second Symphonic Suite, *Largo Sinfonico*: Use of retrograde (bars 89–90)

Skalkottas uses unordered transposed and inverted forms of hexachords. In the *Andante cantabile* he uses sets that derive from inversions and retrograde forms of the referential sets. He also uses set inversions for developmental purposes in the varied Recapitulation of section A and in the Coda, where the retrograde, inversion and retrograde inversion of S1 (RS1, IS1, RIS1) are extensively used (see Chapter 10, 'First Piano Concerto (1931)', pp. 194–6)).

Perhaps unsatisfied with the developmental and structural possibilities offered by this transformational technique, Skalkottas did not use inversions in subsequent works based on a limited number of predominantly linear twelve-note sets. There is some limited and casual use of hexachordal and largely contour inversion for local, motivic developmental purposes in the Piano Trio of 1936, but thereafter inversions are used only sparingly, as a means of set derivation, in certain chamber works after 1945. Examples of passages and melodies in inversion are found in his late chamber music, such as the *First Little Suite* for violin and piano (1946), built on twelve-note collections of largely unordered pitch-class material, and in the Duo for violin and cello (1947). The most substantial use of inversion both for derivational and structural purposes occurs in the Serenata for cello and piano (1949), in which not only individual sets but entire textures are inverted, as will be discussed in some detail in Part III (Chapter 14, 'Serenata for Cello and Piano (1949)', pp. 319–24).

# Chapter 8
# Set Structure and Phrase Structure

Although there is no record of Skalkottas's views on formal structures, his few surviving analytical notes, coupled with evidence from his own compositions, suggest that he was influenced by Schoenberg's tonality-based teaching and ideas on formal articulation, coherence and comprehensibility,[1] and particularly his belief that 'One can understand only what one can keep in mind' (1970/1990, 1991) and that 'understanding is based on remembering […] Remembering is based on recognition and re-recognition' (1995, 133). Thus, in Skalkottas's works continuous repetition of the same motivic segments and harmonic formations saturate the texture and ensure comprehensibility and memorability. Furthermore, as Skalkottas focused on the cultivation of a new harmonic idiom, traditional formal prototypes and tonal elements of construction provided him with predetermined structural frameworks, which he used to create his twelve-note compositions. His formal designs emulate those associated with tonal music, such as sonata, rondo, ternary form and theme with variations. He also uses forms such as minuet, passacaglia, canon and fugue. Traditional textures (melody with accompaniment, imitative counterpoint, and so on) and traditional conceptions of musical continuity (antecedent and consequent phrases, the differentiation of exposition, development and recapitulation of thematic material) continually underpin his music.[2] For Skalkottas, as for Schoenberg (Rosen, 1976b, 96), such

---

[1] In Schoenberg's theory of form, 'the chief requirements for the creation of a comprehensible form are *logic* and *coherence*. The presentation, development and interconnexion of ideas must be based on relationship [and these] ideas must be differentiated according to their importance and function' (1970/1990, 1). In music, comprehensibility refers to conditions that allow the listener to grasp the whole, and in his early writings Schoenberg states: 'something is comprehensible if the whole is surveyable and consists of parts that have relationships not too remote from each other and from the whole' (1994, 22–3). Comprehensibility depends on coherence (1995, 23), which, in *Zusammenhang, Kontrapunkt, Instrumentation, Formenlehre*, he defines as 'that which binds individual phenomena into forms' (1994, 8–9); the principle on which artistic coherence rests is repetition (1994, 16–17). In his late essay 'My Evolution' (1949), Schoenberg extended what he had always taught in his classes about composition to 'composing with twelve tones', which 'is primarily a method demanding logical order and organization, of which comprehensibility should be the main result' (1984, 92).

[2] This practice derives from Schoenberg's beliefs on the issues of old forms and their role in modern music, as given in the article 'Die alten Formen in der neuen Musik' (12 January 1927), which Skalkottas was perhaps familiar with. In this article Schoenberg wrote: '*The old forms in the new music* – their application is thoroughly justifiable and is in accordance

forms are referential rather than organic, and they support comprehensibility amid an otherwise diffuse harmonic vocabulary; they are not style dependent, but are approached as a set of ideal shapes and proportions that can be realized in any of his chosen styles: tonal, post-tonal or dodecaphonic, or a mixture of these.

**Periodicity of the Twelve-note Set-groups to Determine the Small-scale Form**

In most of Skalkottas's dodecaphonic works based on a limited number of sets, the periodicity of the twelve-note set-groups largely constitutes the basis of the phrase structure of a movement. In several of these pieces the unfolding of a set-group frequently coincides with thematic gestures, and demarcates phrase boundaries. The first movement, *Moderato*, of the Second String Trio, which is in sonata form, exemplifies the periodicity of the linear sets *en bloc*, in a set-grid structure, with musical phrases coinciding with the set-group. In the first subject group, the first theme (bars 1–4$^3$) in the violin is based on S1, which is played twice, outlining a periodic phrase structure; the viola, playing S2, and cello, playing S3, accompany contrapuntally (see Example 4.1). In the continuation (bars 4$^4$–12$^1$) the predominant melodic idea, played by the viola, is based on S2, with S1 and S3 providing the contrapuntal accompaniment. Table 8.1 represents schematically the set topography and the correspondence between the twelve-note set structure and phrase structure of the movement.

Similarly, the second movement, *Andante*, which is in rondo form (AA$^1$BACA$^2$Coda), is built on three groups of three twelve-note sets. The set-group recurrence provides coherent pitch-class and harmonic articulations, textural homogeneity, and the basis for phrase delimitation (see Table 8.2). The technique of set-grid presentation is also applied in the third movement, *Presto* (also in rondo form), which is built on the *Moderato*'s sets S1, S2, S3, and the derived sets S4, S5, S6. Table 8.3 represents the set topography and some of the details of its phrase structure.

All musical phrases are therefore essentially a recurrent statement of the section's opening set-group material. The reiteration of common or equivalent segments embedded within the various sets, the recurrence of the theme or fragments of it, the repetition of particular harmonic sequences and chords, not only demarcate the phrase structure, but also help memorability, thus reinforcing relationships and coherence. However, it is not simply the recurrence of the groups that delineates the phrase structure of a section, but the compositional treatment

---

with the principle, set up by me, concerning comprehensibility: If comprehensibility is hindered on the one side, it must be simplified on the other. In the new music the chords and the melodic intervals and their succession are often hard to comprehend. Therefore a form has to be chosen which [...] provides facilitation by establishing a known course. [...] [The advantages of such a form is] to facilitate the comprehension of the ideas by [...] frequent repetition' (von Blumröder, 1982, 101–2).

Table 8.1    Second String Trio, *Moderato*: Set topography and phrase structure

**Exposition**

| Bars | 1–4 | 5–8 | 8–12 | 12 | 13–16² | 16³–17 | 18–19 | 20–23 | 24–5 | 26–7 | 28 |
|---|---|---|---|---|---|---|---|---|---|---|---|
| vln | S1 S1 | S3 | S1 S3 | S1 → | S1 | S1 → | S1 S1 | S3 | S1 S3 | S2 | S3 |
| vla | S2 | S1 | S2 | | S2 | | S3 | S2 | (D♭) | S1 | – |
| vlc | S3 | S2 | S2 S1 S3 | | S3 | | S2 | S1 | S2 | – | S1 |
| | 1st subject group | | | cadence | transition | | | | 2nd subject group | | cadence |

**Development**

| Bars | 29–30 | 31–2 | 33–4 | 35–8 | 39–41 | 42–4 | 45 | 46–7 | 48–9 | 50 | 51–7 | 58–62 | 63–70 |
|---|---|---|---|---|---|---|---|---|---|---|---|---|---|
| vln | S1 | S3 | S2 | S3 S2 S1 | S2 | S1 S2 S3 | S3 → | S2 S2 → | (F) | S3 | S2 S1 | S1 | S1 |
| vla | S2 | S2 | S1 | S1 S3 S2 | S1 | segm | – | – | S2 S1 → | (B♭) | S3 S1 S2 | S2 | S2 |
| vlc | S3 | S1 → | S1 | S3 S1 S3 | S3 | interpol | | | | – | S1 S3 | S3 | S3 |
| | 1st developmental section | | | | | | | | | | 2nd lyrical section | | |

**Recapitulation**

| Bars | 71–3 | 74–5 | 77–81¹ | 81²–6² | 86³–9 | 90–93 | 94–6 | 97–8 | 99–101 | 102 | 103 | 104 | 105–6 | 107–9 |
|---|---|---|---|---|---|---|---|---|---|---|---|---|---|---|
| vln | S1 S1 | S2 S3 → | (B) S2 | S1 | S3 | S3 | S3 S1 | S3 S1 → | S1 S2 | S1 → | – | S3 → | S1 | S1 |
| vla | S2 | S1 | S3 S3 | S2 | S1 | S2 | – S2 | S1 | S2 → | – | S2 → | | S2 | S2 |
| vlc | S3 | S2 | S1 | S3 S3 | S3 | S1 | S1 | S2 | | | | | S3 | S3 |
| | 1st subject group | | | | | | | | 2nd subject group | | | | Coda | |

Table 8.2  Second String Trio, *Andante*: Set topography and phrase structure

| Bars | 1–6 | 7–11 | 12–17 | 18–19 | 20–25 | 26–30 | 31–6 | 37–41 | 42–7 | 48–52 | 53–7 | 58–63 | 64–8 | 68³–73 | 74–8 |
|---|---|---|---|---|---|---|---|---|---|---|---|---|---|---|---|
| vln | S1a | S1a | S1c | S1b | S2a | S2c | S2a | S2a | S1a | S3a | S3c | S3a | S1a | S1c | S1 |
| vla | S1b | S1b | S1b | S1b | S2b | S2b | S2b | S2c | S1b | S3b | S3b | S3b | S1b | S1b | S2 |
| vlc | S1c | S1c | S1a | S1b | S2c | S2a | S2c | S2b | S1c | S3c | S3a | S3c | S1c | S1a | S3 |
|  | Refrain A | | Section A¹ | | | | Section B | | Refrain A | | Section C | | | Section A² | Coda |

Table 8.3  Second String Trio, *Presto*: Set topography and phrase structure

| Bars | 1–6 | 7–11 | 12–14 | 15–18 | 19–24⁴ | 24⁵–9 | 30–34 | 34⁵–9 | 39⁵–48 | 49–52 | 53–4 | 55–7 | 58–62 | 63–9 |
|---|---|---|---|---|---|---|---|---|---|---|---|---|---|---|
| vln | S1 | S3 | S2 | S3→ | S3 S2 | S1 | S2 | S1 | S3 | S3 S2 | S1 | S2 | S1 | S3 |
| vla | S2 | S1 | S3 | S2 | S3 | S3 | S3 | S2 | S1 | S1 S2 | S3 | S1 | S3 | S2 |
| vlc | S3 | S2 | S1 | S1 S2→ | S2 S1 | S2 | S1 | S1 S3 | S3 S2 | S2 S3 | S1 | S3→ | S3 S2 | S2 S1 |
| Sections | | | | A | | | | | B | | | | | |

| Bars | 70–73 | 74–7 | 78–80 | 81–4 | 85–7³ | 87⁴–9⁵ | 89⁶–94 | 95–100 | 101–5 | 106–9 | 110–13 | 114–19 | 120–24 | 125–33 | 134–45 |
|---|---|---|---|---|---|---|---|---|---|---|---|---|---|---|---|
| vln | S1 | S3 | S2 | S1 | S3 | S2 | S4 | S6 | S4 | S5 | S6 | S1/hex1 | S1/hex2 | S3 | S2 |
| vla | S2 | S1 | S3 | → | → | → | S5 | S4 | S5 | S4 | → | S2/hex1 | S2/hex2 | S1 | S3 |
| vlc | S3 | S2 | S1 | | | | S6 | S5 | S6 | S6 | | S3/hex1 | S3/hex2 | S2 | S1 |
| Sections | A¹ | | | | | | C | | | | | A² | | | |
|  | (70–73)=(1–6); (74–7)=(7–11); (78–80)=(12–14) — varied repetition | | | | | | | | | | | (114–124)=(1–6); (125–34)=(7–11); (135–45)=(12–14) — varied repetition | | | |

Table 8.3   concluded

| Bars | 146 | 152 | 159² | 166⁴ | 172 | 176⁵ | 180 | 183 | 186³ | 188⁶ | 195³ | 201³ | 204³ | 211 |
|---|---|---|---|---|---|---|---|---|---|---|---|---|---|---|
| vln | S3 | S2 | S1 | S3 | S2 | – | S1 | S3 | S2 | S5 | S4 | S1 | S3 S2 | – |
| vla | S2 | S1 | S3 | S2 chords | S3 | S3 | S1 | S3 | S2 | S6 chords | S6 chords | S3 | S2 S1→ | S1 |
| vlc | S1 | S3 | S2 | S1 chords | S2 | S2 | S1 | S3 | S2 | S4 | S5 | S2 | S1 S3→ | S3 |
| Sections | B¹ (146–51)=(30–34); (159²–66)=(49–52) – varied repetition | | | | | | A³ (180–82)=(81–4 – S1 unison); (183–6²)=(85–7³ – S3 unison); (186³–8)=(87⁴–9 – S2 unison) | | | C¹ (188⁶–95¹)=(89⁶–94) – varied repetition | | | A⁴ | |

| Bars | 213–16 (=180–82) | 217–22³ (=183–6²) | 222⁴–30 (=186³–8) |
|---|---|---|---|
| vln | S1 | S3 | S2 |
| vla | S1 | S3 | S2 |
| vlc | S1 | S3 | S2 |
| Sections | Coda | | |

the sets receive, together with the manipulation of compositional parameters other than pitch. Each restatement of a twelve-note set-group is reinterpreted in terms of controlled harmonic combinations, instrumentation, registral disposition, dynamics and rhythm, so that the reappearance of each section results in a quite different textural surface, which Skalkottas exploits to create phrase differentiation.

**Tonal Centres**

Furthermore, formal articulation is extensively emphasized by the use of tonal centres. Orga asserts that one of Skalkottas's main contributions was 'the introduction of "tonal" centres', which 'are absent in serialism' (1969, 82), and that he 'evolved a system of "tonal" centres derived from serial principles yet *always* related to a fundamental cosmological law' (38–9, original emphasis). Whatever this law may be, however, such assertions are rather confused and confusing. Skalkottas does create forms by transposing entire sections, thus inviting comparisons with the formal structures of tonal pieces. Nevertheless, Orga appears to mistake this form-building technique with the concept of 'tonal centres', which are individual pitch-classes displaying 'centricity within a given context without necessarily carrying all the implications of the tonal system' (Milstein, 1992, 5). Other twelve-note composers do not abandon tonal functions entirely, and use tonal centres to shape their compositions. As Milstein points out, in Schoenberg's works, 'single pitch-classes or pitch-levels, rendered prominent by virtue of their position as boundaries of groupings, are often made to bear implications formerly pertaining to tonal regions or keys and therefore function as true tonal centres' (*ibid.*). Berg also uses individual pitch-levels and pitch-classes as tonal centres,[3] but as Perle emphasizes, these 'are not generated by diatonic functions and […] have a much more explicit overall importance' (1991, 34).[4] Skalkottas uses individual pitches or pitch collections as tonal centres in the outer voices, the bass line in particular, which are often chosen to invite associations

---

[3] Perle, to avoid explicit references and associations with tonal music, uses the term 'tone centre' and clarifies that 'the term "tone centre" is not intended to suggest any parallel with what is understood by "tonic" in the major–minor system, other than the quality of centricity within a given context' (1980, 134). In contrast, Jarman asserts that Berg's 'use of primary tonal centres in the twelve-note works' and the establishment of such centres and other harmonic collections as referential areas, 'acquire some of the functions associated with a traditional tonic key' (1979, 179).

[4] In attempting to resolve the semantic contradictions that arise from admitting the presence of tone/tonal centres in post-tonal music, Perle draws upon Berger's remarks in discussing Stravinsky's 'pre-twelve-tone' works, while Berger justifies their existence as follows: 'There are other means besides functional ones for asserting pitch-class priority; from which it follows that pitch-class priority per se: 1) is not a sufficient condition of that music which is tonal, and 2) is compatible with music that is not tonally functional' (Berger, 1968, 123).

with traditional tonal compositional practices. They are established and assert their priority by means similar to those encountered in the pieces of Schoenberg (Milstein, 1992, 6) and Berg (Perle, 1980, 131), such as through their registral position (highest and lowest notes in the melodic contour); their temporal position, appearing at the boundaries of groupings; through repetition, duration and/or loud dynamics; and by the functional use of timbre, that is, hierarchically more important notes are played by the same instrument in distinctive registral positions. Such pitch-classes are also reinforced by leading-note and appoggiatura-like semitonal figures, and they are most frequently supported by perfect fifths, suggesting parallels with traditional dominant–tonic harmonic movement. They are often used to highlight important structural junctures, and as aural points of reference for the motivic and harmonic movement of a piece; and their recurrence as centres of attraction throughout a work contributes to formal articulation and general cohesion.

For example, in the *Moderato* of the Second String Trio, certain tonal centres result from the manipulation of the sets, and together with the reiteration of set-groups are used as a means of articulating the large-scale harmonic and formal structure of the movement. Set S3 includes in its internal structure four perfect-fifth intervals: G–D, F–C, A♭–E♭, and F♯–C♯. These are usually positioned in the bass line, which is frequently structured to suggest tonally oriented harmonic movement. Example 8.1 represents schematically the harmonic progression of the bass line in each formal section of the movement.

Throughout the exposition and recapitulation of the first theme, the note C is established as the predominant tonal centre in the bass, through the dominant–tonic-like relationship G–C. In the opening gesture of the second theme, the fifth A♭–D♭ predominates in the voice-leading of the bass line, as if modulating, while in the Coda there is a direction towards and establishment of F♯, the tritone counterpart of C, supported by the fifth C♯–F♯ and ending on an F♯ minor triad. The tritone relationship between the two tonal centres (C and F♯) obscures the overt tonal implications and negates the establishment of a definite sense of key.

## Harmonic Change and Reiteration of Fixed Harmonic Formations to Define the Phrase Structure

The *Thema* of the *Thema con Variazioni* from the First Symphonic Suite, built on a group of four twelve-note sets (S1, S2, S3, S4), outlines a binary structure consisting of four phrases that are largely differentiated by the periodic reiteration of the set-group (see also Part III, pp. 252–5). In terms of harmonic change as a determinant for the organization of the phrase structure, at the opening phrase (bars 1–5), the harmonic support is based on a succession of chordal segments from S4 (see Example 8.2). At the continuation phrase (bars 6–10) the harmony changes to a succession of dyads derived from S3; this regulates the rate of harmonic change and counteracts the vigorous motivic activity of the contrapuntally structured melodic lines. At the contrasting phrase (bars $10^3$–$14^2$), there is a rapid harmonic

Example 8.1  Second String Trio, *Moderato*: Harmonic progression of the bass line

succession of chordal segments from three different sets that are juxtaposed; this enhances harmonic variety and emphasizes the developmental character of the passage. In the last phrase (bars 14³–18) a steady alternation of segments from S2 and S4 stabilizes the rate of harmonic change and counteracts the previous harmonic activity, ending with the same harmonic material as that of the first phrase. Thus, each phrase is characterized by and differentiated from surrounding sections by its individual pitch-class, thematic and harmonic content, which is derived from the new set-group on which it is built, and established by the continuous reiteration of the same succession of motivic and harmonic figures, as well as its texture, rhythmic patterns and orchestration.

In works based on a limited amount of source pitch-class material, but exhibiting a free twelve-note technique, the strict serial reiteration of specific harmonic formations provides the harmonic support that defines phrase structure. For example, the *Passacaglia* from the *32 Piano Pieces* synthesizes Skalkottas's strict use of the serial principle of ordered set reiteration with the free manipulation

Example 8.2  First Symphonic Suite, *Thema con Variazioni: Thema* – schematic pitch-class and harmonic structure

of smaller units of his pitch-class material.[5] Skalkottas superimposes two textural layers, one strictly serial against one that is structured from a limited number of clearly defined pitch-class collections. As shown in Example 8.3, an ordered, eleven-note thematic set (Th-set), B–C–F–E–B♭–A–A♭–E♭–D–G–C♯, functions as

---

[5]  Based on the Baroque form of ground bass, the *Passacaglia* comprises a two-bar theme with twenty variations, and it features elements of both chaconne and passacaglia. Apart from a set of variations, the piece also outlines a ternary form (ABA'), defined by changes in the texture, tempo, dynamics and motivic/thematic repetition. The theme and Variations I–VII comprise section A. Variations VIII–XV, characterized by constant tempo fluctuations and extreme dynamic and mood changes, function as the middle, developmental section B, which ends with a dramatic *pp*, *molto delicato*, *rallentando* variation. Section A' (Variations XVI–XIX) is introduced with an almost exact repetition of the theme. The *Grave* Variation XX, with its chordal texture over the ostinato theme played in octaves, functions as the Coda.

140                  *The Life and Twelve-Note Music of Nikos Skalkottas*

Example 8.3  *Passacaglia* for piano: Harmonic structure of the theme

the ground bass, played by the left hand in all but five variations, where instead it appears in a higher voice (V, VII, VIII, XIV and XV).

The right hand plays a series of six, fixed pitch-class collections of various sizes, shown in Table 8.4, which are continuously repeated in the ensuing variations over the melodic Th-set. For clarity, these pitch-class sets will be referred to here as 'right-hand sets' (RH-sets).

Table 8.4  *Passacaglia* for piano: Right-hand sets

| RH-set 1 | G–D–A♭–E♭–F♯–A |
| --- | --- |
| RH-set 2 | G–D♭–A–E♭–F♯–A |
| RH-set 3 | C–E–A♭–A♭–C♭–E♭–C |
| RH-set 4 | C♭–B♭–F–G–E–E♭–G–D♭ |
| RH-set 5 | D–B♭–C♯–F–A–A♭–C♭–E–A |
| RH-set 6 | C–E♭–G–B♭–G♭–F–B–D–A♭–E–F♯ |

Through rhythm, textural disposition and articulation, each of these six sets is constantly subdivided into smaller fixed segments, shown as numbers [1]–[15] in square brackets in Example 8.3 and in Table 8.5, which presents the relationships between the constituent elements and harmonic structure of the two-bar theme.

These RH-sets are related to one another through common and other associative elements, and they are also associated with the Th-set. For example, in the opening gesture (bar 1), segment [1], g–d$^1$–a♭$^1$–e♭$^2$ (set-class 4–8), is transpositionally equivalent at T$_3$ with the first tetrachord of the Th-set (B–C–F–E), while the first right-hand trichord (g–d$^1$–a♭$^1$) is inversionally equivalent at I$_9$ with the first trichord of the Th-set. In the second phrase (bar 2), the left-hand ground bass is initiated with the tetrachord A♭–E♭–d–G, which is the same as segment [1], while the three-note gesture in the right hand (c♭$^1$–f$^1$–b♭$^1$) is a T$_3$ transposition of the opening trichord (g–d$^1$–a♭$^1$).

The piece is built on a harmonic progression consisting of six 'harmonic groups', which are repeated unchanged throughout the piece. Each harmonic group is constructed from one of the fixed RH-sets and a segment of the Th-set that is associated with it. Within each group Skalkottas preserves pitch-class combinations and specific harmonic relationships, while the continuous, ordered reiteration of these harmonic groups promotes unity and stability. The fixed segments G–D–A♭–Eb [1] and F♯–A [2] of the first RH-set are associated with the first two pitches (B and C) of the Th-set. Similarly, the segments G–D♭–A–E♭ [3] and F♯–A [4] are associated with the third and fourth pitches of the Th-set, and so on. However, the segment E♭–D of the Th-set is occasionally omitted and does not have a harmonic formation of its own; when it appears it is only associated with pitch-class G.

Table 8.5   *Passacaglia* for piano: Six harmonic groups within the theme

|  | Harmonic group 1 |  | Harmonic group 2 |  | Harmonic group 3 |  |
|---|---|---|---|---|---|---|
| Segments of RH-sets | G–D–A♭–E♭ | F♯–A | G–D♭–A–E♭ | F♯–A | C–E–G–A♭ | A♭–C♭–E♭–C |
| Segment number | [1] | [2] | [3] | [4] | [5] | [6] |
| Segments of Th-set | B–C |  | F–E |  | B♭–A |  |
| Th-set order number | 1, 2 |  | 3, 4 |  | 5, 6 |  |
| Bar 1 |  |  |  |  |  |  |

|  | Harmonic group 4 |  |  | Harmonic group 5 |  |  | Harmonic group 6 |  |  |
|---|---|---|---|---|---|---|---|---|---|
| Segment RH-set | C♭, B♭, F G | E E♭ | G–D♭ | D–B♭–C♯ | F–A | A♭–C♭–F♭–A | C–F♭–G–B♭ | G♭–F–B–D | A♭–E–F♯ |
| Segment number | [7] | [8] | [9] | [10] | [11] | [12] | [13] | [14] | [15] |
| Segment Th-set | A♭ |  |  | E♭–D–G |  |  | C♯ |  |  |
| Th-set order number | 7 |  |  | 8, 9, 10 |  |  | 11 |  |  |
| Bar 2 |  |  |  |  |  |  |  |  |  |

Although the segments of the RH-sets within a harmonic group are frequently reordered and progressively interpolated as the variation set progresses, they generally coincide with the appropriate segment of the Th-set. Indicative examples of such pitch-class set reorderings, segment interpolation and superimposition to determine the harmonic support and gradual harmonic change within the phrase structure of Variations II, V and XI can be seen in Example 8.4. These harmonic groups remain constant until Variation X. From Variation XI onwards, through a process of gradual verticalization of pitch-class material and the elimination of pitch duplication, the RH-sets are combined to form chords, several of which include tertiary harmonies. The piece arrives at a chordal climax in Variation XX, which encapsulates the work's essence. Pitch-classes E♭ and D are omitted in the thematic line, which ends on a repeated and sustained C (order number 2). The gradual reduction of surface elements and verticalization of the source pitch-class material to a bare skeleton from which the piece was built is Skalkottas's preferred compositional device in large-scale works, particularly those that include both many ordered twelve-note sets and other pitch-class collections within a rather diffuse harmonic environment.

**Establishment of Harmonic Areas through Segmental Rotation**

At the phrase level, harmonic differentiation through the establishment and alteration of harmonic areas may result from the segmentation, permutation and interpolation of segments of the sets, which thus distinguish these local passages from their surrounding ones, which are also based on the same sets of the group. For example, in the first movement, *Allegro giusto*, of the Third Sonatina for violin and piano, the first theme is built on two twelve-note sets: S1, partitioned into four trichords (ABCD), and S2 (see Example 11.9 in Part III, p. 233). The first phrase of the transitional passage to the secondary theme of the first thematic group (bars 17–26¹) is established by the segmental rotation of S1, which is divided between the two hands of the piano, as shown in Examples 8.5a and 8.5b.

The right hand plays melodic figures based on segments ADBC from S1, with internal pitch-class order (1, 2, 3) (10, 11, 12) (5, 6, 4) (8, 7, 9). The left hand, providing the harmonic accompaniment, is based on a segmental rotation DBCADAD. This segmental presentation produces a new twelve-note context, which suggests the modulatory passages of earlier music. The segmental rotation in the piano right hand results in a twelve-note set that consists of two complementary hexachords, set-class 6–5. The first is formed from segments A and D, while the second from segments B and C. The second hexachord (F♯–C–G–F–C♯–E) is embedded, unordered, within the internal pitch-class structure of S1 (pitch-classes 4 ... 9). This new twelve-note set is combinatorial with its $I_7$ form, and, knowingly or otherwise, Skalkottas creates the first phrase of this transitional passage in a way that approximates combinatorial principles of construction. The two hexachords are arranged so that the left hand accompanies chordally

*Set Structure and Phrase Structure* 143

Example 8.4 *Passacaglia* for piano: Harmonic structure of Variations II, V, XI, XX

144    *The Life and Twelve-Note Music of Nikos Skalkottas*

Example 8.5  Third Sonatina for violin and piano, *Allegro giusto*

(a) Segmental rotation of S1

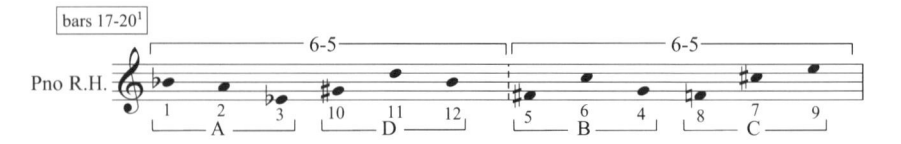

(b) Transition – opening gesture (bars 17–21¹)

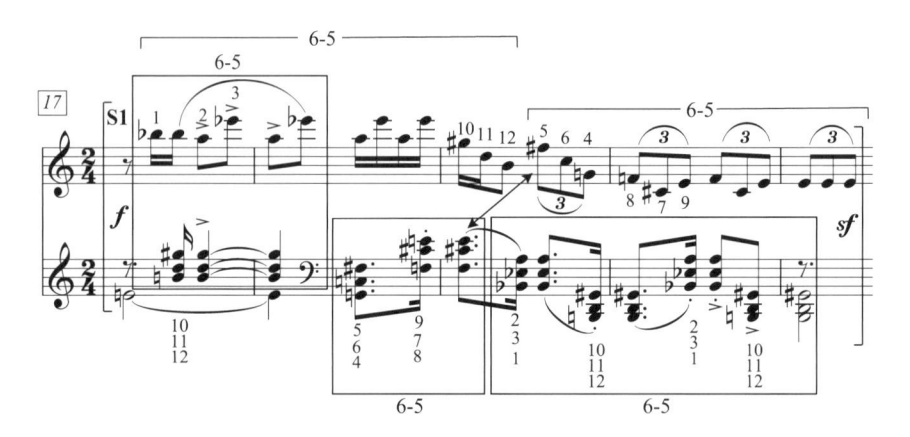

the right hand, with the same hexachords in reverse order. More importantly, this reordering and rotation emphasizes the tonally prominent harmonic progression of the movement at this point. Although dodecaphonic, the *Allegro giusto* inclines towards E♭ major and E major triads, particularly at important cadential points and phrase endings. The transitional passage starts with the implication of E♭ in the right hand, accompanied by the diminished triad G♯–B–D over a bass note E, suggesting an E dominant seventh. This chord frames the transitional passage, not only by initiating it, but also by functioning as its cadence. The reordering of segment C (pitch-class order 8, 7, 9) brings E as its final note in the right hand, and this is reinforced through intense repetition in bar 21¹. The repetition of the chordal segment D after A in bars 20–21¹ in the left hand reinforces the E dominant seventh chord as the goal of the movement's harmonic direction thus far.[6]

There are large-scale consequences to the segmental rotation and pitch-class reordering within each segment of S1, resulting in the two hexachords set-class 6–5. As shown in Example 8.6a, in the third movement, *Maestoso–Vivace*, the opening gesture of the piano part (bars 1–3²) in the *Maestoso* section, is built on the superimposition of two hexachords set-class 6–5, which are transpositionally equivalent at $T_8$ to the 6–5 hexachords of the transitional passage of the *Allegro giusto*.

Example 8.6a  Third Sonatina for violin and piano, *Maestoso–Vivace: Maestoso* (bars 1–12)

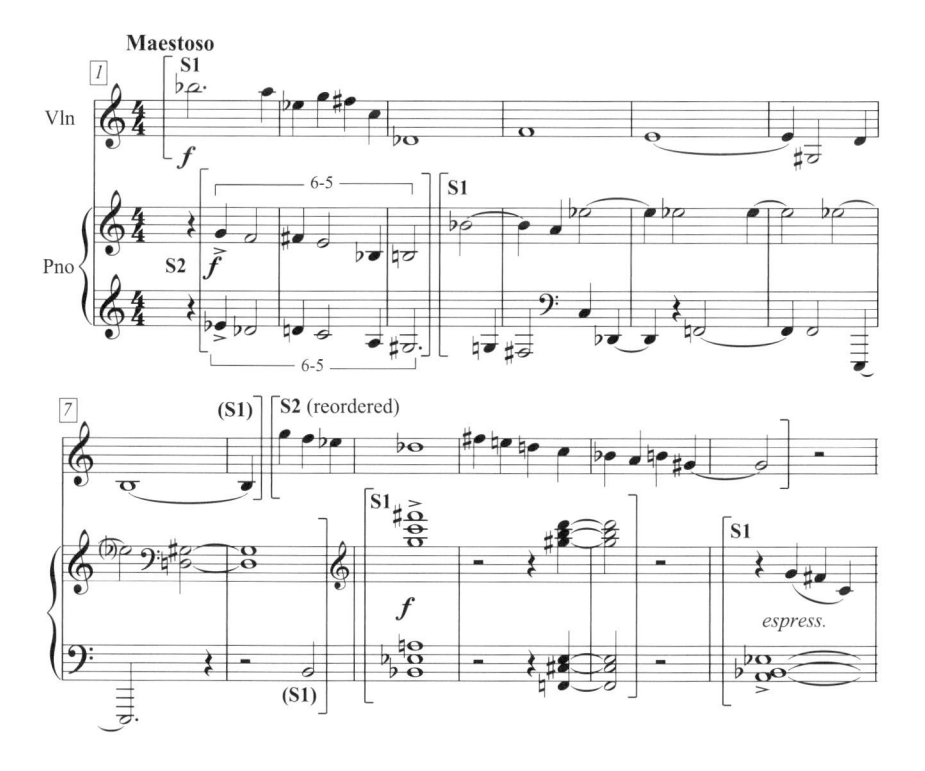

---

[6] In the developmental continuation (bars 21–7) there is further rearrangement of both the notes and the set segments, which results in a new harmonic and motivic surface. The phrase in bars 21²–3 is constructed from the segmentation and partition of S1 between the two hands, resulting in a new twelve-note aggregate, with the right hand playing a six-note melody, e♭²–g¹–f♯²–g♯³–b²–d³ (pitch-classes 3, 4, 5, 10, 12, 11; set-class 6–Z44), and the left hand accompanying with its complement, a–b♭–c¹–d♭¹–e¹–f¹ (pitch-classes 2, 1, 6, 7, 9, 8; set-class 6–Z19). The melodies are inverted in bars 24–7, with the right hand playing the hexachord set-class 6–Z19, and the left hand the hexachord set-class 6–Z44.

These hexachords now result from the segmentation and reordering of S2, with the right hand playing pitch-classes 2, 4, 6, 8, 9, 11, and the left hand the remaining 1, 3, 5, 7, 10, 12. However, the right-hand hexachord is an unordered transposition at $T_8$ of the piano right-hand melodic hexachord in bars 17–21[1], while the left-hand hexachord is a $T_8$ transposition of the first, left-hand hexachord in bars 18[2]–19[1] (see Example 8.6b).

Example 8.6b   Third Sonatina for violin and piano, *Maestoso–Vivace*: Derivation of the hexachords set-class 6–5 from S2

The continuation in the piano (bars 3[3]–8) is built on S1, which is divided between the two hands; the right hand plays pitch-classes 1, 2, 3, 10, 11, 12 (the last note played in the bass clef), while the left hand plays pitch-classes 4, 5, 6, 7, 8, 9. This results in the superimposition of the original two hexachords, set-classes 6–5 (with the second hexachord slightly reordered), from bars 17–20 of the first movement, *Allegro giusto*. Similarly, the pitch-class material of the third phrase (bars 9–17) projects in the piano right hand the hexachord G–C–F♯–G♯–B–D (set-class 6–Z43), which is a reordered retrograde of the third and second trichords of the original twelve-note set of the transition (set-class 6–5), while the left hand plays its first and fourth trichords, with the violin playing S2. This manipulation of initially diverse source material to produce closely related motivic and harmonic structures provides a degree of unity not only within a single movement but also across a multi-movement work, and is characteristic of Skalkottas's compositional style.

**Set Structure and Phrase Structure in 'Free' Twelve-note Works**

In other works based on a large amount of diverse pitch-class material, and which exhibit a free twelve-note technique, each phrase or short passage is built on a different group of new sets. In such works, Skalkottas avoids the immediate sequential repetition of sets and set-groups; phrase boundaries are largely demarcated by the abrupt appearance of a new set-group, and a dramatic change of texture, timbre, register and dynamics, as well as rhythmic and occasionally metric changes.

The Duo for violin and cello is typical of Skalkottas's freer twelve-note technique. It is based on several referential pitch-class groups, with most of the phrases consisting of pitch-class collections that include numerous note repetitions. In the second movement, *Andante molto espressivo*, in particular,

Skalkottas composes with hexachords, and he intermittently employs an idiomatic technique reminiscent of Schoenberg's hexachordal combinatoriality, but one that is freer in conception and use. The movement's opening gesture is built on two unordered chromatic hexachords whose aggregate results in a first order, all-combinatorial set with its $T_6$ and $I_5$ forms. Skalkottas, consciously or otherwise, appears to explore briefly the combinatorial properties of the set to form the harmonic structure of the first theme, by establishing distinct harmonic regions, but he does not make the hexachordal subdivision the normative articulation of the set, and he does not customarily combine polyphonically, or even in succession, set forms with their combinatorial counterparts to produce aggregates.

The opening gesture (bars 1–2) provides the source pitch-class material for large sections of the piece. The opening hexachord of the set ($a^1$–$b\flat^1$–$a^1$–$g\sharp^1$–$g^1$–$f\sharp^1$–$b\flat^1$–b) furnishes the violin melody in the antecedent, which includes note repetitions. Its complementary hexachord is distributed in the cello accompaniment in bar 1, and throughout the texture in bar 2 (see Example 8.7).

Example 8.7   Duo for violin and cello, *Andante molto espressivo*: Opening gesture (bars 1–12)

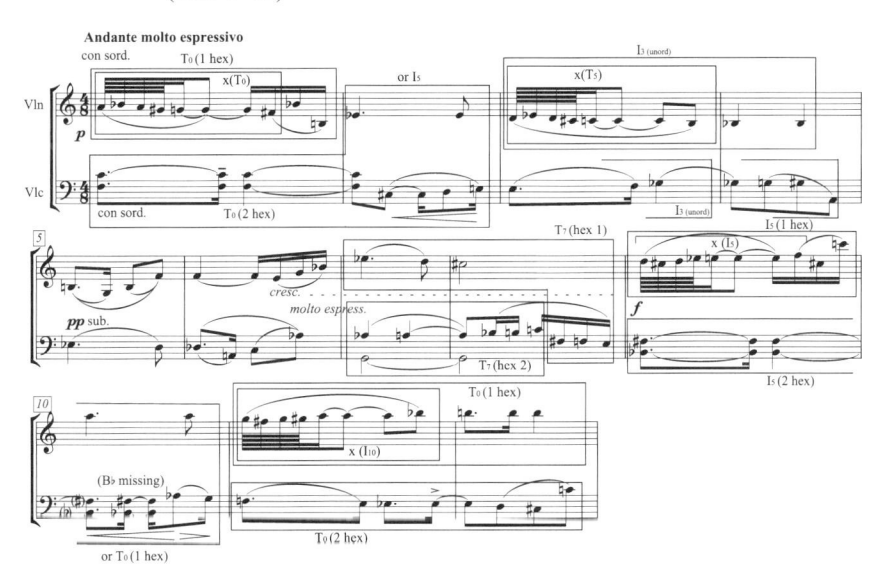

The six-note violin motive $a^1$–$b\flat^1$–$a^1$–$g\sharp^1$–$g^1$–$f\sharp^1$ (bar 1), indicated as **x** in the example, is repeated as a modulatory sequence in the consequent (bar 3), transposed at the perfect fourth ($T_5$) (which is also a reordering of the first pentachord of the $I_3$ form of the hexachord). The remaining heptachord of the set, transposed at $T_5$ or inverted and transposed at the minor third ($I_3$) in bars 3–4, furnishes the cello accompaniment, plus the cadential violin b♭ of the consequent (e–f–g♭–g–g♯–A–b♭). In bars 9–11 Skalkottas repeats motive **x** in the violin, transposed and inverted at $I_5$ (at bar 9), and then at $I_{10}$ (at bar 11), almost as though he wanted to exploit the harmonic possibilities offered by the combinatorial properties of the original set (see Table 8.6).

Table 8.6    Duo for violin and cello, *Andante molto espressivo*: Presentations of motive x (bars 1–11)

| Bars | 1–2 | 3–4 |
|---|---|---|
| Motive x | $a^1$–$b\flat^1$–$a^1$–$g\sharp^1$–$g^1$–$f\sharp^1$ | $d^1$–$e\flat^1$–$d^1$–$c\sharp^1$–$c^1$–$b$ |
|  | $T_0$ | $T_5$ |

| Bars | 9 | 11 |
|---|---|---|
| Motive x | $d^2$–$c\sharp^2$–$d^2$–$e\flat^2$–$e^2$–$f^2$ | $g^2$–$f\sharp^2$–$g^2$–$g\sharp^2$–$a^2$–$b\flat^2$ |
|  | $I_5$ | $I_{10}$ |

At bar 9 the $I_5$ violin melody is accompanied by the remaining pitch-classes of the $I_5$ form, while in the varied repetition of the consequent at bars 10–11 the $I_{10}$ version of the five-note violin melody is included in a reordering of the opening hexachord at its original tonal level ($T_0$), accompanied by the cello playing the second hexachord, which is also reordered. Due to the combinatorial-type relations between the hexachords, further close motivic/harmonic relationships permeate the texture. It is tempting to speculate that Skalkottas experimented with this technique in this late work, but did not go on to refine it to the extent of methodically creating aggregates to determine set succession, which might then have systematically defined the harmonic structure of large sections.

## Other Compositional Parameters – Texture

To articulate and differentiate the formal sections of a movement, such as thematic statements, transitions, developmental passages and cadences, Skalkottas manipulates not only the pitch-class set material to establish new harmonic areas, but also compositional parameters such as texture, instrumentation, timbre, rhythm and dynamics. His writing is normally polyphonic, and thus musical textures consist not merely of independent lines but of distinct subtextures, in a polytextural fabric. The subtextures within one movement are superimposed and move independently, each with its own distinct set content, harmonic structure, and rhythmic and articulative character, while different dynamic levels underline textural and timbral changes. In the chamber works of the mid-1930s he uses as many sets as there are instrumental lines, so, for example, each formal section of a quartet is built on four twelve-note sets, a violin and piano sonata is built on three sets, and so on. In the large-scale orchestral works, he composes with blocks of sound and with more vertical textures, which emerge from the harmonic presentation of the sets. Elements of bitonality or polytonality are found frequently throughout Skalkottas's music, and result from the superimposition of multi-layered textures and the stratification of tonally oriented melodic lines.

Thematic statements have a relatively uncomplicated texture, and are presented in the traditional format of melody with contrapuntal and/or harmonic accompaniment, or in a simple three- or four-part counterpoint. In developmental passages, polyphony predominates while the texture thickens; discrete segments from the different sets of a section may be juxtaposed in quick succession or used simultaneously in different configurations, thus producing a new motivic surface. This enhances harmonic variety and emphasizes the developmental character of these passages. In recapitulations, the original thematic material is varied rhythmically and/or through changes in instrumentation. At cadential points the texture stabilizes, providing a sense of closure.

The main characteristics of Skalkottas's cadential devices include: textural changes; the use of homophony to articulate the cadences of polyphonic passages; intensive repetition of single pitch-classes, small motives and/or chords; motivic liquidation,[7] achieved by the gradual dissolution of the motivic material; the use of melodic direction and contour; the manipulation of timbre, register and dynamics (for example, high registers are usually accompanied by textural density and often homophony and loud dynamics, whereas low registers are characterized by motivic liquidation, textural and rhythmic redundancy, and soft dynamics); rhythmic and/or metric changes; and the use of certain pitch-class collections and/ or chords containing tonal elements to punctuate cadences (for example, the tonally ambiguous tetrachords set-class 4–18 and set-class 4–17 are often used to frame harmonic progressions, either at the beginning of a passage or at its conclusion). Full cadences at the end of significant structural divisions are often based entirely on, or at least include, the twelve-note set that conveys the main thematic idea at the opening of the section, while half-cadences are usually based on another set of the referential set-group on which the relevant section is built.

---

[7] This cadential device arises from tonal practice (see Schoenberg, 1970/1990, 30).

# Chapter 9
# Set Structure and Large-scale Form

As already noted, in the majority of his twelve-note works Skalkottas uses a different set-group for each major section of a piece. The exclusive character of the various sets and set-groups employed, as opposed to the use of one inclusive basic set and its permutations, contributes to the definition of the harmonic structure, and effectively delineates the large-scale form by establishing distinct harmonic regions. Each formal section is differentiated from the surrounding sections by its individual serial, thematic and harmonic content, all derived from the set-group on which it is built, and is established through the sequential reiteration of the same succession of motivic and harmonic figures that arise from the set combination within this group – as well as through its rhythmic structure, texture and orchestration. Skalkottas conceives the set-groups within a single movement as contrasting 'keys', each section being associated with a different group. The group of sets in the opening section of a movement is treated as functionally similar to the tonic region in a tonal composition, and becomes a reference for the ensuing development. Furthermore, the movement always closes in that region. Subsidiary sections are built on either new set-groups or *en bloc* transpositions of the opening thematic set-group, in a manner analogous to modulation. Like Schoenberg in some of his early twelve-note works, Skalkottas uses the stability of the opening referential twelve-note region established by the set-group to create a structural dynamic; the move away from this region creates harmonic instability, which is ultimately resolved by the return of the referential group at the end of the movement, thus effecting closure. This dynamic is more effectively achieved in those pieces where *en bloc* textural transposition is used to define the form. As in traditional sonata practice, where different keys are associated with different themes, regional contrasts in Skalkottas's music are always accompanied by thematic contrasts. This familiar outline facilitates the listener's perception of formal relationships between large sections, and is reminiscent of Webern's approach, except that in Skalkottas's case we may substitute the term 'row' with 'set-group':

> The original form and pitch of the row occupy a position akin to that of the 'main key' in earlier music; the recapitulation will naturally return to it. We end 'in the same key!' This analogy with earlier formal constructions is quite consciously fostered; here we find the path that will lead us again to extended forms. (Webern, 1963, 54)

## Sonata Forms

There are essentially two theoretical approaches to sonata form that twentieth-century composers may adopt; the binary, eighteenth-century structure, and the 'essentially ternary' (Schoenberg, 1970/1990, 200) nineteenth-century equivalent. The two-part, eighteenth-century sonata type is shaped by the polarization of contrasting thematic material, texture and, most importantly, harmonic areas, with the latter being the essential form-generating element. The development of musical language during the nineteenth century led to sonata form being determined more by thematic contrast and thematic repetition, rather than the arrangement of keys (Dahlhaus, 1983, 84). Twentieth-century composers were unable to create sonata forms that arose organically from the harmonic tensions and underlying harmonic structure intrinsic to tonal music. However, by adopting different strategies and ignoring or reinterpreting such issues as the requirement for reconciliation, many composers wrote works in, or suggestive of, sonata form. Although these works derive from adaptation of the original principle, they share no single common practice, but, as Straus suggests, 'they do share a revisionary impulse, a tendency to reshape the form in accordance with post-tonal concerns' (Straus, 1990a, 132; also, 1987).

Skalkottas fashions his twelve-note sonata movements predominantly on a reinterpretation of the eighteenth-century formal prototype, with its contrasting thematic and harmonic material, and in his Notes he describes such movements as binary structures. These sonatas have two subject groups, with at least two clearly defined themes distinguished from each other by their different set structure, texture, rhythm, instrumentation, articulation and often tempo. In the development section Skalkottas closely follows the model described by Schoenberg in *Fundamentals* (1970/1990, 206–9). Although sets from both of the Exposition's two subject groups are used, usually in repeated sequence, they are frequently fragmented, with segments of the various sets being superimposed, juxtaposed, interpolated and often used as independent motives or chords, while the melodic material taken from the Exposition is developed using techniques of diminution, augmentation, fragmentation, contoural inversion, and so on. In works based on a free twelve-note technique with an indeterminate amount of pitch-class material, new sets and/or independent hexachords are introduced in the Development section. Skalkottas also transposes individual sets and entire textures, thus emulating modulatory harmonic movement associated with traditional tonal practice. In the Recapitulations he re-establishes, at some point, the original set-groups at the same 'tonal' level as that of the Exposition, but frequently in a new setting, with voice exchanges and rhythmic variations. In twelve-note works based on a limited number of sets and using a strict twelve-note technique that avoids textural transposition, there is no real sense of functional tonal relationships and resolution of harmonic tension. However, due to the use of tonal sets, triads and other tonally reminiscent material, and the voice-leading movement of the bass line towards a tonal centre, there is frequently an underlying harmonic structure that invites associations with some sort of tonal functionality. In several of his twelve-note movements based on a large amount of pitch-class material and exhibiting his free twelve-note technique, Skalkottas frequently employs symmetrical or arch forms to structure the large-scale formal design, characteristically employing the reversed sonata form,[1] which alters the order of the subject groups in the Recapitulation.

For example, the first movement, *Allegro moderato*, of the First Piano Concerto, which is in reversed sonata form, has two Expositions (I and II), a short Development section, and a Recapitulation that starts with the pitch-class material of the second subject before moving on to a recapitulation of the first subject, as shown in Table 9.1. The Coda, starting with a restatement of the Development's central thematic idea and twelve-note material, misleadingly gives the impression of a second Development section – a technique reminiscent of Beethovenian practice; but soon the development is circumscribed and the first theme reappears to round the movement off.

Similarly, Skalkottas also structures the first movement, *Allegro*, of the Concertino for two pianos as a reversed sonata form, with two Expositions (I and II), and a Recapitulation introduced by the second subject group (see Table 9.2). However, in contrast to the First Piano Concerto, the first movement here is based on only two sets, S1 and S2 – as discussed previously (see pp. 94–7). The first subject group, the transition and the development sections are all built exclusively on S1 and its variant forms, and the second subject group is based on S2.

### Large-scale Transposition as a Form-generating Device

In several of his large-scale orchestral compositions, particularly those based on a significant amount of diverse pitch-class material and which use a free twelve-note technique, Skalkottas establishes the large-scale harmonic and formal structure of a movement by employing not only different twelve-note set-groups in each section, but also their transpositions. The choice of such transpositions appears to be determined by a desire to emulate traditional tonal relationships between main and subordinate subjects, between Exposition and Recapitulation. According to this technique, the Recapitulation invariably repeats the entire Exposition, or large sections of it, transposed *en bloc* at the interval of a perfect fifth ($T_7$) or perfect fourth ($T_5$), creating harmonic movement from a 'tonic-like' area to another 'dominant-like' or 'subdominant-like' one. Furthermore, between the opening and subsequent transposed sections, Skalkottas inserts transitional passages transposed predominantly at the major or minor third ($T_4$, $T_3$), or minor sixth ($T_8$), which are often used as modulatory sequences. At the end of his Recapitulations Skalkottas always returns to the original transpositional level ($T_0$), as if returning to the home key. Although Schoenberg's twelve-note works also exhibit traditional

---

[1] For further discussion of reversed sonata form, see Jackson (1995, 3–29, 1996, 61–111, 1997, 140–208).

Table 9.1  First Piano Concerto, *Allegro moderato*: Formal structure and set structure

| Sections | Phrases | Thematic, set structure |
|---|---|---|
| **Exposition I – orchestral ritornello** (1–66) ||| 
| First subject group | First theme | (1–5): Theme in vln1+vln2 (S1).<br>(6–12): Modified repetition of theme. |
| | Second theme | (13–8): Theme in the upper strings (S2).<br>(19–23): Continuation. |
| | Third theme | (24–30): Contrapuntal theme of triple counterpoint (S3 and S4).<br>(31–3): Codetta – transitional passage. |
| Second subject group | First lyrical theme | (34–41): Lyrical, *ruhig*, first theme in the clarinet (S5).[*]<br>(41–5): Varied repetition of the theme;<br>(46–9) continuation. |
| | Second contrasting theme | (50–56): Assertive, *ff*, *führend* second theme in fls+vlns (S6).<br>(57–61): Liquidated phrase following climactic cadence. |
| | Codetta | (62–6) Material from the first theme (S1). |
| **Exposition II** (67–126) |||
| First subject group | First theme (varied) | (67–74): Variation of first theme in pno RH (S1); new motives in ww; S1 distributed among the instruments.<br>(75–9): New thematic idea in pno – bridge to second theme. |
| | Second theme (varied) | (79$^4$–86): Second theme similar to (13–18); pno RH (S2).<br>(87–90) similar to (19–23). |
| | Third theme (varied) | (91–9) Contrapuntal third theme, similar to (24–30); pno (S3 segms).<br>(100–101): Codetta |
| Second subject group | First theme (varied) | (102–4, 105–10): Gradual transformation and development of pitch content from (34–49). |
| | Second theme (varied) | (111–15$^1$): Transformation of (50–56); new thematic idea in orch.<br>(115–20): Transformation of (57–8); pno predominates.<br>(121–6): Codetta. |
| **Development** (127–54) |||
| | First section | (127–34$^1$): Orchestral ritornello. Theme in tbns reminiscent of the first theme.<br>(134–7) (138–43): New thematic idea in pno (S7). |
| | Second section | (144–9$^1$): Developmental passage.<br>(149–54): Liquidated cadential phrase. |

*Set Structure and Large-scale Form* 155

| | | **Reversed Recapitulation** (155–227) |
|---|---|---|
| Second subject group | First theme | (155–8): Varied recapitulation of (34–41).<br>(159–60): Varied (46–7) and (108).<br>(160–61) pno: varied (48–9) and (109–10 pno RH).<br>(161²–3) orch: varied (48–9 bsn, vlc, db), and (109–10 pno LH). |
| | Second theme | (164–70): varied (50–56) and (111–15 partially); fragmentation and extensive use of chromatic tetrachords. |
| First subject group | First theme | Varied recapitulation of (1–33) and (62–101).<br>(171–9): Truncated first theme in pno LH (S1). |
| | Second theme | (180–88): Truncated second theme in pno RH (S2); (189–200) link. |
| | Third theme (elements) | (201–4): Opening motive A–C (S3). |
| Coda | | (205–10): Restatement of central idea of the Development (S7); varied repetition of (138–43).<br>(211–16): (211 pno RH) = (142 pno RH).<br>(217–27): First theme in strings. |

\* For a more detailed consideration of the pitch-class content of the second subject group, see pp. 190–93 in Part III.

Table 9.2   Concertino for two pianos, *Allegro*: Formal structure and set structure

| **Sections** | **Thematic and phrase structure** | **Sets** |
|---|---|---|
| Exposition I (orch ritornello) | (1–15) First subject group:<br>(1–5) antecedent;<br>(6–11) consequent;<br>(12–15) transition. | S1 |
| | (16–29) Second subject group:<br>(16–20¹) first phrase;<br>(20²–22) continuation. | S2 |
| Exposition II (two pnos and orch) | (30–47) First subject group. | S1 |
| | (48–63) Second subject group. | S2 |
| Development | (64–80) Development of material from first subject;<br>(81–90) retransition. | S1 |
| Reversed Recapitulation | (91–116) Second subject group | S2 |
| | (117–33) First subject group:<br>(117–22) first theme;<br>(123–33) mainly chords S1. | S1 |
| Coda | (134–5) Chordal presentation of S2 and S1. | S2, S1 |

fifth-relationships, these are effected through hexachordal inversional combinatoriality that enabled him to determine the harmonic structure and the large-scale organization of his twelve-note pieces by establishing closely knit groups of set forms, each constituting a harmonic area that functions in a way similar to the tonicized keys in a tonal piece. Because of his use of combinatoriality, Schoenberg was able to modulate from area to area, creating a sense of harmonic movement at the highest structural levels (Straus, 1990b, 158; Haimo, 1992, 10). Although Skalkottas's use of transposition to determine the large-scale harmonic and formal organization of his twelve-note works is comparable to that of Schoenberg, it is less complicated; the tonic–dominant, tonic–subdominant transpositional relationships involve the entire texture, and are used predominantly to differentiate between the Exposition and the Recapitulation.

For example, as shown in Table 9.3, the *Allegro* of the Second Sonatina for violin and piano outlines a reversed sonata form. In the Exposition, the first theme (bars 1–17), combining a Classical-period phrase structure with elements influenced by the subject–answer rhetoric of a Baroque fugue, is based on a twelve-note set (S1). In the antecedent (bars 1–8) the violin melody is based on the first hexachord of S1 (E–F♯–A–A♭–G–F, set-class 6–1), while the consequent (bars 9–16) is constructed from its tritone transposition (B♭–C–E♭–D–C♯–B). This tritone harmonic relationship between the opening two phrases also extends to the accompaniment (see Example 9.1).

Example 9.1  Second Sonatina for violin and piano, *Allegro*: Harmonic structure of the first theme (bars 1–17)

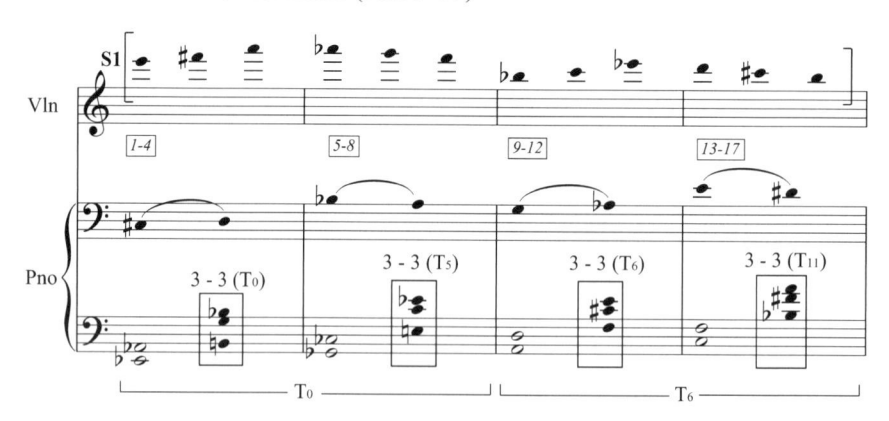

The second theme is based on set S2 that derives from S1 (see Table 6.2a). The Recapitulation starts with the second theme transposed at the fifth ($T_7$), as if it were an extension of the Development section – perhaps the retransition in the dominant. This is followed by a repetition of the second theme at the original tonal level $T_0$, and then the recapitulation of the pitch-class material of the first theme, also at $T_0$, to round off the movement.

Table 9.3  Second Sonatina for violin and piano, *Allegro*: Formal structure and set structure

| Sections | Bars | Themes | Phrase, set structure |
|---|---|---|---|
| **Exposition (1–46)** ||||
| First subject group | 1–17 | First theme | Main thematic idea in vln (S1). (1–8) Antecedent: vln plays first hexachord of S1 (set-class 6–1); pno plays fixed hexachordal pc collections. (9–17) Consequent: transposition at $T_6$ of the antecedent's entire texture – vln plays second hexachord of S1 ($T_6$). |
|  | 18–27 | Varied repetition of first theme | Secondary thematic idea in pno RH-upper voice. (18–27) Varied repetition of (1–16). Unordered segms of S1. |
| Second subject group | 28–41 | Second theme | Main thematic idea in vln (S2). (28–33) Antecedent; (34–39) consequent – repetition of (28–33) at $T_7$; (40–41) bridge. |
|  | 42–6 | Varied repetition of second theme | Theme in pno; vln with new accompanimental melody. |
| Codetta | $46^2$–$51^1$ | Codetta | Modulatory movement: (46) tetrachord set-class 4–13 in pno LH is repeated at $T_7$ in (48). |
| **Development ($52^2$–76)** ||||
|  | $52^2$–64 | First section | ($52^1$–$8^1$) Modified repetition of the first theme in pno only. ($58^2$–64). Varied repetition of (1–16) ($T_0$). |
|  | 65–76 | Second section | Developmental passage, including varied repetition of (22–5) at $T_7$; chordal presentation of material. Retransition. |
| **Reversed Recapitulation (77–106)** ||||
|  | 77–90 | Second subject group at $T_7$ | (77–87) Recap of the second theme (28–33) in pno only at $T_7$; at (82) vln at $T_7$. (83–87) Recapitulation of (34–7) at $T_7$; (88) transposition of (85) at $T_5$, $T_6$, $T_8$. (89–90) Bridge; repetition of (40–41) at $T_0$. |
| $B^3$ | 91–4 | Second theme at $T_0$ | (91–4) Almost exact recap of the second theme as in (42–5) and (28–31) at $T_0$. ($94^2$) Codetta. |
| $A^4$ | 95–102 | First theme | Varied recap of first theme (1–16) at $T_0$. |
| Coda | 103–6 |  | Motivic liquidation. |

Apart from the early pieces (the First String Quartet (1928); the First and Second sonatinas for violin and piano (1929); and the *Presto* of the Octet (1931), to be considered in Part III), this transpositional technique is the predominant structural device in most of Skalkottas's large-scale dodecaphonic works from the third movement of the Piano Trio onwards – up to the mid-1940s.[2]

## Retrograde Presentation of Sets and Large-scale Palindromes to Define the Form

In his chamber music of the mid-1930s, Skalkottas extensively uses retrograde and transposed forms of the source sets to articulate both the small-scale phrase structure and the large-scale form of a movement. The fourth movement, *Finale (Presto)*, of the First Piano Suite provides such an example. It is built on a group of four twelve-note sets, their group transposition at the minor sixth ($T_8$), their retrograde forms ($R_0$), and retrograde transpositions at the minor sixth ($R_8$). The *Finale*'s formal design, which combines a rondo sequence of sections and their varied repetitions (ABA$^1$B$^1$A$^2$CA$^3$ B$^2$A$^4$B$^3$A$^5$) with ternary form (A B A'), is established by the rotation of the set-groups at $T_0$, $T_8$, $R_0$ and $R_8$, as shown in Table 9.4.

Table 9.4    First Piano Suite, *Finale (Presto)*: Formal structure and set-group transpositional and retrograde structure

| Ternary form | A | | | | | B | | | A' | | |
|---|---|---|---|---|---|---|---|---|---|---|---|
| Sections | A | B | A$^1$ | B$^1$ | A$^2$ | C | A$^3$ | B$^2$ | A$^4$ | B$^3$ | A$^5$ |
| Set structure | $T_0$–$T_8$ | $R_8$–($R_0$) | $T_0$–$T_8$ | $R_8$–$R_0$ | $T_0$–$R_8$ | $T_0$–$R_8$–$T_0$ | $T_0$–$T_8$ | $R_0$–$R_8$–$T_0$–$T_8$ | $T_0$–$T_8$ | $R_8$ | $R_0$ |

Changes in texture, rhythmic structure and tempo (*Presto*, *Tempo* and *Prestissimo*) also contribute to the delineation of the large-scale form. In the opening gesture (bars 1–2) the sets unfold as pairs in parallel succession in a two-part texture, with the right-hand sets S1 and S3 supported by the left-hand sets S2 and S4 respectively. The continuation (bars 3–4) is built on their $T_8$ transposed forms, also presented in pairs, S5–S6 and S7–S8. This format is reproduced in all repetitions of the recurring thematic section A (with the exception of the cadential gestures at the end of the ternary sections A and A'). Developmental passages within the B episodes are built predominantly on the retrograde of the transposed

---

[2]   For example, this technique is used in the first movement of the Violin Concerto, the third movement of the Second Piano Concerto, all movements of the Third Piano Concerto, the Fourth String Quartet and *The Return of Ulysses*. The only exception is the Second Symphonic Suite, whose last three movements in particular are closer to a variation form.

forms of the sets (i.e. RS5, RS6, RS7, RS8), while the initial regularity of the set presentation in pairs is interrupted and the speed of set rotation becomes irregular. The developmental middle section C is differentiated from other developmental passages (B, B[1], etc.) by intense motivic elaboration, which results from the segmentation of the sets, extensive reordering within the segments, segmental rotation and chordal textures. The retrograde of the prime forms of the sets (RS1, RS2, RS3, RS4) are used at transitional and cadential passages. Table 9.9 details the set topography and formal structure of the movement.

From the late 1930s Skalkottas became interested in the use of large-scale palindromes as a form-building device. Not only did he use the prime and retrograde forms of single sets consecutively or simultaneously within the texture, but he also built entire sections on the strict retrograde of a complete musical passage. In certain works, he employs palindromes and builds a passage symmetrically around an axis with prime/forward and palindromic forms of the sets. For example, the cadenza of the *Andantino* of the Second Piano Concerto is symmetrically built around a passage featuring the recurrence of the motive $d^1$–$e^1$–$f^1$–$g_b^1$ (bars $126^2$–34), which provides the central axis and a harmonic stasis in the forward–backward movement of the cadenza. As shown in Example 9.2, the thematic and accompanimental material at bars 123–4 are a palindromic presentation of that in bars 120–21 with part-exchanges.

Example 9.2 Second Piano Concerto, *Andantino*: Piano cadenza (bars 120–24)

In several orchestral works a large part of the Recapitulation, in particular, is constructed from a whole section of the Exposition in palindromic motion. For example, the *Ouvertüre Concertante* of the Second Symphonic Suite has a large-scale binary form (AB) defined by the use of a large-scale palindrome. As shown in Table 9.5, Part A – divided into an introduction, two contrasting sections (A, B) and a transition to the second part – is built on the prime form of a variety of

Table 9.5  Second Symphonic Suite: Palindromic structure of the *Ouvertüre Concertante*

| Part A | | Part B | |
|---|---|---|---|
| Sections | Bars | Varied and palindromic repetition of sections | Bars |
| Introduction | 1–7 | Varied Introduction | 142–62 |
| | | Pitch-class material at the original, $T_0$ level. | 142–58 |
| | | Axis for the prime and palindromic presentation of pc material and sections. | 158/159 |
| | | Palindrome of (2–6) | 159–62 |
| Section A | 8–75 | Section A' | 163–205 |
| | | (163–74) = palindrome of (8–17) | |
| | | (175–205) = palindrome of (21–54) | |
| Section B | 76–128 | Section B' | 206–70 |
| | | (218–270) = palindrome of (76–128) | |
| Transition | 129–41 | Coda | 271–96 |
| | | (271–96) = (1–24 at $T_0$) | |

pitch-class material, including independent melodies and twelve-note sets. Part B is a varied repetition of Part A, and is based on a palindromic presentation of several of its sections. The Coda finally returns to the original presentation of the material (at $T_0$) from bars 1–24. As already mentioned, Skalkottas only rarely uses the twelve-note operation of inversion. However, the late Serenata for cello and piano is an exception, and transposition and particularly inversion of the sets and pitch-class material become a significant structural feature of the piece, as will be shown in Part III (see 'Serenata for Cello and Piano (1949)', pp. 319–24).

**Cyclical Forms**

Like other late nineteenth- and early twentieth-century composers, Skalkottas was attracted to cyclical principles of construction as unifying devices and as a way of ensuring systematic formal coherence in large-scale works. This is particularly true of those works exhibiting a free approach to twelve-note technique and built on an indeterminate number of sets. Cyclical procedures involve the often varied recurrence of a first movement's main theme(s), salient motives and rhythmic patterns, and – more significantly – the repetition of entire passages based on specific twelve-note sets (or non-serial pitch-class collections), either exactly or as palindromes, or transposed at different levels, equivalent to modulation. These repetitions invariably occur both within sections of a single movement and between movements, and often feature a developmental treatment of earlier material. Skalkottas paraphrases – and ultimately disintegrates – the main thematic gestures of the first movement, while constantly preserving its pitch-class set structure.

Apart from direct cyclical recurrences of thematic material occurring in more than one movement of a piece, from the mid-1930s onwards Skalkottas frequently uses the twelve-note sets of a first movement to construct an entire multi-movement piece. This approach ensures a high degree of integration of contrasting elements, not only within each section of a movement but also between movements, thus providing a large-scale unified cyclical formal superstructure. The Second String Trio, the Third and Fourth sonatinas for violin and piano, the First Piano Suite, the Third Piano Concerto, the Fourth String Quartet and the Sonatina for cello and piano all typify this approach.

*Second String Trio (1935)*

In the Second String Trio the sense of unity given by the feeling that the three separate movements constitute sub-sections of the whole is reinforced by Skalkottas's manipulation of the set structure. As noted above, the sonata-form first movement, *Moderato*, is built on three discrete, closely related twelve-note sets, which are introduced simultaneously as three superimposed contrapuntal lines at the opening gesture and used throughout only in their prime form (see Table 8.1). The second movement, *Andante*, in rondo form (AA$^1$BACA$^2$Coda), is built on three different groups of three twelve-note sets, one for each of the main sections (A, B and C), while two of the sets from the *Moderato* become the source material for its construction, through the derivation technique of cyclic rotation. Its cadence is built entirely on the three sets S1, S2 and S3 of the *Moderato* (see Table 8.2) This derivation technique provides maximum pitch-class similarity within each section of the *Andante*, and a close motivic and harmonic relationship with the *Moderato*; thus, the second movement functions as a developmental extension of the first. Furthermore, the audibility of the derivation process of these sets ensures not only the necessary contrast in the serial structure, but also unity with the referential twelve-note material of the first movement. The development and contrast of the twelve-note framework is stabilized in the third movement, *Presto*, which is in rondo form. This movement is built on the three sets of the *Moderato* (S1, S2 and S3), although Skalkottas continues the development of this referential material by introducing three derived sets (S4, S5, S6) from it (see Table 8.3).

With regard to the set structure, therefore, the large-scale form of the entire piece outlines a sonata form, with the *Moderato* functioning as the Exposition. The *Andante* is equivalent to the Development section, which not only elaborates motivic and pitch-class material from the Exposition but also introduces thematic ideas based on new dodecaphonic material; its final cadence is analogous to the 'modulatory' retransition to the Recapitulation. The *Presto* functions as this Recapitulation, returning to the same sets as the Exposition; and although the thematic–motivic development continues, it ends 'in the same key'. The use of the same source material throughout such multi-movement works ensures a wide range of integration of themes and contrasts and, in Hans Keller's words, facilitates the inter-related development of the three movements 'into a consistent yet consistently contrasting whole' (Keller, in Wintle (ed.), 1995, 55).

*First Piano Suite (1936)*

Similarly, the substantial, four-movement form of the First Piano Suite outlines a large-scale sonata form with regard to its set structure: the *Preludio* functions as the Exposition, the *Serenade* and *Menuetto* together as the Development, and the *Finale* as the Recapitulation. As already noted, the *Preludio*,[3] outlining sonata form, is built on four twelve-note sets (S1, S2, S3, S4) and their unordered transpositions at the minor sixth ($T_8$) (S5, S6, S7, S8) (see Example II.1 and Table 9.6). The phrases of the first subject group and the transition harmonically oscillate between two key areas, the 'tonic' and the 'minor submediant', established by the use of sets at $T_0$ and $T_8$. The second subject group, exhibiting a developmental character, is built on the prime forms of the four source sets only, while its first theme is established through the segmental rotation of the source sets.

In the *Serenade* and *Menuetto*, varied forms of the *Preludio*'s sets are used, ensuring not only a degree of motivic and thematic variety but also coherence and connection across the suite. The *Serenade*, outlining a simple rondo form (ABA¹B¹A²B²A³) as shown in Table 9.7, is predominantly built on eight sets that derive from the rearrangement of the pitch-class order within each tetrachord of the retrograde forms of the *Preludio*'s eight sets.[4] The set and phrase structure of the *Serenade* is determined by a palindromic-type twelve-note operation. Compared with the set and phrase structure of the *Preludio*, all the phrases of the *Serenade*'s section A, and its varied repetitions, have a retrograde organizational scheme, starting with the set pair RS7a–RS8a, and progress through RS5a–RS6a, RS3a–RS4a to RS1a–RS2a (see Example 9.3).

The phrases of the shorter section B and its curtailed repetitions are built on the slightly varied source sets of the *Preludio*, which are presented in pairs: S2a–S1a, S4a–S3a, S5a–S6a, S7a–S8a. In terms of the set structure and harmonic progression, the movement is open ended, with its final dyad $A_1$–c having a tritone relationship with the opening repeated dyad e♭–g♭. Also, in terms of harmonic groups, the final gesture ends on the set-pair RS4a–RS3a followed by RS3a, giving the impression that it ends with a half-cadence.

The third movement of the First Piano Suite is a traditional *Menuetto* and *Trio*. The *Menuetto*, having a rounded binary form (ABa'),[5] is built on the reordered

---

[3] Other readings of this movement appear in Garmon Roberts (1996, 8–22) and Konstantinou (2001).

[4] The only exception is set RS1a, which although also derived from the unordered retrograde of S1, is constantly presented as a 13-note set, with the note F♯ repeated and a displacement of the pitch-classes D♯ and G in the two hexachords.

[5] Section A represents the first 'phrase' of the rounded binary form, sections B and a' the second and third 'phrases' respectively (see Rosen, 1988, 21).

Example 9.3  First Piano Suite, *Serenade*: Opening gesture (bars 1–4)

prime and retrograde forms of the *Preludio*'s source sets, with section A based on S1–S4, and section B on their retrogrades RS1–RS4, as shown in Table 9.8. The *Trio*, outlining a binary form (AB), is built exclusively on varied presentations of the minor sixth transposed forms ($T_8$) of the source sets and their retrogrades (S5–S8, RS5–RS8), thus suggesting a change of 'key', reminiscent of the *minore* sections of early eighteenth-century *Menuettos*. The cadential passages of both sections (A and B) have the same pitch-class structure, while a smooth transition to the return of the *Menuetto* is achieved through the last melodic gesture in the right hand, $a\flat^2-g^2-f^2-d\sharp^2-c\sharp^2-b^1$, based on S6, which is a curtailed retrograde version of the *Menuetto*'s opening melodic motive $b^1-c\sharp^2-d\sharp-g\sharp^2$. The *Finale (Presto)*, an example of 'Perpetuum mobile', is built on the *Preludio*'s source sets, as if returning to the 'original key' to round off the entire piece (see Table 9.9).

*Fourth String Quartet (1940)*

The Fourth String Quartet, an example of Skalkottas's free approach to his dodecaphonic technique, is representative of all the form-generating processes discussed in this section. Its twelve-note set structure synthesizes groups of pitch-class material, including both twelve-note sets and other pitch-class collections. The thematic sets that furnish the main themes and other important structural passages recur unchanged in the varied repetitions of the thematic sections and in the Recapitulation, thus establishing their structural importance. Several sets are varied representations of previous ones, thus maintaining a degree of motivic similarity, while sets supporting secondary melodic ideas are used only once. As in other free twelve-note works, such as the Violin Concerto and the Third Piano Concerto in particular, in order to unify and control the plethora of material, and to achieve the necessary coherence across the quartet, Skalkottas employs both transposition and palindromes of entire sections as form-generating devices,

Table 9.6  First Piano Suite, *Preludio*: Set topography and formal structure

**Exposition**

| Bars | 1 | 2 | 3 | 4 | 5 | 6 | 7 | 8 | 9 | 11 | 12 | 13 | 14 | 15 | 16 | 17 | 18 | 19 | 20 | 21 | 22 | 23 | 24 | 25 |
|---|---|---|---|---|---|---|---|---|---|---|---|---|---|---|---|---|---|---|---|---|---|---|---|---|
| RH | S1 | S3 | S5 | S7 | S1 | S3 | S6 | S8 | S1 | S5 | S2 | S6 | S1 BCA | S3 BCA | S2 CBA | S3 CAB | S2 | | S4 S1 | S3– S2 | S1– S3 | S1– S2– S4 | S1 | S2 |
| LH | S2 | S4 | S6 | S8 | S2 | S4 | S5 | S7 | S2 | S6 | S1 | S5 | S2 BCA | S4 BCA | S1 CAB | S4 CBA | | S3 | | | | | | |

First subject group | Transition | First theme of second subject group | Second theme of second subj group | Codetta

| | 26 | 27 | 28 | 29 | 30 | 31 | 32 | 33–4 | 35 | 36 | 37 | 38 | 39 | 40 | 41 | 42 | 43 | 44 | 45 | 46 | 47 | 48 |
|---|---|---|---|---|---|---|---|---|---|---|---|---|---|---|---|---|---|---|---|---|---|---|
| RH | S1 | S3–S4 | S2 | S3–S4 | S1 | S3 | S1 | S3 | S1 | S2 | S1–S2–S3–S4 | S1–S2S3–S4 | S2–S1–S3–S4 | S5–S7 | S1 | S3 | S6–S8 | S8 | S1 | S5 | S6–S8 | S8 |
| LH | S2 | | S1 | | | | S2 | S4 | | | | | | S6–S8 | S2 | S4 | S5–S7 | S7 | S2 | S6 | S5–S7 | S7 |

Development

| | 49 | 50 | 51 | 52 | 53 | 54 | 55 | 56 | 57 | 58 | 59 | 60 | 61 | 62 | 63 | 64 | 65 | 66–7 | 68–9 | 70 | 71 | 72 | 73 | 74–5 |
|---|---|---|---|---|---|---|---|---|---|---|---|---|---|---|---|---|---|---|---|---|---|---|---|---|
| RH | S1 | S3 | S2 | S4–S2 | S4–S6 | S8 | S2 | S2–S4 | S4 | S1 | S3 | S5 | S6 | S3 | S4 | S1 | S3 | S2 | S1 | S5 | S6 | S1–S2 | S4 | S1–S2 (segms) |
| LH | | | | | S4–S5 | S7 | S1 | S1–S3 | S3 | S2 | S4 | S6 | S5 | S4 | S3 | | | | S2 | | | | S3 | |

Recapitulation | Coda

Table 9.7  First Piano Suite, *Serenade*: Set topography and formal structure

| Bars | 1 | 2 | 3 | 4 | 5 | 6 | 7 | 8 | 9–11 | 12 | 13 | 14 | 16–17 | 18–19 | 20 |
|---|---|---|---|---|---|---|---|---|---|---|---|---|---|---|---|
| RH | RS7a | RS5a | RS3a | RS1a | RS7a–RS5a | RS5a–RS3a | RS1a | RS7a–RS5a | RS3a–RS2a | RS7a | RS5a | RS4a | RS2a–RS1a | RS8a–RS6a–RS4a | RS2a |
| LH | RS8a | RS6a | RS4a | RS2a | RS8a | RS6a–RS4a | RS2a | RS8a–RS6a | RS4a–RS1a | RS8a | RS6a | RS3a | RS1a–RS2a | RS7a–RS5a–RS3a | RS1a |

Section A

| | 21 | 22 | 23 | 24 | 25–7 | 28 | 29 | 30 | 31 | 32 |
|---|---|---|---|---|---|---|---|---|---|---|
| RH | S2a | S4a | S5a | S7a | S2a | S4a | S3a | S5a | S7a | RS8a |
| LH | S1a | S3a | S6a | S8a | S1a | S3a | S4a | S6a | S8a | RS7a |

Section B

| | 33 | 34 | 35 | 36–7 | 38–9 | 40 | 41 | 42 | 43 | 44 |
|---|---|---|---|---|---|---|---|---|---|---|
| RH | RS6a | RS4a | RS2a | RS7a | RS5a–S6a (interpol) SS3a | RS4a–RS2a | S1a | S3a | S5a | S7a |
| LH | RS5a | RS3a | RS1a | RS8a | | RS3a–RS1a | S2a | S4a | S6a | S8a |

Section A[1]

| | 45–7 | 48–9 | 50 | 51–2 | 53–4 | 55–6 | 57 | 58 | 59 | 60 | 61 | 62–3 | 64 | 65 |
|---|---|---|---|---|---|---|---|---|---|---|---|---|---|---|
| RH | RS7a–RS5a | RS5a/RS6a (interpol) | RS2a | RS7a BCA | RS5a BCA | RS3aC–RS1a | RS1a | RS7a CAB | RS5a CAB | RS3a CAB | S1a | RS8a–S7a | RS5a–RS3a | RS1a |
| LH | RS8a–RS7a | RS3a–RS a | RS1a | RS8a BCA | RS6a BCA | RS4a BCA | RS3aA | RS8a C/BA | RS6a CAB | RS4a CBA | S2a | RS7a–RS8a | RS6a–RS4a | RS2a |

Section A[2]

| | 66 | 67 | 68 | 69–70 | 71–2 | 73 | 74 | 75–7 | 78 | 79 | 80–84 |
|---|---|---|---|---|---|---|---|---|---|---|---|
| RH | S1a | S4a–S5a | S6a–S7a | RS8a | RS5a | RS3a | RS2a | RS7a | RS5a | RS5a | RS3a |
| LH | S2a | S3a–S6a | S6a–S8a | RS7a | RS6a–RS4a | RS4a–RS3a | RS3a | RS8a | RS5a | RS4a | RS4a–RS3a |

Section B[2]

Section A[3]

Table 9.8    First Piano Suite, *Menuetto–Trio*: Set topography and formal structure

**Menuetto**

Phrase structure and set structure (source sets)

| Bars | 1–3 | 4–5 | 6–7 | 8–10¹ | 10²–14 | 15–17 | 18–20 | 21–2 | 23–5 | 26–8 | 29–30 | 31–2 | 33–5 |
|---|---|---|---|---|---|---|---|---|---|---|---|---|---|
| RH | S1 | S3 | S2 | S4 | RS4–RS2 | RS3 | RS4–RS2 | RS2 | RS3–RS1 | S1 | S3 | S2 | S4 |
| LH |  |  |  |  |  | RS3–RS1 | S1–S3 | S2 | RS4 |  |  |  |  |

Melodic structure (derived sets)

| RH | IIIa | IIIc | RIIIc | RIIIb | RIIIc | RIIIa | IIIa | IIIc |
|---|---|---|---|---|---|---|---|---|
| LH | IIIb | IIId | RIIId | RIIIa | IIIb | IIId | IIIb | IIId |
|  | Section A |  | Section B |  |  |  | Section A' |  |

**Trio**

|  | 36–7 | 38–9 | 40–42 | 43 | 44–5 | 46–9 | 50–52 | 53 | 54–6 |
|---|---|---|---|---|---|---|---|---|---|
| RH | S6 | S8 | S5 | S5 | S6 | RS7 | RS5 | S5 | S6 |
| LH | S5 | S7 | S6 |  |  | RS8 | RS6 |  |  |
|  | Section A |  |  |  |  | Section B |  |  |  |

Table 9.9  First Piano Suite, *Finale (Presto)*: Set topography and formal structure

| Bars | 1 | 2 | 3 | 4 | 5 | 6 | 7 | 8 | 9 | 10 | 11 | 12 | 13 | 14 | 15 | 16 | 17 | 18 |
|---|---|---|---|---|---|---|---|---|---|---|---|---|---|---|---|---|---|---|
| RH | S1 | S3 | S5 | S7 | S1 | S3 | S5 | S7 | | RS7 | | RS5 | RS3 | RS1 | RS7 | RS7–RS5 | RS3 | RS1 |
| LH | S2 | S4 | S6 | S8 | S2 | S4 | S6 | S8 | RS8 | RS6 | RS4 | | RS2 | | RS8 | RS6 | RS4–RS2 | RS2 |

Section A — Section B

| | 19 | 20 | 21 | 22 | 23 | 24 | 25 | 26 | 27–8 | 29 | 30 | 31 | 32 |
|---|---|---|---|---|---|---|---|---|---|---|---|---|---|
| RH | S2 | S2–S4–S6 | S6–S8 | S8 | RS8 | RS6 | RS4 | RS2 | RS2 | RS7 | RS5 | RS3 | RS1 |
| LH | S1 | S3 | S5 | S7 | | RS7 | RS5 | RS3 | RS1 | RS8 | RS6 | RS4 | RS2 |

Section A[1] — Section B[1]

| | 33 | 34 | 35 | 36 | 37 | 38 | 39 | 40 | 41–42 | 43–44 | 45 | 46 | 47–9 | 50–52 | 53–5 |
|---|---|---|---|---|---|---|---|---|---|---|---|---|---|---|---|
| RH | S1 | S3 | S5 | S7 | S1 | S3 | S5 var | S7 var | S1BCA | S3BCA | S5BC | | S7 | S2 | S3 |
| LH | S2 | S4 | S6 | S8 | S2 | S4 | S6 var | S8 var | S2 | S4 | S6AB | S2C | S8 | S1 | S4 |

Section A[2] — Section C — Transition to A[3]

| | 56–62 | 63–6 | 67–71 | 72–3 | 74 | 75 | 76 | 77 |
|---|---|---|---|---|---|---|---|---|
| RH | S1 | S3 | S5 | S7 | S1 | S3 | S5 | S7 |
| LH | S2 | S4 | S6 | S8 | S2 | S4 | S6 | S8 |

Section A[3]

*continued*

Table 9.9  concluded

|    | 78–80 | 81–3 | 84–7 | 88–90 | 91–3 | 94–6 | 97    | 98     | 99–100 | 101–2 | 103 |
|----|-------|------|------|-------|------|------|-------|--------|--------|-------|-----|
| RH | RS3   |      |      |       | RS1  |      | S2var | S4 var | S5     |       | S7  |
| LH | RS7   | RS5  | RS8  | RS6   | RS4  | RS2  | S1 var| S3 var | S6     | S2C   | S8  |
|    | Section B² |  |  |  |  |  | Transition to A⁴ |  |  |  |  |

|    | 104–10 | 111–14 | 115–23 | 124–5 | 126–7 | 128–9   | 130 | 131–6 | 137–9 | 141 |
|----|--------|--------|--------|-------|-------|---------|-----|-------|-------|-----|
| RH | S1     | S3     | S5     | S7    | RS7   | RS7–RS5 | RS3 |       | RS1   |     |
| LH | S2     | S4     | S6     | S8    | RS8   | RS6     | RS4 | RS2   | S2A   |     |
|    | Section A⁴ |  |  |  |  | Section B³ |  |  | Section A⁵ |  |

Set Structure and Large-scale Form        169

together with cyclical procedures. The latter operate both within each movement and across movements, and include the recurrent repetition of certain thematic sets, either exact or slightly varied, and specific melodic and rhythmic motives. For example, in the first movement, *Allegro molto vivace*, the first theme is built on three twelve-note sets (S1, S2, S3) and certain independent segments, shown in Example 9.4a.

Example 9.4a    Fourth String Quartet, *Allegro molto vivace*: First theme – opening gesture (bars 1–7)

The second theme (bars 65–79) outlines three phrases, each based on a different set-group of four sets (S5–S8, S9–S12, S13–S16) (Example 9.4b). Apart from these consistently identifiable thematic sets, the developmental process involves the ever changing use of pitch-class material in the form of entire twelve-note melodies and chords, and independent motives not easily identified as a segment of a set. The diffuse pitch-class content of the movement is bound together by the recurrence of a particular motivic figure – the melodic motive $d^1$–$b^1$–$b\flat^2$–$g^2$–$e^2$ (the first pentachord of the thematic set S1), which has a characteristic wave-like contour and is constantly presented in an upbeat semiquaver pattern.[6]

Example 9.4b  Fourth String Quartet, *Allegro molto vivace*: Second theme (bars 65–79)

---

[6]  This motive appears throughout the texture in twenty-four slightly varied forms, but with identical rhythm. In each presentation it belongs either to a new twelve-note melody, or to a variant of the original source set, or it is used as an independent motive.

In terms of its formal structure, the *Allegro molto vivace* outlines a reversed sonata form with a subdominant recapitulation, as shown in Table 9.10. The latter is introduced with the second subject group followed by the first subject group, with the exposition's pitch-class content transposed at the fourth ($T_5$), implying a movement from a 'tonic' region to a 'subdominant' one. The short Coda recapitulates the first theme at its original tonal level ($T_0$) to round off the movement.

Table 9.10 Fourth String Quartet, *Allegro molto vivace*: Set structure and formal structure

| Sections | Bars | Thematic structure | Set structure |
| --- | --- | --- | --- |
| Exposition | 1–132 | | |
| | 1–64 | First subject group (1–7) First theme. | S1, S2, S3, S4. Several variants of the main thematic sets. |
| | 65–132 | Second subject group (65–79) Second theme. | (65–70): S5, S6, S7, S8. (71–3): S13, S14, S15, S16. (74–9): S13, S14, S15, S16. Other independent sets S17, S18, S19; diverse pc material different in each phrase. |
| Development | 133–257³ | | A plethora of groups of twelve-note sets and other pc collections. |
| Recapitulation | 257⁴–403² | | |
| | 257⁴–335 | Second subject group at $T_5$. | S9–S16 ($T_5$) and varied repetition of pc material from Exposition at $T_5$. |
| | 336–403² | First subject group at $T_5$. | S1–S3 ($T_5$) and varied repetition of pc from Exposition at $T_5$. |
| Coda | 403²–11 | First theme at $T_0$. | S1 ($T_0$) |

Large-scale unity across the entire quartet is achieved through cyclical procedures. These involve the varied recurrence and progressive transformation of the first movement's theme and its sets, particularly the thematic set S1, which, in slightly varied forms, is used as the main source for all four movements. In the second movement, *Thema con Variazioni*, the opening gesture of the *Thema* (*Andante molto espressivo*) (bars 1–3) is predominantly built on set S1 (see Example 9.5a).

This set is now segmented, with the first eight pitch-classes played by the first violin while the viola plays the retrograde of the last tetrachord as an ostinato figure. The continuation (bars 4–5) is based on new material, which is a variation of the opening phrase, with the thematic violin melody accompanied by an ostinato figure in the violas similar to that of bars 1–3. The opening gestures of

Example 9.5 Fourth String Quartet, *Thema con Variazioni*

(a) *Thema*: Opening gesture (bars 1–4)

(b) Var.I and Var.III – opening gestures (bars 23–4 and 85–6)

both Variation I (bars 23–4) and Variation III (bar 85) are built entirely on S1, partitioned between all four parts (see Example 9.5b). The continuation features similar textural and rhythmic content but is now based on the material of the *Thema*'s continuation phrase.

Skalkottas uses a large-scale palindrome to construct Variation V, *Andante lyrico* (bars 181–220). Bars 181–204 are an exact retrograde of the pitch-class content of bars 1–22 of the *Thema* (*Andante molto espressivo*), with part exchanges and variations in articulation and rhythm. Bars 205–20 are a varied representation of the twenty-two-bar-long *Thema*, with the material in its prime form. Example 9.5c shows the opening section of Variation V, with the pitch-class material of the *Thema* (bars 1–4) appearing first in retrograde and then in prime form around the axis of bar 204.

(c) Var.V (bars 181–6 and 200–06)

The opening gesture (bars 1–5) of the third movement, *Scherzo*, is built on a varied presentation of S1, whose segments are distributed among the four instruments (see Example 9.6).

Finally, the unifying cyclic relationship is fully manifested in the construction of the fourth movement, *Allegro giusto (e ben ritmato)*. Whereas the first thematic set S1 of the first movement is used as the starting point of the second and third movements, the opening of the fourth movement is based on the pitch-class material of the first movement's second subject group. The entire first 17 bars of the *Allegro giusto* are a varied repetition of the first movement's bars 65–79 (see Example 9.7). The linear arrangement of the three different set-groups comprising four sets each is maintained, although there are variations in the set presentation (including incomplete sets), articulation and rhythm, and some notes of the sets appear later in the theme.

Overall, the first movement has a structure similar to other large-scale pieces, such as the first movements of the Second and Third piano concertos and the Violin Concerto, with its form being defined by the *en bloc* transposition of sections. The second and third movements are developmental elaborations of the first one. The fourth movement is a varied recapitulation, starting with the second

Example 9.6  Fourth String Quartet, *Scherzo*: Opening gesture (bars 1–6)

Example 9.7  Fourth String Quartet, *Allegro giusto*: Opening gesture (bars 1–6)

subject group at the original tonal level, and progressing towards a reminiscence of the first theme in the cadence, which rounds off the entire piece. With regard to the set and thematic structure, and similar to the Third Piano Concerto, the piece is a large-scale reversed sonata form, with the first movement functioning as the Exposition, the second and third movements the Development, and the fourth movement the reversed Recapitulation. A schematic presentation of this reading is given in Table 9.11.

Finally, a distinctive feature of Skalkottas's music is not so much his adherence to traditional forms but his methods of constructing and evolving his formal designs based on tonal archetypes. Fugal procedures and Classical-style periodic phrases are constantly reassessed and fused to produce new narrative gestures at the small-scale structural level. Similarly, sonata and/or ternary structures are continually challenged and frequently combined with other forms (rondo, variations), as will be discussed in Part III. Such formal syntheses derive from the nineteenth- and early twentieth-century tradition of formal experimentation in instrumental and symphonic compositions, but they also reflect the conscious distortion of formal prototypes suggested by theorists Anton Reicha and A.B. Marx, for example.

Table 9.11    Fourth String Quartet: Large-scale formal structure and set structure

| Large-scale Sonata form | Fourth String Quartet | Thematic structure | Set structure |
| --- | --- | --- | --- |
| Exposition | *Allegro molto vivace* | Exposition: First subject group ($T_0$) – Second subject group ($T_0$). Development. Reversed Recapitulation: Second subject group ($T_5$) – First subject group ($T_5$). Coda ($T_0$). | First subject group: S1, S2, S3, S4. Second subject group: S5–S16, and many independent twelve-note melodies appearing only once. |
| Development | *Thema con variazioni* | *Thema*, Variations I–VI. | Both movements start with main thematic set S1, and include a variety of groups of new sets. |
|  | *Scherzo* | Scherzo–Trio–Scherzo. |  |
| Reversed Recapitulation | *Allegro giusto* | Rondo ABA$^1$CA$^2$Coda. It starts with the first movement's second subject group. It ends with a reminder of the first theme. | Sets S9–S16 and many independent twelve-note melodies appearing only once. Ends with S1. |

This practice occasionally results in formal ambiguity, and as Dahlhaus has noted in another context, 'it leave[s] open the question whether the ambiguity is to be assessed as differentiation or uncertainty, as sign of emancipation or formal decay' (Dahlhaus, 1983, 76). In Skalkottas's case, the stylistic corruption that arises from the merging of two styles and the reinterpretation of traditional forms leads to new and interesting musical structures.

# PART III
# Twelve-Note Compositional Development: Case Studies

*May you stop at Phoenician markets*
*and their fine things to buy,*
*mother of pearl and coral, amber and ebony,*
*[…]*
*May you visit many Egyptian cities*
*to learn and learn from their scholars.*
(Konstantinos Kavafis, *Ithaca*)

# Introduction to Part III

Throughout his compositional career Skalkottas developed various versions of his idiosyncratic twelve-note technique, occasionally using different approaches even within a single multi-movement work. These versions are predominantly distinguished by the number and handling of twelve-note sets and other pitch-class collections used within a piece. Although, conceptually, he had formulated the basic precepts of his approach before his studies with Schoenberg, his adoption of a twelve-note method evolved gradually during the late 1920s, and was fully established in the works of the mid-1930s. In particular, chamber music works from 1931 to around 1936, and again in 1948–49, are composed with a predetermined number of sets, largely superimposed as melodic lines in a polyphonic texture. Generally, but not exclusively, a different group of sets is used in each major section of a movement. The sets are reiterated as a group, defining both the small-scale phrase structure and the large-scale form. The 'strict' serial process in these pieces involves not the ordered rotation of an individual set's pitch-classes, but the ordered cyclical repetition of the set-group as a unit, and the reiteration of certain predetermined harmonic formations that result from the methodical pairing and association of sets and their segments. In some large-scale works, such as the First and Second Symphonic Suites, Skalkottas employs a predetermined number of various melodic and chordal sets, each defined by the neighbourhood relationships within their constituent segments. Such sets are used both linearly, superimposed in several parts, and successively, each distributed in the entire texture of a short temporal unit (for example, one bar).

In the large-scale works of the late 1930s and early 1940s, such as the Violin Concerto and the Overture for large orchestra (*The Return of Ulysses*), Skalkottas composed 'freely' with a very large number of sets of various types, different in each major phrase or passage of a movement, and predominantly defined by their segmental content. The sets are used more strictly in thematic statements, while elsewhere, particularly in developmental passages, they are used freely and unordered, while twelve-note melodies may appear only once. In works characterized by the expansion of the twelve-note material and the postponement of immediate set and set-group repetition, in order to establish the identity of the thematic groups, regulate the harmonic structure and define the form, Skalkottas used large-scale palindromes and/or transpositions of the entire texture of sections, predominantly at the perfect fifth ($T_7$) or perfect fourth ($T_5$).

From the late 1930s onwards, while simultaneously writing small-scale pieces based on his 'strict' twelve-note technique and large-scale works based on 'free' twelve-note techniques, Skalkottas also composed a series of short, characteristic chamber music pieces, such as the concert cycle for winds and piano,[1] the *Ten Sketches* for strings and the *32 Piano Pieces*. Although these exhibit the same principles of construction as the dodecaphonic works (that is, the linear, contrapuntal presentation of the material, textural stratification, and repetition or reiteration of groups of pitch-class collections, melodies and distinct harmonic formations), they are not built systematically on sets (twelve-note or otherwise), although the occasional twelve-note melody can be found in the texture. For lack of appropriate terminology, I describe such pieces as 'atonal'. Notwithstanding its limitations, this appears a more appropriate term than Papaioannou's and Demertzis's 'post–dodecaphonic', which implies a stylistic evolution beyond a clearly defined period of dodecaphonism. However, the compositional principles and techniques used in these atonal pieces are not discussed here, as they are beyond the scope of this book.

---

[1] This concert cycle includes the Concertino for oboe and piano (1939) (there is also a version for oboe and chamber orchestra), the First and Second Quartets for oboe, trumpet, bassoon and piano (1941–43), the Concertino for trumpet and piano (1941–43), and the *Sonata Concertante* for bassoon and piano (1943).

# Chapter 10
# Berlin Works

**Early Development from Composition with Groups of Unordered Pitch-class Collections to Twelve-Note Themes**

Skalkottas's early surviving Berlin works demonstrate the development of his harmonic language from advanced chromaticism to dodecaphonism, and they exhibit, in an embryonic form, many of the motivic, harmonic and formal techniques and compositional features employed in later twelve-note works. They are examples of the young Skalkottas's attempts to progressively reassess and re-accommodate the traditional within the new musical environment he was endeavouring to create. From an early stage he sought to synthesize Baroque and Classical formal procedures. He extensively used polyphonic textures, contrapuntal (particularly fugal) writing and bitonality, and he also experimented with traditional homophonic forms, all alongside the incorporation of dodecaphonic elements. The characteristic compositional processes established here include the use of:

1. distinct groups of referential pitch-class material, which are different in each section of a piece;
2. a limited number of thematic, ordered twelve-note sets, and groups of unordered pitch-class collections;
3. fixed set-segments, which are defined by their pitch-class content;
4. polyphonic writing and multi-layered textures, with each line or subtexture having its own rhythmic and harmonic structure and moving independently from the others, often resulting in conflicting harmonic events;
5. tonally centred melodic lines;
6. one intervallic motive (the minor third) that saturates the texture, providing motivic integration;
7. the abrupt juxtaposition of distinct harmonic regions, resulting from the use of groups of pitch-class material, each coinciding with the beginning of a major formal section and creating its own continuity and identity;
8. the transposition *en bloc* of the pitch-class content of a formal section, predominantly at $T_7$ and $T_5$, as a means of harmonic and formal differentiation.

The earliest surviving Berlin works (dating from 1924), the tonal *Greek Suite* for piano and two suites for two pianos,[1] are youthful experiments in elaborating and

---

[1] One of the two-piano suites is a transcription of two movements of the *Greek Suite* (*Tango* and *Vivace*), and the other is in two movements (*Presto, Fox-Trot*).

reworking a limited amount of source material in different movements to provide motivic and thematic integration. Such economization at the most fundamental compositional level remained a feature of Skalkottas's compositional technique throughout his career. This technique is found fully developed in several mature twelve-note works, with multi-movement pieces built on the twelve-note sets established at the opening of the first movement, such as, for example, in the Second String Trio, the Third and Fourth Sonatinas for violin and piano, the First Piano Suite, the Third Piano Concerto and the Second Symphonic Suite. The more advanced Sonata for solo violin (inscribed 'Sommer 1925'), in four movements related through cyclical elements, is characterized by a more advanced chromatic language than the earlier piano pieces, and could be considered a precursor to Skalkottas's linear approach to composition, with several melodic lines employed simultaneously and contrapuntally, often momentarily creating bitonal effects.[2] The works of 1927 exhibit a more advanced harmonic language, and incline towards atonality. In the surviving works of 1928–29 Skalkottas consolidated the basic premises of his compositional technique, which would feature almost unchanged in his later dodecaphonic works.[3] The First String Quartet in particular demonstrates a decisive step towards his linear approach to twelve-note composition.

### 15 Little Variations *for Piano Solo (1927): Composing with Groups of Unordered Pitch-class Sets*

The *15 Little Variations* (inscribed '24–26 July 1927'), Skalkottas's last composition before undertaking lessons with Schoenberg in the autumn of 1927, is a seminal work featuring the use and controlled manipulation of a referential group of unordered, but clearly defined pitch-class sets; this is a definitive moment in the evolution of his mature compositional technique. The piece comprises a set of character variations within the superstructure of an extended rounded binary form (A–BC–A'), shown in Table 10.1. Skalkottas closely follows the principles of the nineteenth-century prototype in that the harmonic scheme and formal plan of the theme remain fixed in the following 15 variations, while the thematic motives, part-writing, rhythm, tempo, mood and dynamics are all modified or new.

The *Thema*, outlining a binary phrase structure (bars 1–4, 5–8), consists of two unordered ten-note collections (F–G–D♯–G♯–B–B♭–F♯–E–A–D, and E♭–F–A–D–G–F♯–E–G–C–B♭) presented as a harmonic skeleton of two pairs of pentachords (set-classes [5–26] – [5–30], and [5–24] – [5–28]), as shown in Example 10.1. At the end of section A (bar 4), the linear motive B–C–A (set-class 3–2) functions

---

[2] The opening thematic material of the first movement is quasi-dodecaphonic and is used as the thematic source for the entire sonata. For a brief discussion of the early piano pieces and the violin sonata, see Mantzourani (1999, 155–60).

[3] The Second Sonatina for violin and piano has already been discussed in Part II. For a detailed discussion of the only surviving movement, *Andantino*, of the First Sonatina for violin and piano, see Mantzourani (1999, 176–84).

Table 10.1   *15 Little Variations* for piano: Formal structure

| Sections | Theme and variations | Thematic, phrase structure |
|---|---|---|
| A (1–62) | *Thema* | Exposition of thematic material in the form of a harmonic 'skeleton' (set-classes [5–26]–[5–30]–[5–26] – [5–24]–[5–28]–[5–24]). |
| | Var.I | Part-writing exchange. Introduction of new motivic ideas, with ascending melodic contour. |
| | Var.II | Transitional passage to Var.III. |
| | Var.III | Exposition of new secondary theme, accompanied by a change of tempo. |
| | Var.IV | Transitional passage to Var.V. Exchange of part-writing. |
| | Var.V | Retardation of tempo (*Moderato*). Introduction of 'foreign' notes.* |
| | Var.VI | Cadential passage, characterized largely by descending motivic contours and a unique cadential simultaneity, f♯–a–e♯$^1$–g♯$^2$. |
| B (63–98) | Var.VII | 'Lyrical' theme; metric change (3/4); slow tempo (*Andantino*). |
| | Var.VIII | Developmental passage; use of 'foreign' notes; faster tempo (*Allegro*). |
| | Var.IX | Transitional passage with a 'light' character, leading to section C. |
| C (99–154) | Var.X | New thematic ideas. Change in the harmonic structural skeleton with the chords presented in reverse order ([5–30]–[5–26]–[5–30] – [5–28]–[5–24]–[5–28]). Superimposition of a ternary melodic-phrase structure on the supporting harmonic framework, which retains its established binary scheme. Use of 'foreign' passing notes. |
| | Var.XI | Change of tempo, intense rhythmic activity, busy polyphony, use of high registers. |
| | Var.XII | Polyphonic, rhythmically active section; climax of the variation set. |
| | Var.XIII | Cadential passage; use of progressively slower tempos and longer note values. |
| A' (155–97) | Var.XIV | Recapitulation of the thematic material, in chordal presentation similar to the *Thema*. |
| | Var.XV | Lengthy cadential passage; change of tempo, and extensive use of pedal points. |
| Coda | | Motivic elaborations based on the initial A♭ minor chord. |

* In this context 'foreign' notes indicate notes that are not members of the fixed pitch-class collections that constitute the thematic material.

Example 10.1  *15 Little Variations for piano solo: Thema*

as the connective motive with section A′, and the chromatic pentachord G–G♯–E♯–A–F♯ in bar 8 connects with the following variation.

Each of the four pentachords is constantly divided into two segments, a dyad and a trichord, designated in Example 10.1 as a, b, and a′, b′. Throughout the piece, within these two-note and three-note segments the order of the pitch-classes can be changed and presented in any permutation that maintains the identity of the segment, a technique Skalkottas also employs almost exactly in all of his twelve-note works. Notwithstanding the triads embedded within the pentachords (G♯/A♭ minor, D minor, C major and C dominant seventh), in the *Thema* the chord succession does not exhibit any tonal functionality.[4] There is instead a static reiteration of the chord progression and, within each part of the binary structure, each chord is circled by its neighbouring one, as follows:

---

[4]  Whatever tonal tendency these chords may have is undermined by the supporting bass. The lower notes of the chords do not belong to the triads above them, and they do not function as a bass line that supports or establishes a key.

([5–26]–[5–30]–[5–26]) – ([5–30]–[5–26]–[5–30])
([5–24]–[5–28]–[5–24]) – ([5–28]–[5–24]–[5–28])

Furthermore, apart from changes in the surface motivic structure, Skalkottas establishes the large-scale formal design of the piece by assigning a different tempo and rhythmic patterns to each section, a technique he later also employed in the *Thema con Variazioni* of the First Symphonic Suite for large orchestra and the *Finale (Presto)* of the First Piano Suite, among other pieces. The use of referential pitch-class sets to build a piece, the extensive pitch-class reordering within fixed segments and the motivic developmental technique are also employed almost exactly in the *Passacaglia* from the *32 Piano Pieces*. Furthermore, the use and strict sequential presentation of sets (here four pentachords), with each set-statement encompassing the entire texture, becomes the predominant compositional device in certain large-scale orchestral works, such as several movements from the First and Second Symphonic Suites.

*First String Quartet (1928): Composing with unordered pitch-class collections and ordered twelve-note sets*

All three movements of the First String Quartet are built on several independent, linear twelve-note and non-twelve-note melodies, superimposed in as many voices, while the large-scale form is delineated through the unfolding of groups of pitch-class sets and their transpositions. In the first movement, *Allegro giusto*, modelled on the eighteenth-century sonata form prototype with a repeated exposition, Skalkottas uses the groups of pitch-class material in a manner that heralds the strict twelve-note practices of his Third String Quartet. Each instrument plays a melody based on a pitch-class set featuring several note repetitions (see Example 10.2).

Example 10.2   First String Quartet, *Allegro giusto*: Opening gesture (bars 1–5)

These melodic sets are treated as independent entities and are established through their continuous exact or slightly varied reiteration, while transposition articulates both the phrase structure and the large-scale form. For example, as shown in Table 10.2, within the first subject group, the consequent (bars 6–9) is built on the pitch-class material of the antecedent transposed at $T_{10}$, an unusual transpositional relationship between the two thematic phrases that is not used elsewhere – Skalkottas preferred the more traditional tonal relationships of $T_7$ or $T_5$ in establishing antecedent–consequent phrase structures. In the Recapitulation the second subject group is recapitulated transposed at $T_5$, thus emulating the secondary

Table 10.2  First String Quartet, *Allegro giusto*: Formal structure

| Thematic structure | Phrase and harmonic structure |
| --- | --- |
| **Exposition (repeated) (1–40)** ||
| First subject group | (1–5) First phrase (antecedent): theme in vln1; vln2+vla: parallel major thirds; vlc: melodic semitonal dyads; ends on an E♭ minor triad. (6–9) Second phrase (consequent): varied repetition of antecedent at $T_{10}$ with voice exchanges. (10–11¹) 'Modulatory' passage: vlc plays vln's melody at (4–5¹) transposed at $T_7$. |
| Transition | (11²–15) First phrase; (16–23¹) second phrase. |
| Second subject group | (23²–9¹) New group of pitch-class material; each instrument plays an independent melody. (29²–35) Repetition of (23²–9¹) with voice exchanges. |
| Codetta | (36–9¹) Repetition of the pitch-class content of (1–2) in vln2, vla, vlc with voice exchanges. (39–40) Modulatory transition: as (2–3¹) transposed at $T_5$. |
| **Development (41–76)** ||
|  | (41–54) First section. (41–2): modulatory sequential treatment of the opening motive: f♯²–g♯²–a²–d² (55–66) Contrasting section. (67–76) Material from first theme – retransition. |
| **Recapitulation (77–126)** ||
| First subject group | (77–80) First phrase; varied recapitulation of (2–5) with voice exchanges and rhythmic variations. (81–6¹)Second phrase with modulatory movement and voice exchanges. (82)=(78, or 2) at $T_3$; (83)=(79, or 3) at $T_5$; (84)=(8) at $T_3$; (85)=(9) at $T_5$; (86–7¹)=(10–11¹) at $T_5$. |
| Transition ($T_5$) | (86–96¹)=(11²–13) and (16–23¹) at $T_5$. |
| Second subject group ($T_5$) | (96²–102¹)=(23²–9¹) at $T_5$. (102²–8)=(29–35) at $T_5$. |
| Codetta ($T_5 - T_0$) | (109–11)=(36–7) at $T_5$. (112) vln1+vln2 at $T_5$, vla+vlc at $T_0$. (113–14) Continuation at $T_0$. |
| Coda | (114²–26) Based predominantly on vln2+vla material from (1) in parallel sixths. |

development section often found in late eighteenth-century sonatas, where the 'second phrase' appears transposed in the subdominant (Rosen, 1988, 288–9). Skalkottas also applied this technique in the third movement, *Allegro (ben ritmato) vivace*, and in the mature, large-scale Third Piano Concerto and the Fourth String Quartet.

The second movement, *Andante con variazioni*, consists of a theme and three variations. The theme outlines a ternary form, A (1–12) – B (13–20) – A' (21–8), with each section based on a different group of linear pitch-class material, treated as independent melodic lines (see Example 10.3). The harmonic skeleton of the theme is preserved in Variations I and II, while the developmental Variation III introduces new pitch-class collections.

Similarly, each section of the third movement, *Allegro (ben ritmato) vivace*, is built on a different group of unordered pitch-class sets and independent melodies (see Example 10.4).

Example 10.3    First String Quartet, *Andante con variazioni*: Opening gesture
                (bars 1–6)

Example 10.4    First String Quartet, *Allegro (ben ritmato) vivace*: Opening gesture
                (bars 1–4)

As shown in Table 10.3, its formal design combines a rondo (ABA[B¹] CA'B'C'A'') with a large-scale rounded binary form (ABa'), the latter suggested by the *en bloc* transposition of consecutive sections at $T_5$, and the return to the original tonal level ($T_0$) at the end of the movement.

Table 10.3   First String Quartet, *Allegro (ben ritmato) vivace*: Formal structure

| Rounded binary form | Sections Rondo form | Phrase structure |
|---|---|---|
| A ($T_0$) | A | Rounded binary phrase structure: a (1–4); b (5–9); a' (9⁴–13)=(1–4). |
|  | B | a (14–16¹); b (16²–17)=(14); b' (18)=(15–16¹ ($T_5$)). a (19–20); a' (21)=(19–20); a'' (22)=(18 ($T_6$)); b (24–33). |
|  | A | Repetition of (1–13) with voice exchanges. |
|  | [B¹] | Codetta with rhythmic material similar to those of section B. |
|  | C | Developmental section. a (52–5); (56–7)=(52–3 ($T_6$)); (58–9). b (60–73). |
| B (A($T_5$)) | A' | (74–86)=(1–13 ($T_5$)) with voice exchanges. |
|  | B' | (87–101)=(14–28 ($T_5$)); (110)=(50 ($T_5$)). |
|  | C' | (111–20¹)=(52–61¹ ($T_5$)). |
| a' ($T_0$) | A'' | a (132–38): (134–35)=(132–33 ($T_0$)). b (139–43): (139–41)=(11–12); (142)=(11–12). |

**First Piano Concerto (1931): An Experiment in Free Twelve-note Composition**

The First Piano Concerto is an ambitious experiment in Skalkottas's fledgling dodecaphonic technique, in which he simultaneously tries out several diverse ways of dealing with the treatment of twelve-note sets and the possibilities for development they offer. In later dodecaphonic works he adapted and refined several of the techniques tested here, but he only used each one individually in any given movement.

*First Movement*, Allegro Moderato: *Twelve-note Set Structure and Developing Variation*

The first movement, *Allegro moderato*, is structured as a reversed sonata form with double Exposition. Each section of the Exposition and the Development is built on several sets, which are treated linearly and contrapuntally throughout. In the orchestral Exposition I, the first subject group (bars 1–33) outlines three thematic ideas, each based on new, closely related twelve-note sets (thus giving the impression that each theme is a varied repetition of the previous one), and a plethora of other pitch-class collections (predominantly unordered hexachords) that are different in each phrase (see Example 10.5).

Example 10.5  First Piano Concerto, *Allegro moderato*: First subject group – opening gestures of first, second and third themes

An ascending glissando in the cellos initiates the decisive first theme, based on the twelve-note set S1 and played by the first and second violins (bars 1–5). The orchestral accompaniment is built on different pitch-class collections, largely hexachords, which are used freely throughout the thematic passage. The second theme, played by the upper strings (bars 13–18), is based on a new ten-note set S2; during its exposition it includes the repetition of the six pitch-classes D–C♯–B–B♭–G–A, in order to reinforce the structural importance of this hexachord (set-class 6–Z10), which features prominently in the motivic development of the movement. The third theme is built on the triple counterpoint of two twelve-note sets, S3 and S4. The main thematic idea, based on S3, is played as a canon at the octave between the first violins and the violas, and is supported contrapuntally by the second violins playing S4.

The lower strings accompany with dyads that derive from two hexachords (set-classes 6–Z11 and 6–Z39).

The second subject group (bars 34–66) delineates two main thematic ideas, the first one conveying the first, calm (*ruhig*), lyrical theme in the clarinet (bars 34–41). As a whole, the section is segmented into small phrases discreetly punctuated by contrasting instrumental colours, with the linear sets that controlled the first subject group here replaced by shorter motivic cells. This section is built on two unordered complementary hexachords (set-class 6–Z38/6–Z6), but for clarity this is referred to here as set S5. Skalkottas uses not only the unordered hexachords of the original source set in their prime form, but also the hexachords of the inverted form transposed at the minor third ($I_3$). He partitions the set into four, three-note, unordered segments, which are dispersed in the orchestral texture. More importantly, he manipulates not only the pitch-class order within each segment but also its pitch content, to produce new 'iridescent' sets. 'Iridescent' sets, a term coined by Alsmeier (2001, 122–8), consist of set segments that gradually change their pitch-class content. Specifically, each trichordal segment of the source set, S5, is submitted to a transformational process by gradually replacing a single note; in consecutive phrases, the identity of the trichord is maintained by preserving two of its notes and changing the third. The newly resulting segment thus deviates only minimally from that used in the immediately preceding phrase. Apart from the transformation within each trichord, the order of the trichords also changes occasionally. Example 10.6 represents schematically the pitch-class content of the first theme of the second subject group, and the distribution of the trichordal segments in the texture.

The contrasting *ff* second theme of the second subject group, indicated as *führend* (leading) (bars 50–56), and played in unison by the flutes and upper strings, is based on set S6, which consists of two unordered hexachords (set-classes 6–Z38 and 6–Z6($T_{10}$)) that result from the transformational treatment of the trichordal pitch-class content thus far. This segmental transformation occurs not only within the second subject group in Exposition I, but also at the equivalent sections in Exposition II and the Recapitulation. Table 10.4 represents schematically the set structure and gradual transformation process within each unordered trichord of the source twelve-note set (S5) at equivalent passages in these sections.

The use of such 'iridescent' sets demonstrates Skalkottas's version of developing variation technique. It is possible that, in order to control the large amount of diverse pitch-class material he was using in this movement, Skalkottas adapted Schoenberg's principle that 'relationships of parts to the whole and to one another are close at hand when at least one of the most essential parts is contained in the other' (Schoenberg, 1994, 22–5); that is, Skalkottas felt that the gradual transformation of the segments, whereby two parts of the whole remained the same and one changed, provided relationship to the connecting parts and ensured coherence and comprehensibility.

The Development proper is short (bars 127–54), and Skalkottas, abruptly interrupting the developmental technique used in the second subject group, returns

Example 10.6  First Piano Concerto, *Allegro moderato*: First theme of the second subject group – distribution of the pitch-class trichordal segments in the texture (bars 34–45)

to the linear approach of the first subject group and explores further the serial properties of the various pitch-class collections used there. The source pitch-class material comprises predominantly unordered hexachords, used not only in their prime form but also in transposed and inverted forms. The most prominent thematic idea, first introduced by the piano right-hand in bars 138–9 is based on a new set S7. Its first hexachord in particular (6–Z36) is the most distinctive melodic feature of the Development and is used as an independent six-note melody transposed and inverted throughout the section.

However, the compositional approach of the movement as a whole lacks consistency and cohesiveness in respect of a unifying twelve-note technique. In the first subject group there is only localized serial treatment of the pitch-class

Table 10.4   First Piano Concerto, *Allegro moderato*: Set structure and set transformation process

| Exposition I | Exposition II | | Recapitulation | | |
|---|---|---|---|---|---|
| First subj group | First subj group | | First subj group | | |
| Bars 1–33 | 67–101 | | 171–204 | | |
| S1 (1–12)<br>S2 (13–18)<br>S3–S4 (24–9) | S1var (67–74)<br>S2var (79–86)<br>S3–S4var (91/99–100) | | S1 (171–9)<br>S2 (181–8)<br>S3 (elements) (201–4) | | |
| Second subj group | Second subj group | | Second subj group | | |
| 34–41 | 102–4 | | 155–8 (pno) | 155–8 (ww) | 157–8 (pnoRH/ tbn/str) |
| E–B–G<br>F–C–G♭<br>D–B♭–G♯<br>E♭–C♯–A | E–B–F♯<br>F–C–G<br>D–B♭–A♭<br>E♭–C♯–A | | E–B–C<br>F–F♯–G<br>D–C♯–G♯<br>A–B♭–E♭ | E–C–G<br>F–F♯–B<br>D–B♭–A<br>A♭–D♭–E♭ | E–B–F<br>F♯–C–G<br>D–B♭–G♯<br>A–C♯–E♭ |
| 41–5 | 105–6 | 107 | 155–8 | | |
| E–C–G<br>F–C–G♭<br>D–B♭–A<br><br>E♭–A♭–D♭ | E–C–B<br>F–G–F♯<br>D–E♭–A<br><br>E♭–A♭–D♭ | E–C–G<br>F–B–F♯<br>D–E♭–A<br>(D–B♭–A)<br>A♭–D♭–B♭–<br>(A♭–D♭–E♭) | E–C–B<br>F–G–F♯ | | |
| 46–7 | 108 | | 159–60 | | |
| E–C–B<br>E♭–B♭–G♭<br>D–F–A<br>A♭–D♭–G | E–C–B<br>E♭–B♭–G♭<br>D–F–A<br>A♭–D♭–G | | E–C–B<br>E♭–B♭–G♭<br>D–F–A<br>A♭–D♭–G | | |
| 48–9 (orch) | 109–10 (pno RH) | | 160–61 (pno) | | |
| E–C–F♯<br>D♯–A♯–B<br>A♭–A–F<br>D–C♯–G | E–C–F♯<br>D♯–A♯–B<br>A♭–A–F<br>D–C♯–G | | E–C–B<br>E♭–B♭–G<br>A♭–D♭–F<br>D–F♯–A | | |

| 48–9 (vlc/kb/bsn) | 109–10 (pno LH) |  | 161–3² | 163³⁻⁴ |
|---|---|---|---|---|
| E–C–B<br>E♭–B♭–G<br>D–F♯–A<br>A♭–D♭–G | E–C–B<br>E♭–B♭–G<br>D–F♯–A<br>A♭–D♭–G |  | E–C–A<br>E♭–B♭–F<br>D–F♯–B<br>A♭–D♭–G | E–C–D<br><br>A–F♯–B |
| 50–56 | 111–5 |  | 164–70 (pno) |  |
| G♯–C–F♯<br>E♭–B♭–E<br>D–F–A<br>B–C♯–G | A♭–C–G<br>E♭–B♭–E<br>D–F–A<br>B–C♯–F♯ |  | B♭–C–F<br>D♯–B–G<br>D–F–A<br>G♯–C♯–F♯ |  |
| 50–56 (vln/fl) | 111–5 (vln/fl) |  | 165 (ww) |  |
| A♭–C–G<br>E–B♭–F<br>D–E♭–A<br>B–C♯–F♯ | B–C–G<br>D–B♭–F<br>E–E♭–A<br>G♯–C♯–F♯ |  | B–C–C♯<br>C–B♭(E)–F<br>E–E♭–D |  |
| 57 | 115–17 |  |  |  |
| G♯–C–C♯<br>G♭–B♭–F<br>D♭–E♭–E<br>D–C♯–D♯–E | A♭–C–D♭<br>G♭–B♭–F<br>D♭–E♭–E<br>D–C♯–D♯–E |  |  |  |

material. There are motivic similarities and correspondences between the sets, but overall the material is difficult to absorb owing to the lack of immediate repetition, the complexity of the texture and the size of the movement. In the second subject group Skalkottas abandons linear twelve-note writing and explores instead a motivic developmental technique. Although the significant number of gradually changing motivic cells within the small-scale phrase structure is logically controlled, this technique cannot be considered strictly dodecaphonic, as it can equally be used to compose atonal or even tonal works. Furthermore, the expansion and profusion of gradually changing trichordal pitch-class segments, and the composition with a large number of hexachords, results in an unfocused harmonic structure. In contrast to later works (also based on a free twelve-note technique and using large numbers of sets), here Skalkottas does not use block transposition of entire sections to shape the form and define the harmonic structure of the movement. And if we are to believe that there was ever a disagreement between Schoenberg and Skalkottas about this concerto (as discussed in Part I, pp.37–8), it might have been about this somewhat disjointed compositional approach, or rather the lack of compositional consistency in one movement. If so, although Skalkottas did not revise this particular piece, in later works he did not use again in such a rigorous and sustained way the transformation technique he applied in the second subject group.

*Second Movement,* Andante Cantabile

The *Andante cantabile* as shown in Table 10.5, outlines an expanded Andante form (AA¹BA'B'Coda), which Schoenberg in his *Fundamentals* groups with the rondo forms (1970/1990, 190).

Table 10.5   First Piano Concerto, *Andante cantabile*: Formal structure and set structure

| Sections | Thematic and set structure |
|---|---|
| **Exposition (1–35)** ||
| A (orch ritornello) | First theme<br>(1–5) First phrase (antecedent). First theme: ob+hn (S1); countermelody: bcl (S2); accomp: strings (S1a).<br>(6–10¹) Second phrase (consequent). Melodic continuation of first theme: vln1 (S2). String accomp (S1 and S1a).<br>(10²–13) Codetta: S1 divided among ww and strings; (S1a segments). |
| A¹ (pno and orch) | Varied repetition of first theme<br>(14–20) pno RH upper melody (RS1a); pno LH (S1).<br>(20–31) ww and hn (S2).<br>(21) Change of metre to ¾; pno and strings (S2).<br>(22–4) pno solo (S1).<br>(25–8): pno RH (S1a); pno LH (S1).<br>(29–35) Cadential phrase of A¹. (33–4) Pno and strings (S1, S1a, S2). |
| B (pno and orch) | Second theme<br>(36–40²) Second theme based on four new twelve-note sets (S3, S4, S5, S6), and RS6.<br>(40³–45²) Continuation; pno (RS6); fl1 (S3); fl2 (S4).<br>(45–8) Climactic cadence. S6 saturates the texture of the last phrase. |
| **Recapitulation (49–76)** ||
| A' | First theme<br>(49–53) Rhythmically varied repetition of (1–5); first theme: fl (S1). S1a divided between ww and brass; xylophone (S2); strings (S1a) (*pizzicato*). |
| | (54–8) Varied repetition of (6–10). Use of inversion, and retrograde of the inversion of the sets pno RH upper melody (IS1); pno RH middle melody (IS2); pno LH (S1b); at (55) vln1 (RS2 trichords); at (56) ww: (IS1 segms). |
| | (59–65) Metric changes.<br>(63–65) Cadential phrase of A' based on S1. |
| B' | Second theme<br>(66–69) pno solo with second theme; pno RH upper melody (S3); pno RH middle melody (S4); pno LH (S5). |
| | (70–76) orch and pno. pno: chords in (70⁴–72¹); sets of the second theme. |
| Coda | (77–83) Varied repetition of the first theme. Use of retrograde and inversion of sets (S1a, S1b).<br>(77–79) pno (S1a); (80–81) S1a and IS1 segms; (82–3): S1.<br>(84–85¹) pno RH (IS1 second hex); pno LH (IS1 first hex).<br>(85–91) Built entirely on new set S7. |

Here Skalkottas applies a more homogeneous twelve-note technique, which involves groups of twelve-note sets that are different in each major section of the movement. The sets, however, are not treated strictly; they are usually partitioned into segments distributed freely in the texture and frequently used unordered as independent motives. Skalkottas also experiments with the use of transposition, inversion and retrograde forms of these sets, together with the generation of derived sets. For example, as shown in Example 10.7, the opening gesture of the movement is built on three sets: S1 (played by the woodwinds and horns), S2 (played by the bass clarinet and having its last pentachord played chordally by the upper strings and upper woodwinds), and S1a (played by the strings).[5]

Example 10.7  First Piano Concerto, *Andante cantabile*: First theme – opening gesture (bars 1–5)

In the varied repetition of the first theme's second phrase (bars 54–8), the piano enters playing three sets: the upper right-hand melody is based on the ordered inversion of S1 (IS1), while the lower right-hand countermelody plays IS2; the left hand plays S1b.[6] (see Example 10.8).

---

[5]  Set S1a derives from a pitch-class reordering within each trichord of the retrograde form of S1, as follows:

| S1 | 1 2 3 4 5 6 | 7 8 9 10 11 12 |
|---|---|---|
| S1a (RS1) | 11 12 10 9 7 8 | 5 4 6 1 3 2 |

[6]  Set S1b derives from a reordering within each trichord of the retrograde inversion of S1 (RIS1), as follows:

| IS1 | 1 2 3 4 5 6 | 7 8 9 10 11 12 |
|---|---|---|
| S1b (RIS1) | 12 11 10 7 8 9 | 5 6 4 1 2 3 |

Example 10.8  First Piano Concerto, *Andante cantabile*: Piano entry at bars 54–8

The second theme (bars 36–48) is built on four new, closely connected sets, S3, S4, S5 and S6, and the strict retrograde RS6;[7] these are used linearly and contrapuntally throughout. The treatment of the sets is not strict and includes segment repetition and interpolation within a set, together with the free distribution of segments in the texture.

*Third movement,* Allegro vivace

Skalkottas's experimentation with his twelve-note compositional technique continues yet more intensely in the third movement, *Allegro vivace*, which is in sonata form, shown in Table 10.6. Similar to the previous two movements, each section is built on a different group of a large number of pitch-class sets, superimposed in several textural layers; some of these sets are used only fleetingly in one section, while several derive from sets of the first movement, thus reinforcing cyclic references and connections across the concerto.

The first subject group is built on six closely related sets (S1, S1a, S2, S3, S4, S5).[8] The second subject group is built on three sets, S6, S7, S8, which are presented simultaneously and treated contrapuntally,[9] and the Development introduces three

---

[7]  S3 includes the hexachord C–D–E–F♯–C♯–D♯ (set-class 6–2), which is a $T_{11}$ transposition of the hexachord set-class 6–2 of S1b. S4 includes the hexachord C♯–F–E♭–A♭–A–D (set-class 6–Z17), which is a $T_8$ transposition of the equivalent hexachord of S1a. S3 and S4 share the hexachord A–B–C–D–E–F♯ (set-class 6–33). S5 has eleven different pitch-classes, with the D repeated and the C♯ missing; its first tetrachord is a $T_5$ transposition of the last tetrachord of S2b. S6 has several common trichords and tetrachords with other sets.

[8]  Set S1a derives from the retrograde of S1 through pitch-class reordering within each trichord. S2 is an unordered transposition at $T_{10}$ of S1 of the first movement, while S3 is an unordered transposition at the tritone ($T_6$) of S8 of the first movement. S5 is constantly presented as a set of six dyads.

[9]  Set S6 derives from the ten-note set S6 of the first movement (piano RH, bars 138–9); its first hexachord (set-class 6–Z36) is an exact transposition at the minor sixth of

new derived sets, S9, S10, S11.[10] Skalkottas continues the development in the Recapitulation, and although he predominantly recycles the sets of the Exposition, with S1, S1a, S2 and S3 being thematically prominent and most frequently used, he also introduces three derived sets (S12, S13, S14).[11] The sets are used thematically as melodies to be varied and developed in the traditional sense. Perhaps because Skalkottas was aware by this point that the relentless transformation of a plethora of source material would diffuse the piece as an organic entity, he uses several cyclical correspondences between the first movement, *Allegro moderato*, and this third movement. In both, the interval of a descending third predominates in the melodic shape of the first subject, while the second theme is a transposed cyclic repetition, with the same rhythm and melodic contour of the secondary thematic idea of the first movement's Development section (bars 138–9).

As in the first movement, here there is a proliferation of source and derived sets, and a lack of strict serial treatment to control the diverse pitch-class material. Although Skalkottas applies a similar compositional technique in the large-scale dodecaphonic concertos of the late 1930s, with the free treatment of a plethora of different sets in each section of a movement, the predominant thematic sets are treated strictly, and are frequently used as signposts throughout the movement. Their segments are more easily recognizable as structural, melodic and harmonic units, often associated with particular instrumental colours and always remaining in the vicinity of the other segments of the set, thus reinforcing neighbourhood relationships. Meanwhile, the transposition and/or palindromes of entire sections control the harmonic structure and contribute to the definition of the form.

## Octet (1931): Consolidation of the Twelve-note Technique

The Octet, scored for woodwinds (flute, oboe, B♭ clarinet and bassoon) and string quartet, marks a decisive step in Skalkottas's efforts to hone his version of composing with twelve notes. In terms of its dodecaphonic serial treatment, the second and third movements, in particular, consolidate some of the compositional

---

the corresponding first hexachord, while the common tetrachord of the second half is also a $T_8$ transposition of the equivalent segment of S6. S7 derives from the retrograde of the $I_6$ form of S2 through a reordering within the hexachords; its first pentachord is an unordered presentation of pitch-classes with order numbers 7,..,11 of S2 (at $T_0$). S8 shares five pitch-classes within each hexachord of RS6.

[10] S10 is a 'derived' set, consisting of three diminished tetrachords (set-class 4–28), each a semitone higher than the previous one. S11 is first presented as six dyads; in its linear presentation, however, it derives from a reordering within each hexachord of the $I_7$ form of S6.

[11] S14 has eleven different pitch-classes (the E is doubled and the B is missing); it derives from S6, through an exchange of unordered hexachords, while each of its hexachords also has an $I_4$ inversional relationship with each hexachord of S3.

Table 10.6   First Piano Concerto, *Allegro vivace*: Formal structure and set structure

| Thematic structure | Phrase and set structure | Sets |
|---|---|---|
| \multicolumn{3}{c}{**Exposition** (1–80)} | | |
| First subject group (1–50) | | S1, S1a, S2, S3, S4, S5 |
| pno solo (1–14) | First theme (1–5) (a) Antecedent; pno RH$^1$ (S1); pno RH$^2$ (S2); pno LH (S1a). | S1, S1a, S2 |
| | (5$^2$–10) (b) Consequent; new pitch-class material same rhythm as (a). | S3 |
| | (11–14) (a′) Varied repetition of (a); pno LH (S1); pno RH (interpolation of S1a and S2); S1, S1a, S2 (interpol of segms). | S1, S1a, S2 |
| orch ritornello (15–21$^1$) | (15–21) New material in the orch (S4). | S4 |
| pno and orch (21$^2$–42) | (21$^2$–8) Thematic material in pno; first phrase based on (S4). (29–32) Second phrase based on (S5). | S5; unord segms S1, S2, S1a |
| | (33–6) Continuation. | S1a, S1, S5 (segm interpol) |
| | (37–42) Third phrase; (S3) distributed in orch; pno (S1, S1a segms). | S3, S1, S1a. |
| | Codetta (43–50) Motivic liquidation and textural reduction. (44–8) S1, S1a, S2; (49–50) S1 (segms). | S1, S1a, S2. |
| Second subject group (51–80) | | S6, S7, S8 |
| orch ritornello (51–67) | Second theme (51–7) First phrase (S6, S7, S8); cyclic material from the first movt. (58–67) Varied repetition; contrapuntal treatment of sets, particularly S6 first hexachord. | S6, S7, S8 |
| pno exposition (68–80) | (68–75) Second theme varied; interpolation of set segms; minimal orch accomp. | S6, S7, S8 (segms) |
| | (76–80) Cadential passage (held notes in tpt). | S6, S7 |
| \multicolumn{3}{c}{**Pno cadenza in place of Development** (81–98)} | | |
| Cadenza (81–98) | (81–85) New material in pno (S9, S9a). Minimal orch accomp (held notes in bsn and hns). | S9 (dyads), S9a, S8 (chordal tetrachords) |

| Thematic structure | Phrase and set structure | Sets |
|---|---|---|
| | (86–9) Cadenza proper (S10, S10a). | S10, S10a (S10a=RS10 in chordal tetrachords) |
| | (90–96) Phrase based on (S11). | S11 (pno dyads), S11(linear), S10 (segms) |
| | (97–8) Retransition to the Recapitulation. Metric modulation. | S1 |
| **Developmental Recapitulation (99–196)** | | |
| First subject group (99–172) | | S1, S1a, S2, S3, S4, S5, S12, S13 |
| | (99–102) pno solo – first theme; varied recap of (1–5); pno RH$^1$(S1); pno RH$^2$ (S2); pno LH (S1a). | S1, S1a, S2 |
| | (103–7) Developmental passage in orch + pno. | Independent set-segms |
| | (108–13$^1$) (a) Varied recap (1–5); same sets in orch; new pno theme (S12, S13). | S1, S1a, S2, S12, S13 |
| | (112$^2$–7) (b) Varied recap (6–10). | S3 |
| | (118–21) (a′) Varied recap (11–14); pno (S12, S13). | S1, S1a, S2, S12, S13 |
| | (122–32) Developmental equivalent to (15–21); (133–8) = equivalent to (21–5); (139–40) = equivalent to (26–8). | S4 |
| | (141–4) pno solo; varied repetition of (29–32). | S1, S1a, S5 |
| | (145–8) pno and vlc in theme–countertheme contrapuntal texture. | S3 (pno), S14 (vlc) |
| | (149–55) Continuation. | S1, S1a |
| | (156–73) orchestral recap of Expo's first subj group (36–50). Codetta (166–71): varied repetition of (44–8); (172)=(49–50). | S1, S3, S1a, S2 |
| Second subject group (173–92) | (173–5) pno recap second theme. Varied repetition of (51–7). | S6, S7, S8 |
| | (176–92) Varied repetition of (58–67); (176–82): pno with minimal orch accomp; (183–92) contrapuntal treatment of sets in orch. | S6, S7, S8 |
| | (193–6) Cadence; solo pno: varied recap of (37–41). | S3 |
| **Coda (*Presto*) (197–221)** | | |
| | (197–8) pno: repetition of (49–50). | S1 |
| | (199–208) Varied (1–5). | S1, S1a, S2 |
| | (207$^2$–11) Varied (6–10). | S3 |
| | (212–21) Varied (29–36). | S1, S1a, S2, S4 |

processes tried out in the First Piano Concerto. In all three movements Skalkottas employs his established set-group technique, with each section being identified by its set content. In contrast to the Concerto, however, here the treatment of the sets is strict, with the development circumscribed and evolving organically out of the primary material. Textural and timbral changes, resulting from the juxtaposition and rapid alternation of instrumental groupings, coincide with the successive reappearance of the set groups and contribute to the delineation of the small-scale form.

Each of its three movements explores a different aspect of Skalkottas's twelve-note technique. The *Allegro moderato*, although featuring some twelve-note melodies, is not exclusively dodecaphonic, and its multi-sectional design integrates two different forms. By contrast, the *Andante cantabile* is entirely dodecaphonic, and establishes the linear, polyphonic technique that will also be used in most of the mid-1930s and late 1940s chamber works. The *Presto* is built on a large number of sets, and its formal design is predominantly determined by the operation of transposition – a technique similarly but not as comprehensively employed in the earlier First String Quartet and the First and Second Sonatinas for violin and piano.

*First Movement,* Allegro Moderato: *A Study in Formal Synthesis*[12]

At first glance, the *Allegro moderato*'s form appears to outline a combination of rondo (ABA$^1$CA$^2$B$^2$A'B'C'Coda[A$^3$B$^3$A$^1$]) and a ternary structure (Parts I, II, III, Coda), demarcated by Skalkottas's double bar lines at the ends of sections C, B$^2$, and C', as shown in Table 10.7.

Table 10.7　Octet, *Allegro moderato*: Reading of the formal design as a combination of rondo and ternary forms

| Sections | A | B | A$^1$ | C | A$^2$ | B$^2$ | A' | B' | C' | A$^3$ | B$^3$ | A$^1$ |
|---|---|---|---|---|---|---|---|---|---|---|---|---|
| Parts | I ||| | II || | III ||| Coda |||

Each section of Part I establishes a referential group of pitch-class material, motivic figures and harmonic formations that reappear in Part III, as if returning to the 'home key'. Section A outlines a period structure, largely defined by texture and timbre, in which the strings play the antecedent while the repetition of the theme in the consequent is given to the winds. The thematic melody, played by the first violin (bars 1–4$^1$), is based on a tonal twelve-note set (S1) whose internal structure contains the A♭, G, and A major triads. The second violin, playing the countermelody, is based on a pitch-class collection that features several note repetitions, while the viola and cello accompany contrapuntally in similar rhythmic patterns with independent melodies (see Example 10.9).

---

[12]　Sections of the following discussion appear in Mantzourani (2004b, 73–86).

Example 10.9  Octet, *Allegro moderato*: Section A – opening gesture (bars 1–4¹)

Section B, introduced by an abrupt change of texture and mood, presents a new thematic idea in the bassoon (bars 7⁴–11), based on a new twelve-note set S2 (see Example 5.1). Section A¹ is characterized by a dense, antiphonal texture between the winds and strings; there is a clear break at the end of this section, as abrupt textural, timbral and articulative changes introduce section C. Here, the slower and more lyrical main thematic melody in the first violin (bars 23³–28) is based on S3, which derives from the pitch-class material of section A;[13] as noted in Chapter 4, 'Incomplete and Irregular Twelve-note Sets' (p. 97), this does not include twelve different pitch-classes in its internal structure.

Part II is shorter than the outer parts and is divided into two sections (A², B²), each loosely based on the pitch-class material of the principal themes of sections A and B in Part I. The main thematic idea of section A², played by the oboe, is based on a twelve-note set that is an exact transposition at the fourth ($T_5$) of the thematic set S1, and the dance-like thematic melody of section B² in the first violin is a varied presentation of S2, through a reordering of its trichordal segments. The introduction of new melodies, which might at first seem arbitrary, can be traced back to a few basic and characteristic motives of Part I.

Part III, introduced with abrupt changes in texture, timbre, dynamics and mood, is a varied repetition of Part I, without the reappearance of A¹ between sections B and C. Skalkottas reinforces the final cadence with a tempo change (*langsamer werden*), and the final chord is based on S1.

However, the movement's textural and motivic layout, the thematic organization with contrasting themes, the cadential structure at the end of each

---

[13]  The first hexachord of S3 (f¹–e²–d²–c♯²–d♯²–c²) is an unordered transposition at $T_5$ of the six-note second violin melody in the cadential bars 7–8¹, while the second hexachord (b♭¹–a¹–b¹–c²–e²–e♭²) has an $I_4$ relationship with the accompanimental viola melody in bars 1–2.

section, and, in particular, the tonally oriented bass line, all invite a reading of the overall form as modified sonata with cyclical rondo elements. Although the bass is an independent line within the polyphonic texture, Skalkottas constructs it in a manner comparable to tonal bass lines. His treatment of register, timbre and articulation asserts the notes G, C, F and B♭$_1$ as the predominant tonal centres, often approached by perfect fifth and semitonal voice-leading movement, and Skalkottas exploits the tonal allusions resulting from the voice-leading in the bass line to control and delineate the large-scale form. As shown in Example 10.10,[14] the large-scale movement in the bass (cello and bassoon), even decontextualized, presents an interplay of tension and resolution analogous to traditional tonal patterns of harmonic movement in sonata form.

Example 10.10   Octet, *Allegro moderato*: Large-scale movement in the bass line

Taking this bass line into account, section C can be perceived as an integral section of Part II, if we disregard Skalkottas's double bar line at its end and consider instead the natural break of the music at the end of section A$^1$, the character and textural layout of the different themes, and the continuous musical flow between sections C and A$^2$. Thus sections A and B can be seen as the 'first subject group', with the voice-leading of the bass line in sections A, B and A$^1$ implying a movement from G (at the cadence of section A) to C (at the final cadence of section A$^1$), reminiscent of a V–I tonal movement. Section C, with its lyrical thematic idea, can now be seen as the 'second theme', which establishes the note F as the predominant tonal centre in the bass, thus implying a move to the 'subdominant'. According to this reading, sections A$^2$ and B$^2$ function as the Development section. Section A$^2$ has a transpositional relation at the fourth (T$_5$) with the opening section A, albeit a tenuous one, and is comparable to an episode in the subdominant, often used in Classical sonata rondos and sonata forms. Section B$^2$, with its thin texture, predominantly semitonal motivic structure and the relatively long pedal point on note G, functions as the retransition leading to the recapitulation of the first part of the movement. The Recapitulation (Part III) returns to the opening thematic material; the cadential structure of all sections (A'B'C') is similar to that of Part I, albeit now more clearly defined, with section A' cadencing on G (V), and both sections B' and C' cadencing on C (I). Overall, therefore, the placement of the double bar lines at the ends of sections C, B$^2$ and C' appear to demarcate the Exposition, Development and Recapitulation of the

---

[14]   In the example, the slurs connecting two notes indicate the support of a note by a linear fifth relationship, and crotchets represent tonal centres.

sonata form. Such an interpretation of the piece suggests that Skalkottas sought to integrate the Exposition and Development sections. This perhaps explains why, in the Recapitulation, section C is the least developed, helping to readjust the balance required by the formal prototype. Table 10.8 represents schematically the formal and cadential structure of the *Allegro moderato* under this different interpretation.

Table 10.8   Octet, *Allegro moderato*: Reading of the formal design as a sonata form

| Parts | I | | | | II | | III | | | Coda |
|---|---|---|---|---|---|---|---|---|---|---|
| Sections | A | B | A¹ | C | A² | B² | A' | B' | C' | A³B²A¹ |
| Tonal centres | G | C | C | F | F–B♭ | G | G | C | C | C |
| Cadences on | V | | I | IV | (IV) | V | V | I | I | I |
| Sonata form | | Exposition | | | Development | | Recap. in 'I' | | | |
| | | 1st subj. group | | 2nd theme in 'IV' | | | | | | |

*Second Movement,* Andante Cantabile: *Texture, Motive and Twelve-note Set Structure*

The *Andante cantabile*, outlining a simple ternary form (ABA') shown on Table 10.9, is Skalkottas's first, tightly-structured dodecaphonic piece, and a case study in his use of textural and timbral change combined with set-group reiteration to define both set boundaries and phrase structure.

The musical fabric of the movement consists of two textural complexes, winds and strings, which constantly compete yet progress independently, each with its own rhythmic and harmonic content. These complexes converge in the outer sections (A, A') at cadential points, which are enhanced by homophony and the intense repetition of certain single notes and short motives. Apart from their similar textural, harmonic and cadential structures, sections A and A' provide coherence through the derivation of different pitch-class sets from one source set, and the close motivic similarities such sets share. Section A is built on a group of sets all deriving from the source set S1a.[15] S1a includes in its internal structure three forms of the set-class 3–3 and two of set-class 4–7, the most important building blocks of the movement, which permeate the texture and provide continuity and coherence. As shown in Example 10.11, the main theme in the flute is based on S1a. The countertheme in the viola is based on set S1b, each hexachord of which is a slightly reordered retrograde of the corresponding hexachord of S1a. By changing

---

[15] There has been a misunderstanding about the twelve-note structure of this movement, which arises from a printing error in the published score. The third note in the flute line (set S1a) has been printed as c♯², instead of the correct d♯² (in the manuscript this note is d♯²). Orga, overlooking the errors in the published score, misinterprets the internal structure of the sets, seeing 'two tone rows – one of 11 and one of 12 notes' (Orga, 1969, 38).

Table 10.9  Octet, *Andante cantabile*: Formal structure, texture and set structure

| Sections | Phrase structure | Sets | Texture and set structure |
|---|---|---|---|
| A | (1–4) Antecedent. | S1a, S1b, (S1c)=I, II, III | Three-layered polyphonic texture: Theme: fl (S1a); accomp: ob+cl (I, II); countertheme: vla (S1b); contrapuntal accomp: vlc (III). (1–2) first hexachords of sets. (3–4) second hexachords of sets. |
|  | (5–7) Consequent. Compressed, rhythmically modified repetition of the antecedent. | S1a, S1b, RS1a, I, II, III | Thematic block: vla, vlc (S1a, S1b); new melody: bsn (S1c=RS1a); accomp: ww, vln1, vln2. Textural complexes contrasted in rhythmic and articulative character: legato phrasing of the main thematic block in lower strings against staccato accomp of ww. |
|  | (8–9) Codetta. | S1a reordered | Recessive texture. |
|  | (10–13) Developmental passage. | RS1a reordered, S1a | Superimposition of two-textural blocks. Linear polyphony in ww (RS1a); chordal string accomp (S1a). |
|  | (14–18) Modified recurrence of the antecedent. | S1b (chords), S1a, I, II, III | Polyphony in ww+vlc (S1a, I, II, III); chordal homophony in strings (S1b). (17–18) Cadence (S1a). |
|  | (19–22) Transition to section B. | S1a, S1a (reord), S1b (reord), III | Melody: vla (S1a); countermelody: vln1 (III, S1a)+fl (III); accomp (S1b, III, S1a reord). |
| B | (23–28[1]) Contrasting middle section. (23–4) Statement of new thematic material. (25–8) Continuation. | S2 (chords), S3, S4 | Two antiphonal textural blocks: homophonic, texturally thick, rhythmically intense strings (S3, S4), against slow, registrally low, dynamically *p* ww (S2). |
|  | (28–33[1]) New thematic ideas in ww. | S3, S4, S2 (chords) | Polyphonic ww (fl+bsn (S3) – cl+ob (S4)) against chordal stings (S2). Textural reduction to syncopated chords; gradual liquidation of the string textural block (S2) to simultaneity E♭–e–g (set-class 3–3). |
|  | (33–36) New thematic group in four-part counterpoint in ww. | S2 (linear), S3, S4 | Two-layered texture. Polyphonic ww (S2–linear, S3, S4) against chordal strings (S2). Recessive cadence; motivic liquidation. |
|  | (37–43[1]) Contrasting passage. Climax. | S2 (chords), S3, S4 | Two antiphonal, contrasting textures. Predominant demisemiquaver rhythm in ww (S3, S4) against quaver, chordal strings (S2). |

| Sections | Phrase structure | Sets | Texture and set structure |
|---|---|---|---|
| A' | (43⁴–7) Modified reappearance of antecedent. | S1a, S1b, I, II, III | Rhythmic intensity; rhythmic figures carried on from the previous climatic phrase. |
|  | (48–54¹) Modified consequent with cadential passage. | S1a, S1b, RS1a, I, II, III | Multilayered texture; chordal passage (51) prior to cadence (52–3), established by recessive chordal homorhythm, liquidation of motivic material, and descending melodic contour in fl melody (fl+strings S1a reordered). |
|  | (54⁴–5) Codetta, pc material derive from developmental passage (10–13). | S1a (reordered) | Homophonic and homorhythmic passage in ww. |
|  | (56–62) Modified recurrence of (14–18). | S1a, S1b (chords), I, II, III | Textural exchange of (14–18); polyphony in strings (S1a, I, II, III); chordal homophony in ww (S1b, S1a). |
| Coda | (63–6) pc material and motivic ideas from section B. | S3, S4 (reordered) | Antiphony between strings (S3 chordal) and ww (S3, S4 linear). |

Example 10.11   Octet, *Andante cantabile*: Section A – opening gesture (bars 1–4)

the order position of d¹ and b in S1b, the motivic construction of the countertheme is affected, with both melodic phrases in the viola cadencing with motives that have the same intervallic structure, and a T₇ transpositional relationship: e♭–d¹–b (set-class 3–3) in bar 2, and g♯–g¹–e¹ (3–3) in bar 4. The homorhythmic accompaniment in the oboe and clarinet consists of melodic segments based on the eight-note set I, and six-note set II, respectively, while the bass line is based on the eight-note set III. These set segments derive from set S1c, which itself derives from the unordered retrograde of S1a (RS1a), and is partitioned between the oboe, clarinet and cello (bars 1–4). They are continuously presented throughout the movement in this segmented form, establishing their own motivic/harmonic identity. The note succession in each derived set is not determined by twelve-note considerations, but appears to underline the motivic similarities between them, as for example the equivalent tetrachords c²–e²–c♯²–g¹, a¹–g♯¹–f¹–d¹, c♯²–g¹–e²–c² (set-class 4–18) and the trichords c²–e²–c♯², g¹–b♭¹–b¹, a¹–g♯¹–f¹ (set-class 3–3).

Although the texture consists exclusively of twelve-note material, Skalkottas also employs tonal elements in both the internal structure of the sets and the overall harmonic fabric, and he relies on functional analogues to construct the form. The combination of different textural complexes within the polyphonic fabric frequently results in simultaneities that consist of two functionally contradictory chords, each implying a different key. As shown in Example 10.12, the consequent of section A cadences at bar 7 with the superimposition of two chords: C major, and B minor/diminished, whereas the climactic cadence of section A (bars 17–18) is built on their inverted position (B minor/diminished and C major chords, including the predominant trichord, set-class 3–3). The final cadential gesture of the movement (bar 66) combines a B diminished seventh chord with the trichord E♭–g–e¹ (set-class 3–3). Although the B major/minor and C major harmonies are integrated into the pitch-class structure of the source set S1a, the C major and B minor/diminished triads that conclude the opening section of the movement arise from the simultaneous statement of six independent sets (S1a, S1b, S1c[RS1a], I, II, III). Thus, despite any traditional associations they might suggest, these chords are bound by the twelve-note structure from which they emerge.

Section B is built on three new sets, S2, S3, S4. It is characterized by an antiphonal texture created from the juxtaposition of contrasting blocks of sound, the unfolding of the thematic material alternating between chordal and polyphonic textures, rhythms that get progressively faster, a relatively static harmony and recessive cadences characterized by textural thinning. The woodwind thematic idea is based on the twelve-note set S2, which is partitioned into four trichords and is constantly presented as a block of four three-note chords (B♭–f♯–c¹, D–a–d♭¹, G♯–b–f¹, and D♯–g–e¹) (see Example 10.13). During the course of the section this textural block changes timbre (between woodwind and strings), but remains at the same registral level throughout, thus establishing both B♭–A♭–E♭ as the predominant motivic configuration in the bass line and the note E♭ as the tonal centre of the section. The homorhythmic string block consists of the twelve-note sets S3, which is partitioned between the first violin and cello, and S4, partitioned

Example 10.12   Octet, *Andante cantabile*: Harmonic structure of section A

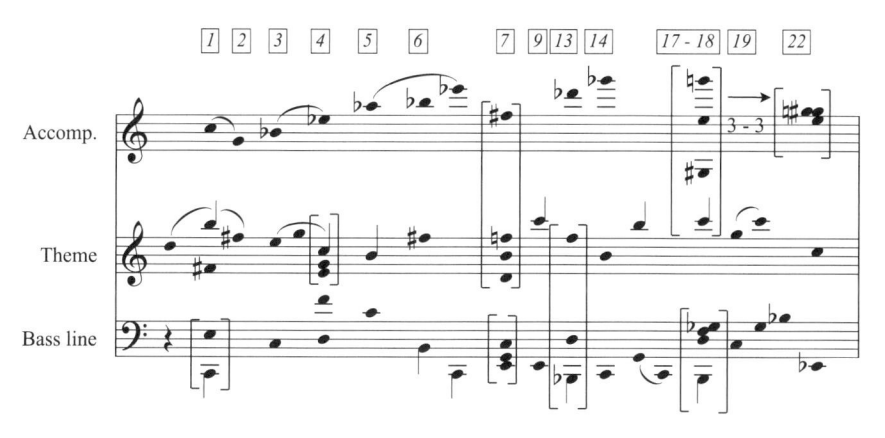

Example 10.13   Octet, *Andante cantabile*: Section B – opening gesture (bars 23–4)

between the second violin and the viola. These sets are closely related through invariant segments, particularly the trichord set-class 3–2.

Although section B is rhythmically and texturally active, there is a compensatory stasis of harmonic rhythm. As shown in Example 10.14, a large-scale neighbouring-note motive (E♭–E–E♭), resulting from the registral exchange of the thematic complexes, and supported by neighbouring-note trichords (E♭–g–e¹ (set-class 3–3) – E–f♯–g (set-class 3–2) – E♭–g–e¹), is reiterated throughout the section, which ultimately cadences on an E♭–g–e¹ simultaneity.

Example 10.14   *Andante cantabile*: Harmonic structure of section B

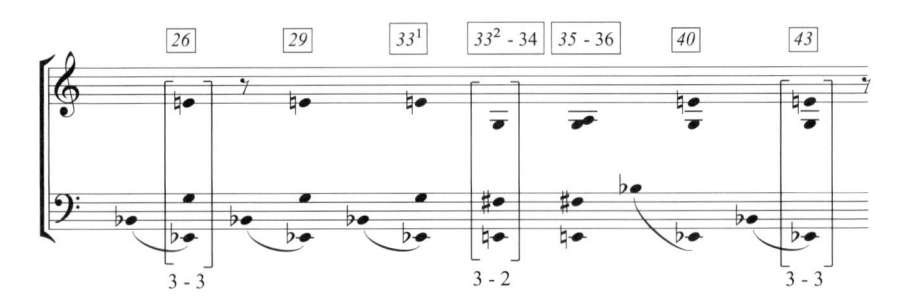

Overall, the multilayered texture of the *Andante cantabile* is reminiscent of the earlier two sonatinas for violin and piano. Two textural complexes, winds and strings, constantly compete yet progress independently, each with its own rhythmic and harmonic content. These complexes converge in the outer sections (A, A') at cadential points, which are further enhanced by homophony, the superimposition of two tonally reminiscent chords, and the intense repetition of certain single notes and short motives. In contrast, the cadences of section B, with its static and clearly defined harmonic structure, are based on non-triadic simultaneities, which also result from the simultaneous unfolding of different melodic lines.

Furthermore, there is an extensive network of motivic relationships throughout the texture that underpins the harmonic/motivic structure of the movement and provides compositional integrity. Within each individual phrase, and throughout the larger sections, the textural differentiation and superimposition of harmonically contradictory elements are counterbalanced and made less obtuse by the unifying power of the motive set-class 3–3, which is a particularly distinctive feature of the *Andante*. As noted above, it is included in the internal structure of all sets and appears in various motivic forms, predominantly as A–D♭–C, E–G♯–G, E♭–E–G; it emerges both as a triadic simultaneity and as a component of particular chords punctuating cadences.[16]

---

[16]   For example, the cadence at bar 7 ends with the motive G♯–G–E in the bass (vlc). In the cadential bars 17–18 the linear motive $a^3$–$d♭^4$–$c^4$ generates the flute line, while the triad $g♯$–$e^2$–$g^3$ forms part of the supporting chord in the upper strings. In bar 22 the motive a–$d♭^2$–

## Third Movement, Presto: *Large-scale Transposition as Determinant of Form*

In the *Presto* Skalkottas revisits certain compositional aspects explored in previous pieces, such as *en bloc* transposition to determine form, and the deployment of a large number of different sets in each section of the movement. The fusion of traditional forms is again evident here, with the incorporation of a large rondo form within the superstructure of a rounded binary form. Similar to the *Allegro moderato*, the *Presto* is divided into three parts (I, II and III), each comprising a number of sections (ABACA'B'A'C'A). The rounded binary form is suggested by the transposition of sections of Part I (ABAC) at the fifth ($T_7$) in Part II (A'B'A'C'), implying a harmonic movement from a 'tonic' region to a 'dominant' one, and then the return to the 'tonic' in Part III (A). Table 10.10 gives an overview of the movement's formal structure and set structure.

Section A (the refrain) is built on a set-group including three closely related twelve-note sets and three derived ones (S1, S2, S3; derived sets I, II, III). As shown in Example 10.15, the theme in the flute is based on S1; its second and fourth trichords (G–E♭–G♭ and B♭–C♯–D), having a transpositional relationship of a fifth ($T_7$), punctuate the melodic cadential structure of the two opening phrases (bars 1–5¹, 5–10), suggesting a harmonic relationship comparable to the tonic–dominant form of a sentence. This is accompanied by the clarinet and bassoon playing S2 and S3 respectively, sets that share several invariant dyads and trichords. The strings play fragments of S2 and S3, which, as discussed in Part II (pp. 118–19), results in the derived sets I, II, III. Skalkottas's motivic signature, the trichord B♭–C♯–D (set-class 3–3) predominates throughout, defining the melodic cadences of section A and each of its modified returns.

Section B (the first episode) is built on a group of six new sets (S4–S9), closely related through the association of a high number of invariant dyads. It has an 'etude-like' character, with the sets used freely as melodies, albeit ones that contain all the twelve notes. Section C is divided into three phrases, largely defined by abrupt textural changes; it is more developmental than the other two sections and is predominantly built on a group of eight new sets (S10–S17).

A sudden textural reduction marks the opening of Part II. Section A' is sparse, almost pointillistic compared with Skalkottas's general tendency towards complex, polyphonic textures. The entire thematic and pitch-class set content of the refrain is repeated here transposed at the fifth ($T_7$). The remaining sections (B', A', C'[C($T_0$)]) recapitulate a liquidated version of their main thematic statements. Part II ends with phrase c2 of section C', in its original twelve-note

---

c² in the viola is emphasized with *sf* and *ff* dynamics, while two *sf* and *ff* triads, e²–g²–g♯², accompany in syncopated rhythm. Similarly, the trichord E♭–g–e¹ forms the cornerstone of the harmonic structure of section B. It is the last simultaneity of the thematic block, based on S2, and the last element that remains in the liquidation process of the second developmental phrase of the section. It also punctuates the cadences at bars 33¹ and 43¹.

Table 10.10  Octet, *Presto*: Formal structure and set structure

| Parts | Sections | Phrases | Thematic and phrase structure | Set structure |
|---|---|---|---|---|
| I | A Refrain | a1 | (1–10) Antecedent. Main theme: fl (S1); chordal accomp. | S1, S2, S3, I, II, III |
| | | a2 | (11–16) Consequent. Canonic repetition of theme in vln1+vla (S1); polyphonic accomp. | S1, S2, S3, I, II |
| | | a3 | (17–24) Transition. Increasingly thick texture. | S1, S2, S3, III |
| | B First Episode | b1 | (25–35) Thematic gesture with glissandi figures in va+vlc (S4). | S4, S5, S6, S7, S8, S9 |
| | | b2 | (36–51) Continuation. | S4, S5, S6, S7, S8, S9 |
| | A Refrain | a1 | (52–63) Theme in canon (ob+bsn). Irregular 2/2+3/4 metre. | S1, S2, S3, I, II, III |
| | | a4 | (64–76) Cadence; motivic liquidation. | S1, I, II, III |
| | C Second Episode | c1 | (77–83) Thematic idea: vla (S10); countermelody in fl+ob. | S10, S11, S12, S13, S14 |
| | | c2 | (84–92) Continuation; new sets. | S10, S11, S12, S13, S14, S15, S16, S17 |
| | | c3 | (93–101) Cadence; motivic liquidation. | S10, S11 |
| II | A' ($T_7$) | a'1 | (102–9) Rhythmically modified theme in bsn. | S1, S2, S3, I, II, III ($T_7$) |
| | | a'2 | (110–18) Varied, canonic repetition of theme. | S1, S2, S3, I, II, III ($T_7$) |
| | | a'3 | (118–23) Modified transition. | S1, S2, S3 ($T_7$) |
| | B' ($T_7$) | b'1 | (124–36) Modified repetition of b1. | S4, S5, S6, S7, S8, S9 ($T_7$) |
| | A' ($T_7$) | a'1 | (137–45) Modified and liquidated repetition of a1. | S1, I, II ($T_7$) |
| | C' ($T_7$–$T_0$) | c'1 | (146–52) Modified reappearance of c1 | S10, S11, S12, S13, S14 ($T_7$) |
| | | c2 | (153–65) Retransition. Modified repetition of c2. | S10, S12, S13, S15, S16, S17, S11, S14 ($T_0$) |
| III | A ($T_0$) | a1 | (166–75) Exact statement of a1. | S1, S2, S3, I, II, III ($T_0$) |
| | | a5 | (176–89) Motivic variations on the theme. | S1 ($T_0$) |
| | | | (190–96) Coda. | S1 ($T_0$) |

Example 10.15   Octet, *Presto*: Section A – opening gesture (1–10)

setting ($T_0$ form of the sets used), thus functioning as the retransition to the final return of section A at its original tonal level.

Bailey, discussing Webern's music, questions whether the rondo form can be successfully integrated in a twelve-note context, since 'the basic premise of the technique' – the avoidance of establishing any tonal preference through the literal repetition of the same set of rows at the places where the refrain was expected – 'and the essential requirements of the rondo are incompatible' (Bailey, 1991/1994, 237–8). Skalkottas, perhaps conscious of this inherent incompatibility, endeavours to make the structural outline of this rondo aurally identifiable. The refrain, although rhythmically varied upon its returns (except for its final restatement in Part III), is easily discerned by the recurring, linear ordered sets, particularly the thematic set S1. Furthermore, each section is distinguished by its individual twelve-note set-group structure, texture and articulation, and certain characteristic thematic ideas and rhythmic figures, as, for example, the descending glissandi figures associated with section B, and dotted rhythms with section C.

In the *Presto*, through the use of transposition at $T_7$, which evokes traditional, tonal expectations of tonic–dominant polarization and resolution to control the diffused dodecaphonic harmonic vocabulary, Skalkottas established the technique that he would go on to use extensively in the large-scale orchestral works of the late 1930s and early 1940s, notwithstanding that these exhibit a freer approach to twelve-note composition.

# Chapter 11
# Linear Serialism of the Mid-1930s: 'Strict' Twelve-Note Technique

The completion of a large number of entirely dodecaphonic works in 1935 marks a significant juncture in Skalkottas's stylistic development. The sheer quantity of large-scale complex dodecaphonic works – demonstrating different approaches to twelve-note composition and featuring both the consolidation of his linear serial composition, using a limited number of fixed sets, and the expansion of his twelve-note technique to include chordal sets, supersets and sets defined by their unordered segments – suggests that he must have been working on these pieces during the period when he was supposedly depressed and barely composing.

The Third String Quartet and the Second String Trio consolidate his strict approach to twelve-note technique, according to which fixed twelve-note sets within each formal section are predominantly presented linearly, superimposed as melodic lines. The pitch-class order within each set segment is maintained, with only occasional pitch-class reorderings at developmental passages. The Third and Fourth sonatinas for violin and piano indicate a developmental extension of this compositional technique. Although the linear approach to presenting the sets in distinct textural layers (violin, piano right hand and piano left hand) is maintained, the sets are partitioned into segments, which are progressively used freely, with frequent permutations of their pitch-class order, and, after being established, the rearrangement of the segments themselves. Despite the progressively free manipulation of the sets, both sonatinas outline a large-scale unified formal structure arising from the cyclical use of the source twelve-note sets, which circumscribes and controls the developmental digressions from the strict serial treatment of the original material. The First Piano Suite combines elements of both compositional approaches used in the chamber works of 1935, together with the technique of transposition and retrograde of set-groups to define the form.

**Third String Quartet (1935): Linear Use of a Limited Number of Sets**

The Third String Quartet provides a case study of Skalkottas's strict use of his version of twelve-note composition. The twelve-note sets, treated as ordered series, are used both in their prime form and, in a few instances, in retrograde and transposed forms. It is notable that in this piece the composer pays homage to his classical inheritance through his use and reinterpretation of traditional sonorities, tonal harmonies, motives and gestures. The inclusion of tonal elements within the twelve-note texture is striking, and deliberately done to show the fusion of two styles (twelve-note and tonal) – a fusion that was to become the defining characteristic of his harmonic language and compositional style.

*First Movement,* Allegro Moderato*: Homage to Beethoven*

As in previous works, each section of the *Allegro moderato* is built on a different set-group, while the form of the movement combines the sequential presentation of two sections, A and B, and their varied repetitions, with that of a sonata movement, as shown in Table 11.1.

Table 11.1   Third String Quartet, *Allegro moderato*: Formal structure and set structure

| *Allegro moderato* | Sonata movement | Thematic structure | Set structure |
|---|---|---|---|
| Section A | Exposition | First subject group. First theme: three-phrase period. (1–14) Antecedent; $(14^4–23^2)$–$(23^3–7)$ consequent. $(28–33^1)$ Varied and condensed repetition of antecedent. $(33^4–42^1)$ Transition and chordal cadence. | S1, S2, S3, S4 |
| Section B | | Second subject group. Second theme: $(42^2–51)$ Antecedent; $(51^4–60)$ consequent. (61–4) (65–75) Developmental passage. $(76–9^2)$ $(79^4–82^2)$ Cadence. | S5, S5($T_3$), S6, S7 |
| Section A[1] | Development | Material from the first subject group. $(82^4–90^3)$ $(90^4–101)$ (102–6) $(106^4–17)$ $(117^4–21^3$ cadence). | S1, S2, S3, S4 |
| Section B[1] | | Material from the second subject group. $(121^4–8)$ $(128^4–34)$ (135–41) $(141^4–8)$ (149–55 cadence). | S5, S5($T_3$), S6, S7 |
| Section A' | Truncated Recapitulation | First subject group. $(156–68^2)$ Antecedent; $(168^4–76)$ consequent. (177–83) Continuation and cadence. | S1, S2, S3, S4 |
| Section B' | | $(184–7^1)$–$(187^3–90^1)$. Recapitulation of the second theme's extended cadential passage/(Coda). | S5, S5($T_3$), S6, S7 |
| Section A" | Coda | (190–91) Chords based on pitch-class material from the first theme. | S1, S2, S3, S4 |

Section A is built on a group of four sets, S1, S2, S3, S4. The assignment of sets to individual instruments is a distinctive characteristic of this section, with each set played by the same instrument throughout both the exposition and the recapitulation of the section; the first violin plays set S1, the second violin S2, the viola S3 and the cello S4 – thus each set is identified with a particular instrumental colour. However, in the Development there are some part exchanges, which to some extent differentiate this section from those surrounding it. In an approach deriving from the *15 Little Variations* for piano, where the material substructure of the piece first appears as a skeleton and is then progressively elaborated, section A is characterized by the exposition of the twelve-note pitch-class material initially presented one note at a time, then progressively as chords (bars 1–14), followed by the compositional 'realization' of this material (see Example 11.1).

Example 11.1  Third String Quartet, *Allegro moderato*: Section A – opening gesture (bars 1–14)

In the slow opening gesture, each of the first three notes of the sets (order numbers 1, 2, 3) is presented sequentially at one-bar intervals, which ensures aural clarity and comprehensibility, but also sets out the compositional properties of the movement. As shown in Example 11.2, which outlines the harmonic structure of the opening gesture, this slow presentation in bars 1–10 results in three tetrachords, starting with the descending chromatic tetrachord g$^2$–f♯$^2$–f$^2$–e$^2$ (set-class 4–1), followed by the whole-tone tetrachord e♭$^2$–d♭$^2$–c♭$^2$–a$^1$ (set-class 4–21), and concluding with the diminished seventh g♯$^1$–f$^1$–d$^1$–b (set-class 4–28). The remaining pitch-classes are presented as nine tetrachords with the same order number sounding together, establishing the harmonic premise of the section (which includes the frequent reiteration of harmonically equivalent chords) against which the thematic material unfolds. These tetrachords frame section A, and in all its varied repetitions constitute its cadential gesture.

Example 11.2   Third String Quartet, *Allegro moderato*: Harmonic structure of the opening gesture

Apart from the exploitation and expansion of the sonic space (from the minor third, e$^2$–g$^2$, of the first chord to an octave plus a minor seventh, D♯–c♯$^1$), the atonal–tonal implications and associations that permeate this piece are already established in the opening four chords of the movement. It is as though the piece grows out of a concentrated, semitonal tetrachord to the most versatile chord of tonal music, the diminished seventh. This latter chord, often used as a device for creating mystery, confusion or unpredictable modulation, is used here as a stable chord, a point of arrival after the progressive opening-out of the harmony. In this context, paradoxically, it both unbalances the dodecaphonic expectations established by the opening two tetrachords and creates a degree of stability and rest. A harmonic resolution to the G♯ diminished seventh in first inversion (and thus a release from the previous escalation of tension) is provided on the downbeat of bar 11 by the tonally ambiguous tetrachord a♯–c♯$^1$–e$^1$–a$^1$ (set-class 4–18). The rate of chord progression increases, ending in bar 14 on the tetrachord D♯–e–g♯–c♯$^1$; the bass note, D♯, played by the cello, functions as a leading-note to the following e$^1$, which initiates the melodic exposition of the section's thematic material. Thus, by juxtaposing and presenting in a condensed form his dodecaphonic and diatonic material, Skalkottas sets out his compositional principles from the beginning and makes clear to the listener the contrasts upon which the piece is predicated.

The unfolding of the set-group and the music's contour and harmonic rhythm all determine the phrase structure of section A. The opening 27 bars outline a phrase structure comparable to a three-phrase period. The antecedent outlines the opening-out of the pitch-class material and the main musical 'idea' (G–F♯–F–E) in bars 1–10, followed by 'contrasting motive-forms' of staccato chords. The first consequent phrase (bars 14⁴–23²) is introduced with the opening gesture inverted and metrically displaced. The melodic theme (bars 18–27), played by the first violin and comprising two consecutive statements of S1, outlines an antecedent–consequent-like periodic phrase structure. The cadence of the thematic passage at bar 27 is established through changes in articulation (the accompanying strings playing arco), contour direction in the final motivic gesture (ascending major sixth motive, $e^2$–$c♯^3$, as opposed to the previous descending minor third $e^1$–$c♯^1$), and motivic liquidation to the final trichord E♭–g♯¹–$e^2$ (set-class 3–4).

Section B is composed from the group of four new sets, S5, S5(T₃), S6, S7, while its contrapuntal texture, dance-like character, fluid phrase rhythm and overtly tonal character contrast notably with the homophonically constructed section A. The second, 'lyrical' theme, structured as a trio (first and second violins and cello), is initiated with an expanded, 'diatonic' idea, C–B–A–G, as opposed to section A's chromatic G–F♯–F–E (see Example 11.3). Set S7 is introduced later (in the developmental passage, bars 61–8), supporting the bass line of the four-part texture.

In contrast to the strict serial treatment of section A, section B exhibits a freer approach to the handling of the sets, all of which include insertions and repetitions of segments that temporarily interrupt the linear presentation of their pitch-class order. In the main thematic idea played by the first violin, the motive $c^2$–$b^1$–$a^1$–$g^1$–$g^1$–$g^1$ is a direct quotation from the fourth movement of Beethoven's Fifth Symphony. Not only does this permeate the motivic surface of this movement, but also, in this particular gestural presentation, it is the thematic idea of the second subject in the Recapitulation, transposed into the tonic, C major. Its obsessive reiteration within section B, which constitutes the second subject group in this sonata movement, ensures that the listener does not miss the reference to Beethoven, whose symphonic originality Skalkottas greatly admired.[1] In bars 61–8, the opening gesture of the C major/minor theme, played by the upper strings (bars 61–2), is accompanied contrapuntally by the cello playing an arpeggio based on pitch-classes with order number 1 … 10 of S7 (Example 11.4).

This cello part includes the motivic tetrachord c♯¹–f♯¹–f¹–e♭¹ (set-class 4–11), transposed at the tritone, while its final motivic gesture outlines the tonally reminiscent tetrachord e♭¹–g¹–c¹–b (C minor with added major seventh), which shares three pitch-classes (g¹–c¹–b) with the C–B–A–G tetrachord. Aurally the motive is resolved in the viola melodic line, which on the last quaver of the bar plays a¹ of S6, approached by the leading-note movement g♯²–a¹. The completion of S7 in the cello (pitch-classes A, G♯) is reserved for the cadential gesture at

---

[1] Skalkottas believed that imitation in the context of an original work is episodic, and his justification for such a quotation is that it can be inserted 'in small phrases and as an element which does not disturb, but stylistically reminds us of a classical music episode worthy of attention and imitation' (Skalkottas, 'Originality and Imitation', MS essay).

218   *The Life and Twelve-Note Music of Nikos Skalkottas*

Example 11.3   Third String Quartet, *Allegro moderato*: Section B – opening gesture (bars 42–52)

Example 11.4   Third String Quartet, *Allegro moderato*: Section B (bars 61–8)

bar 68; this is a recurring feature within section B (and each of its repetitions), with the dyad A–G♯ punctuating its final cadence. Furthermore, the final tetrachord of S7, C–B–A–G♯, is not only a motivic variation of the segments C–B–A–G of S5, C–B–G–G♯ of S2 and C–B♭–A–G♯ of S3 (thus further reinforcing motivic connections in the musical fabric across contrasting sections),[2] but also another direct reference to the fourth movement of Beethoven's Fifth Symphony.[3]

The motive C–B–A–G/C–B–A–G♯, being the first and last melodic gesture of section B, emphasizes both the compositional significance of associative relationships between the different sets of the group and the unifying power of Skalkottas's developmental motivic technique, which integrates the contrasts between the opening phrase and the more loosely constructed developmental

---

[2]   There are several associative relationships between the different sets of the two sections. For instance, the last hexachord of S6 (F–G–B–C–B♭–F♯, set-class 6–Z6) is an unordered transposition at the tritone ($T_6$) of the second hexachord of S1, while the first tetrachord of S6 (D♭–E♭–E–G♯), played by the cello in the lower register, is exactly the same as the final cadential chord of section A (D♯–E–G♯–C♯).

[3]   This motive (C–B–A–G♯) derives from the third motivic unit of the second subject in the Exposition of Beethoven's *Allegro*, and, played by the first violin, is used as the melodic cadence of the final developmental phrase of both sections B and B′ (bars 74³–5 and 147³–8) before the forceful, chordal cadence to these sections.

passages of the section. Such integration is further emphasized by the pervasive use of the tetrachord set-class 4–11, which frames the section, being both its opening gesture and its last cadential tetrachord, presented as two consecutive dyads, (f♯$^1$–e$^2$)–(A–g♯) (see Example 11.5).

The precompositional considerations that determine the construction of the different sets not only ensure coherence of contrasting structural elements, but also serve Skalkottas's developmental motivic technique; this further reinforces relationships between contrasting events, since these events can be understood to originate from changes made in the repetition of earlier motivic gestures. Although such motivic repetition and variation ensures coherence, the episodic structure of the movement, outlining diverse twelve-note harmonic regions provides the necessary contrasts. Each harmonic region, besides its different serial content and structure, is further differentiated by the tonally suggestive harmonic movement within its boundaries.

Example 11.5   Third String Quartet, *Allegro moderato*: Harmonic structure within sections A and B

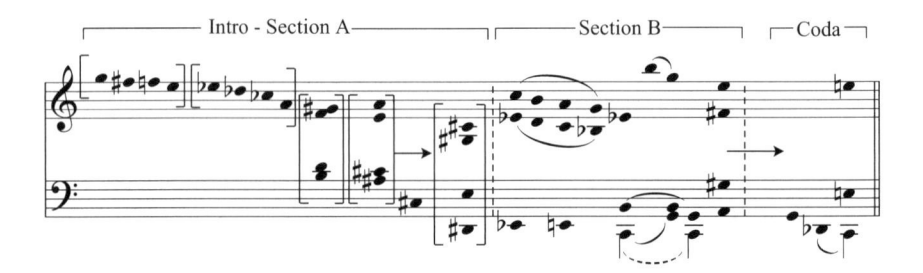

Overall, as shown in Example 11.5, the harmonic structure of section A outlines a movement from the opening semitonal tetrachord to a diminished seventh chord, and the latter's subsequent resolution to an A major/A♯ diminished tetrachord, then to a C♯ minor triad included in the cadential chord, rendering section A open-ended. In section B the tonal emphasis shifts, and the harmonic movement, although predominantly centred on C (emphasized by its temporal position and supported by a G–C dominant–tonic-like progression in the bass and the C major/minor motivic gestures in the upper voices), eventually cadences on a *ff*, rhythmically augmented and texturally prominent note A, coupled with its leading-note G♯. The last cadential tetrachord of the section, and its varied repetitions, has a major sixth (T$_9$) transpositional relationship with the opening recurring melodic tetrachord C–B–A–G. This surprising, 'quasi-interrupted' type of cadential gesture shifts the harmonic emphasis from C to A, thus frustrating the expectations that Skalkottas has created in the course of the section. This aural surprise is repeated unchanged at the end of each varied repetition of section B, becoming a structural feature of the piece. As the listener becomes accustomed to the established pattern of harmonic events, Skalkottas frustrates expectations yet again at the very end of the piece. The Coda, built on the set-group material from section A, cadences with a C in the bass, while the final chord of the piece is built on the diatonic C–E dyad and includes a C major triad in its internal structure.

These tonal/serial interactions, and the ensuing tension and relaxation they create, are played out against the background of sonata form. Although no real harmonic conflict and resolution exists in the traditional sense, the sonata form is emphasized here through clear, contrasting themes and harmonic regions, and the tension and relaxation created by textural change. Skalkottas skilfully establishes contrasts between statements and developments, between homophonic dodecaphony in the opening gesture and throughout section A, and contrapuntal dodecaphony in section B and the development section, as well as by the use of two harmonic areas within a well-defined harmonic framework. Furthermore, the rondo formal design, with the final reappearance of the opening twelve-note material presented in the dense, cadential chordal texture associated with section B, unifies the entire structure and ensures the integration of themes and contrasts.

*Second Movement,* Andante: *Set Structure and Tonal Phrase Structure*

Tonal/serial interaction and overall traditional functional connotations are also prevalent in the *Andante*, which outlines a simple rondo form ABA[1]B[1]. Each section is built on a different set-group, and here, for the first time, Skalkottas systematically employs the retrograde and transposed forms of the source sets to structure the small-scale form. Table 11.2 represents schematically the set topography and phrase structure of the movement, with the letters a, b, c, a1, b1, c1, b2 indicating the phrases.

Section A is built on two twelve-note sets (S1, S2) and their retrogrades (RS1, RS2), which include several tonal elements, and its set structure outlines a ternary design (aa′–bb′–a). Within each phrase the sets are presented as a duet between two instruments, each playing one set in its original and retrograde forms, which alternate, thus delimiting phrase boundaries. As shown in Example 11.6, in the antecedent (bars 1–6) the duet is presented between the first violin playing S1–RS1–S1 and the cello playing S2–RS2–S2, a circling technique first used in the *15 Little Variations* for piano. In the consequent (bars 7–12) the duet is played between the second violin and viola with an alternation of the sets (S2–S1)–(RS2–RS1)–(S2–S1).

The contrasting middle passage (b b1) is characterized by the predominance of the retrograde forms of the sets. The first violin–cello duet returns with a reversed circling repetition of the first phrase in bars 13–18: (RS1–RS2)–(S1–S2)–(RS1–RS2), which in turn is followed in bars 18[4]–23 by the second violin–viola duet with (RS1–RS2)–(S1–S2)–(RS1–RS2). In bars 24–30[2] the duets are played in canon, while the pitch-class structure of the phrase retains its ternary outline.

Section B introduces a new theme and is built on two new sets, S3 and S4, and their various transpositions, indicated as S3a [S3($T_5$)], S3b [S3($T_{10}$)], S3c [S3($T_3$)], S4a [S4($T_3$)], S4b [S4($T_2$)]. Each of the transposed forms of S3 ($T_5$, $T_{10}$ and $T_3$) is a perfect fourth higher than the previous one, and Skalkottas uses these

Table 11.2  Third String Quartet, *Andante*: Set topography and phrase structure

Section A

| | 1–2 | 3–4 | 5–6 | 7–8 | 9–11 | 11–12 | 13–14 | 15–16 | 17–18 | 18⁴–19 | 20–22³ | 22⁴–3 | 24–5 | 26–7 | 28–30² | 30⁴–32 |
|---|---|---|---|---|---|---|---|---|---|---|---|---|---|---|---|---|
| Vln1 | S1 | RS1 | S1 | | | | RS1 | S1 | RS1 | | | | S1 | RS1 | S1 | |
| Vln2 | | | | S2 | RS2 | S2 | | | | RS1 | S1 | RS1 | S2 | RS2 | S2 | S2 |
| Vla | | | | S1 | RS1 | S1 | | | | RS2→ | RS2 S2→ | S2 RS2 | S1 | RS1 | S1 | |
| Vlc | S2 | RS2 | S2 | | | | RS2 | S2 | RS2 | | | | S2 | RS2 | S2 | S1 |
| Phrases | a | | | a1 | | | b | | | b1 | | | a (canon) | | | cadence (7–8) |

Section B

| | 33–6 | 37–40 | 41–7 | 47⁶–50³ | 50⁴–58¹ | 58⁴–64³ |
|---|---|---|---|---|---|---|
| Vln1 | | S3a S3a | S4b | S3a S3b | S4a S4b | |
| Vln2 | S3 S3 S3 | | S3b S3b S3b | S3 S3b | S3b S3c | |
| Vla | S4/1hex | S4/2hex | S3c | S3a | S3b S3c | S4 |
| Vlc | | S4a/1hex | S4a/2hex | S3 S4 | S3b S3c | S3 S3 S3 |
| Phrases | a | | b | | b1 | a1 |

## Section A¹

| | $64^4$–6 | $67$–8 | $69$–70 | $71$–2 | $73$–4 | $75$–6 | $77$–8 | $79$–$80^4$ | $80^5$–$81^3$ | $81^4$–$2^3$ | $82^4$–4 | 85 | $86$–7 | $88$–9 | $90$–$92^3$ | $92^4$–$4^2$ |
|---|---|---|---|---|---|---|---|---|---|---|---|---|---|---|---|---|
| Vln1 | S1 | RS1 | S1 | | | | RS1/1hex | RS1 | | | RS1 | RS2 | S1 | RS1 | S1 | |
| Vln2 | S2 | RS2 | S2 | | | | RS2/2hex | RS1 | RS1 | | RS2 | RS1 | S2 | RS2 | S2 | S2 |
| Vla | | | | S2 | RS2→ | RS2 S2 | RS1/1hex | RS2 | | RS1 | RS1 | RS2 | S1 | RS1 | S1 | |
| Vlc | | | | S1 | RS1 | S1 | RS1/2hex | RS2 | RS1 | RS1 | RS2 | RS1 | S2 | RS2 | S2 | S1 |
| | | | | | | | RS2/1hex | | | | | | | | | |
| | | | | | | | RS1/2hex | | | | | | | | | |
| Phrases | a (bs.1–6) | | | | a1 (7–12) | | | c | | | c1 | | a (canon) (24–30) | | | cadence (30–32) |

## Section B¹

| | $94^3$–$7^2$ | $97^3$–103 | $104$–$6^3$ | $106^4$–9 |
|---|---|---|---|---|
| Vln1 | S3 S4 | S3c S4b | S3c | S3b |
| Vln2 | S3 S4 | S3c S4b | S3c | S3b |
| Vla | S3a | S3b S4a | S3b | RS3a |
| Vlc | S3a | S3b S4a | S3b | RS3a |
| Phrases | b2 (48–58¹) | | | 'Tonal cadence' |

Example 11.6  Third String Quartet, *Andante*: Opening thematic gesture (bars 1–12)

sets consecutively, thus producing a traditional modulatory sequential movement within section B. This distinguishes it from section A, which has a rather static and oscillating harmonic structure, the result of the contiguous use of prime and retrograde forms of its sets. The set structure of section B outlines an arch form, with phrases (a) and (a1) based on the source sets S3 and S4, and phrases (b) and (b1) built predominantly on different combinations of their transposed forms. It starts as a duet between the second violin and the viola (bars 33–6), and introduces a new, tonal thematic gesture, arpeggiating four triads (B major, G minor, D♭ major and A minor) played three times by the second violin. The continuation (bars 37–40) is structured as a trio, with the first violin playing S3a [S3($T_5$)] twice, the viola playing the second hexachord of S4, and the cello the first hexachord of S4a [S4($T_3$)]. Although the sets are used linearly as superimposed contrapuntal voices, there is an overall, form-generating modulatory movement, starting with a

B major triad in the second violin (bar 33) and ending with a C minor seventh at the end of the passage (bar 47).

Section A¹ is a varied repetition of section A, featuring a developmental, climactic passage in bars 77–85 (indicated as c and c1 in Table 11.2); this is built entirely on the retrograde forms of sets S1 and S2, featuring extensive partitioning and interpolation of the hexachords between the instruments and chordal presentation of the segments, all culminating in the octet texture of the climactic *mf–ffff–ff*, bars 79–84. Section B¹ ends with a cadential gesture built on RS3a and S3b, which outlines a sequence (and at places a superimposition) of tonal triads, as shown in Table 11.3. Overall, a sense of bitonality prevails throughout section B and its varied repetitions, reminiscent of the earlier polyphonic Berlin works, but the piece unequivocally ends on a B major triad in first inversion.

Table 11.3   Third String Quartet, *Andante*: Tonal cadence (bars 106–9)

| Bars | 106⁴ | | 107 | | 108 | | 109 |
|---|---|---|---|---|---|---|---|
| vln1 | | | E  A | F  A♭ | G  B♭ | F♯ → B → | F♯  B |
| vln2 | | | | D♭ | D | D♯ → | D♯ |
| vla | F | G♭ | G  C | G♯ → | | | |
| vlc | A  D | B♭  D♭ | C  E♭ | B →  E → | | | |
| Harmon progr vln1–vln2 | | | A_m | D♭_M | G⁶/⁴_m | B⁶_M | B⁶_M |
| Harmon progr vla–vlc | D_m | G♭⁶/⁴_M | C⁶_m | E_M | | | |

*Third Movement,* Allegro Vivace (Rondo): *Development in Set Structure and Phrase Structure*

The *Allegro vivace (Rondo)*, built on eight twelve-note sets and characterized by a high concentration of derived sets of various types, outlines a large-scale rondo form (ABA¹B¹A²). Within this design, each section, built on a different set-group, is also structured as a rondo with a refrain and episodes, as shown in Table 11.4. Table 11.5 gives a detailed presentation of the set topography within the phrase structure.

Section A is built on four sets, S1, S2, S3, S4. The refrain (bars 1–8¹), consisting of a recitative-like main theme played in unison by all four instruments,[4] is based

---

[4]   In Schoenberg's Fourth String Quartet (1936), composed a year later than Skalkottas's Third String Quartet, the third movement, *Largo*, also begins with a recitative played in unison by all four instruments (Schoenberg, 'Notes on the Four String Quartets' in Rauchhaupt, 1971, 61). However, any connection or imitation between the two pieces should be dismissed, as the two composers had not had any contact for over three years.

Table 11.4  Third String Quartet, *Allegro vivace (Rondo)*: Formal structure and set structure

| Rondo | Rondo subsections | Bars | Thematic structure and set structure |
|---|---|---|---|
| A | Refrain a$^a$ | 1–8$^1$ | Refrain of section A: S1 played by the four instruments in unison. Slow waltz rhythm. |
| | | 8$^3$–19$^1$ | Phrase (a1): Introduction of all four sets. Thematic idea in vln1 ( S1); countermelody in vlc (S4); chordal accompaniment vln2 (S2) and vla (S3). |
| | Episode b$^a$ | 19$^2$–31 | (b1): Trio texture with triple counterpoint between S1, S3, S4. Introduction of waltz rhythmic motive identified with the second theme of the section. |
| | | 31$^2$–9$^1$ | (b2): *Die Fledermaus*-waltz theme in vln1 (S2) (31$^2$–7). Waltz rhythm based on the rhythmic pattern of phrase b1. |
| | Refrain a$^a$ | 39$^2$–44 | Refrain: S1 played in unison, with new quaver rhythm. |
| | Episode c$^a$ | 45–53$^1$ | (c1): New thematic idea in vln1 (S3), with ascending *glissando* gesture. |
| | | 53–60 | (c2): Varied repetition of the *glissando* thematic idea (S3) in vlc. Introduction of semiquaver rhythmic patterns. |
| | | 61–9 | Cadential phrase (c3): Melodic idea based on the simultaneous unfolding of S2 (vln2) and S3 (vla). |
| | Episode c$^{a'}$ | 70–86 | (c′): Third thematic idea, based on a simultaneous unfolding of S2 (vln1) and S3 (vlc), and using the ascending *glissando* motive of phrase (c1). |
| | Refrain a$^a$ | 87–90 | Refrain of A: Theme: *pizzicato* by solo vla (S1). |
| | Episode b$^{a'}$ | 91–103$^1$ | (b1/c′): Trio texture, similar to phrase (b1); melodic duet between vla (S2) and vlc (S3), similar to the thematic structure of phrase (c′). |
| | | 103$^2$–19 | (b2): Second, 'waltz', thematic idea (S2). Final cadence (111–19) established by textural and motivic liquidation; 'tonal' cadential gesture on a C seventh. |
| B | Refrain a$^{b1}$ | 120–27 | (a1): Tonally oriented antecedent. Main thematic idea played by the vla (S6); vlc accompaniment in perfect fifth dyads (S5a). |
| | | 128–35 | (a2): Duet between vln1 (S5) and vln2 (S6). |
| | Refrain a$^{b2}$ | 136–42 | (a3): Chromatic response to phrase (a1). The main thematic idea, played by the vla (S8), is similar to the second, 'waltz' theme of section A; vlc accomp in minor seventh dyads (S7a) |
| | | 143–9$^2$ | (a4): Response to phrase (a2). Duet between vln1 (S7) and vln2 (S8). |

| Rondo | Rondo subsections | Bars | Thematic structure and set structure |
|---|---|---|---|
| | | 149–56² | Link: Predominant melodic idea with *glissando* motive of phrase (c1) in the vlc (S6); contrapuntal accompaniment by vla in ascending arpeggiated triads (S5b), vln2 in descending major seconds in (S7a), and vln1 in major sevenths (S8a). |
| | Episode b^b | 156³–63¹ | (b1): Trio texture. Main thematic idea in vlc (S8). Introduction of continuous semiquaver rhythmic motives. |
| | | 163–9 | (b2): Developmental passage, with increased rhythmic activity. |
| | | 170–83 | (b3): Trio texture. Main melodic idea (S5) divided between vln1 and vln2. |
| | Refrain a^b1 | 184–91 | (a1): The same structure as (120–27). |
| | | 192–200¹ | (a2): Duet between vln1 (S5) and vln2 (S6). |
| | Refrain a^b2 | 200²–06¹ | (a3): Response to phrase (a1). Main thematic idea in vlc (S8), accomp by vln1 and vln2 playing segments of S7a. |
| | | 206³–14 | (a4): Variation of phrase (a2): (S8 and S7b). E major, 'tonal' cadential gesture. |
| A¹ | Refrain a^a' | 215–20² | Varied refrain: Duet between vln1, playing the first theme (S1) and vln2 (S2). |
| | | 220–24¹ | (a1): Presentation of all four sets. |
| | Episode d^a | 224–32¹ | (d1) Canonic treatment of melodic ideas based on S1 and S3 and played as duets between vln1–vln2 and vla–vlc chordal accompaniment (S2, S4). |
| | | 232–9² | (d2): Main thematic idea played as a duet between vla and vlc. |
| | Episode e^a | 239³–48 | (e1): Developmental passage, with increased semiquaver rhythmic and textural activity similar to phrase (b2) of section B. |
| | | 248³–57¹ | (e2): Melodic gesture in the vlc (S1); continuous semiquavers in the bass, accompanied by chords in vln1 and vln2. Liquidated cadence. |
| | Episode c^a'' | 257²–63 | (c1''): Duet between vln2 (S3) with ascending *glissando* motive and vlc (S1). New, triplet rhythmic patterns in vln1 and vla. |
| | | 264–71 | (c2''): Predominant thematic idea in the vlc (S2). Rhythmic dialogue between semiquaver and triplet rhythmic motives. |
| | | 272–81¹ | (c3''): Varied repetition of phrase (c'); excessive use of trills. |
| | Episode b^a'' | 281²–9¹ | (b2'): Varied repetition of phrase (b2) with the second, 'waltz' theme played simultaneously by vln1 (S2), and vln2 (S1). |

*continued*

Table 11.4   *concluded*

| Rondo | Rondo subsections | Bars | Thematic structure and set structure |
|---|---|---|---|
|  |  | 289–99 | Cadential phrase to section A[1]. Textural and motivic liquidation; 'tonal' cadential gesture on C major seventh. |
| B[1] | Episode d[b] | 300–07[2] | (d[b]1): Contrapuntal treatment and interpolation of segments from different sets. |
|  |  | 307[3]–13[1] | (d[b]2): Developmental continuation. |
|  |  | 312[3]–20 | (d[b]3): Overlapping phrases. Contrapuntal treatment of the sets. Predominant melodic gesture: *pizzicato* vln2 (S5b); taken over by vln1 (S8) in (315). |
|  | Refrain a[b1'] | 321–6 | (a1'): Only the first phrase is stated. Second thematic idea in the vla (S6). The dyads of S5a are divided between vln1 and vln2. |
|  | Refrain a[b2'] | 327–31 | (a3): Only the first phrase is used. Predominant thematic idea in vlc (S8); the dyads of S7a are divided between vln1 and vln2. |
| A[2] | Episode b[a] | 332–42 | (b1): Reduced, trio texture. Duet between vlc (S4) and vla (S3). |
|  |  | 342–52[1] | (b2): Overlapping phrases. Duet between vln1, playing the second, 'waltz' theme (S2), and vla (S1). |
|  | Refrain a[a] | 352[2]–8 | Refrain of A: First theme (S1) played in unison. |
|  |  | 359–60 | Two twelve-note chords (S1). Each instrument plays a trichord of S1. |

on S1 only, thus reinforcing the importance of this set and ensuring the audibility of the refrain's rondo appearances within section A (see Example 11.7).

In the continuation (bars 8[3]–19[1]), the main thematic idea, based on S1, is played by the first violin and outlines a series of perfect fifths – implying a continuous tonic–dominant melodic progression, which, however, remains unresolved. The cello accompanies with a countermelody based on S4,[5] while the second violin and viola provide the chordal accompaniment with the simultaneous unfolding of S2 and S3 respectively (see Example 11.8). The sets are closely connected and, as usual, Skalkottas employs segmental association to guarantee coherent relationships between the four independent voices. Consequently, the texture is saturated by equivalent motivic segments, particularly the trichord set-class 3–2. The trichord set-class 3–5, outlining an upper appoggiatura-like semitonal gesture followed by the interval of a perfect fifth (with its inherent dominant–tonic tonal connotations), also determines the opening and closing gestures of the phrase. It initiates the first violin thematic line (bars 8[3]–12[1]); it appears reordered and

---

[5]   Set S4 has eleven different pitch-classes and one doubled (E).

Example 11.7  Third String Quartet, *Allegro vivace (Rondo)*: Opening thematic gesture (bars 1–8)

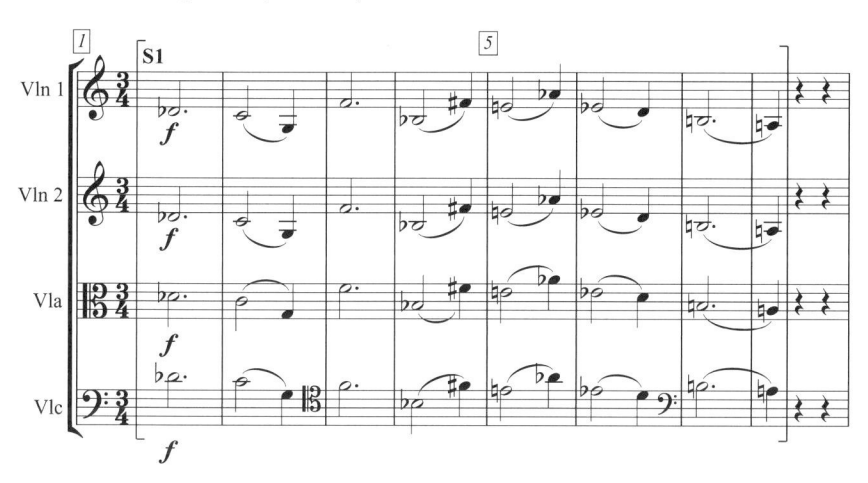

Example 11.8  Third String Quartet, *Allegro vivace (Rondo)*: Thematic gesture (bars $8^3$–$19^1$)

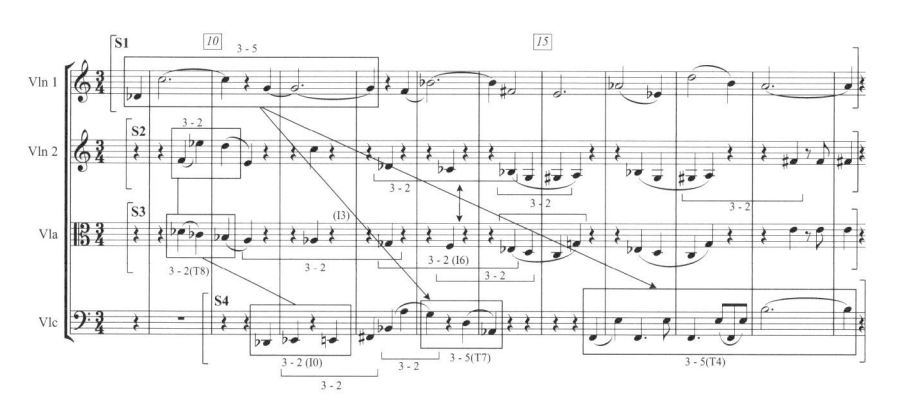

transposed at the fifth ($I_7$) in the bass line at bars 13–$14^1$; and finally, transposed at the major third ($T_4$), it establishes the last cadential gesture in the cello in bars $15^3$–$19^1$.

The loose construction, characteristic of last-movement rondo forms, and the developmental yet still controlled treatment of the source material, is also projected in the dance-like rhythmic motives and gaiety of the movement's character, and is perhaps intended to counteract the gravity of the quotation from Beethoven's Fifth Symphony in the first movement. The first episode (b[a]) introduces the rhythmic motive in phrase b[1] which is identified with the second theme of the section. In

Table 11.5  Third String Quartet, *Allegro vivace* (Rondo): Set topography and phrase structure

| Bars | 1–8¹ | 8³–19¹ | 19²–31 | 31²–9¹ | 39²–44 | 45–53¹ | 53–60 | 61–9 | 70–86 | 87–90 | 91–103¹ | 103²–119 |
|---|---|---|---|---|---|---|---|---|---|---|---|---|
| Vln1 | S1 | S1 | – | S2 *Die Fledermaus* waltz theme | S1 | S3 *Glissando* theme | S2 | S1 | S2 | – | S1 | S2 S1 Second 'waltz' theme (S2) |
| Vln2 | S1 | S2 | S1 | S4 (dyads) | S1 | S2 | S4 | S2→ | S2 S4 (dyads) | – | S2 | S1 S3 |
| Vla | S1 | S3 | S3 | S1 | S1 | S4 | S1 | S3→ | S3 S1 (dyads) | S1 | – | S3 S4 |
| Vlc | S1 | S4 | S4 | S3 (dyads) | S1 | S1 | S3 | S4 | S3 | – | S3 | S4 |
| Phrases | Unison theme | a1 | b1 | b2 | Unison theme | c1 | c2 | c3 | c' | | b1/c' | b2 |
| Rondo subsections | Refrain aᵃ | | Episode bᵃ | | Refrain aᵃ | | Episode cᵃ | | Episode cᵃ¹ | Refrain aᵃ | | Episode bᵃ¹ |
| Large-scale Rondo | Section A |||||||||||

| Bars | 120–27 | 128–35 | 136–42 | 143–9² | 149–56² | 156³–63¹ | 163–9 | 170–83 | 184–91 | 192–200¹ | 200²–06¹ | 206³–14 |
|---|---|---|---|---|---|---|---|---|---|---|---|---|
| Vln1 | – | S5 | – | S7 | S8a | S6 | S8 S7b | S5 → | – | S5 | S7a → | – |
| Vln2 | – | S6 | – | S8 | S7a (linear) | S5b | S7b S8 (dyads) | | – | S6 | | – |
| Vla | S6 | – | S8 | – | S5b | S7a S6→ | S6 S6 (dyads) S8 | S8 S6 S8 | S6 | – | – | S8 |
| Vlc | S5a | – | S7b | – | S6 | S8 | S5a S5 S7a | S7b S6 S7b | S5a | – | S8 | S7b |
| Phrases | a1 | a2 | a3 | a4 | link | b1 | b2 | b3 | a1 | a2 | a3 | a4 |
| Rondo subsections | Refrain aᵇ¹ | | Refrain aᵇ² | | | Episode bᵇ | | | Refrain aᵇ¹ | | Refrain aᵇ² | |
| Large-scale Rondo | Section B |||||||||||

| Bars | 215–20² | 220–4¹ | 224–32¹ | 232–9² | 239³–48 | 248³–57¹ | 257²–63 | 264–71 | 272–81¹ | 281²–91¹ | 289–99 |
|---|---|---|---|---|---|---|---|---|---|---|---|
| Vln1 | S | S1 | S2 (dyads) S3 | S1 | S3 S4 S2 S1 | S1 (dyads) S4 (dyads) | S2 | S3 | S2 | S2 | S1 |
| Vln2 | S2 | S2 | S1 S4 (dyads) | S2 | S2 (dyads) S1 S2 | S1 (dyads) S3 (dyads) | S3 | S4 | S3 | S1 | S3 |
| Vla | – | S3 | S1 S4 (dyads) | S3 | S1 (dyads) S3 S4 | S1 | S4 | S1 | S4 | S3 (dyads) | S4 |
| Vlc | – | S4 | S2 (dyads) S3 | S4 | S4 (dyads) S3 (dyads) S4 | S3 S2 | S1 | S2 | S1 | S4 (dyads) | – |
| Phrases | | a1 | d1 | d2 | e1 | e2 | c1″ | c2″ | c3″ | b2′ | |
| Rondo subsections | Refrain aᵃ′ | | Episode dᵃ | | Episode eᵃ | | Episode cᵃ″ | | | | Episode bᵃ″ |
| Large-scale Rondo | | | | | Section A¹ | | | | | | |

| Bars | 300–7² | 307³–13¹ | 312³–20 | 321–6 | 327–31 | 332–42 | 342–52¹ | 352²–8 | 359–60 |
|---|---|---|---|---|---|---|---|---|---|
| Vln1 | S8a | S6 (dyads) | S8 S7b | S5a | S7a | – | S2 | S1 | S1B |
| Vln2 | S7b S5b S7b | – | S5b S7a S8 (dyads) | S5a | S7a | S1 | S4 (dyads) | S1 | S1A |
| Vla | S±b S7? S5b | S7a | S6 S6 (dyads) S8 (dyads) | S6 | S8 | S3 | S1 | S1 | S1C |
| Vlc | S8a S6 | S8 | S5a S5 S7a | a1' | – | S4 | S3 (dyads) | S1 | S1 D |
| Phrases | dᵇ1 | dᵇ2 | dᵇ3 | | a3 | b1 | b2 | Unison theme | |
| Rondo subsections | | Episode dᵇ | | Refrain aᵇ¹″ | Refrain aᵇ²″ | | Episode bᵃ | Refrain aᵃ | Chordal cadence |
| Large-scale Rondo | | Section B¹ | | | | | | Section A² | |

phrase b² it exposes the most distinctive melody of the movement, a parody of the waltz theme from Johann Strauss's operetta *Die Fledermaus*, played by the first violin (bars 31²–7) and based on the chromatic set S2. The second episode, cᵃ, presents a new thematic idea with an ascending *glissando* gesture, played successively by the first violin and based on S3. A variation of the waltz theme (identified in Tables 11.4 and 11.5 as the second waltz theme) appears in phrase b² of the episode bᵃ′, now incorporating the *glissando* figures of the second episode's theme (in phrase c¹).

Section B is built on four source sets (S5, S6, S7, S8) and five derived ones (S5a, S5b, S7a, S7b, S8a).[6] The refrain, introducing the main theme of the section, has a periodic structure of two double, antecedent–consequent-type phrases with contrasting harmonic content. The first (refrain aᵇ¹) consists of two duets: between viola and cello – the viola playing S6 with the ubiquitous opening motive set-class 3–2, accompanied by the cello playing the tonal set S5a (bars 120–27); and between the first and second violins, playing S5 and S6 respectively (bars 128–35). The duets are repeated in refrain aᵇ² (bars 136–49²) with the cello and viola unfolding the chromatic sets S7a and S8, and the first and second violins sets S7 and S8.

---

[6] Set S5 is a 'derived' set, generated from four equivalent trichords, set-class 3–8 ($T_0$, $I_2$, $T_5$, $I_7$). Set S5a, constantly presented as a sequence of six, perfect-fifth chordal dyads, results from the superimposition of the two hexachords of S5. This chordal dyadic form, always played by the cello, frequently provides the harmonic accompaniment of the opening gesture of the phrases, thus imbuing the bass line with tonal associations and a directed movement towards a C major/minor goal. The tonal set S5b derives from the linear presentation of each perfect-fifth dyad of S5a. It includes several major/minor triads (B♭–D–F, D–F–A, E–G♯–B, G♯–B–D♯, B–D♯–G♭[F♯]) and two major seventh tetrachords in its internal structure, while its last trichord (D♭–C–G) is the same as the first trichord of S1. Set S6, accompanied by S5 and S5a, furnishes the predominant thematic line of the section, while its opening motivic gesture (set-class 3–2) creates aural associations with section A. Set S7 is a 'derived' set, generated from four equivalent trichords, set-class 3–3 ($T_0$, $I_9$, $T_2$, $I_{11}$). Identical to the set derivation technique of S5a, set S7a results from the superimposition of the two hexachords of S7, and is constantly presented as a sequence of six minor-seventh dyads. In this format, played always by the cello at the same registral level as S5a and following the latter's presentation, it counteracts the overt tonal implications of the consecutive perfect fifths of S5a. Similar to S5b, set S7b derives from the linear presentation of the dyads of S7a, and it consists of three transpositionally equivalent chromatic tetrachords (set-class 4–1 at $T_0$, $T_4$, $T_8$). Set S8 comprises two chromatic hexachords (set-class 6–1), and it derives from the $T_5$ form of S2 through a reordering of the pitch-class order within each hexachord. At the developmental episode in bars 149–56, a rearrangement of the pitch-class order, resulting in the retrograde presentation of each dyad within each hexachord of S8, creates a new twelve-note melody (indicated as S8a) that outlines a series of five descending major sevenths (a²–b♭¹, g²–a♭¹, f²–g♭¹, d²–e♭¹, c²–d♭¹), ending with a repeated chordal perfect fifth, e¹–b¹.

## Third Sonatina for Violin and Piano (1935): Linear Serialism and Tonal Principles of Construction

The first movement, *Allegro giusto*, outlines a reversed sonata form, shown on Table 11.6. The first subject group is built on two twelve-note sets, S1 and S2. The first theme (bars 1–12), played by the violin, is based on S1, while the piano accompanies with S2; the latter is distributed between the piano's two hands and is initially presented as a series of dyads, with the pitch-class order of each dyad varying in subsequent linear presentations of the set. The two sets S1 and S2 are closely connected through their common dyadic structure (E♭–G, D♭–F, F♯–C, B♭–A) (see Example 11.9).

Example 11.9   Third Sonatina for violin and piano, *Allegro giusto*: First theme (bars 1–12)

The second theme (bars 46²–54), also played by the violin, is based on S3 (which derives from S1; see Part II, p. 120), and the piano accompanies with S4 (see Example 11.10).

Apart from the extensive use of set segmentation, permutation and interpolation of segments to differentiate harmonic regions and to articulate its small-scale formal organization, the movement is based on tonal principles of construction, which have structural implications for the entire piece. Overt tonal elements give direction to individual textural lines, which converge at the ends of phrases or sections, while the large-scale harmonic structure oscillates between E♭ major/minor triads (the opening sonority of several phrases) and E dominant seventh (their concluding harmonic gesture). For example, S1 includes the notes B♭, E♭, G, F♯, which are grouped together via temporal and registral means to

Table 11.6  Third Sonatina for violin and piano, *Allegro giusto*: Formal structure and set structure

| Large-scale sonata form | Third Sonatina for vln and pno | Formal structure | Set structure |
|---|---|---|---|
| Exposition | *Allegro giusto* | **Reversed Sonata form** | |
| | | (1–74) Exposition | |
| | | (1–46¹) First subject group: (1–12) First theme (S1); (13–18) continuation; (18²–27) transition to secondary theme (segmental rotation). (28–35) Secondary theme (S2). (36–46¹) Transition to second subject group. | S1, S2 |
| | | (46²–74) Second subject group: (46²–54¹) Second theme (S3); (54–61) continuation; (62–72) secondary theme. | S3, S4 |
| | | (74²–96¹) Development | |
| | | Extensive juxtaposition, interpolation and simultaneous presentation of segments from S1, S2. (93–6¹) Retransition to Recapitulation (S1, S3, S4). | S1, S2 (S3, S4) |
| | | (96²–123) Reversed Recapitulation | |
| | | (96²–100) Second theme (pno solo) | S3, S4 |
| | | (101–8) First theme; (106–12¹) continuation; (112²–16¹) transition to second theme (segms from S1, S3, S4). | S1, S2 (S3, S4 segms) |
| | | (116²–23) Second theme. | S3, S4 |
| | | (124–41) Coda | |
| | | (124–30) Chordal passage; (131–41) final cadence. | S1, S2, S3, S4 |
| Development | *Andante* | **Ternary form** | |
| | | (1–19) Section A. | S1a, S2a |
| | | (20–43²) Section B. | S3a, S4a |
| | | (43³–66) Section A'. | S1, S2 |

| Large-scale sonata form | Third Sonatina for vln and pno | Formal structure | | Set structure |
|---|---|---|---|---|
| Retransition–Recapitulation | *Maestoso–Vivace* | **Rondo form** | | |
| | | (1–17) *Maestoso*: Retransition (1–3²) First phrase; (3³–8) second phrase; (8²–17) continuation. | | S1, S2 |
| | | (18–154) *Vivace*: Recapitulation | | |
| | | (18–44) Section A. | | S1, S2 |
| | | (45–77¹) Section B. | | S3, S4 |
| | | (77–125³) Section A¹. | | RS1, RS2, S1, S2 |
| | | (125⁴–42¹) Section B¹. | | S3, S4 |
| | | (142²–54) Section A². | | S1, S2 |

Example 11.10   Third Sonatina for violin and piano, *Allegro giusto*: Second theme – opening gesture (bars 46²–52)

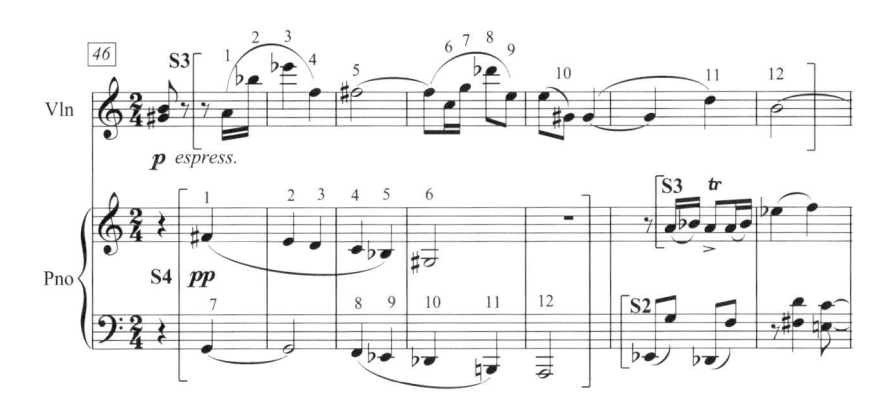

create Skalkottas's signature sound: E♭ major and E♭ minor triads. The set's last tetrachord (E–G♯–D–B), an E major dominant seventh (set-class 4–27), functions not only as the cadential gesture of the thematic line, but also as the final goal of the harmonic progression of the entire movement.

The transition to the second subject group outlines a movement from an E♭ major to an E dominant seventh, which traditionally requires resolution to an A major/minor harmony. Such a resolution is implied in the second theme, where the accompaniment to the violin's thematic line (outlining E♭ minor), based on S4, emphasizes an A major area. In the Recapitulation the E♭ minor area predominates in the upper line, while the first theme is recapitulated over an A₁ in the bass, which, however, is not consolidated as the resolution of the previous harmonic progression. The triadic conception of the work is fully exemplified in the final cadence (see Example 11.11).

Example 11.11  Third Sonatina for violin and piano, *Allegro giusto*: Final cadence (bars 131–41)

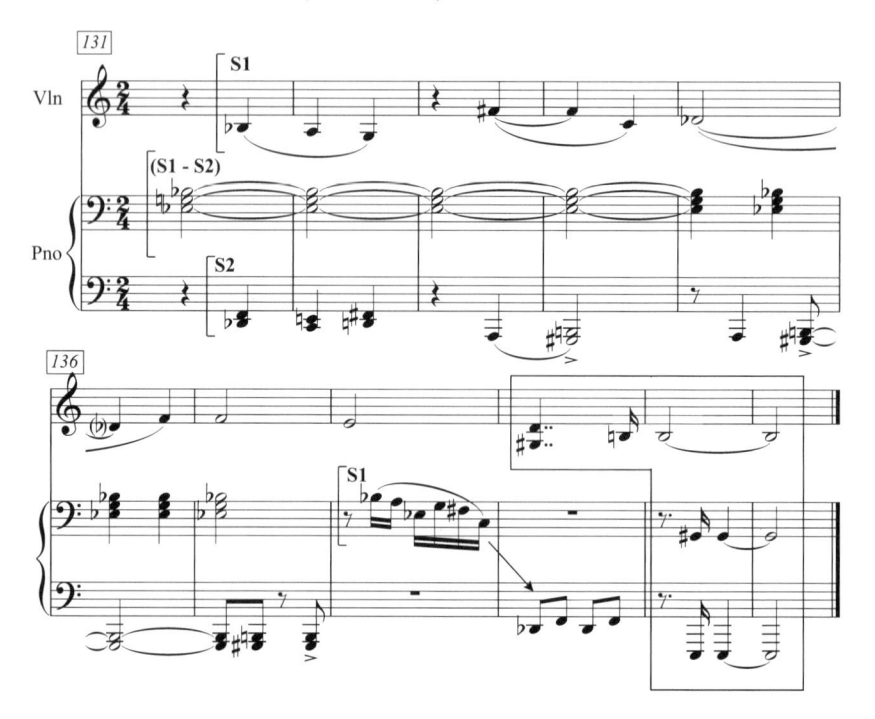

In bars 131–7, a sustained E♭ major triad in the piano right hand is formed through the merging of S1 and S2, using the common dyad E♭–G and the note B♭. In bars 134–7 this triad is accompanied by the dyad G♯$_1$–B$_1$ (approached by an appoggiatura A$_1$), anticipating the E dominant seventh, which itself is completed at the closing gesture (bars 140–41) through a rearrangement of the last tetrachord of S1. This tonal cadence built on triadic harmonies – notwithstanding their derivation from the manipulation of the movement's twelve-note set structure – encapsulates Skalkottas's notion of serialism and his treatment of explicit tonal references within a twelve-note context.

The second movement, *Andante*, in simple ternary form (ABA′), is built on the four sets S1a, S2a, S3a, S4a, which are varied presentations of the pitch-class order of the first movement's sets.[7] Its final gesture, recalling the retransition of the traditional formal prototype, is built entirely on the source sets S1 and S2. Overt reference to the tonal E♭ major/minor and E major sonorities of the previous movement are replaced here by non-triadic simultaneities. There is no break at the end of the movement and the music continues uninterrupted into the following *Maestoso*.

---

[7] See discussion in Part II, Chapter 6, 'Derived Sets through Source Trichords and Tetrachords' (p. 116), and 'Interchanging One Pitch-class in each Hexachord' (p. 120).

The third movement, *Maestoso–Vivace*, in simple rondo form (ABA¹B¹A²), is built on the original sets of the first movement, as if returning to the home key; however, for variety and further development within section A¹, Skalkottas uses the retrograde forms RS1 and RS2. This set structure also suggests that the movement outlines an arch form of linear, forward projection of the sets around the axis of a central section (A¹) built on their retrograde presentation. As already noted in Part II (pp. 142, 144–6), with its close harmonic relationship with the *Allegro giusto*'s transition section, the *Maestoso* section functions as the modulatory retransition to the Recapitulation proper, which starts at the *Vivace*. This is emphasized by a metric change to 6/8 and is initiated with a chordal E♭ major triad. The expected direction towards an E dominant seventh does not clearly materialize until the end of section A¹ (bars 120–25), where it repeatedly accentuates its cadential gesture. As if resolving this dominant harmony, section B¹ starts with a single, exposed note a¹ in the violin. The movement ends on an A₁ in the piano left hand, approached by an appoggiatura B♭₁ (the first two pitch-classes of S1); it is accompanied harmonically by its leading-note diminished triad on g♯, played as two dyads g♯–b/b–d¹ by the piano right hand and the violin respectively (both dyads are segments of the last trichords of S1 and S2). This final harmony, establishing A as the predominant tonal centre in the bass line and the goal of the harmonic progression, casts a different light on the large-scale harmonic structure of the entire piece; it renders the A major/minor chord as the structural goal and predominant key of the piece, and it reinforces the reading of the entire sonatina as a large-scale sonata form, organically developed from tonal harmonic functions. Example 11.12 presents the harmonic structure of the Third Sonatina for violin and piano as a large-scale sonata movement.

In summary, the *Allegro giusto* functions as the Exposition, which finally ends on an E dominant seventh, continuously approached within the phrase structure by its leading-note-like E♭ (major/minor). According to triadic functions, this needs resolution to an A major/minor tonic; but this is never established convincingly either during or at the end of the movement, which thus remains unresolved. The *Andante*, with its clear avoidance of triadic harmonic relationships, is comparable to the Development section, which not only elaborates and develops pitch-class material from the Exposition, but also delays resolution. Its final section, based on the original source sets of the first movement, functions as the retransition, which continues in the opening short section of the third movement, *Maestoso*. The Recapitulation, initiated by the *Vivace* section, returns to the twelve-note material of the first movement, but now it avoids the incessant E♭–leading-note – E–dominant-seventh harmonic progression within each phrase. The E dominant seventh gains structural significance in the middle of the movement and is finally resolved at its closing cadence.

Example 11.12　Third Sonatina for violin and piano: Large-scale harmonic and formal structure

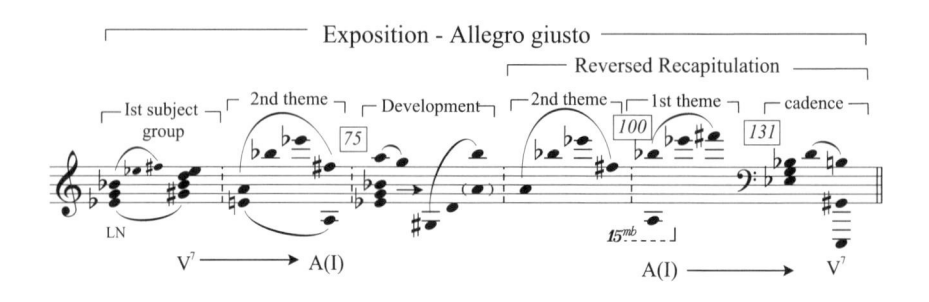

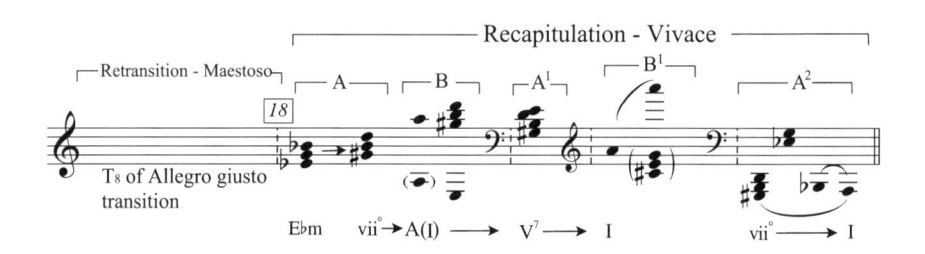

## Fourth Sonatina for Violin and Piano (1935): Development in 'Strict', Linear Twelve-Note Technique

The Fourth Sonatina for violin and piano outlines a large-scale reversed sonata form: the first movement, *Moderato*, functions as the Exposition, the second movement, *Adagio*, the Development, including a retransition, and the third movement, *Allegro moderato*, the reversed Recapitulation, starting with the sets of the first movement's second subject group and progressing to the recapitulation of the first subject group.

Similar to the *Allegro moderato* of the Third String Quartet, the *Moderato*, consisting of two sections (A and B) and their various repetitions, outlines a design that combines a simple rondo with a modified sonata form, as shown in Table 11.7,

Table 11.7  Fourth Sonatina for violin and piano, *Moderato*: Set topography and formal structure

| | 1–5 | 6–13¹ | 13²–19 | 19–25 | 26–30¹ | 29–32 | 33–6 | 36–42 | 42²–6 | 47–9 | 50–55 | 56–61 |
|---|---|---|---|---|---|---|---|---|---|---|---|---|
| vln | – | S3 ABC | S2 | S1 | RS4 | S5 | S6 | – | S4 | S1 | S3 | S2 S3 |
| pno RH | S1 | RS1 | S3/1hex S1 (chords) | S2 S3 | RS4→ | RS4 S5 S6→ | S6/2hex RS4→ | RS4 S5 S6 | RS6 | S2 | S1 S3 S1var | S1 S3 S2 |
| pno LH | S2 | RS2 | S3D S1 S3/2hex | S2 S1 | S4→ | S4 RS5 | RS6 | RS4 S5 S6→ | S6 RS5 | S3 | S1 S2 | S3 S3 S2 |
| Sections | A | | | | | | B | | | | A¹ | |
| Sonata form | Exposition – First subject group | | | | | Exposition – Second subject group | | | | | Development → | |

| | 61–3 | 64–70¹ | 73³–8¹ | 70–73 | 78–81 | 82–4 | 85–90 | 91–3 | 94–6 | 97–101 (=1–5) | 102–10 | 111–116 | 116–122 |
|---|---|---|---|---|---|---|---|---|---|---|---|---|---|
| vln | S4 | RS5 RS6 | S6 RS4ABC | RS4 S5 | – | S6 | S1 | S3 | – | – | S3 S1 | S1 | pedal f¹ |
| pno RH | RS4 S5(5–10) | S6 | S6 | RS4 S5 | RS4D S6 | S4 RS6 | S2 RS1→ | RS1 RS2→ | S1 S3/2hex | S1 | RS1 S2 S3 (segms) | RS4 S4 RS5 S5 (segms) | RS6BC |
| pno LH | S4 | S5(1–4, 11–12) | S6 RS5→ | S4 RS5 | RS5 S6 | RS5 | S3 | RS2 S3→ | S2 | S2 | RS2 RS1 | S4 RS5 RS6A | Pedal RS6A |
| Sections | B¹ | | | | | | A² | | | | | B² | |
| Sonata form | Development | | | | | | Recapitulation – First subject group | | | | | Coda – Recap of elements from second subject group | |

*Note*: In this table, the letters ABCD following certain sets (for example, S3ABC, S3D) indicate the four trichords of the set (pitch-classes (1, 2, 3) (4, 5, 6) (7, 8, 9) (10, 11, 12) respectively).

which outlines the set topography and formal structure of the movement.[8] In the Exposition, section A (the first subject group) is built on three sets, S1, S2, S3,[9] and the retrogrades of S1 and S2 (RS1 and RS2). As shown in Example 11.13, in the antecedent (bars 1–5), the piano right hand plays S1 accompanied by the left hand playing S2 in dyads. In the consequent (bars 6–13[1]), the thematic violin line, based on the first three trichords of S3, repeats the piano's right-hand opening thematic three-note motive, first transposed a tone lower and then reordered at the original tonal level; it is accompanied by RS1 and RS2, thus rounding off the first theme with the same harmonic material as that of its opening gesture. Although there is substantial segmentation of the sets and distribution of the segments among the three voices, the phrase structure is determined not only by the rotation of the sets as a group, but also by textural changes and contoural articulation.

Section B, the second subject group, is built on three new sets, S4, S5, S6, and their retrogrades, RS4, RS5, RS6. Sections A[1] and B[1], characterized by free treatment of the sets, function as the Development section, and section A[2] acts as the truncated Recapitulation, including a varied repetition of the first theme. The final passage of the movement (bars 111–22), based on elements from section B presented largely as segments distributed between the two piano hands, merges the curtailed recapitulation of the second theme within the Coda space.

The second movement, *Adagio*, an extended ternary form (A–BC–A' –D), is built on the three sets of the *Moderato*'s section A and their retrogrades, S1, S2, S3, RS1, RS2, RS3. The sets of the *Moderato*'s section B appear only in the last section of the movement (D), which functions as the retransition, equivalent to traditional dominant preparations leading to the Recapitulation (see Table 11.8). As noted previously (Example 5.6, p. 108), Skalkottas employs a freer twelve-note technique, composing with the largely unordered segments of the different sets. Metric changes, coinciding with the set-group reiteration and the thematic cadential structure, contribute to phrase articulation. There is a steady oscillation

---

[8] George Zervos reads the movement as a sonata form with Exposition (bars 1–46), short Development (bars 47–61), Recapitulation (62–108), and Coda (109–22), and he demarcates the Recapitulation to begin with the second subject group (Zervos, 2001, 31). However, such a reading, although neatly outlining a symmetrical form with the Exposition and Recapitulation consisting of 46 bars each (*ibid.*, 39–53), appears misguided. It does not take into consideration the textural layout of the different themes and other textural and rhythmic changes (contributing to sectional definition), the melodic contoural articulation (contributing to the cadential phrase structure), the continuous developmental process and gestural connectiveness around bar 61 (end of section A[1] and beginning of B[1]), and the natural break of the music at the end of section B[1], before the truncated recapitulation of the first subject group only (section A[2]).

[9] Set S1 has the note C♯ missing and B presented twice; its first trichord, A–E–D♯ (set-class 3–5), is a distinctive motive in the movement; S3 includes three versions of this motive at $T_{10}$ (D–C♯–G), $T_0$ (E♭–A–E) and $I_8$ (F–B–B♭). S2 includes in its internal structure three equivalent trichords, set-class 3–4 (at $T_0$, $T_3$, $I_6$), and it shares the trichord G–F♯–D (set-class 3–4) with S1.

Linear Serialism of the Mid-1930s: 'Strict' Twelve-Note Technique 241

Example 11.13  Fourth Sonatina for violin and piano, *Moderato*: First theme – opening gesture (bars 1–14)

*Note*: In bar 8 of the published score, the chord in the piano right hand is presented arpeggiated as g–c¹–b¹. In Skalkottas's manuscript it is written as presented in Example 11.13 (c¹–g¹–b¹).

between 12/8 and 9/8, with 12/8 supporting the stable thematic and cadential gestures, and 9/8 the more developmental passages.

In the third movement, *Allegro moderato*, Skalkottas composes with segments. By this point the sets have established their identity and the compositional

Table 11.8  Fourth Sonatina for violin and piano, *Adagio*: Set topography and formal structure

|        | 1–2    | 3    | 4–5   | 6–8        | 9–10       | 11–12 | 13–15       | 16                         | 17                         |
|--------|--------|------|-------|------------|------------|-------|-------------|----------------------------|----------------------------|
| vln    | S2 S3→ | S3   | S2    | –          | –          | –     | RS1 RS2 RS3 | –                          | S1 S2 S1 segm interpol     |
| pno RH | S1     | S2   | S3 →  | S1 RS1 S3  | S2 S3 S1   | S1 S3 | S3 S1 S2    | S1 S2 RS3 segm interpol    | S1 S2 S1 segm interpol     |
| pno LH | S3→    | S1→  | S3 S1→| S2 S2      | S2 S3→     | S3 S2 S1 | S1 S2 S3 | S1 S2 RS3 segm interpol    | RS3 S2 S1 segm interpol    |
| Metre    | 12/8 |      |       | 9/8        |            | 12/8  |             | 12/8                       | 9/8                        |
| Sections |      |      |       | A          |            |       |             | B                          |                            |

|        | 18       | 19          | 20          | 21        |
|--------|----------|-------------|-------------|-----------|
| vln    | S1 S2 S3 → | S1 S2 S3 →  | S1 S2 S3 →  | S2 chords |
| pno RH | →        | →           | →           | S3 chords |
| pno LH | →        | →           | →           | S1 chords |
| Metre    | 9/8    |             |             | 12/8      |
| Sections |        | C           |             |           |

|        | 22–4         | 25–6⁶       | 26⁷–8                          | 29–30                  | 31                        | 32–4                 |
|--------|--------------|-------------|--------------------------------|------------------------|---------------------------|----------------------|
| vln    | S1 S3 S2→    | S2          | –                              | –                      | –                         | S4A S5C S6C          |
| pno RH | S1 S3 S2→    | S2          | S1A S3A S1B S3B S1C S3C        | S4 S5 S6 → chords      | S4 S5 S6 → chords         | S4C chord | S5A chord | S6A chord | S4B chord | S5B chord | S6B → chord |
| pno LH | S2 S3 | S2 | S1 S3 S1 | S2(segms) S1 | S1 S3D                     |                        |                           |                      |
| Metre  | 12/8         | 6/8         | 12/8                           | 9/8                    | 12/8                      | 9/8                  |
| Sections |            | A′          |                                |                        | D (Retransition)          |                      |

*Note*: In this table, the letters ABCD following S1 and S3 (for example, S1ABC, S3ABC) indicate the four trichords of these sets only. The letters ABC following the sets S4, S5 and S6 indicate their three tetrachords (pitch-classes (1, 2, 3, 4) (5, 6, 7, 8) (9, 10, 11, 12), respectively)..

technique here involves not only the occasional free treatment of the set order, but also consistent manipulation of the sets, including extensive partitioning, segmental rotation, missing notes, octave doublings and the use of segments as independent motives, or chords. The movement has a complicated formal design, combining a rondo within the superstructure of a large-scale ternary form (ABA'), symmetrically built around a middle section B; section A is 57 bars long, section B 21 bars, and section A' 57 bars. Table 11.9 represents the set topography and formal structure of the movement. Section A of the large-scale ternary form – itself having a small-scale rondo structure (ABA$^1$C) – is built on the sets of the *Moderato*'s section B (S4, S5, S6, RS4, RS5, RS6). The retrograde forms of the sets, in chordal formations, predominate in subsection B, while in subsection C the sets S4, S5 and S6 are freely distributed in the two-part piano texture over a long pedal a$^3$ played by the violin. The middle section B of the large-scale ternary form, also indicated as D in the internal small-scale rondo form, is built on sets S1, S2 and S3 of the *Moderato*'s section A. Ternary section A' consists of a sequential, truncated presentation of the rondo sections A and D, each alternating the sets of the two thematic groups. It is the most developmental and climactic section of the entire movement, and is characterized by the predominantly chordal appearance of set segments distributed among the three-part texture.

Table 11.9  Fourth Sonatina for violin and piano, *Allegro moderato*: Set topography and formal structure

| | 1–5¹ | 5²–8¹ | 8²–12 | 12–15¹ | 15²–17¹ | 17²–19¹ | 19²–23 | 24–8 | 29–32 | 33–6¹ | 36²–9 | 40–43 |
|---|---|---|---|---|---|---|---|---|---|---|---|---|
| vln | RS4 | S5 | S6 | – | S5 | – | RS4 S5 | S4 RS5 S4 | – | – | – | RS4 S5 S6 reorderings |
| pno RH | S4 → | RS5 | RS6 → | S4var | | S6 | RS4 S5 → | RS4 → | S5ACB → | S4CAB | RS4 | S5 | S6 |
| pno LH | | | | RS4 | RS5 | S6CAB | S6 | S5 | | S4 | RS5 | RS6 | |
| Phrases | a | | | | a' | | b | | | a (=bs.1–12) | | a' (cadence) |
| Rondo | A | | | | | | B | | | | | A¹ |
| Ternary form | Section A → | | | | | | | | | | | |

| | 44–6 | 45²–50 | 51–6 | 57–60 | 61–4 | 65–73 | 74–7 |
|---|---|---|---|---|---|---|---|
| vln | S4(dyads) | S6(dyads) S4B | pedal a³ | S1 | | S3 | S2 |
| pno RH | S4 → | S6 | S6 S4(segms) | S5 | S6 | S4 | S5 S4 → | S4 | S2 S3 → | S2 S3 → | S3 | S1 S3 segm interpol | S1 → |
| pno LH | | | | | | S3 S2 | S2 → | | |
| Phrases | c | | c' | | d' | | d' |
| Rondo | C | | | | D | | |
| Ternary form | ←A | | | | B | | |

| | 78–82¹ | 82²–5 | 86–7 | 88–9¹ | 89²–90 | 91–4 | 95–9 | 100–04 | 105–12 | 113–16 | 116–24 | 125–30¹ | 131–4 |
|---|---|---|---|---|---|---|---|---|---|---|---|---|---|
| vln | S5var | S6 → | S1 → | S2 → | S3(segm) | S4 S6 (segms) | S5 | – | – | S4var S5var → | S5v S6 | S3 S2A | RS4 S5 S6 (segms) |
| pno RH | RS4 → | | | | ←S2 | S4 S5 S6 → (segms) | RS4 | S1 S3 → | S2 → | RS4 S5 S6 | S4 | S5 S6 → | S1 S3 → | S2 RS4 S5 S6 → |
| pno LH | | | | | S3(segm) → | S3 S4 S5 S6 (segms) | S5A S6C | | S4 RS5 RS6 | S4 S5 (segms) | | | |
| Rondo | A² | | | D¹ | | | A³ | D² | | A⁴ | | D³ | A⁵ |
| Ternary form | | | | | | | A' | | | | | | |

*Note*: In this table, the letters ABC following the sets S4, S5 and S6 indicate their three tetrachords (pitch-classes (1, 2, 3, 4) (5, 6, 7, 8) (9, 10, 11, 12), respectively).

# Chapter 12
# Expansion of the Mid-1930s 'Strict' Twelve-Note Technique: First Symphonic Suite (1935)

The First Symphonic Suite for large orchestra, in six movements (*Ouvertüre*, *Thema con Variazioni*, *Marsch*, *Romance*, *Siciliano–Barcarole* and *Rondo–Finale*), is Skalkottas's first surviving entirely dodecaphonic large-scale orchestral work. In the Foreword to his Notes to the piece, Skalkottas states that he '*composed* [it] *in 1929 in Berlin*',[1] although the surviving manuscript and the Notes themselves date from 1935, when, according to Papaioannou, there was the possibility of a performance of it by an orchestra in Athens.[2] Papaioannou, evoking comparisons with the legendary anecdotes about Mozart's memory, misleadingly asserts that Skalkottas 'rewrote it from memory from the 1929 version' (1974, 219). Skalkottas's correspondence, however, casts doubt on Papaioannou's assertions. In a letter to Matla Temko dated November 1935, enumerating his compositions to date, Skalkottas wrote that he had '***finished*** *a large orchestral work (a Suite in 6 large movements, lasting 3/4 of an hour) of which I had already composed – sketched the themes only in Berlin, right or left next to Schoenberg*' [my emphasis].[3] This suggests that he received guidance from Schoenberg – or perhaps they discussed twelve-note compositional processes – when sketching the themes of the 'orchestral piece' mentioned in Schoenberg's report for the summer semester of 1929 (APrAKB, 128). Skalkottas also mentioned such a piece in a 1931 letter to Benakis, confirming that he did not finish it at the time because of ill health (Thornley, 2002a, 200).

Certainly, the First Symphonic Suite as we now know it cannot have been composed and completed in 1929. The other surviving works of that period, the First String Quartet and the First and Second sonatinas for violin and piano, show

---

[1]   Skalkottas, 'Notes to the Ouvertüre' in 'Accompanying Notes to the First Symphonic Suite' (MS, Skalkottas Archive). Skalkottas wrote sketchy programme notes, in both Greek and German, which remain unedited and unpublished, but give an insight into his compositional strategy. However, it appears that he was not always sufficiently careful in his writing, and there are several contradictions between his descriptions and the music itself. Henceforth all quotations taken from these Notes appear in italics without further citation.

[2]   The piece was never performed during Skalkottas's lifetime. It was premiered on 28 April 1972 by the City of Birmingham Symphony Orchestra conducted by Marius Constant.

[3]   The last phrase is typically ambiguous, but I take it to mean that Schoenberg was beside him, i.e. tutoring him, as he sketched the themes.

an early stage in Skalkottas's compositional development which is incompatible with the breadth, sophistication and confident use of twelve-note technique in this suite. Moreover, in the Octet and the First Piano Concerto of 1931, Skalkottas clearly experiments with different approaches to his developing composition with twelve notes, approaches that would only be consolidated and expanded in the chamber music of the mid-1930s. The First Symphonic Suite exhibits more advanced twelve-note techniques than those tried out in these smaller pieces, and it establishes a compositional approach that Skalkottas would develop further in large orchestral works of the early 1940s, such as the Second Symphonic Suite and *The Return of Ulysses*.

In this suite Skalkottas explores a different compositional approach in each movement, although he still composes with a limited number of twelve-note set-groups; as he clarified in his Notes: '*The twelve-note harmony dominates in all movements and is strictly connected with the development of the themes.*' The *Ouvertüre* and *Thema con Variazioni* are built on superimposed, predominantly linear sets. The *Marsch* and *Romance* use both linear and chordal sets. In the *Siciliano–Barcarole* the multidimensional arrangement and vertical harmonic presentation of set segments, and the use of a superset, are explored for the first time. The *Rondo–Finale* consolidates this technique by systematically employing a superset.

Significantly, in this large-scale orchestral suite, as in other compositions of 1935, harmonic and formal differentiation are not dependent on transpositions of the pitch-class content of entire sections, as was the case in several works he composed in Berlin (such as the Second Sonatina for violin and piano, the First String Quartet and the *Presto* of the Octet), and Skalkottas observes in his Notes that '*Unlike* [other] *works (especially those of diatonic harmony) harmonic transpositions here are avoided.*' Furthermore, despite the twelve-note polyphony and multilayered structures of the piece, he asserts that '*The appearance of the score is mainly transparent, its sound coming from a new world, another sphere.*' This statement may have its roots in Schoenberg's analysis of his own song op.22 no.4, *Vorgefühl*, in which he described the orchestration as 'preponderantly soloistic and, despite the frequently high number of parts [...] mostly *transparent*' (1968, 43-4).[4]

### First Movement, *Ouvertüre*: Twelve-note Set Structure and Harmonic Structure[5]

Skalkottas claims that the *Ouvertüre* '*is written in sonata form*', and he describes it as a binary structure consisting of two sections: the first section conveys '*the first*

---

[4] For a discussion of the compositional processes and orchestration of this song see Schoenberg's lecture-analysis accompanying the first performance of op.22, given at Radio Frankfurt on 21 February 1932 (Schoenberg, 1952/1968, 43–4); also Dunsby (1977, 137–49).

[5] For a detailed discussion of this movement, see Mantzourani (1999, 274–319); also (2004a, 49–57) and (2006, 73–81).

theme', while the second section '*starts with the second theme* [...] *is completely contrasting* [...] *and is found in great musical opposition to the first section* [...] *with a tendency to move towards the preparation of the first theme*'; it also includes a curtailed repetition of the first theme (section A') and a short coda. These sections are distinguished from each other by their different twelve-note set content, rhythm, instrumentation, articulation and character. However, this formal outline implies an andante form (ABA'), with each section outlining a ternary structure consisting of three subsections aba'; these in turn, at thematic statements, are further subdivided into three phrases, as shown in Table 12.1, and in more detail in Table 12.2.

Table 12.1   First Symphonic Suite, *Ouvertüre*: Schematic presentation of formal structure and set structure

| Andante form |||||||||
|---|---|---|---|---|---|---|---|---|
| **Sections** | A ||| B ||| A' |||
| | First subject group ||| Second subject group ||| Curtailed first subject group |||
| Subsections | a | b | a' | a | b | a' | a | b | a' |
| Phrases | aba' | aba' | | aba' | | | | | |
| | First theme | Contrapuntal passage | Modified a | Second theme | Contrasting passage | Modified a Retransition | First theme | | Coda |
| Sets | S1, S2, S3, S4 ||| S5, S6, S7, S8 ||| S1, S2, S3, S4 |||

Although Skalkottas writes that '*the first theme consists of three twelve-note sets*', section A, the first subject group (bars 1–61), is in fact built on four closely connected sets (S1, S2, S3, S4), as shown in Example 12.1.[6]

Within section A, the first theme in its opening appearance is characterized by a striking textural contrast between solo motives and large chords. The opening chord, D–A–e–b♭–e♭$^1$–g♭$^1$ (set-class 6–Z17), provides one of the most distinctive sounds of the movement, and is used throughout as a harmonic landmark. It is followed by a distinct motto-like melody played by the horns, which Skalkottas claims '*has the character of a signal*'; it appears three times (bars 1, 13, and 32), each time introducing the next phrase of the theme's ternary form. In bars 3$^4$–4$^2$ a reordering in the second hexachord of S2, bringing the signature trichord b♭–e♭$^1$–g♭$^1$ (order position 10, 12, 11) before d♭–a♭–c♭$^1$[b] (9, 8, 7), and superimposing this segment on G–c–f (4, 5, 6), creates harmonic conditions similar to those of

---

[6] All the musical examples from the *Ouvertüre* are presented in reduced form to facilitate the reading of the set structure.

Table 12.2   First Symphonic Suite, *Ouvertüre*: Formal structure and set structure

| Sub-sections | Thematic, phrase and set structure | Set combinations |
|---|---|---|
| | **Section A** | |
| a | (1–4²) First phrase (a). Antecedent (1–6); motto-like thematic idea: hns (S1). | a (S1+S2) |
| | (4³–6) Consequent; varied repetition of the thematic idea: basses (S4). | b (S3+S4) |
| | (7–9²) Varied repetition of theme: vln1 (S1). | a |
| | (9³–11) Continuation; thematic idea (S4), similar to (4³–6). | b |
| | (11⁴–12) Closing passage; 'perfect' cadence to the first phrase of the theme's ternary design. | a |
| | (13–15¹) Second phrase (b); motto-like thematic idea: hns (S1). | a |
| | (15³–17³) Continuation; predominant thematic idea: cl (S3). | c (S1–S4 segms) |
| | (17³–22¹) (22–5²) (25²–8¹) phrases with new melodic ideas in two-part counterpoint (vln1+tpt, vlns+tbn); (28–9³). | c¹, c², b, a |
| | (29³–31) 'Half' cadence to the phrase with liquidation of motivic and textural material. | b |
| | (32–4¹) Third phrase (a'); motto-like thematic ideas: hns (S1). | a |
| | (34–7) Continuation with liquidation of motivic and textural material. | a [b] |
| | (37⁴–9¹) Introduction of 'rhythmic episode'. | a |
| | (39¹–41²) Rhythmic episode functioning as 'half' cadence to the theme's ternary design. | b |
| | (41³–3) Closing gesture; last appearance of modified thematic idea: db (S1). | a |
| b | (44–6) '*Contrapuntal section of double counterpoint*'; theme in two-part counterpoint: fl+vln1, ob+vln2 (S3). | b¹ (S3) |
| | (46–50¹) 'Answer' (S4). | b² (S4) |
| | (49⁴–53) Continuation leading to the reappearance of the main thematic idea. | c³ |
| a' | (53⁴–5) Modified repetition of main theme; motto-like thematic idea: fl+ob+vla. | a |
| | (56–8²) Continuation with predominant thematic idea (S4), similar to (9–11). | b+c |
| | (58³–61) Closing gesture to section A. | a+b |
| | **Section B** | |
| a | (62–5) First phrase (a); theme, in two-part counterpoint: cl (S5) – ob (S6); accomp (S7, S8). | d [e] (S5+S6) |
| | (66–70¹) Varied repetition of the theme. | d [e] |
| | (70–72) Second, contrasting phrase (b); introduction of new motivic ideas (S5, S7). | e [d] (S7+S8) |
| | (73–5) Third phrase (a'); modified appearance of the theme (fl+ob). | d [e] |

| Sub-sections | Thematic, phrase and set structure | Set combinations |
|---|---|---|
| | (76–81) Developmental continuation. | f (S5–S8 segms) |
| | (82–4) Closing passage to subsection **a**; textural changes. | d [e] |
| **b** | (84⁴–6¹) Contrasting, rhythmically active middle section. | d [e] |
| | (86–7)( 88–91²) ( 91³–3¹) (93²–5²) Continuation. | e [d], d, f¹, f² |
| | (95²–100¹) Fugato cadence to subsection **b**. | d [e] |
| **a'** | (100–02) Modified repetition of the section's theme in ob+cl (S6) and tpt (S5). | d [e] |
| | (103–8) Cadence with motivic and textural liquidation; retransition to section A'. | d [e] |
| | **Section A'** | |
| **a** | (109–11) Modified and truncated recap of main theme. Motto-like thematic idea: tba (S1). | a |
| | (112–15) Slow formation of the hallmark harmony (E♭ minor + D–A–E trichord). | a |
| | (116–19) Chordal interlude. | a |
| | (120–21) Repetition of thematic idea (S4), similar to (4³–6). | b |
| | (122–4¹) Modified reappearance of thematic material from (7–9). | a |
| | (124–5) Repetition of material from (9⁴–12). | b |
| | (126–7²) Similar to (37⁴–8). | a |
| | (127³–9³ ) 'Half' cadence similar to (39–41). | b |
| **b** | (129³–32) Contrasting middle section; contrapuntal thematic idea: vln1–vln2 (S3). | b¹ |
| | (133–4) Thematic idea: fl1+fl2 (S4). | b² |
| | **Coda** | |
| **a'** | (135–6) Last repetition of main theme. Motto-like thematic idea: solo vln1 (S1 only). | a (S1) |
| | (137–9¹) Continuation: vln1+vla (S3 only). | b (S3) |
| | (139–41) 'Perfect' cadence to subsection **a'**. | a |
| | (142–4) Six-note chords. | x |
| | (145—8) twelve-note chords. | y |

bars 1–2; the upper woodwind and upper strings play an E♭ minor triad (reminiscent of the harmonic structure of the Third Sonatina for violin and piano), which has the double function of being both the opening and cadential chord of the thematic gesture. The basses accompany with the trichords G–c–f and d♭–a♭–c♭, forming the hexachord set-class 6–Z43, the complement to the opening chord. The consequent, built on the superimposition of S3 and S4, has similar rhythmic structure and textural layout to the antecedent.

In subsection **b** the splitting off of S3 followed by S4 results in '*a purely contrapuntal section of double counterpoint*' (see Example 12.2), while the canonic

Example 12.1  First Symphonic Suite, *Ouvertüre*: First theme – opening gesture (bars 1–7)

Example 12.2  First Symphonic Suite, *Ouvertüre*: Subsection **b** – opening gesture (bars 44–7)

entries of the voices and the dovetailing of the phrases maintain momentum and keep the music in a state of flux.

Section B, the second subject group, which has a '*calm, dolce, espressivo*' character, contrasting thematic material and a thinner texture, is built on a group of four new sets (S5, S6, S7, S8) (Example 12.3). In contrast to the first theme, the orchestration is essentially soloistic, with large passages written for small instrumental ensembles and the texture tending to thin out at cadences.

Section A', introduced following a long tutti pause, is a truncated recapitulation of section A. It ends with a short coda based on long six-note *pp* and twelve-note *ppp* chords, played by the lower woodwind, brass and strings. This is the first instance of vertical serialism in Skalkottas, and this condensed, chordal presentation of the twelve-note material as the final gesture of the movement is also used in the following movements of the suite.

Example 12.3　First Symphonic Suite, *Ouvertüre*: Second theme – opening gesture (bars 62–6)

Harmonic cohesion is achieved in the *Ouvertüre* through the combination of certain twelve-note sets and/or their trichordal and tetrachordal segments, which form distinct harmonic units that recur at regular intervals within the sections. A short phrase presenting the opening gesture of the main thematic idea, or its varied repetition, is always based on S1 and S2 (as in bars 1–4²). These sets are always presented together, with an E♭ minor triad being both the opening and closing gesture of the phrase they support. This set combination, when used at the closing phrase of a larger section or at cadential points, functions as a 'perfect' cadence; in Table 12.2 it is symbolized as 'a'. This is generally followed by another short phrase, based on S3 and S4 (as in bars 4³–6). When used at cadential points, this set combination functions as a 'half' cadence; it is symbolized as 'b' in Table 12.2. In subsection **b** of the first theme, passages whose thematic material is based predominately on S3 are symbolized as 'b¹', while others based on S4 are represented as 'b²'. At developmental passages discrete segments from all four sets are juxtaposed in quick succession or used simultaneously in different formations; these are represented as 'c', 'c¹', 'c²' and 'c³' respectively. Similarly, in section B the sets are largely employed as pairs, S5–S6 and S7–S8. Here, contrary to section A, all four sets are used simultaneously within a phrase. However, at each reappearance of the group a particular set combination predominates by supporting the main thematic idea of the passage. The letter 'd' represents phrases in which S5 and S6 predominate or convey the main thematic idea, while segments of S7 and S8 provide the accompaniment. The letter 'e' represents phrases in which S7 and S8 convey the main thematic lines, while S5 and S6 accompany. As in section A, at developmental passages discrete segments from all four sets are juxtaposed, combined and used simultaneously, and these are represented as 'f'. In passages where the variations are so extensive that set-segment identities are blurred, the harmonic combinations are stated as 'f¹', and 'f²'. The six-note and twelve-note chords of the coda are shown as 'x' and 'y' respectively.

As in most of Skalkottas's works thus far, tonal elements within the twelve-note texture of the *Ouvertüre* (particularly the E♭ minor triad) are important structural features. The opening chord consists of the superimposition of an E♭ minor triad and the quartal trichord D–A–E. These two harmonies not only frame the entire movement, they also contribute to the harmonic definition of formal sections. As shown in Example 12.4, within section A the harmonic movement is static, and it is framed by the E♭ minor triad in the upper textural stratum and the quartal D–A–E trichord in the lower one. Section B, with its contrapuntal texture and developmental character, does not establish a strong tonal centre, although the E♭ environment is felt throughout. In section A', the recapitulation of the first theme starts with the same minor-quartal sonority, which is now inverted, with the E♭ minor triad in the lower register. It clearly ends with an E♭ minor chord at bar 134, thus asserting the latter's priority as the 'tonic' of the piece. Typically, however, Skalkottas undermines this event in the coda, which is underlined by a sustained pedal of an E♭ minor triad in second inversion, over an E♮ in the bass, a temporal dislocation of the D–A–E trichord. The final six- and twelve-note chord progression is based on a descending linear voice-leading movement to the final D–A.

Example 12.4   First Symphonic Suite, *Ouvertüre*: Schematic presentation of the harmonic structure

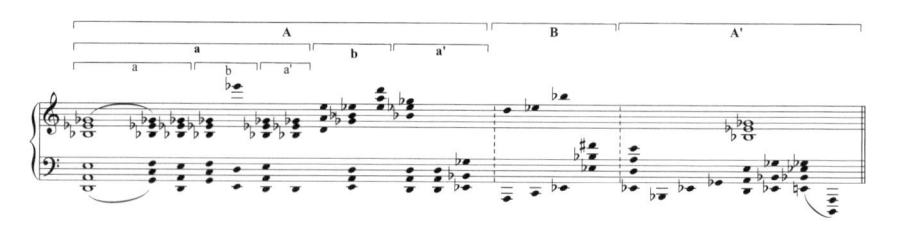

## Second Movement, *Thema con Variazioni*: A Study in Variation Form

Skalkottas was aware of the two opposite ways of constructing variations, either on a structural plan (wherein the formal design of the theme is preserved in the variations) or on a free plan. In the *15 Little Variations* for piano (1927) he had already used the structural plan within an atonal context. In the *Thema con Variazioni* of the First Symphonic Suite, his first large-scale orchestral variations, he used similar compositional principles but now within a twelve-note context. The movement consists of a theme with three variations and a short coda, as shown in Table 12.3. The formal outline of the *Thema* largely remains constant in the variations, while the thematic motives, part-writing, rhythm, tempo, mood and dynamics are all modified or new.

The 3/8 *Thema* has a dark, subdued sound arising from a small ensemble of predominantly low instruments. As discussed previously (Part II, Chapter 4, 'Set-groups Consisting of Several Discrete, Closely Related Twelve-note Sets in Polyphonic Combinations', pp. 88–9 and Chapter 8, 'Harmonic Change and Reiteration of Fixed Harmonic Formations to Define the Phrase Structure', pp. 137–9), it is built on a group of four twelve-note sets, and Skalkottas combines a twelve-note polyphonic texture of three melodic lines, each playing a different set,

Table 12.3   First Symphonic Suite, *Thema con Variazioni*: Formal structure and set structure

| Sections | Phrases | Thematic and set structure |
|---|---|---|
| | | **Thema** |
| A | a | (1–5) First thematic-melodic phrase: cl (S1); countertheme: bcl (S2); contrapuntal accomp: cbsn (S3); harmonic accomp (S4). |
| | a¹ | (6–10) Continuation; varied repetition of phrase a with rhythmic variations. Exchange of set material and rhythmic motives: thematic line: cl (S2); countertheme: bcl (S1); contrapuntal accomp: cbsn (S3) and vlc (S4). Harmonic accomp (S3). |
| B | b | (10³–14²) Contrast. New thematic phrase: fl+vln (S4) |
| | a² | (14³–18) Repetition of the initial thematic phrase; duet between db (S1) and cl (S3); harmonic accomp (S2 and S4 segm interpol). |
| | | **Variation I** |
| A | a | (19–22) New theme; duet between hn (S2) and db (S3); harmonic accomp as in (1–4). |
| | a¹ | (22²–8) Continuation; duet between vlns1+2 (S2) and hn (S2); harmonic accomp similar to (6–10). |
| B | b | (28–32) Contrast; new thematic phrase in tpt (S1), replacing S4 of phrase b in *Thema*. (33–6¹) Phrase extension; duet between tpt (S3), and vlc (S2); harmonic accomp (S4). |
| | a² | (36–49) Modified repetition of duet between tpt (S2) and vlns1+2 (S3); chordal cadence. |
| A′ | a | (49²–56¹) Modified representation of (19–28). Thematic phrase in ob and cl (S2); harmonic accomp (S1, S3, S4 segm interpol). |
| | a¹ | (56²–60) Continuation with phrase variation (S3). |
| B′ | b | (61–7) Modified repetition of (28–32); thematic line: vln1+vln2 (S1). |
| | a² | (68–75) Modified repetition of (19–27); thematic duo in cbsn+db (S3) and vlns1+2 (S2). |
| | | **Variation II** |
| A | a | (76–80) Reworking of (1–5); varied presentation of melodic phases on S1, S2, S3. |
| | a¹ | (81–6) Continuation similar to (6–10); thematic idea in vlc (S3). |
| B | b | (87–91) Contrasting phrase similar to (11–14²); melodic duet between vln1 (S4) and vln2 (S3). |
| | a² | (92–5) Final statement of duet between db (S1) and cl (S3) as in (14³–18). |
| | | **Variation III** |
| A | a | (96–9) Varied repetition of Variation I, structurally and harmonically similar to (19–22); thematic melody in hn (S2). |
| | a¹ | (100–06) Continuation; varied representation of (23–8); duet between hn (S2) and vlns1+2 (S2). |
| B | b | (106–11) Contrast; varied repetition of thematic idea: hns and tpt (S1) similar to (28–32). |
| | a² | (112–15) Varied repetition of the thematic duet between vlc (S2) and tpt (S3) as in (33–6); (116–20) chordal cadence. |
| | | **Coda** |
| | | (121–31) Varied repetition of the *Thema*'s phrase a²; final cadence with liquidation of motivic, textural and sound material. |

with dodecaphonic homophony in the form of a chordal accompaniment in the horns and trombones (see Example 12.5).

Example 12.5  First Symphonic Suite, *Thema con Variazioni: Thema* – opening gesture (bars 1–7)

The *Thema* outlines a binary structure consisting of four phrases (aa¹ba²), which are differentiated by the periodic reiteration of the set-group and the '*change of the compositional position of the theme*'. In the opening phrase **a** (bars 1–5), the thematic idea, based on S1, is played by the clarinet, while the bass clarinet plays the countertheme with S2. In phrase **a¹** (6–10), a varied repetition of the opening phrase, the thematic clarinet gesture outlines S2 with a similar rhythm to the contrapuntal bass clarinet line in the first phrase. The contrasting phrase **b** (10³–14²), initiated by an abrupt textural change and orchestration, introduces a new thematic gesture played by the flutes and violins based on S4. In phrase **a²** (14³–18), the thematic segment in the basses (on S1) is played as a duet with the clarinet (on S3), and has an identical rhythm to the thematic clarinet line in bars 2–5. Preserving this rhythm enables changes to the pitch-class content of the thematic line, thus facilitating further variation. This last phrase provides the source material for the subsequent variations. The melodic duet between the basses and the clarinet becomes the predominant feature for Variations I and III, while the glissandi of the accompaniment in the lower strings shape the indistinct sound and texture of Variation II.

Variation I, in 2/4 metre, having a '*transparent*' sound and an animated '*dance-like character*', is a double variation – in essence two variations dovetailed by expanding the binary formal design of the *Thema* (AB–A'B'). Variation II, returning to 3/8 and a rather indistinct and subdued sound, represents the slow, middle section of the set. In its section A, the thematic melody and its contrapuntal accompaniment dissolve as individual lines. Although occasional motivic references persist, their identity is so disguised through glissandi and tremolos that they are scarcely perceptible. In contrast, to compensate for this lack of clarity, section B is an almost exact repetition of the second half of the *Thema*. Variation III (in 2/4 metre), '*also dance-like in character with a humorous content*', is a variation of Variation I, whose formal design and phrase and thematic structure it largely follows. However, this is curtailed by the omission of the second part of the earlier variation. To round off the movement, Skalkottas returns to its original pitch-class set and thematic, textural and timbral material in a slow-paced coda (bars 121–31).

### Third Movement, *Marsch*: Composing with Instrumental Colours

The *Marsch* is built on three twelve-note sets (S1, S2, S3), and it outlines a traditional Scherzo with Trio, as shown in Table 12.4. Here, Skalkottas not only creates a twelve-note polyphonic texture, with each textural layer having its own set, rhythmic and melodic structure, but he also develops his version of *Klangfarbenmelodie*: he substitutes the single notes of a set with trichordal segments, both linear and chordal, each played by a different instrument, while the set is defined by blocks of instrumental colour. The superimposition of the sets and the use of syncopated rhythms result in the interpolation of their segments, producing a 'hocketed' accompaniment split between two or more instruments or instrumental families, which play the segments alternately.[7] As shown in Example 12.6, the opening, antecedent phrase of the first theme is played by the cellos and double basses (bars 1–5) and is based on S1; this is repeated in condensed form in the bass clarinet (bars 5–6). It is accompanied sequentially by a countermelody based on S2, played fragmented first by the viola and then as an ascending arpeggio by the oboe and clarinet; the violins, playing chordal trichords of S3, provide the harmonic accompaniment. The consequent is announced by a twelve-note chord, based on S3, in the woodwind and brass. The thematic line is now played by the trumpets (bars 7–10) accompanied contrapuntally by the bassoons playing the countermelody based on S2; and then it is repeated by the flutes (bars 11–12). Owing to the syncopated, march-like rhythm, in bars 7–10 the hocketed chordal accompaniment consists of the interpolation of trichordal segments from S3 (played by the upper strings) and S2 (played by the violas and cellos); in bars 11–13 segments from S3 are played consecutively by the upper strings, trombones, trumpets and the woodwind (oboes, clarinets and bass clarinet).

The longer, second theme (bars 16–18), based on S2, is played as a duo between the first and second violins, and exhibits a contrapuntal technique that accentuates the tonal references that underline the movement. As shown in Example 12.7, the first violin, starting with a four-quaver rhythmic figure on note D♯ [E♭] (the most

---

[7] This technique would be used by Stravinsky in his serial works of the 1950s and 60s, and has been widely discussed with reference to works such as *Canticum Sacrum*, *Abraham and Isaac*, and *Variations*.

Table 12.4  First Symphonic Suite, *Marsch*: Formal structure and set structure

| Thematic, phrase structure and set distribution | Set structure |
|---|---|
| **A – Scherzo** ||
| (1–5²) First theme: vlc+db (S1); countermelody: vla (S2); three-note chordal accomp: upper strings (S3). | S1, S2, S3 |
| (4³–6) Canon in ww between ob+cl (S2) and bcl+bsn (S1). Link with repetition of first theme. | S1, S2 |
| (7–10) Repetition of first theme: tpt (S1). Accomp. (S2, S3 segms). | S1, S2, S3 |
| (10⁴–12) First phrase of the transition; intense, quaver melody in fl (S1); accomp (S2, S3 segm interpol). | S1, S2, S3 (segms) |
| (13–15) New thematic idea: vla (S3); accomp: three-note chords (S2), and melodic embellishments in ww. Final twelve-note chord: ww–brass (S3). | S3, S2 |
| (16–48) Second theme: vln1+vln2 (S2). Accomp: ww+brass (interchanging chordal and melodic segments, S1+S3). Climax emphasized by the use of percussion. Final, long, *f*, twelve-note chord (S2). | S2–S2 in counterpoint; S1, S3 (segms) |
| (49–57) Three-part chordal rhythmic ostinati in bsn+cbsn+vlc+db (S3, S2, S1, each played three times); restless melodic motives: ww. | S1, S2, S3 |
| (58–65³) Continuation: strings only. | S1, S2, S3 (segms) |
| (65⁴–70) Segment distribution in whole orch. | S1, S2, S3 (segms) |
| (71–3) Cadential melody divided between vln1+vln2 (S2). Cadential chords ww+brass (S1, S2, S3). | S1, S2, S3 (segm interpol) |
| **B – Trio** ||
| (74–82) Trio theme: vlc+vla in canon (S2); countermelody: cbsn+db (S2); chordal accomp (S3). | S2 in canon; S1, S3 chords |
| (83–8) Theme repetition: cl (S2+S1 played simultaneously and homorhythmically): accomp: chords (S3). | S2–S1, S3 |
| (89–96) Theme repetition: ob (syncopated homorhythmic S2, S1). | S2–S1, S3 |
| **A' – Scherzo (modified)** ||
| (97–106) Reappearance of quaver rhythmic motive; motives divided linearly and sequentially in upper strings (S1, S2, S3). | S1, S2, S3 |
| (106⁴–11) vln1+vln2: repeated quaver figure on D♯; tpt+ob (S2 in counterpoint). | S2, S3 |
| (111³–17) First theme: vlc+db (S1); accomp chords (S3). Final twelve-note chord (S1). | S1, S2, S3 |
| (118–26) First theme: vln1 (S1) + vln2 (S2) played simultaneously and homorhythmically, similar to (83–8). Chords (S3) played three times. | S1–S2, S3 |
| (127–39) Duo – transition; contrapuntal, canonic presentation of the notes within each set. At (127–9) duo between tpts (S1) (130–33): (S2); (134–9): (S3). | S1, S2, S3 |
| (140–52) Second theme (S2): two-part counterpoint in hns+ww, and then tpt+tbn. Pedal note D♯ in upper strings. Climactic passage with continuous march rhythms in percussion. | S2, S1, S3 |
| **Coda** ||
| (152⁴–9) Long diminuendo chords in tbn, bsn and then vlns+vla. | S1, S2 |
| (160–165) Chorale-like presentation of superimposed trichords from S1, S2, S3. | S1, S2, S3. |

Example 12.6  First Symphonic Suite, *Marsch*: First theme – opening gesture (bars 1–12)

prominent sound in the entire suite), progressively (during bars 16–39) introduces each note of the first hexachord of S2; each is held for almost four bars as a pedal point. The exposition of the second hexachord is faster. Underneath this prolonged presentation, the second violin contrapuntally plays S2 eight times. In each appearance of S2, however, there is one note missing, this note being played by the first violin.

Each set presentation is separated from the following one by rests, which determine the phrase structure of the second theme. Within each phrase, the

Example 12.7    First Symphonic Suite, *Marsch*: Second theme – opening gesture (bars 16–31)

woodwind and brass accompany with three-note chords and melodic motives based on S1 and S3, also manipulated to produce Skalkottas's version of *Klangfarbenmelodie* and a hocketed texture. Table 12.5 represents the twelve-note polyphonic texture and phrase structure of the second theme as delineated by the unfolding of the sets and the instrumentation.

In the cadential phrase to the Scherzo section (bars 71–3), which outlines two contrapuntal melodies with a chordal accompaniment, the twelve-note set, melodic and harmonic material is distributed in a three-layered texture, each layer having a distinctive rhythmic, timbral and articulative character (see Example 12.8). A broad, arch-like melodic gesture based on S2, with the ascending movement played by the first violins and the descending one by the second violins, is accompanied by a rhythmically compressed melody based on S3, with each tetrachord played by a different flute. Although the sound colour is the same, the move from one player to the next is felt, emphasizing not only the segmental structure of the set but also the hocketing technique explored in this movement. In bars 71–3[1], the melodic three-note segments in the flutes are accompanied by chordal trichords of S1 played by the oboes, clarinets and contrabassoon, while the closing gesture in bar 73 is punctuated by interpolated segments from S2 and S3 in syncopated and interchanging upper woodwind (flutes, oboes, clarinets) and brass (horns, trombones) timbres.

The final cadence of the movement (bars 160–65) is structured as a three-part chorale with each part consisting of a three-note chord, as shown in Example 12.9. Skalkottas superimposes the trichords of each set, which are played in unison by two different instrumental families. Thus the chordal trichords of S1, providing the bass part of the chordal cadence, are played by the lower woodwind and brass and lower strings. The trichords of S2, supporting the inner part of the chordal texture, are played by the middle-register woodwind and high trombones. The trichords of S3, furnishing the upper part of the harmonic texture, are played by the upper strings and upper woodwind. The superimposition of chordal segments of

Table 12.5  First Symphonic Suite, *Marsch*: Second theme (bars 16–48) – set presentation and instrumentation

16–19

|  | S1AB ob | S1C cl | S1D fl | S3AB cl | S3C ob | S3D fl |
|---|---|---|---|---|---|---|
| ww | S1AB ob | S1C cl | S1D fl | S3AB cl | S3C ob | S3D fl |
| hn+ tba | S3ABA | | | S3C | S3E | |
| Brass | | | | | | |
| vln1 | D♯ | | | | E | |
| vln 2 | S2 (–D♯) | | | | S2 (–E) | |

20–22

| S3C ob | S1AB |
|---|---|
| S1AB | |

23–7²

| S1AB bcl | S1D ob–cl | S1D ob–cl |
|---|---|---|
| | | S1C bcl |
| S3AB | | S3CD |
| A | | |
| S2 (–A) | | |

27⁴–31

| S1D ob–cl → | S1A bcl |
|---|---|
| S3AB tbn | S3AB tbn | S1AB tpt | S1ABC tpt | S3CD tbn |
| C | | | | |
| S2 (–C) | | | | |

32–5³

| S3ABCD (chords) fl |
|---|
| S1BCD (melod reord) cl |
| G |
| S2 (–G) |

35³–9³

| S3AB (melod) fl | S3AB (melod) cl |
|---|---|
| S1AB (chord) ob–c♯ | S1CD (chord) |
| | |
| B | |
| S2 (–B) | |

39²–43

| | S1A tpt1 | S1B tpt2 | S1C tpt3 |
|---|---|---|---|
| | | | S1D tbn1 |
| F♯ F D | | | |
| S2 (–F♯) | | | |

44–8

| S3AB | S1A tbn1 | S1BC | S3C tpt1–3 | | S3D cl → | | | | S2 chord → |
|---|---|---|---|---|---|---|---|---|---|
| | | | | S1D tbn3 | S3A tbn1 | S3B tpt2 | S3C tpt1 | S3D fl–ob | |
| B♭ D♭ A♭ | | | | | | | | | |
| D♯ E A C G B F♯ | | | | | | | | | |

Example 12.8   First Symphonic Suite, *Marsch*: Cadential gesture to the Scherzo (bars 71–3)

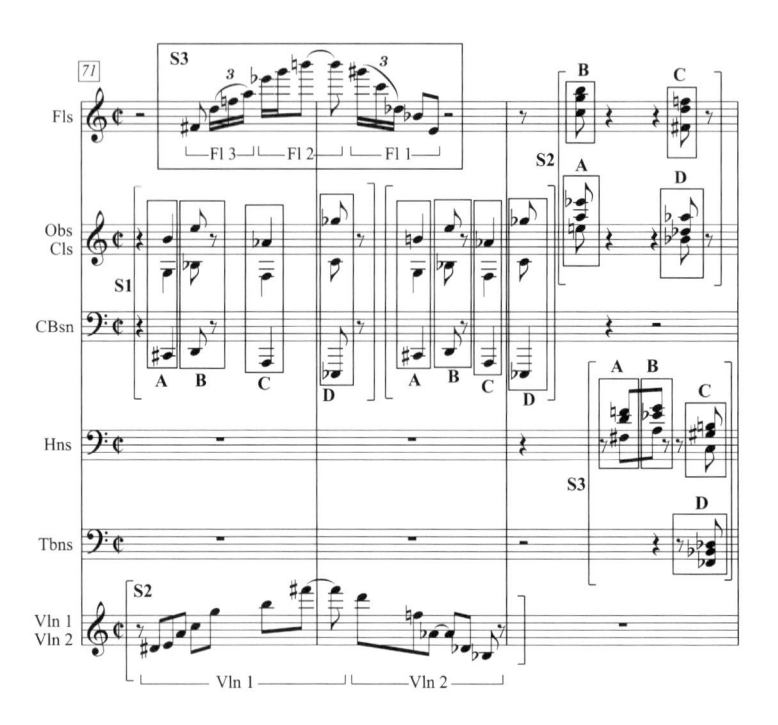

Example 12.9   First Symphonic Suite, *Marsch*: Final cadence (bars 160–65)

the sets, each identified with a particular instrumental colour, became a favourite cadential compositional device for Skalkottas: he used it also in other large-scale symphonic works, such as the fourth movement of the Second Symphonic Suite, *Largo Sinfonico*, and *The Return of Ulysses*.

## Fourth Movement, *Romance*: Splitting off and Verticalization as Compositional Process

In the *Romance*, perhaps reflecting the movement's title, Skalkottas creates a pervasive tonal ambience through the consistent use of overt tonal elements. The movement, which outlines a ternary form – A (bars 1–29) – B (30–44) – A' (45–70) – coda (71–80) – is built on an E♭ pedal, and there is extensive use of an E♭ major triad, resulting from the superimposition of several sets. In his Notes, Skalkottas misleadingly writes: '*Five Reihen, three divided as three-note chords and the other two moving freely and starting from the same note E♭, reveal little by little the shape of the first theme.*' However, as already discussed in Part II (Example 4.4), the movement is in fact built on six twelve-note sets: the melodic S1 and S2, sharing the first note E♭, and the chordal sets S3, S4, S5, S6, which are constantly presented as four three-note chords (apart from bars 20–27, where they are presented linearly), but with the last trichord generally missing – reserved to punctuate important structural cadential points, such as in the cadence to section A (bars 27–9), the cadence to section B (bars 41–4) and in the coda (bars 71–80).

Throughout section A, the periodic presentation of the thematic material is as a sequence of two-bar antecedent–consequent phrases in a duet texture first between the bass clarinet and the cellos (bars 1–22) and then between the violas and the cellos (bars 23–7), which alternately play segments of the melodic sets S1 and S2. The melodic phrases are accompanied harmonically throughout the first ten bars by the upper strings and violas sequentially playing chordal trichords of S3–S6 (see Example 12.10).

Here Skalkottas also employs a compositional technique that involves the splitting off and verticalization of a set's pitch-class content to determine the phrase structure. Throughout section A, the note E♭ is used as a pedal in the basses. Following their initial presentation, the two melodic sets S1 and S2 are gradually transformed into chords through the verticalization of single notes, which are superimposed on the pedal E♭. Within each short phrase, the progressively shorter melodic motives are accompanied by gradually larger chords, culminating in the final twelve-note chords at the end of the section. In section B, the pedal E♭, played by the woodwind (oboe and clarinet) as an inverted pedal, supports the melodic gesture in the cellos, based on S1 and S2. At its cadence (bars 41–4), all four trichords of the four chordal sets are presented complete for the first time, played as pizzicato chords in the brass and strings, and are interpolated with chordal segments from S1 and S2. In section A' the original set presentation and phrase format is repeated, with the pedal E♭ played by the timpani, while the duet,

Example 12.10  First Symphonic Suite, *Romance*: Section A – opening gesture (bars 1–10)

based on S1 and S2, is now played between the first and second violins. The slow verticalization of the melodic sets S1 and S2 gradually culminates in two long, *ff* twelve-note chords, S1 (bar 68) and S2 (bar 69), which punctuate the end of section A'. Table 12.6 represents the set and phrase structure of sections A and B, and the splitting off and verticalization of the melodic sets S1 and S2 within section A.

Table 12.6  First Symphonic Suite, *Romance*: Sections A and B – set structure and phrase structure

| | Section A ||||||||
|---|---|---|---|---|---|---|---|---|
| Bars | 1–2 | 3–4 | 5–6 | 7–8 | 9–10 | 11–12 | 13–14² | 14³–16² | 16³–17 |
| Melodic set (bcl) | S1 | | S1 | | S1 | | S1 | | S1 |
| Melodic pc segments | 2–12 | | 2–12 | | 3–12 | | 4–12 | | 5–12 |
| Melodic set (vlc) | | S2 | | S2 | | S2 | | S2 | |
| Melodic pc segments | | 2–12 | | 3–12 | | 4–12 | | 5–12 | |
| Accomp | S3 | S4 | S5 | S6 | S6 | S3 | S4/S5 | S5 | S6 |
| Pedal + gradual verticalization of S1 | E♭ | | | A E♭ | | G♯ A E♭ | | F♯ G♯ A E♭ | |
| Pedal + gradual verticalization of S2 | | | B E♭ | B E♭ | B♭ B E♭ | | G B♭ B E♭ | | F♯ G B♭ B E♭ |
| Chordal pcs | 1 | 1 | 1–2 | 1–2 | 1–3 | 1–3 | 1–4 | 1–4 | 1–5 |

*continued*

Table 12.6   *concluded*

| Bars | 18 | 19 | 20 | 21 | 22 | 23 | 24 | $25^{1-2}$ | $25^{3-4}$ |
|---|---|---|---|---|---|---|---|---|---|
| Melodic set (bcl) | | S1 | | S1 | S2 | | S2 | | S2 |
| Melodic pc segments | | 6–12 | | 7–12 | 8–12 | | 9–12 | | 10–12 |
| Melodic set (vlc/vla) | S2 | | S2 | | | S1 | | S1 | |
| Melodic pc segments | 6–12 | | 7–12 | | | 8–12 | | 9–12 | |
| Accomp | S6 | S6 | S3 | S3 | S4 | S5 | S5 | S6A | S6A |
| Pedal + gradual verticalization of S1 | F F♯ G♯ A E♭ | D F F♯ G♯ A E♭ | B D F F♯ G♯ A E♭ | C B D F F♯ G♯ A E♭ | G C B D F F♯ G♯ A E♭ |
| Bars | 18 | 19 | 20 | 21 | 22 | 23 | 24 | $25^{1-2}$ | $25^{3-4}$ |
| Pedal + gradual verticalization of S2 | | | | | E | D E | | D♭ D E | |
| | | F F♯ G B♭ B E♭ | | F F♯ G B♭ B E♭ | | F F♯ G B♭ B E♭ | | F F♯ G B♭ B E♭ | |
| Chordal pcs | 1–5 | 1–6 | 1–6 | 1–7 | 1–7 | 1–8 | 1–8 | 1–9 | 1–9 |

*Expansion of the Mid-1930s 'Strict' Twelve-Note Technique* 265

| Bars | 26¹⁻² | 26³⁻⁴ | 27 | 28–9 |
|---|---|---|---|---|
| Melodic set (bcl) | | S1 | | |
| Melodic pc segms | | 10–12 | | |
| Melodic set (vlc/vla) | S1 | | S1 | |
| Melodic pc segms | 10–12 | | 10–12 | |
| Accomp | S6A | S6A | S6B/S4AB | S4D/S6D |
| Pedal + gradual verticalization of S1 | | G C B D F F♯ G♯ A E♭ | | |
| Pedal + gradual verticalization of S2 | C C♯ D E F F♯ G B♭ B E♭ | | | |
| Chordal pcs | 1–10 | 1–9 | | |

| Section B ||||||||
|---|---|---|---|---|---|---|---|
| Bars | 30 | 31–2 | 33–4 | 35 | 36–7 | 38 | 39–40 |
| Pedal in ww | D♯[E♭] | D♯ | D♯ | D♯ | D♯ | D♯ | D♯ |
| Chords | | S3 (1–9) | S4 (1–9) | | S5 (1–9) | S6 (1–9) | S1 |
| Melodic set | S1 (2–12) | | | S2 (2–12) | | | |

| Bars | 41 | 42 | 43 | 44 |
|---|---|---|---|---|
| Chords | S3(1–12) S1(2–7) | S4(1–12) S1(8–12) | S5(1–12) S2(1–6) | S6(1–12) S2(7–12) |

## Fifth Movement, *Siciliano–Barcarolle*: Tentative use of a Superset

The *Siciliano–Barcarole*, continuing the tonally imbued '*lyrical character*' of the *Romance*, and projecting '*a lyrical mood towards the audience*', outlines a traditional large-scale ternary form (*Siciliano–Barcarole–Siciliano*), as shown in Table 12.7.

The *Siciliano* section is based on a group of seven independent twelve-note sets (S1–S7), with S1 repeated to frame the eight-set thematic group, or superset (S1–S2–S3–S4–S5–S6–S7–S1). S1–S6 have their last dyads always played chordally, thus defining the boundaries of each set. Despite Skalkottas's statement

Table 12.7  First Symphonic Suite, *Siciliano–Barcarole*: Formal structure and set structure

| Bars | Phrase structure | Set structure |
|---|---|---|
| *Siciliano* | | |
| 1–17 | a¹: Exposition of material. Theme: vln1+vln2 (pcs 1–8 of S1–S5; 1–10 of S6, 1–8 of S1); countertheme: cbsn+db (S7 melodic); harmonic accomp: vla (continuous dyads). | S1 S2 S3 S4 S5 S6 S7 S1 |
| 18–28 | a²: New presentation of thematic material; melodic ideas in fl+cl, then vln1+vln2. | S1 S2 S3 S4 S5 S6 S7 S1 |
| 29–37 | a³: Overlapping phrases. (26–8) S1 belongs to both phrases a² and a³. | S2 S3 S4 S5 S6 S1 (S7 elements only) |
| 38–44 | a⁴: vla with soloistic motives (segm interpol of pc 9–10 of S1–S2, S3–S4). (44–46): Cadence (S1 chordal and melodic presentation, twice). | S1 S2 S3 S4 S5 S6 S1 (S7 not used) |
| *Barcarolle* | | |
| 47–61 | b¹: New theme first in bcl then in cl; *Barcarolle* semiquaver rhythmic figures; contrapuntal new melodies: upper strings (pcs 5–10 of S4, S5, S6 and S7); harmonic accomp: dyads as in *Siciliano*. | S1a S2a S1a S2a S3a S4a S5a S6a S7a S1a |
| 62–9 | a⁵: Interpolation of *Siciliano*'s set-group; each set is distributed within one bar; harmonic dyads: fl+vln2. | S1 S2 S3 S4 S5 S6 S7 S1 |
| 70–88 | b²: Three sub-phrases: (70–5³) thin, ww texture; melodic presentation of material in ob1 (S7)+ob2 (S1a, S2a segms); (75⁴–82) harmonic presentation of sets; (83–8) cadence to the *Barcarolle*, transition to *Siciliano*: ww melody (S1a), strings (S7). | (70–5³): S1a S2a S7 (75⁴–82): S1a S2a S3a S4a S5a S6a S7a (83–8): S1a S7 |
| *Siciliano* | | |
| 89–100 | a⁶: *Siciliano* rhythm; melody distributed in cl+bcl (S1, S2), ob+cl (S3, S4), fls (S5, S6); similar set structure as in (1–17). | S1 S2 S3 S4 S5 S6 S7 S1 (S7 melodic) |
| 101–11 | Coda: Chordal presentation of sets, similar to (38–40). | S1 S2 S3 S4 S5 S6 S1 (S7 not used) |

in his Notes that the piece is built on '*eight sets*' (seven-plus-one-repeated), the contrasting *Barcarolle* section is built on seven new sets (S1a–S7a), each sharing the same final chordal dyad with its equivalent set of the *Siciliano*. This is the first movement in Skalkottas's compositional output thus far in which, although the pitch-class material is organized in distinct textural layers, the twelve-note sets are arranged multidimentionally; they are largely treated as unordered pitch-class collections, and they are partitioned into segments of various lengths which are distributed in the orchestral texture in block presentations (see Example 12.11).

Throughout the *Siciliano* and its varied repetition, the twelve-note process involves the strict, sequential presentation of the entire set-group, which is repeated nine times. Apart from S7, which is used only intermittently, and predominantly

Example 12.11   First Symphonic Suite, *Siciliano–Barcarole: Siciliano* – first theme (bars 1–17)

in the *Barcarole* section, the sets are always reiterated in order (S1–S6), with S1 frequently repeated after S6 to indicate phrase closure. This establishes the harmonic rhythm, and contributes to the delineation of the phrase structure in a way similar to harmonic change in tonal phraseology. In terms of the sequential set presentation, and its motivic and rhythmic content, the 17-bar theme outlines a traditional, periodic phrase structure, as shown in Table 12.8.

Table 12.8   First Symphonic Suite, *Siciliano–Barcarole*: First theme (bars 1–17) – set structure and phrase structure

| Bars | Motivic structure | Set structure |
| --- | --- | --- |
| 1–2 | Main thematic rhythm ♪. ♪ ♪♪ ♪ presented in prime and inverted forms. | S1 |
| 3–4 | Partial retrograde of the thematic rhythmic motive. | S2 |
| 5–6 | Remote motive forms; new melodic gesture cadencing with inverted version of opening motive on e♭². | S3 |
| 7–9 | Starting with a partial retrograde of the main rhythmic and pc motive of (2). | S4 |
| 10 | Cadential gesture, established by partial retrograde variation of the main rhythmic motive and descending melodic contour. | S5 |
| 11–14 | Contrasting passage based on motive ♩♪, played in prime and retrograde forms. | S6, S5 |
| 15–17 | Truncated and varied repetition of opening gesture. | S1 |

In terms of the melodic structure, the first theme is composed of sequential segments from six different sets (pcs 1–8 from S1–S5, pcs 1–10 from S6, and pcs 1–8 from S1), which are played in unison by the first and second violins. The choice of these segments produces motivic gestures that recall traditional phraseology. For example, the opening thematic melody (bars 1–6) starts with the trichord e♭¹–a–g of S1, and ends with its inversion ($I_0$) b²–a²–e♭² (pcs 6, 7, 8 of S3). Phrase a¹ (bars 7–10) starts with the motive f²–b¹–e²–c² of S4 (the same as the second tetrachord of S1), which was first played as the second motivic gesture of the opening melody in bar 2. The melody in bars 11–14, based on pitch-classes 1–10 from S6, deviates from the previously established eight pitch-class set segments, so that this melodic phrase ends with an a♭¹. This provides a tonal-like, ascending-fifth melodic movement between the penultimate and the closing phrase (bars 15–17), which starts with the note e♭³ (of S1). However, each repetition of the thematic set-group engenders a gradual reshaping of the initial 17-bar theme.

Overall, contrary to his hitherto established linear twelve-note technique, here Skalkottas does not compose with independent linear sets, but with the sum total of the twelve-note pitch-class material as presented in the opening seventeen bars. This is his first attempt at treating the set-group as a superset, a technique he would consolidate in the following *Rondo–Finale* and in the Second Symphonic Suite.

**Sixth Movement, *Rondo–Finale*: Composing with a Superset**

In his accompanying Notes, Skalkottas declares: '[There is an] *absolute dominance of twelve sets in the Rondo.*' As noted in Part II, the movement is built on a superset

*Expansion of the Mid-1930s 'Strict' Twelve-Note Technique* 269

consisting of twelve independent twelve-note sets used sequentially, S1 to S12. Each set is partitioned into four segments, and is initially presented as four three-note chords, each defined by its initial vertical ordering (see Example 4.5). There is an exception to this chordal presentation, with the first hexachord of S3, the second hexachord of S11 and the first of S12 all appearing as four linear trichords. Example 12.12 illustrates the presentation of the superset at the opening gesture of the *Rondo*'s introduction (bars 1–19[1]). Tonal elements abound in the texture, with major and minor triads, particularly E♭ minor, predominating in the set-group structure and saturating the texture with a quasi-tonal ambience.

The repetition of the superset largely defines the large-scale form, as shown in Table 12.9. However, similar to the previous three movements, abrupt textural change and changes in melodic articulation, timbre and orchestration also contribute to the delineation of the phrase structure. The movement outlines a

Example 12.12  First Symphonic Suite, *Rondo–Finale*: Introduction – opening gesture (bars 1–19[1])

large-scale binary formal design, A (bars 1–252) – A' (253–376), which also features sonata form elements. Each section consists of rondo repetitions, not so much of a refrain and episodes, but of the twelve-note superset.

The '*opening* [bars 1–43] *has a strict introductory character*'; it consists of two subsections (A$^1$ A$^2$), each unfolding the superset. The first thematic area (bars 44–104$^2$), outlining two subsections B$^1$, B$^2$, also consists of the presentation twice

Table 12.9  First Symphonic Suite, *Rondo–Finale*: Formal structure and set structure

| | Introduction |||||||||
|---|---|---|---|---|---|---|---|---|---|
| Bars | 1–6$^1$ | 6$^2$–8$^1$ | 8$^3$–10 | 11–15$^1$ | 15$^2$–19$^1$ | 19$^2$–26 =1–6$^1$ | 27–31 =6$^2$–8$^1$ | 32–6$^1$ =8$^3$–10 | 36$^2$–40 =13–19$^1$ | 41–3 =15$^2$–19$^1$ |
| Sections | A$^1$ |||||  A$^2$ |||||
| Sets | S1–S3 | S4–S5 | S6–S7 | S8–S9 | S10–S12 | S1–S3 | S4–S5 | S6–S7 | S8–S9 | S10–S12 |
| Superset | S1–S12 ||||| S1–S12 |||||

| | First thematic area ||||||| 
|---|---|---|---|---|---|---|---|
| Bars | 44–53 | 54–58 | 59–67 | 68–72 | 73–83$^1$ | 83$^2$–91 | 92–104$^2$ |
| Sections | B$^1$ |||| B$^2$ |||
| Sets | S1–S5 | S6–S8 | S9–S11 | S12 | S1–S5 | S6–S8 | S9–S12 |
| Superset | S1–S12 |||| S1–S12 |||

| | Transition | Second thematic area |||||
|---|---|---|---|---|---|---|
| Bars | 104$^3$–11 =21$^4$–31 | 112–21 | 122–33 | 134–50 | 150–61 | 162–71$^1$ |
| Sections | | C$^1$ || C$^2$ |||
| Sets | S1–S5 | S6–S9 | S10–S12 | S6–S9 (S1–S4 segms) | S10–S11 | S12 |
| Superset | S1–S5 | S6–S12 || S6–S12 |||

| | Third theme ||||
|---|---|---|---|---|
| Bars | 162–71$^1$ | 171$^2$–80 | 181–91 | 192–97 |
| Sections | D$^1$ || D$^2$ ||
| Sets | S12(CDBA) | S1–S2 | S3–S8 | S9–S12 |
| Superset | S1–S12 ||||

| | Development |||
|---|---|---|---|
| Bars | 198–209 | 210–15 | 216–52 |
| Sections | B$^3$ | D$^3$ | A$^3$ |
| Sets | S1–S8 (segms) | S9–S12 | S1–S12 (segms) |
| Superset | (S1–S8) S9–S12 || S1–S12 |

|  | Varied repetition of Rondo |  |  |  |  |  |  |  |
|---|---|---|---|---|---|---|---|---|
|  | (Third?) First theme | Second theme | Introduction | | First thematic area | | | Coda |
| Bars | 253–66 | 267–81 | 282–300 | 301–11 | 312–16¹ | 316²–32 | 333–49 | 349–61 | 362–76 |
| Sections | B⁴ | C³ | A⁴ | | B⁵ | B⁶ | B⁷ | |
| Sets | S1–S8→ | S1–S12 (segms) | S6–S9 (S1–S4 segms) | S1–S8 | S9–S12 | S1–S12 | S1–S12 | S1–S12 (segms) | S1–S12 (chords) |
| Superset | S1–S12 | | S6–S12 | S1–S12 | | S1–S12 | S1–S12 | (S1–S12) | S1–S12 |

of the superset. However, the sets are now partitioned into unequal segments, distributed in a three-layered texture. The predominant thematic idea, according to Skalkottas the '*first theme*', is played in unison by the oboes and first violins in bars 44–72 (see Example 12.13).

This 'first theme' is accompanied by continuous quaver dyads played by the second violin, while harmonic support is provided by the lower strings playing sustained, three-note chordal segments. The section ends (bars 100–04²) with a cadential gesture, punctuated by repeated E♭ minor and F minor triads, played forcefully by the brass; the *Ouvertüre*'s signature quartal trichord ($e^2$–$a^2$–$d^3$) is included in the final chord.

Bars 104³–11, a condensed repetition of bars 21⁴–31, featuring an abrupt textural reduction with the strings playing S3–S5, function as a '*brief preparation*' (transition) to the second, *dolce* theme (bars 112–33). This is based on sets S6–S12, the 'second hexachord', as it were, of the superset; it has a reduced, antiphonal texture, and is characterized by an abrupt juxtaposition of instrumental colours and a periodic phrase structure in which each melodic phrase is played by a different woodwind instrument (oboe, flute, clarinet) (see Example 12.14).

The subsequent section is difficult to define, and Skalkottas's description of it is confusing. He indicates that the passage starting at bars 162–71¹ is the third theme, which '*is free, virtuosic and contrasting with the previous one* [and is] *frequently interrupted by the different entries of the instruments*'. However, the predominant, lyrical, thematic idea of the section is played by the solo first violin in bars 192–7, based on melodic segments from sets S9–S12 with distinct triplet rhythmic motives. According to Skalkottas's Notes, bars 198–252 outline the development of the themes. Yet there is no development as such of motivic figures. Although the bassoons enter with melodic gestures based on S1 (bars 198⁴–207¹), and the oboe and bassoon (210–15) reply with the lyrical melodic gesture of bars 192–7, the rest of the passage is a note-by-note sequential presentation of pitch-classes, punctuated by chordal segments from different sets – but in a way that obscures their identity. The held notes progressively build to a climactic *ff* played by the entire orchestra, based on S11. An abrupt *pp* gesture in bars 249–52, played by

Example 12.13  First Symphonic Suite, *Rondo–Finale*: First theme (bars 44–72)

the strings and woodwind and based on a chordal presentation of S12, including E♭ minor and F minor triads and the quartal E–A–D trichord, functions as the cadence to this developmental section.

The rest of the movement, introducing a new march tempo, is a varied repetition of the *Rondo*. Skalkottas rather misleadingly suggests that '*the repetition of the Rondo is reversed: third, second, and first themes*', and that

Example 12.14   First Symphonic Suite, *Rondo–Finale*: Second theme (bars 112–33)

it is introduced by '*a new theme which is the realisation of the third theme*'. However, the section in bars 253–81 is a varied repetition of the first theme, with the melodic line in the clarinets altered in rhythm and articulation (bars 253–66). The second theme, now divided between the violins and the flutes, is a varied repetition of bars 134-50, with reduced harmonic accompaniment. As in the previous movements, the coda (bars 362–76) is based on all twelve sets, played sequentially as twelve-note chords. The constituent trichordal segments are superimposed within the chordal texture, and each is played by a different instrument or instrumental family.

# Chapter 13
# Towards a Free Dodecaphonic Technique

Following the consolidation of the 'strict' treatment of his twelve-note technique in the chamber works and the First Symphonic Suite of 1935, the search for new ways of dealing with twelve notes and an increasing sense of compositional freedom led Skalkottas away from the use of a small number of set-groups, consisting of independent and clearly defined twelve-note sets, to employing large groups of pitch-class material. These include thematic twelve-note sets and a plethora of pitch-class collections – frequently different in each phrase – that are not necessarily repeated in subsequent passages. Several melodic sets may appear only once, while others are varied representations of thematic sets, thus maintaining a degree of motivic similarity. The various sets establish their identity when an entire section is repeated in the Recapitulation, occasionally as a palindrome, or transposed, usually at $T_7$ and/or $T_5$. Overall, in almost all orchestral dodecaphonic works of the middle Athenian period, the vertical set arrangement becomes the predominant compositional principle. In these works, Skalkottas's approach is that of composing with twelve notes related to one another, rather than with ordered twelve-note sets.

**Second Piano Concerto (1937–38)**

*First Movement,* Allegro Molto Vivace*: Composing with One Source Set*

Within the context of his free dodecaphonic technique, and similar to the First Piano Concerto of his formative years, in the Second Piano Concerto Skalkottas experiments with various approaches to manipulating his source twelve-note material. The first movement, *Allegro molto vivace*, outlines a reversed sonata form, shown in Table 13.1. In this movement Skalkottas explores the use of one source twelve-note set (S1) and its variations. The set is used as a frame of reference of twelve notes, with the neighbourhood relationships between adjacent notes ensuring coherence and unity in the derivation of the varied set statements, and other secondary melodies and harmonic formations. The developmental process reaches the point of free composition, as motives are only tentatively connected with the source thematic material. However, the development is circumscribed by the return of the opening formal sections transposed in a manner similar to that used in the Berlin works. At the outset of the movement, Skalkottas emphasizes the referential importance of the source set by presenting it sequentially several times in its prime and retrograde forms. In its initial presentations the pitch-class order of the

Table 13.1   Second Piano Concerto, *Allegro molto vivace*: Formal structure

| Bars | Thematic and phrase structure |
|---|---|
| **Orchestral Exposition I** ||
| 1–9 | First theme: vln1 (S1); countermelody: vla (S1); chordal accomp: vln2 (RS1). |
| $9^3$–14 | Transition. |
| 15–22 | Second theme: (15–16) Thematic melody: cl (starting at pc 3); accomp: db (RS1 chordal dyads); (17–19): cl (RS1); accomp vln1+vln2 (S1 chordal dyads); (20-22) melody divided between fl–cl–bsn, each playing segms of S1. |
| 23–6 | Continuation; second theme in db. |
| 27–35 | New melody: hns (pcs 9–11). |
| 36–40 | Link to the third theme, in the form of a fanfare (hns). |
| 41–7 | Third theme: hns (S1, contrapuntal treatment of unordered segms). |
| 48–52 | Cadence. |
| **Exposition II (pno and orch)** ||
| 53–82 | Pno entrance with chordal presentation of the pitch-class material of the first theme. |
| 83–96 | First theme in orch. |
| 97–120 | Second theme: pno RH (S1); LH accomp (RS1). (116–20): cadence to the exposition: pno (S1 second hexachord). |
| **Development** ||
| 121–232 | Development of first and second themes; intense pno cadenza (198–211); chordal cadence (S1). (224–32)=(9–14) (varied section repetition). |
| **Reversed Recapitulation** ||
| 233–40 | Second theme at $T_{10}$ and $T_8$. Modulatory movement: (233–4)=(15–16 ($T_{10}$)); (235–$6^2$)=(17–$18^2$ ($T_8$)). |
| 241–79 | Second theme at $T_7$. (241–5)=(25–30 ($T_7$)); (246–56)=(47–57 ($T_7$)); (257–60)=(95–8 ($T_7$)); (261-4)=115–18 ($T_7$)); (265–78)=(133–46 ($T_7$)). |
| 280–94 | Pno cadenza. |
| 295–305 | Elaboration; developmental passage. (295–305)=(147–57 ($T_0$)) |
| 306–37 | Closing passage, initiated with the third theme: (306–26)=(41–59); (326–37)=(82–92). |
| 338–50 | First theme at $T_0$. |
| 351–6 | Coda starting with second thematic idea. |

set is maintained and reinforced through repetition, regardless of the texture. Chords result from the verticalization of segments, and in the case of counterpoint the order of the notes is determined linearly. Following its establishment, the set is manipulated so that new sets derive from it, while entirely new ones are fleetingly used only in developmental passages. In the opening gesture of the first theme (bars 1–$4^1$), the first violins convey the predominant thematic idea based on an ordered, linear presentation of S1 contrapuntally accompanied by a countermelody in the viola,

Example 13.1  Second Piano Concerto, *Allegro molto vivace*: First theme – opening gesture (bars 1–9)

also with S1 (see Example 13.1). The second violins accompany with chordal dyads of the retrograde RS1, followed contrapuntally by chordal dyads in the woodwind, with the flutes playing the first tetrachord, and the oboes and clarinets the second and third tetrachords. In the continuation (bars 4–5) there is some reordering and distribution of the segments among the strings. The third phrase (bars 6–9) features a duet between the first violin (playing reordered set segments) and the viola (playing ordered segments).

The second theme (bars 15–22), played by the solo clarinet, is based on two varied presentations of the set. Its opening melodic gesture in bars 15–16 (based on pitch-class numbers 3…11) is accompanied by the double bass playing chordal dyads of RS1, while in bars 17–19 (with similar rhythmic patterns) it is based on a partial reordering of RS1; it is now accompanied by the first and second violins playing chordal dyads of S1 (see Example 13.2).

Example 13.2  Second Piano Concerto, *Allegro molto vivace*: Second theme – opening gesture (bars 15–19)

The third, closing theme, played by the horns (bars 41–7), is based on a varied presentation of S1. It is a duet, with the upper voice playing sequentially, a fanfare-like reordering of the first tetrachord, while the lower voice comprises a reordering of – predominantly – the second tetrachord. It is accompanied by the strings playing arpeggiated segments of RS1 (Example 13.3).

Example 13.3  Second Piano Concerto, *Allegro molto vivace*: Third theme – opening gesture (bars 41–5)

In the Development the reshaping of the set reaches its climax. Coherence, however, is provided by the reiteration of the second tetrachordal segment E♭–A–D♭–C, which saturates the texture and is the pre-eminent component of all the main thematic ideas; even at points of extensive reshaping and variation this tetrachord is the common denominator that refers back to the source set S1. Following a dense piano cadenza, the cadence to the section is a chordal outburst played by the entire orchestra, characterized by harmonic stasis. Sequential modulatory movement follows, blurring the boundaries of the retransition and the reversed Recapitulation, the latter appearing as an extension of the Development. It starts with the second theme played by the first violins first at $T_{10}$, accompanied by the basses playing harmonic dyads based on its retrograde $RS1(T_{10})$ (bars 233–4), and then at $T_8$, progressing to the piano entrance of the theme transposed at $T_7$. Gradually the material moves to the third theme, played by the horns (bars 306–37), which leads back to the recapitulation of the first theme (bars 338–50) at its original tonal level. The short Coda (bars 351–6) is initiated with a brief reminder of the second thematic idea, and the movement appears open-ended.

*Second Movement,* Andantino

The second movement, *Andantino*, in binary form (AA′), is predominantly built on one thematic set S1 and several other pitch-class collections. The thematic set, first played by the cello at the opening gesture of the movement (bars 1–8) shares its last tetrachord with that of S1 of the first movement (B–G–A♭[G♯]–E). Here Skalkottas also explores the technique of transposing entire passages, together with limited use of palindromes, to define the large-scale form. Section A outlines three thematic groups. Section A′ is introduced with the pitch-class material of the first thematic group transposed at the fifth, and then progresses to the repetition of the pitch-class and thematic material at the original tonal level. Other short passages and melodies also appear transposed in section A′, while the piano cadenza is built on palindromic principles, as discussed in Part II (see Example 9.2). Table 13.2 represents the formal structure of the second movement.

*Third Movement,* Allegro moderato: *Composing with Set-groups and Pitch-class Collections*

The *Allegro moderato* is also in sonata form; but in contrast to the first movement, each of its three subject groups is based on a different group of twelve-note sets and a variety of other pitch-class collections. This large amount of material is controlled by cyclical devices and, following the technique already employed in the *Presto* of the Octet and the *Molto vivace* of the Piano Trio, by the transposition of entire sections. In the Recapitulation the three subject groups are repeated in varied form and transposed at the fifth ($T_7$). In place of a Coda, the first theme is played complete, at the original tonal level ($T_0$). However, this abrupt modulatory change is not convincing, as there is still the impression that the entire concerto

Table 13.2  Second Piano Concerto, *Andantino*: Formal structure

| Bars | Thematic structure |
|---|---|
| \multicolumn{2}{c}{Section A} ||
| 1–14 | First thematic group (1–36).<br>First theme: (1–8) thematic melody in vlc (S1). Accomp: vln1+vln2+vla; (9–10) link;(11–14) continuation: strings. |
| 15–18 | Transition to the piano introduction; change of metre (2/4); strings. |
| 19–27 | Pno entrance with a variation of the main thematic material. New thematic idea in cls. |
| 28–36 | Continuation; (33–6) pno plays the cl melodic line. |
| 37–45 | Second thematic group (37–65).<br>Second theme in pno RH; fanfare motive fls+obs+cls (40–42). |
| 46–52 | Continuation. Elaboration of the material. |
| 53–6 | Varied repetition of (11–14). The passage ends with the first thematic melody in pno LH (S1). |
| 57–65 | Transition. (57–9)=(15–18). |
| 66–89 | Third thematic group (66–119).<br>(66–76) pno predominates; (76–89) melodic ideas in ww. |
| 90–99 | Varied repetition of (66–76). |
| 100–08 | New melodic ideas in vln1+fl. |
| 109–19 | Chordal, *ppp* cadence in pno and strings. |
| 120–35 | Pno cadenza (palindromic structure). |
| 136–47 | Cadential passage to section A.<br>pno: (140–45)=(120–24 (R)). |
| \multicolumn{2}{c}{Section A'} ||
| 148–58 | First theme ($T_7$).<br>(148–58)=(1–14 ($T_7$)). |
| 159–66 | Varied repetition of (11–21) at $T_0$. |
| 167–72 | Varied repetition of (43–52). |
| 173–84 | Second theme at $T_0$.<br>Varied repetition: (173–9)= (37–42); (180–81)=(60–3); (182–4)=( (64–5); (184)=(64/65 at $T_7$). |
| 185–99 | Third theme at $T_0$.<br>Varied repetition: (185–7)= (66–8); (188–93)=(66–70 at $T_7$). |
| 200–14 | Coda; varied repetition of (28–37); material from first thematic group. |

ends in a different 'key' from that in which it started. The technique of *en bloc* transposition to determine the form would be refined in the subsequent Violin Concerto and Third Piano Concerto. Table 13.3 represents the formal structure of the *Allegro moderato*.

Table 13.3   Second Piano Concerto, *Allegro moderato*: Formal structure

| Bars | Thematic and phrase structure |
|---|---|
| | **Exposition** |
| 1–47 | First subject group. |
| 1–15 | First theme: vla+vlc+cl+bsn (unison) (S1, S2, S3, S4). |
| 16–30 | Theme repetition: pno solo. |
| 31–47[1] | Transition. |
| 47–114 | Second subject group. |
| 48–57 | First theme of second subj group in orch. (48–51) main thematic idea: fl; (54–7)=(48–51) (section repetition): fl+vln1. |
| 58–82 | Second theme of second subj group: pno; (62–6)=(58–62 ($T_{10}$)); (67–8)=(58–9 ($T_7$)); (79–82)=(58–62). |
| 83–114 | Developmental continuation. (83–90)= 48–53); (91–4)=(48–51); (99/100)=(52/53 ($T_3$)); (101–04)=(48–51 ($T_3$)); (105–10)=(48–53); (111–14)=(48–51). |
| 115–68 | Third subject group. |
| 115–18 | Introductory thematic idea: fl. |
| 119–32 | Third theme: vlc. |
| 133–46 | (133–46)=(119–32) Varied repetition of third theme: pno. |
| 146–68 | Continuation and short piano cadenza. |
| 169–93 | Orchestral development of the material. |
| | **Development** |
| 169–79 | New thematic idea: solo cl. |
| 180–88 | (180–88)=(1–82) Curtailed repetition of first theme: partitioned between tba+lower strings. |
| 189–93 | Link to second section. |
| 194–235 | Predominantly orch section. |
| 194–97 | New theme: pno. |
| 198–214 | Varied repetition of new pno theme: (198–200)=(194–6 ($T_{11}$)); (203–5)=(194–7 ($T_7$)); (206–9)=(194–6 ($T_6$)). |
| 215–35 | Pno cadenza. Closing passage. |
| | **Recapitulation at $T_7$** |
| 236–45 | First subject group ($T_7$). |
| | (236–40)=(16–20 ($T_7$)). First theme: pno at $T_7$. |
| | (240–45)=(25–30 ($T_7$)). Continuation at $T_7$. |
| 246–60 | Second subject group ($T_7$). |
| | (246–56)= 47–57 ($T_7$)). First theme of second subj group at $T_7$. |
| | (257–60)=(95–8 ($T_7$)). Developmental continuation at $T_7$. |
| 261–90 | Third subject group ($T_7$). |
| | (261–4)=(115–18 ($T_7$)). Introductory thematic idea of third subj group: pno solo. |
| 265–91[1] | (265–78)=(133–46 ($T_7$)). Varied repetition of third theme: pno. |
| | (277–90)=(119–32 ($T_7$)). Third theme: vln1. |
| 291[4]–312 | Coda. First theme: fls+vln1 at $T_0$. |

## Violin Concerto (1938)

*First Movement,* Molto appassionato: *An Experiment in Free Twelve-Note Technique*

In the Violin Concerto Skalkottas experiments with a free use of his twelve-note technique, which is diametrically opposite to that explored in the first movement of the Second Piano Concerto. In the first movement, *Molto appassionato*, in particular, he abandons the self-imposed limitations of the predetermined set-groups and instead adds new sets and/or other pitch-class collections in each formal gesture. At the small-scale structural level, coherence is achieved through motivic and thematic means, repetition of harmonic groups, rhythmic figures and articulation, rather than through the unifying power of a limited number of constantly reiterated sets. At the macro-structural level, Skalkottas employs cyclical procedures, including the slightly varied repetition of certain passages, together with transposition of the pitch-class content of entire sections, to define the harmonic and formal structure of the movement.

The *Molto appassionato* is in sonata form, with each phrase built on a new collection of pitch-class material, including twelve-note sets and their variations (see Table 13.4). Although the thematic sets of the first and second subject groups are used more strictly in order to establish their thematic predominance, the transitional and developmental passages feature extensive segment interpolation, new sets and several twelve-note melodies that appear only once. The most striking feature of the piece, however, is the avoidance of the immediate block repetition of the pitch-class content of a phrase or passage to define the small-scale phrase structure. The dodecaphonic premise of the set complexes in Exposition I only become clear in Exposition II and in the Recapitulation. Furthermore, there is an extensive free treatment of the sets, similar to the troping technique used in the Concertino for two pianos, albeit not as systematically employed.

The orchestral Exposition I (bars 1–66) is built on a large amount of pitch-class material, including linear, chordal and derived sets, and aggregates resulting from the pairing of hexachords. The first subject group (bars 1–13) is built on eight different sets. Rhythm and motivic contour are the predominant unifying features in this passage, which exemplifies Skalkottas's version of developing variation technique; he preserves sufficient motivic and rhythmic elements to ensure connection and logic while changing other elements to produce variety, development and growth. As shown in Example 13.4, the antecedent phrase (bars 1–5) is built on three twelve-notes sets (S1a, S2a, S3a). The main thematic line, with a wave-like melodic contour and a distinctive initial descending gesture played by the first violins, is based on S1a; it is accompanied contrapuntally by the second violins playing a melody with a similar initial descending contour, based on S2a; the cellos accompany with continuous syncopated harmonic thirds, based on S3a. The continuation (the remote motive forms of bars $5^3$–7) adds a fourth set, S4a, which is played chordally by the woodwind and violas. The consequent

Example 13.4  Violin Concerto, *Molto appassionato*: First subject group (bars 1–5 and 8–13)

(bars 8–13), starting as a varied repetition of the antecedent with some intervals transposed at the tritone, perfect fifth and major sixth, is built on four new sets (S5a–S8a), and has an internal structure similar to that of the opening thematic phrase. The melody and countermelody, played by the first and second violins and based on S5a and S6a respectively, have similar descending contours to the opening thematic gestures. The cellos accompany with syncopated harmonic dyads (S7a), while a third accompanimental voice in the violas is based on S8a.[1]

The first phrase of the transition (bars 14–19) is built on three sets, S9a–S11a.[2] Although this is timbrally different from the previous phrases, with the thematic/melodic line given to the woodwind, its part-writing remains the same, with melody and countermelody played contrapuntally by the first and second clarinets, while the bassoons accompany with syncopated thirds. The latter function as a rhythmic ostinato, binding the phrases together and providing a degree of unity that counteracts the diffused dodecaphonic context of the first subject group. The linear presentation of the sets is abandoned in the second phrase of the transition (bars 20–34). The clarity of the opening first theme is replaced by the equivalent of a musical puzzle, a bewildering fabric of independent voices exhibiting a

---

[1]   Each hexachord of S6a is an unordered transposition at $T_4$ of S2a, while each hexachord of S7a derives from the unordered transposition at $T_5$ of S3a.

[2]   The predominantly chordal S11a is an unordered transposition at $T_3$ of S10a. Each hexachord of S9a is an unordered transposition at $T_8$ of S3a, and it also has a $T_3$ transpositional relationship with S7a; thus, there is a modulatory-like movement in minor thirds within each phrase of the first theme.

Table 13.4  Violin Concerto, *Molto appassionato*: Formal structure and set structure

| Sections | Thematic and phrase structure | Set structure |
|---|---|---|
| \multicolumn{3}{c}{**Exposition I**} | | |
| First subject group | First theme. (1–5) Antecedent: vln1 (Sa); countermelody: vln2 (S2a); harmonic accomp: vlc (S3a). | S1a, S2a, S3a |
| | (5³–7) Continuation – remote motive forms. | S1a, S2a, S3a, S4a |
| | (8–13) Consequent; vln1+vln2 (contrapuntal melodies); vla (melodic triplet accomp); vlc (harmonic thirds). | S5a, S6a, S7a, S8a |
| Transition | (14–19) First phrase; melodic idea: cl+fl. | S9a, S10a, S11a |
| | (20–34) Second phrase; intense segmental interpolation. | Trichordal and hexachordal segms |
| Second subject group | (35–50) Second theme: fl+ob (S1b, S3b, S7b, S10b). | S1b, S2b, S3b, S4b, S5b, S6b, S7b, S8b, S9b, S10b, S11b |
| | (51–5) Continuation built on superimposed set segments. | S1b, S2b, S3b, S4b, S7b |
| | (56–66) Closing section. Predominantly S11b: each dyad played in order by ob–cl–bsn–tbn–tba+cbsn–fl. | S11b, S7b, S1b (segms) |
| \multicolumn{3}{c}{**Exposition II**} | | |
| First subject group | (67–70)=(1–5) First theme: solo vln (S1a); accomp: S3a dyads. | S1a, S3a |
| | (71–6)=(8–13) Thematic line: solo vln (S5a); accomp (S8a dyads). | S5a, S8a |
| | (77–81)=(14–19) Solo vln in dyads: upper line S9a ($T_{10}$), lower line S10a ($T_{10}$). The last three notes of both sets at $T_0$. | S9a ($T_{10}$–$T_0$), S10a ($T_{10}$–$T_0$) |
| | (82–7)=(1–8) Thematic line (S2a); countermelody: solo vln; accomp (S3a dyads). | S2a, S3a |
| | (88–92¹)=(8–13) Thematic line (S6a); countermelody: solo vln. | S6a |
| | (92²⁻⁴)=(14–19) harmonic accomp: solo vln (S11a; originally played by the bsn). | S11a |
| | (93–103)=(1–19) Use of material from the first theme. | S1a – S11a, RS1a, RS2a |
| | (104–22) New pc complex; extensive use of palindromic forms of melodies. (104–5)=(106–7 (R)). (110–12)=(113–15 (R)). (116–19²)=(119³–22³ (R)). | |

| Sections | Thematic and phrase structure | Set structure |
|---|---|---|
| Transition | (123–33)=(20–34 exact pitch repetition). (134–45) New material. | |
| Second subject group | (146–77)=(35–66) Second theme. | |
| | (178–84) New material; predominant intervallic motive of a third. | |
| | (185–92) Cadential passage. | |
| **Development** | | |
| | (185–230) Development of previous material; introduction of new material appearing just once. | |
| **Recapitulation (predominantly at $T_7$)** | | |
| First subject group | (231–41)=(1–13 ($T_7$)) First theme at $T_7$. | |
| | (242–44)=(30–2 ($T_7$)) End of transition at $T_7$. | |
| Second subject group | (245–82)=(35–76 ($T_7$)) Second theme at $T_7$. | |
| | (283–8)=(104–9 ($T_7$)) Material from the first subject group at $T_7$. | |
| | (289)=(109) at $T_4$. Modulatory gesture. | |
| | (290–6)=(109–15($T_0$)) Material from the first subject group at $T_0$. | |
| | (297–306)=(123–33) at $T_0$. | |
| | (308–14)=(128–33) at $T_0$. Partial repetition of transition. | |

kaleidoscope of motivic figures. This is a strikingly contrasting passage, built on the complex interpolation of many set segments in their prime form and a few transposed at $T_7$, the latter largely trichords and hexachords. Their combinations result in eleven new aggregates, most of which are presented only once. However, the associative elements between the set segments, together with the motivic, rhythmic and contoural treatment, ensure cohesion and connection. The transition ends with a brief reminder of the thematic idea based on S1. The second subject group (bars 35–66), returning to the textural layout of the first theme, is built on several thematic twelve-note sets and other pitch-class collections different in each phrase. Four of these thematic sets (S1b, S3b, S7b, S10b)[3] support the second theme (bars 35–50), which is played in unison by the flutes and oboes and which outlines a two-part extended periodic, antecedent–consequent-type phraseology (see Example 13.5).

The melodic first phrase (bars 35–7), played in unison by the flutes and oboes, is based on S1b and is accompanied by the chordal S2b. The continuation (bars 38–42) features a duet between the divided flutes and oboes playing S3b and a

---

[3] Set S10b derives from a reordered presentation of each hexachord of the $I_6$ form of S3b.

Example 13.5   Violin Concerto, *Molto appassionato*: Second theme (bars 35–50)

segment of S4b, and introduces a countermelody in the second violins (the first seven notes of S4b), which responds to the dotted rhythmic gesture of the opening phrase. The clarinets take over the rhythm in an ostinato accompaniment derived from S6b, while the lower strings provide the harmonic support with S5b. Bars 43–5 function as the closing phrase of the first part of the theme; the melodic gesture is built on S7b and is accompanied by S8b in the clarinets (a dyadic and reordered presentation of each chromatic hexachord of S7b); the harmonic support is now based on S9b. The second, consequent-like, part of the theme opens as a major sixth ($T_9$) transposition of the first part, but then continues freely. In bars 46–50, the thematic melody in the flute and oboe is based on S10b. Thereafter it continues playing a different twelve-note melody in each phrase. The continuation (bars 51–5) is built on new twelve-note sets and various set segments, conventionally superimposed as independent lines in the overall texture. The third phrase of the second subject group starts with a new thematic idea (bars 56–61), based on S11a. In a technique reminiscent of the opening gesture of the Third String Quartet, each dyad of the set is gradually introduced by a different instrument.

In Exposition II (bars 67–192), which is an expanded and varied repetition of the pitch-class and thematic material of the orchestral Exposition I, all the sets used previously are now played by the solo violin, but in different configurations and order, while there is a limited use of palindromic presentations of melodies and phrases. Following a short Development section, the Recapitulation is based on a transposition of the pitch-class material of the Exposition at the fifth ($T_7$), with cyclical but varied repetitions of its melodic/thematic and rhythmic elements. Towards the end, within the second subject group space (bars 288–90), and via a brief modulatory movement from $T_7$ to $T_4$, the pitch-class material returns to the original transpositional level of the Exposition ($T_0$) to round off the piece. The initial strict use of earlier dodecaphonic material does not last long, however, and Skalkottas produces freer compositional arrangements, featuring new twelve-note melodies played just once, together with the recapitulation of material from the equivalent section in the Exposition.

### Third Concerto for Piano and Ten Wind Instruments (1939): Synthesis of Free Dodecaphonic Techniques and Tonal Structure – a Study in Cyclical Form

The Third Concerto for Piano and Ten Wind Instruments, commonly known as the Third Piano Concerto, is a large-scale mature work for a small chamber orchestra of ten wind instruments (flute, oboe, B♭ clarinet, English horn, bassoon, contrabassoon, horn in F, trumpet, trombone, tuba), percussion (used sparingly) and piano. Here Skalkottas combines the developmental processes of the compositional techniques he explored in the Second Piano Concerto (experimenting with the use of one source set) and the Violin Concerto (using a very large number of sets and pitch-class collections). His free dodecaphonic technique involves the use of three thematic sets, which function as the generative source for the entire concerto, and numerous other unordered sets (largely deriving from the thematic ones), while at developmental passages set segments (usually hexachords) are often employed independently. Free dodecaphonic and atonal passages co-exist and alternate with passages built on strict serial processes. Skalkottas employs *en bloc* transposition of entire sections as a form-generating device, as well as cyclical procedures; the latter operate both at the structural level within each movement and as a means of connecting first-movement elements to the other movements. Such cyclical procedures across the entire concerto involve the varied recurrence (and progressive metamorphoses) of the first movement's two main themes, of certain rhythmic patterns and salient motives associated with a particular instrumental colour, and the repetition of entire passages either exact, or transposed, or as palindromes.

The first movement, *Moderato*, outlines a sonata form, as shown in Table 13.5. In the orchestral Exposition I, the first theme of the first subject group is built entirely on the twelve-note set S1 (see Example 13.6). The set is partitioned into segments that are distributed throughout the texture as contrapuntal motives. Its most striking feature is the opening three-note motive $f^1$–$e^1$–$a^1$, which, repeatedly

Table 13.5    Third Piano Concerto, *Moderato*: Formal structure

| Sections | Thematic structure | Phrase structure |
|---|---|---|
| | | **Exposition** (1–159) |
| Exposition I (orch ritornello) | First subject group | (1–2) First theme ((S1); thematic melody: ob–cl. (16–20) S1 ($T_6$); (24–6): S1 ($T_0$). |
| | Second subject group | (27–8) Second theme: ob (S2); accomp S2 ($T_7$). (36–41) Passage with metric fluctuation and predominance of major sevenths. (46–50) Repetition second theme: hn; accomp: (S2 dyads at $T_3$, $T_7$, $T_{10}$). |
| Exposition II (pno and orch) | First subject group | (51–70) New chordal theme: pno (S1 ($T_2$)); orch accomp: three-note motives derive from different forms of S1. (71–6) Gradual transformation of first theme. (80–86) Transition (predominantly S2). (85–6) Closing cadence with statement of first theme. |
| | Second subject group | Second theme in pno. (87–90/1) pno (S2 ($T_0$))=(27–31). (94–6)=(33–5 (S2 ($T_1$)). (97) New thematic idea. (126–9) Material from first theme. (147–53)=(17–23) Short pno cadenza. (158–9) Cadence: motives from both themes. |
| | | **Development** (160–239) |
| orch ritornello | | First part. (160–71) Opening gesture. |
| pno and orch | | (172–173) Develop of first theme: pno. (185–7) Develop of second theme (S2 ($T_5$)). |
| | | Second part. (220–21) New theme: tpt. (239) Cadence on motives from S1 ($T_0$). |
| | | **Recapitulation predominantly at $T_7$** (240–436) |
| Exposition I (orch ritornello) | First subject group | (240–51) =(1–14 ($T_7$)) First theme at $T_7$. (252–63)=(12–23 ($T_0$)). (264–5) Modulatory sequence: (264=263 ($T_3$)) ; (265=264 ($T_3$) [263 ($T_7$)]). (266–8)=(24–6 ($T_7$)). (269–70)=(1–3 ($T_0$)) Bridge. |
| | Second subject group | (271–94)=(27–50 ($T_7$)) Second subject at $T_7$. |
| Exposition II (pno and orch) | First subject group | (295–305)=(51–61 ($T_7$)) Chordal theme: pno at $T_7$. (306–24)=(68–86 ($T_7$)). |

| Sections | Thematic structure | Phrase structure |
|---|---|---|
| | Second subject group | Second subject group with develop passages at $T_7$.<br>(325–43)=(87–105 ($T_7$)).<br>(344–79)=(115–50 ($T_7$)).<br>(380–83)=(151–52 ($T_0$)).<br>(384)=(154 ($T_0$)).<br>(385–8)=(156–9 ($T_7$)). |
| | | Pno cadenza: Material from the end of Exposition II and Development at $T_7$.<br>(387–8)=(158–9 ($T_7$)); (389–94)=(165–71 ($T_7$)). |
| | | Orch and pno<br>(395)=(157 ($T_0$)) End of second theme; pno at $T_0$; accomp at $T_7$.<br>(396–401) End of section in pno. |
| Coda | | ($401^4$–03) orch.<br>(404–7)=(212–15 ($T_0$)) Recycling material from Development at $T_0$.<br>(415)=(57 ($T_0$)) pno entry; cyclical references to the initial pno entry.<br>(435–6) First thematic gesture at $T_0$. |

Example 13.6 Third Piano Concerto, *Moderato*: First theme – opening gesture (bars 1–3²)

played by the oboe throughout the entire concerto, is used as a motto at important structural points, either initiating or closing formal sections. This is answered by the motive $eb^1$–$g^1$–$c^1$–$f\#^1$, played by the clarinet, an instrumental colour also associated with thematic statements.

The transition, fulfilling its harmonic modulatory function, is built on the same set transposed at the tritone ($T_6$). The second theme (bars 27–35) is built on two sets. The predominant melodic set S2,[4] partitioned between the oboe and contrabassoon, also has a motto-like opening three-note motive $d^2$–$eb^1$–$c^2$; it is

---

[4] Set S2 derives from the $I_5$ form of S1 by interchanging the notes F♯ and D within each hexachord.

accompanied by the harmonic set S3, which is presented mainly as a series of dyads (Example 13.7).

Example 13.7   Third Piano Concerto, *Moderato*: Second theme – opening gesture (bars 27–8)

Following their exposition, the three sets are used freely, with their segments and pitch-classes distributed in the texture to produce new melodic configurations, which in turn undergo further transformation. Several other derived sets are used to introduce new secondary thematic ideas. The piano writing is percussive throughout, and in Exposition II, the piano part, based on the $T_2$ form of S1, starts with a virtuosic chordal gesture totally contrasting in character to the melodic orchestral themes of Exposition I. Thereafter every passage is based on new pitch-class material, most of which derives from the transformational processes of the previously used thematic sets.

The curtailed Development, justified by the long developmental passages between the two main themes and those following their exposition, requires little further elaboration. In the Recapitulation the pitch-class material of the entire Exposition is repeated transposed at the fifth ($T_7$), with some instrumental exchanges and rhythmic variations, implying a movement from a 'tonic' region to a 'dominant' one. However, following the initial appearance of the first theme at $T_7$, part of the first subject group is repeated, as an interlude, at its original tonal level ($T_0$) (bars 252–63). The movement ends with a final appearance of the first theme at $T_0$.

The second movement, *Andante sostenuto*, has a similar structure to that of the *Moderato*, but with noticeable rondo elements within each section of its overall reversed sonata form, resulting predominantly from cyclical repetitions of pitch-class material and motives (see Table 13.6). The first theme, played by the clarinet and based on the source set S1, is a varied repetition of the *Moderato*'s first theme (Example 13.8).

In the opening 12 bars of the thematic passage the varied reappearances of the thematic melody are accompanied by gestures based on seven new sets, which

Example 13.8   Third Piano Concerto, *Andante sostenuto*: First theme – opening gesture (bars 1–2)

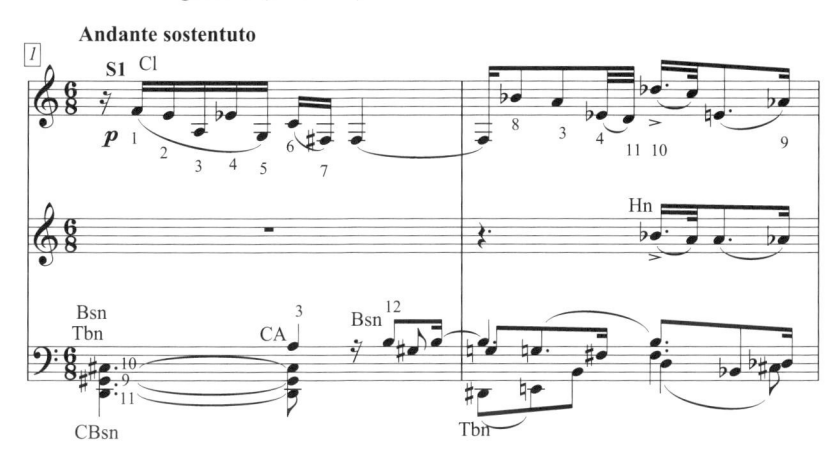

Example 13.9   Third Piano Concerto, *Andante sostenuto*: Second theme – opening gesture (bars 7–8)

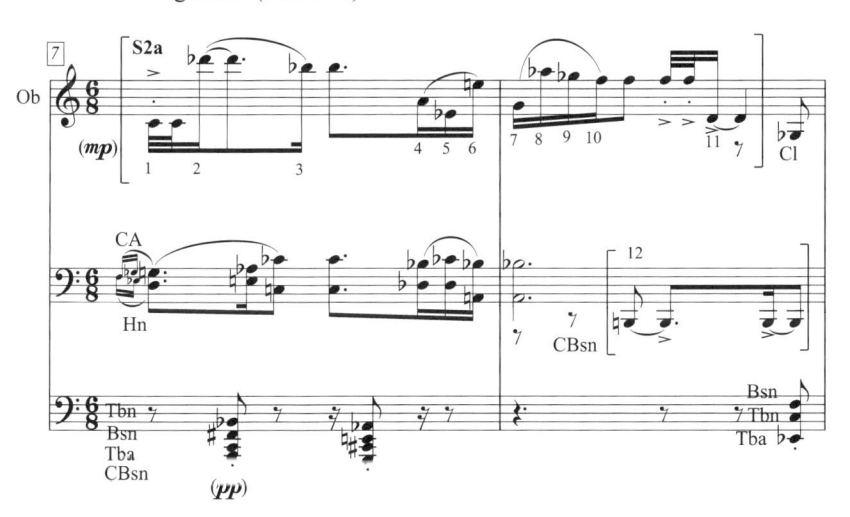

are used freely as pitch-class collections. In keeping with the cyclical processes established so far, there are colouristic references to the first movement. The second thematic idea, played by the oboe, is based on S2a, which derives from the $T_{10}$ form of the *Moderato*'s S2, and shares with it the first tetrachord (set-class 4–3) and the last diminished trichord (set-class 3–10) (see Example 13.9).

Within Exposition II, the pitch-class content of entire passages is used in palindromic form ($R_0$) and transposed at $T_9$. In the short Development section,

Table 13.6   Third Piano Concerto, *Andante sostenuto*: Formal structure

| Sections | Rondo sections | Phrase and set structure – Sectional repetitions |
|---|---|---|
| \multicolumn{3}{c}{**Exposition** (1–91)} |||
| Exposition I (orch ritornello) | A | (1–6) First theme: cl (S1). |
|  | B | (7–12) Second theme: ob (S2a). |
|  | A$^1$ | (13–18)=(1–6) Varied repetition of first theme. (19) Bridge. |
| Exposition II (pno and orch) | A$^2$ | (20–25)=(1–6 (T$_0$)) First theme: pno only; new orchestral material. |
|  | A$^3$ | Varied repetition of A transposed at T$_9$. (26–2)=(1–6 (T$_9$)): pno; (26–9)=(20–22/24 (T$_9$)): orch. |
|  | B$^1$ | (30–33)=(7–12 pno (T$_9$)). Second theme at T$_9$: pno. |
|  | B$^2$ | pno (34–7)=(7–12 (T$_0$)). Varied second theme at T$_0$. |
|  |  | (38–51) Developmental passage. (41) pno RH chords: (S2 of First Symphonic Suite). (52)=(19 (R$_0$)) Bridge. |
|  | A$^4$ | (53–8)=(1–6 (R$_0$)) Palindromic presentation of first theme in orch. |
|  | B$^3$ | (59–64)=(2–17 (R$_0$)) Palindromic second theme in orch. |
|  | A$^5$ | (56–71$^2$)=(53–8)=(1–6 (R$_0$)) Palindromic first theme in orch. |
|  | A$^6$ | (71$^3$–4$^3$)=(1–6 (T$_0$)) Varied first theme in orch at T$_0$. |
|  | B$^4$ | (74$^4$–84)=(7–19 (T$_0$)) Varied second theme in orch at T$_0$. (85) Bridge. |
|  | Codetta | (86–91) Codetta. (88)=(38 partial restatement) |
| \multicolumn{3}{c}{**Development** (92–124)} |||
| First part |  | (92–105) Development of first theme in orch. |
| Second part |  | (106–7) First theme: pno inner voice at T$_9$. (122–4) Orch retransition. |
| \multicolumn{3}{c}{**Reversed Recapitulation** (T$_7$) (125–97)} |||
| Exposition I (orch ritornello) | B$^5$ | (125–30)=(7–12 (T$_7$)) Second theme: orch at T$_7$. |
|  | A$^7$ | (131–3)=(13–15 (T$_7$)) First theme at T$_7$. (134–6)=(4–6 (T$_7$)). (137–8)=(19 (T$_7$)) Bridge. |
| Exposition II (pno and orch) | A$^8$ | (139–44)=(20–25 (T$_7$)) pno: first theme at T$_7$. |
|  | pno cadenza | (145–6)=(76–7 (T$_7$))=(10–11(T$_7$)) Variation of second theme at T$_7$. |
|  | B$^6$ | (170–79)=(76–85 (T$_7$)) orch and pno. Material from second theme at T$_7$. (180) Bridge. |
| Coda | A$^9$ | (181–92) Coda starts with first theme at T$_0$ in orch+ pno. (193–7)=(102–4 (T$_0$)) Material from the end of Development's first part at T$_0$. |

passages are constructed by the free treatment of the pitch-class material, particularly by juxtaposing, superimposing and interpolating linear segments of different forms of the sets. The reversed Recapitulation is introduced by the second theme and recapitulates the entire pitch-class material of the Exposition transposed at $T_7$, while the Coda returns to the original tonal level ($T_0$).

The third movement, *Allegro giocoso*, outlines a partially reversed sonata form,[5] in which, as shown in Table 13.7, the Recapitulation and Coda are elided, with the recapitulation of the first subject group material doubling as the Coda. The first theme of the Exposition is a varied recapitulation of the *Moderato*'s second theme at the original tonal level ($T_0$), based on varied forms of S2 and S3 (see Example 13.10).

Example 13.10   Third Piano Concerto, *Allegro giocoso*: First theme – opening gesture (bars 1–4)

The cyclical transformation process is further observed in the second theme, which is also played by the oboe and based on set S2b, which derives from S1 of the *Moderato*'s first theme (see Example 13.11).

The predominant cyclical characteristic of this theme is its opening trichord, which is an exact retrograde (A–E–F) of the original set's opening trichordal motto (F–E–A). Following the piano entry with a new thematic idea, in bars 120–25 the piano elaborates the first theme of the orchestral exposition transposed at $T_8$, as a

---

[5] For a discussion of the partially reversed recapitulation, see Jackson (1997, 141).

Example 13.11    Third Piano Concerto, *Allegro giocoso*: Second theme – opening gesture (bars 42–6)

modulatory interlude before the varied reappearance and further transformation of both themes at $T_0$.

The Development starts as a false recapitulation, predominantly elaborating motivic gestures from the first subject group, before the piano and orchestra separate, each introducing new material. In the Recapitulation, initiated with the second theme, Skalkottas revisits a formal/harmonic technique he used ten years earlier in the first and third movements of the First String Quartet; the pitch-class content of the Exposition is now recapitulated transposed predominantly at the fourth ($T_5$). This movement implies a subdominant recapitulation, with the 'tonic' becoming the goal rather than the point of departure (Rosen, 1988, 288–9). Eventually the music moves to the original tonal level ($T_0$), via a modulatory passage at $T_9$. The Coda is initiated by the movement's first theme, which is the *Moderato*'s second theme at $T_0$, and it progresses to a texturally modified yet exact – in terms of its pitch-class structure – repetition of material from the movement's Exposition and the beginning of the Development, also at its original tonal level. The Coda ends with a reminder of the movement's first theme to round off the entire piece.

Table 13.7  Third Piano Concerto, *Allegro giocoso*: Formal structure

| Sections | Thematic structure | Phrase, motivic, set structure – sectional repetitions |
|---|---|---|
| **Exposition** (1–210) ||| 
| Exposition I (orch ritornello) | First subject group | (1–41) First theme: cl (S2); accomp (S3):varied repetition of *Moderato*'s second theme.<br>(33–6)=(1–4 (T$_0$)) with new additions. |
|  | Second subject group | (42–76) Second theme: ob and cl (S1b); varied repetition of *Moderato*'s first theme.<br>(49–51$^2$)=(42$^3$–5$^1$ (T$_8$)) Varied repetition of theme: fl+cl at T$_8$; new accomp. |
| Exposition II (pno and orch) | New theme | (77–119) pno entry; new motives and pitch-class material; percussive pno part; soloistic, melodic, thin orch accomp. |
|  | First theme (pno) | (120–25)=(1–6 (T$_8$)) Varied first theme at T$_8$: pno. |
|  |  | (126–43) Developmental passage. |
|  |  | (144–55)=(15–26 (T$_0$)); (156–60)=(38–41(T$_0$)) pno: material from first theme at T$_0$. |
|  | Second theme (pno) | (162–8)=(42–8 (T$_0$)) pno: material from second theme at T$_0$. |
|  |  | (169–210) Cadential passage. |
| **Development** (211–309) ||| 
| pno solo | First theme | (211–14)=(1–4 (T$_0$)) False recapitulation of first theme.<br>(215–23$^1$) Cadenza-like continuation: pno. |
| orch ritornello |  | (223–33) Contrasting passage with chordal and scalic gestures.<br>(234–7) First thematic idea treated sequentially at T$_5$ (ww + brass).<br>(238–52) Continuation. |
| pno and orch |  | (253–75) Thin, soloistic orch accomp.<br>(276–90) pno solo cadenza.<br>(291–309) pno and orch. |
| **Reversed Recapitulation predominantly at T$_5$ (310–422)** ||| 
| Exposition I (orch ritornello) | Second subject group | Second theme: cbsn at T$_5$.<br>(310–16)=(42–8 (T$_5$)).<br>(317–20)=(49–52 (T$_7$)) modulatory bridge at T$_7$.<br>(322–37)=(58–73 (T$_5$)) Varied second theme material at T$_5$.<br>(338)=(4 (T$_3$)) Modulatory bridge at (T$_3$). |
|  |  | (339–46)=(7–14 (T$_5$)) Displaced retransition to recap of first theme: cl at T$_5$. |

*continued*

Table 13.7   *concluded*

| Sections | Thematic structure | Phrase, motivic, set structure – sectional repetitions |
|---|---|---|
| Exposition II (pno and orch) | First subject group | (347–72)=(144–69 ($T_5$)) Varied first-theme: pno material at $T_5$. |
|  |  | (373–6)=(173–6 ($T_5$)) Varied second thematic material from Exposition's cadence at $T_5$. |
|  | pno cadenza | (376–88) pno solo. (376)=(176 ($T_5$)). |
|  | From second subject group | (389–403)=(196–210 ($T_5$)) Varied second subject group material at $T_5$. |
|  | From first subject group | Varied repetition of material and modulatory passages from the first subject group. (404–9 pno)=(1–6 ($T_5$)). (404–16)=(120–32 ($T_9$)). (417–18)=(131–2 ($T_0$)). (419–20)=(133–4 ($T_0$)) in orch+pn RH; pn LH ($T_3/T_4$). (421)=(135 ($T_0$)) in pn – ($T_9$) orch. (422)=(136 ($T_0$)) all except for piano LH. |
| **Coda (423–51)** |||
| orch |  | (423–6)=(75–6 ($T_0$)) *Moderato*'s thematic motto at $T_0$. |
| pno and orch |  | (427–51) pno entry at $T_0$. (427–8³)=(77–8 ($T_0$)). |
|  |  | Modulatory passage; pno and orch at $T_3$ and $T_0$. (428⁴–32)=(83⁴–7 ($T_3$)). (433–6)=(93–6 ($T_3$)). (437)=(81 ($T_0$)). |
|  | pno cadenza | pno solo. Varied repetition of material from the Development at $T_0$. (438–40²)=(223–5² ($T_0$)). (440³)=(226¹⁻² ($T_0$)). (441–2)=(226³–8² ($T_0$)). (443–6)=(228³–33 ($T_0$)). |
|  |  | (447–51) Final cadence and elements of the movement's first theme; i.e. the *Moderato*'s varied second theme. |

Within the stylistic requirements of twelve-note or even atonal music, the unconventional harmonic structure of each of these three movements, the employment of the twelve-note sets and their transpositions, and the cyclical reappearance of the themes from the first movement in varied forms, may be explained with regard to the formal structure of the Third Piano Concerto as a whole, which outlines a large-scale reversed sonata form. As such, the *Moderato* functions as a large-scale Exposition section. Contrary to normative sonata form, the opposition between thematic and harmonic material takes place between the two outer sections, so that the *Moderato*'s exposition takes the place of the first subject group (with principal and secondary themes), its short Development that of the transition, and its Recapitulation the second subject group 'in the dominant'; the Coda functions as a transitional, modulatory passage (at $T_0$) to what follows. The *Andante sostenuto* functions as a Development section, which not only elaborates and expands thematic and motivic material from the Exposition, but also introduces new twelve-note sets and ideas. The *Allegro giocoso*, starting with a variation of the second theme (based on S2) at its original tonal level and gradually progressing towards the first thematic material, functions as the reversed Recapitulation of the entire piece, resolving the harmonic, 'tonic–dominant'-like opposition established in the first movement between the Exposition (large-scale first subject group) and Recapitulation (large-scale second subject group).

The *Allegro giocoso*'s reversed Recapitulation in the 'subdominant' is a reference to (or paraphrase of) eighteenth- and nineteenth-century sonata practices. Although in the previous two movements the Recapitulation in the 'dominant' needs resolution, which is not fulfilled within the boundaries of each movement, in the *Allegro giocoso* the variant reversed Recapitulation is largely in the subdominant, which traditionally, when used in sonata finales, needs no resolution and 'acts itself as a force for resolution, an antidominant' (Rosen, 1988, 288). At the large-scale structural level, this local subdominant recapitulation functions as the 'secondary Development' section within the entire concerto's large-scale Recapitulation; in several traditional sonata forms, this kind of section often starts with the second phrase soon after the beginning of the Recapitulation, eventually returning to one of the themes of the first subject group (Rosen, 1988, 289). Within the boundaries of the large-scale sonata form, this 'secondary development' lowers harmonic tension and provides harmonic equilibrium, as well as satisfying Skalkottas's desire for further variation.

Although this work is largely dodecaphonic, Skalkottas's choice of transpositions of the pitch-class material of entire sections, and the strategic placement of thematic gestures across the entire concerto to determine its large-scale form, deliberately suggests tonal readings and provides a sense of unity and coherence in this long and complex piece.

## Second Symphonic Suite – *Largo Sinfonico* (1942–44/46/49): Composing with a Superset – Unity and Diversity in the Construction of the Musical Space

The Second Symphonic Suite, similar to the First, is in six movements: *Ouvertüre Concertante, Toccata, Promenaden–Marsch, Largo Sinfonico, Thema con Variazioni, Perpetuum mobile (Rondo)*.[6] The *Largo Sinfonico*, in particular,

---

[6] Skalkottas started the orchestration of the Second Symphonic Suite in 1946 – with the instrumentation of the Athens State Orchestra in mind – and completed the first four movements; in 1949, a few months before he died, he orchestrated the fifth movement, but he never finished the orchestration of the sixth movement.

with its length and breadth, epitomizes Skalkottas's conception of musical space and twelve-note composition. It is characterized by expansiveness and a multidimensional arrangement of numerous clearly defined twelve-note sets. The movement is built on a superset consisting of sixteen different but closely related twelve-note sets (S1–S16).[7] Similar to the hexachordal partitioning of an ordered twelve-note series, the superset is partitioned into two halves of eight sets each (S1–S8, S9–S16), with each half delineating formal sections. Each set of the first half has at least one common tetrachord with the corresponding set of the second half, thus providing a degree of connection between the two halves of the superset. Each set is constantly partitioned into three tetrachordal segments (indicated as A, B, C in the examples), defined by the neighbourhood relationships between the constituent notes of the segment; these are always grouped together and establish their motivic/harmonic identity through rhythm, articulation and orchestration.

The formal design of the *Largo Sinfonico* combines a set of variations with sonata form, typical of Skalkottas's synthesis of antithetical formal prototypes. It is built on the continuous and strictly ordered repetition of the sixteen sets (S1–S16) of the superset, which is reiterated thirty times, outlining a sixteen-bar theme with twenty-nine variations. The variations maintain the segmental partitioning of the sets, while each presentation of the superset is characterized by dramatic textural changes, as well as changes in orchestration, dynamics and mood. Table 13.8 represents schematically the large-scale formal, thematic and set structures of the piece.

Here Skalkottas uses a procedure reminiscent of Schoenberg's isomorphic partitioning;[8] he partitions the sets identically in order to articulate phrases – not by interval succession and interval replication from one set form to an inversionally related one, but by consistent segmental repetition, including motives with certain note duplications and other memorable harmonic formations. As shown in Example 13.12, throughout the exposition of the superset in the variation theme (bars 1–16), the first tetrachord (segment A) of each set is played by the clarinets as dotted harmonic dyads, in an uninterrupted, pedal-like harmonic accompaniment. The extended melodic line of the first theme, based on successive segments B and

---

[7] All sixteen sets are closely connected through common and transpositionally or inversionally related segments, and several derive from reorderings within each hexachord of previous sets. For example, each hexachord of S8 is an unordered presentation of the retrograde form of S6, transposed at $T_4$ ($R_4S6$); similarly, S10 is a reordering of S2 transposed at $T_{11}$; S13 is an almost exact transposition at the tritone of S5 ($T_6$); each hexachord of S14 is both a reordering of the $I_6$ form of S2 and of the $I_3$ of S10. However, each set is used consistently with the new segmental ordering, thus establishing its own identity as a different set, though it belongs to the same set-class as the source set.

[8] For a detailed discussion of Schoenberg's use of isomorphic partitioning, according to which two or more set forms of the basic set are partitioned identically in order to articulate phrases by systematic intervallic relationships, see Haimo and Johnson (1984, 47–72), and Haimo (1992, 22–6).

Table 13.8  Second Symphonic Suite, *Largo Sinfonico*: Formal structure and set structure

| Variations | Thematic structure | Phrase structure | Set structure |
|---|---|---|---|
| | Sonata Exposition (1–129³) |||
|  | | First subject group | **Sequential presentation of S1–S16** |
| Theme | First theme | (1–8) Antecedent. | Melody: S1BC–S8BC<br>Accomp: S1A–S8A<br>One set per bar. |
|  |  | (9–16) Consequent. | Melody: S9BC–S16BC<br>Accomp: S9A–S16A<br>One set per bar. |
| I |  | (17–22) First phrase. | Melody: S1BC–S8BC<br>Accomp: S1A–S8A<br>Two sets per bar. |
|  |  | (23–7) Second phrase. | Melody: S9BC–S16BC<br>Accomp: S9A–S16A<br>Two sets per bar. |
| II |  | (28–9) First phrase. | Melody: S1A–S8A<br>Accomp: S1BC–S8BC<br>Four sets per bar. |
|  |  | (30–33¹) Second phrase. | Melody: S9A–S16A<br>Accomp: S9BC–S16BC<br>Four sets per bar. |
| III |  | (33–5) Transitional passage with duet thematic line. | Melody: S1BC–S16BC<br>Accomp: S1A–S16A<br>Interpolation of segments. |
| IV |  | (36–9) Developmental passage with thick texture. | Melody: S1A–S16A<br>Accomp: S1BC–S16BC<br>Four sets per bar. |
| V | Secondary theme of first subj group | (40–47) First phrase. | Melody: S1BC – S8BC<br>Accomp: S1A–S8A, S1B–S8B, S1C–S8C<br>One set per bar. |
|  |  | (48–56³) Second phrase. | Melody: S9BC–S16BC<br>Accomp: S9A–S16A, S9B–S16B, S9C–S16C<br>One set per bar. |
| VI |  | (56¹–66) Harmonic episode. | Superimposition of S1BC–S16BC on S1A–S16A<br>Two sets per bar. |
| VII |  | (67–74) Transition and liquidated cadence. | S1A–S16A |

*continued*

Table 13.8  concluded

| Variations | Thematic structure | Phrase structure | Set structure |
|---|---|---|---|
| | | Second subject group | Sequential presentation of S1–S16 |
| VIII | Second theme | (75–8) First phrase. | Melody: S1A–S8A<br>Accomp: S1BC–S8BC<br>Two sets per bar. |
| | | (79–84) Second phrase. | Melody: S9A–S16A<br>Accomp: S9BC–S16BC<br>Two sets per bar (S16 over two bars) |
| IX | | (85–94) First phrase. | Melody: Duet S1BC–S8BC and S1CB–S8CB<br>Accomp: S1A–S8A<br>One set per bar (S8 over three bars). |
| | | (95–104) Second phrase. | Melody: Duet S9BC–S16BC and S9CB–S16CB<br>Accomp: S9A–S16A<br>One set per bar (S16 over three bars). |
| X | | (105–11) Liquidated cadence. | Soloistic use of set-segments. |
| XI | Secondary theme of second subj group | (112–15) First phrase. | Melody: Duet between S1A–S16A<br>Accomp: Segms S1BC–S16BC<br>Superimposition of four sets per bar. |
| XII | | (116–20$^1$) Developmental continuation. | Melody: S1A–S16A<br>Accomp: S1BC–S16BC<br>Segm superimposition; four sets per bar. |
| XIII | | (120$^2$–29$^3$) Varied repetition of secondary theme; extended cadence on S16. | Melody: Duet between S1A–S16A<br>Accomp: S1BC–S16BC<br>Two sets per bar (S16 over two bars). |
| | | Development (129$^3$–79) | |
| XIV | First section | (129$^3$–32) First phrase. | S1–S16: segm interpol over an A♭ pedal. Predominant S1A–S16A. |
| | | (133–4) Climactic second phrase. | S9–S16: segm interpol over an A♭ pedal. |
| XV | Second section | (135–46) First phrase. | S1–S16: segm interpol. |
| XVI | | (147–9$^2$) Second phrase; climax with a brass fanfare. | S1–S16 |
| XVII | Third section | (149$^3$–58) First phrase; false recapitulation of first theme; soloistic treatment of thematic segms A. | Melody: S1A–S16A<br>Accomp: S1BC–S16BC |

| Variations | Thematic structure | Phrase structure | Set structure |
|---|---|---|---|
| XVIII | | (159–64) Second phrase. | S1–S16: fragmentation; segm interpol. |
| XIX | | (165–72) Third phrase with sparse texture and melodic harp feature. | Melody: S1BC–S16BC<br>Accomp: S1A–S16A |
| XX | | (173–9) Closing section – retransition. | Melody: S1A–S16A<br>Accomp: S1BC–S16BC (interpol)<br>Two sets per bar. |
| **Recapitulation** (180–265) ||||
| **First subject group** ||||
| XXI | First theme | (180–95) Almost exact recap of first theme; part exchanges and canonic presentation of thematic material. | Thematic line: Canon S1A–S16A<br>Harmonic accomp: S1BC–S16BC<br>One set per bar. |
| XXII | | (196–206) Almost exact recap of Var I; part exchanges and canonic presentation of thematic material. | Melody: Canon S1BC–S16BC<br>Accomp: S1A–S16A<br>Two sets per bar. |
| XXIII | | (207–11) Recap of Var II. | Melody: Canon S1A–S16A<br>Accomp: S1BC–S16BC<br>Four sets per bar. |
| XXIV | | (212–16) Recap of Var VI; harmonic episode. | Superimposition of S1BC–S16BC on S1A–S16A |
| XXV | | (217–21) Condensed recap of Var VII; transition and liquidated cadence. | S1A–S16A |
| **Second subject group** ||||
| XXVI | Second theme | (222–31) Recap of second theme (Var VIII) with minor rhythmic changes and thicker texture. | Melody: S1A–S16A<br>Accomp: S1BC–S16BC<br>Two sets per bar. |
| XXVII | | (232–51) Almost exact recap of Var IX. | Melody: Duet S1BC–S16BC and S1CB–S16CB<br>Accomp: S1A–S16A<br>One set per bar. |
| XXVIII | | (252–8) Recap of Var X; liquidated cadence. | Soloistic use of segments. |
| XXIX | Coda | (259–65) Chordal cadence. | Chordal presentation of S1–S16 |

C of sets S1–S8, is played by the cor anglais in bars 1–8; in bars 9–16, based on segments B and C of sets S9–S16, it is played in unison by the oboes and first violins.

Example 13.12   Second Symphonic Suite, *Largo Sinfonico*: Variation theme – set structure (bars 1–16)

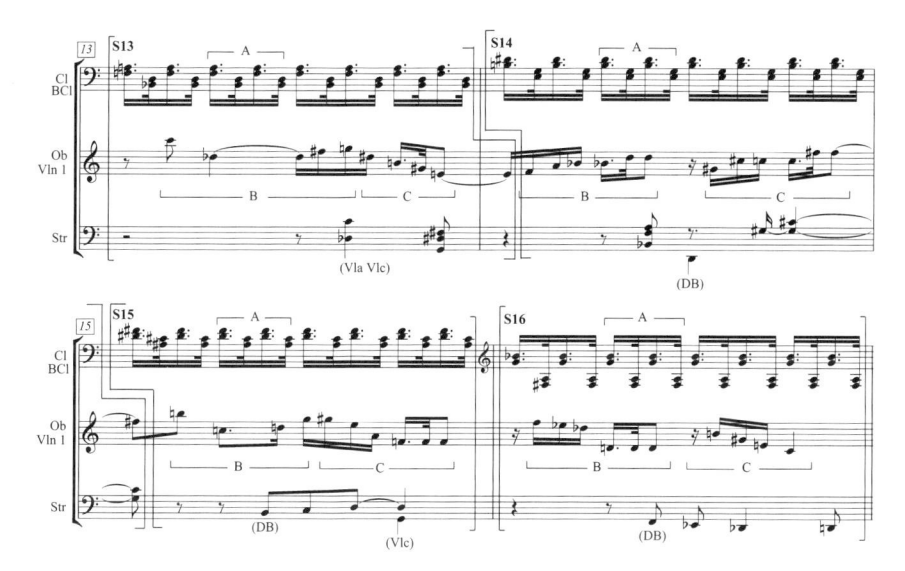

The segmental partitioning, together with the orchestration, texture and rhythm, divides the theme into regular, square phrases. Thus the variation theme, which also functions as the first theme of the sonata form, outlines two, eight-bar, antecedent–consequent phrases (bars 1–8, 9–16), while each of the 16 sets is exposed at one-bar intervals. Each periodic phrase is articulated into two subphrases (**a**, **b**), which are further subdivided into four phrases each (a, b, c, d), as shown in Table 13.9.

Table 13.9  Second Symphonic Suite, *Largo Sinfonico*: Variation theme (bars 1–16) – phrase structure and set structure

| | Antecedent ||||||||
|---|---|---|---|---|---|---|---|---|
| Subphrases | a |||| b ||||
| Phrases | a || b || c || d ||
| Sets | S1 | S2 | S3 | S4 | S5 | S6 | S7 | S8 |
| Melody (CA) | S1BC | S2BC | S3BC | S4BC | S5BC | S6BC | S7BC | S8BC |
| Accomp (cls) | S1A | S2A | S3A | S4A | S5A | S6A | S7A | S8A |
| Bars | 1 | 2 | 3 | 4 | 5 | 6 | 7 | 8 |

| | Consequent ||||||||
|---|---|---|---|---|---|---|---|---|
| Subphrases | a |||| b ||||
| Phrases | a || b || c || d ||
| Sets | S9 | S10 | S11 | S12 | S13 | S14 | S15 | S16 |
| Melody (ob+vln1) | S9BC | S10BC | S11BC | S12BC | S13BC | S14BC | S15BC | S16BC |
| Accomp (cls) | S9A | S10A | S11A | S12A | S13A | S14A | S15A | S16A |
| Bars | 9 | 10 | 11 | 12 | 13 | 14 | 15 | 16 |

In the first variation (bars 17–27) the rotation speed of the sets increases, with the presentation of two sets per bar (see Example 13.13). The texture thickens as the oboes, first violins and violas play in unison the dotted thematic melody of the section, based on set segments B and C, while the cor anglais, bass clarinet, bassoons and harp provide the harmonic accompaniment, now based on segments A in continuous quaver motives.

Example 13.13    Second Symphonic Suite, *Largo Sinfonico*: Variation I – opening gesture (bars 17–20)

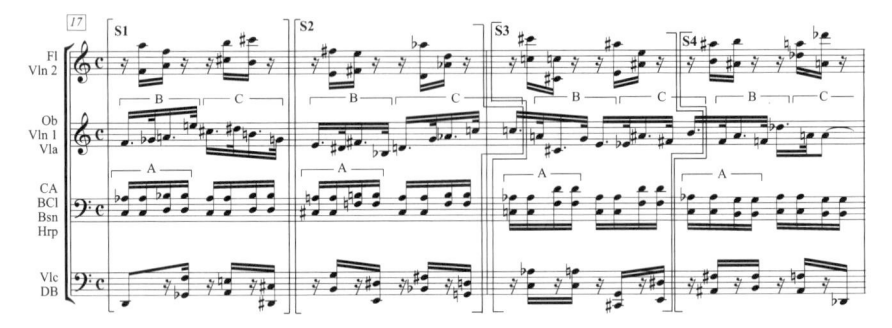

In the following variation (bars 28–33[1]), based on the third presentation of the superset, the set rotation accelerates further, with four sets per bar distributed vertically in the texture (see Example 13.14). In terms of instrumentation and rhythm, the thematic/melodic line, a continuation of the thematic line of the previous variation, is now based on frequently reordered segments A, while the harmonic accompaniment consists of the chordal presentation of segments B and C.

Example 13.14    Second Symphonic Suite, *Largo Sinfonico*: Variation II – opening gesture (bars 28–9)

Further manipulation of the constituent sets occurs in the secondary thematic idea of the first subject group, at the opening gesture of the fifth variation (bars 40–56³). As shown in Example 13.15, segments A are now played by the lower woodwind, harp and lower strings as long chords. The thematic line, played by the cellos in their high register, outlines segments B and C, each with a new internal ordering; it is accompanied by a chiastic superimposition of the same unordered segments, with the second violins playing continuous, scalic segments B and C, and the upper woodwind playing dotted chordal segments C and B.

Example 13.15  Second Symphonic Suite, *Largo Sinfonico*: Variation V – opening gesture (bars 40–41)

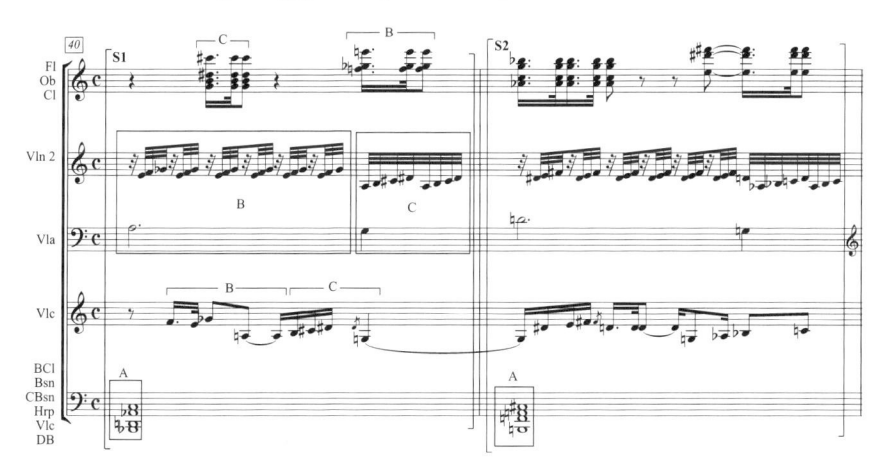

The second lyrical theme (bars 75–84), also structured as an antecedent–consequent phrase and played in unison by the flutes and first violins, consists of consecutive unordered segments A, accompanied chordally by harmonic tetrachords B and C, as shown in Example 13.16. The sets rotate swiftly, at two sets per bar, apart from the elongated cadence of the thematic section, based on S15 and S16.

In the Development, which comprises three sections, the set segments are used freely, often interpolated and juxtaposed in the texture, while there is frequent use of segments A only. The first section ends with a climactic gesture as the whole orchestra plays dense rhythmic motives, whereas the third section is introduced by an abruptly reduced texture; it starts as a false recapitulation of the first theme, with soloistic motives based on segments B and C played by the trombones.

The Recapitulation is an almost exact repetition of large sections of the Exposition, but with a thicker texture resulting from the tetrachordal segments being played simultaneously with their retrograde presentations, and the thematic melodies appearing in canon (see Example 13.17).

Example 13.16  Second Symphonic Suite, *Largo Sinfonico*: Second theme – variation VIII (bars 75–84)

Example 13.17    Second Symphonic Suite, *Largo Sinfonico*: Recapitulation – opening gesture of first theme (bars 180–81)

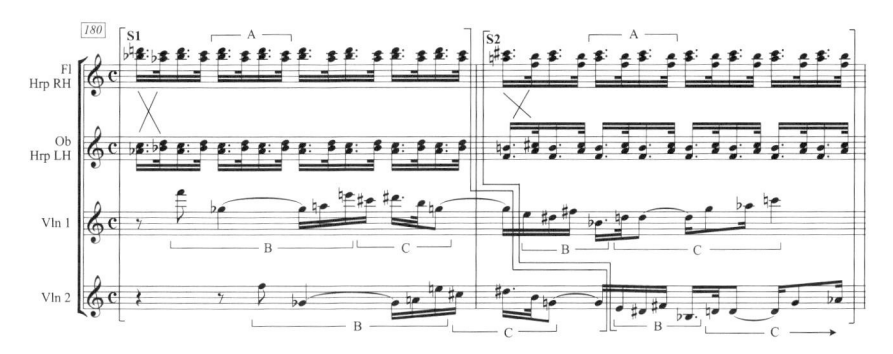

In a technique similar to the one used in several movements of the First Symphonic Suite (and which would be used again in *The Return of Ulysses*), the *Largo Sinfonico* ends with a Coda built on the sixteen twelve-note sets presented as sixteen *pianissimo* twelve-note chords (see Example 13.18).[9]

Example 13.18    Second Symphonic Suite, *Largo Sinfonico*: Coda (bars 259–65)

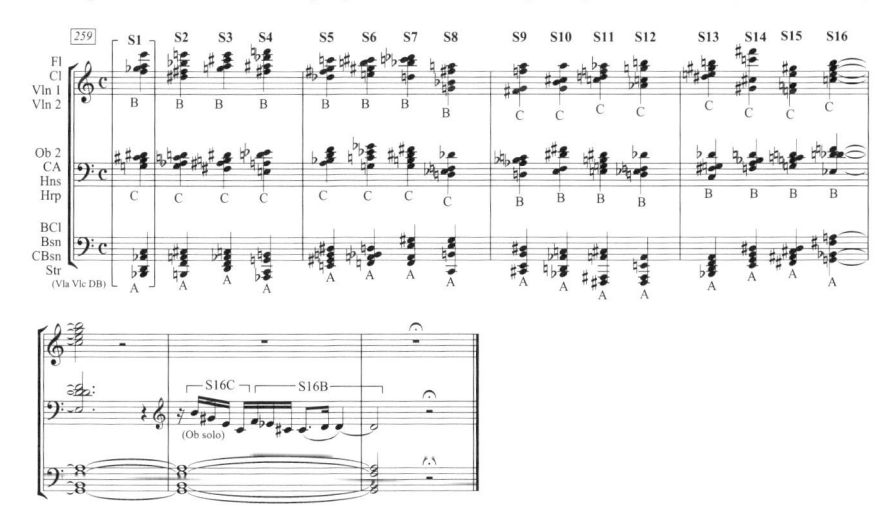

Each set is divided into a three-layered texture marked by orchestration and timbre. In bars 259–60, instruments with brighter timbres (flutes, clarinets and violins) play segments B of S1–S8; instruments with darker timbres (oboe, cor anglais, horns and harp) play segments C; the bass instruments (bass clarinet,

---

[9]    The score reduction of this passage has been taken from Skalkottas's own manuscript short score (MS Skalkottas Archive).

bassoons, contrabassoons, cellos and double basses) play segments A. The segmental disposition changes in bars 261–3, with the brighter instruments playing segments C, the darker instruments playing segments B, and the bass instruments continuing to play segments A. Above a fading segment of the last chord, which includes G minor and D major triads, a low solo oboe gesture rounds off the piece.

Overall, orchestration, textural change and part-writing have important articulating functions, and, together with set repetition and thematic–melodic gestures, these frame the variations and outline the form. Furthermore, the large-scale form is underlined by the harmonic rhythm (that is, the change of speed of set rotation within a variation), which produces waves of tension and relaxation and controls the ebb and flow of the music during the unfolding of the piece. In the Exposition, within the first subject group, there is a gradual increase in the harmonic rhythm – accompanied by changes in orchestration – from one set per bar in the variation theme, to two in variation I, to four in variation II. This is followed by a climactic passage (variations III, IV) that precedes the secondary theme of the first subject group, which returns to the regularity of one followed by two sets per bar (V, VI), before a liquidated cadence (VII) that leads to the second subject group. The latter has a reverse harmonic rhythm to the first subject group. The second theme moves from two sets (VIII) to one set (IX) per bar, and the secondary theme, preparing for the Development, starts with a superimposition of four sets (XI, XII) and concludes with two sets per bar (XIII). In the Development, the first short section (XIV) is based on a sustained A♭ pedal, and the second (XV, XVI), with its intense segmental activity, dense texture and percussive sounds, functions as the climactic middle section. It is followed by a long anticlimactic section (XVII–XX) featuring set fragmentation. In the truncated Recapitulation the original harmonic rhythm of the main sections is resumed, ending with a liquidated cadence (XXVIII). The chordal Coda contains the harmonic material that sustains the work and encapsulates Skalkottas's compositional approach in the entire Second Symphonic Suite.

**Overture for Large Orchestra (*The Return of Ulysses*) (1942–44/49): The Pinnacle of Skalkottas's Integration of Free Dodecaphonic Technique and Tonal Structure**

Skalkottas composed the large-scale Overture for large orchestra[10] in 1942–44, and in 1949 he produced a reduction for two pianos, from which the examples presented here are taken. This Overture is popularly known as *The Return of*

---

[10] The score includes: three flutes (and piccolos), three oboes, cor anglais, D clarinet, two B♭ clarinets, bass clarinet, two bassoons, contrabassoon, six horns, cornet, three trumpets, four trombones, tuba, timpani, percussion, celesta, harp, and strings. The horn section includes two bass horns, which in his unpublished *Treatise on Orchestration* Skalkottas refers to in passing as being a relative of the tuba family. In modern recordings the bass horn parts are performed on Wagner tubas.

*Ulysses* or 'Symphony in one movement' – two descriptive titles ascribed to the piece after the composer's death. In his accompanying Notes to the work, written in German, Skalkottas attributes the inspiration and composition of the Overture to a yet to be written opera, called 'Die Rückkehr Odysseus in seiner Heimat' ('The Return of Odysseus to his Home/Homeland').[11] However, he never received the libretto or composed the opera; therefore, any interpretation of particular themes or passages as representations of various mythological characters or events is purely conjectural.

The piece epitomizes Skalkottas's free dodecaphonic technique and his predilection for integrating traditional formal prototypes and fusing Baroque and Classical compositional processes. The formal design outlines an expanded, five-section sonata form, shown in Table 13.10. Table 13.11 presents the main themes of the Overture, as given by Skalkottas in his Notes. A distinctive compositional feature of the work is the number and rate of change of the pitch-class material used, with groups of pitch-class collections different not only in each phrase, but frequently in each bar of a section. In his accompanying Notes Skalkottas writes that, '*The harmony from the beginning to the end moves strictly and freely in twelve-note sets.*' Indeed, the Overture is based on a very large number of sets of various types (comprising a few ordered twelve-note sets, their variations, derived sets, and sets that include note repetitions and interpolation of segments), a plethora of independent hexachords, and other collections consisting of more than twelve notes.[12] Their identity is frequently established at their varied repetitions within a section, and/or in the Recapitulation. Although segmental partitioning is not employed here as methodically as it is in, for example, the *Largo Sinfonico*, sets are frequently partitioned into segments of various sizes, which are presented multidimensionally as harmonic dyads and/or three-note chords, or as tetrachordal and hexachordal melodic gestures.

The broad, slow introduction (*Molto adagio*) demonstrates the conflicting compositional styles Skalkottas employs in this piece by presenting twelve-note material within a clearly implied tonal context. As shown in Example 13.19, the atmospheric opening starts with a traditional tonic–dominant diatonic relationship through two interchanging open perfect fifths in the horns (C–G, G–D), which progress (in bar 4) to the chromatically altered diminished fifth (C–G♭), while further chromatic distortions continue throughout the section. On top, superimposed in a different tonal sphere, the thematic melody is constructed from three different sets.

---

[11] Heimat is a difficult word to define and translate into either English or Greek; several possibilities include 'home', 'homeland', 'fatherland', 'nation' and 'birthplace'. For further discussion on the idea of *Heimat*, see Spranger (1923/1967), Bastian (1995), Boa and Palfreyman (2000), Blickle (2004).

[12] Papaioannou misleadingly asserts that: 'The Symphony in one movement [*sic*] breaks all records in twelve-note complexity: the "complex [of rows]" consists of 18 independent rows, and sometimes four different rows are presented simultaneously' (1969b, 615).

Table 13.10  Overture for large orchestra (*The Return of Ulysses*): Formal structure

| Sonata form | Bars | Thematic groups | Thematic, formal structure within each thematic group |
|---|---|---|---|
| Introduction | 1–45 | *Molto adagio* | |
| Exposition | 46–274 | First subject group (*Allegro molto vivace*) | ABA' (46–162). A: First theme 1 (*Haupt-Thema* 1) (46). B: Second theme 1 (*Neben-Thema* 1) (71). A': Varied first theme 1 (135). |
| | | Second subject group (*Sehr ruhig–esspressivo*) | ABA' (163–274). A: First theme 2 (*Haupt-Thema* 2) (163). B: Second theme 2 (*Neben-Thema* 2) (214). A': Reminiscences of first theme 2. |
| Development | 275–429 | First section | A: Fugue 1 (275–328). |
| | | Second section | B: Fugue 2 (329–73). |
| | | Third section | A': Double Fugue (374–429). |
| Truncated Repetition (Recapitulation) | 430–602 | First subject group ($T_7$) (*Allegro molto vivace*) | (430–587) =(46–206 ($T_7$)). First theme 1 at $T_7$. Second theme 1 at $T_7$ (458). |
| | | Second subject group ($T_7$–$T_0$) (*Sehr ruhig–espressivo*) | First theme 2 at $T_7$ (541). Transitional episode (577–87). Second theme 2 at ($T_0$) (588–602)=(259–74 ($T_0$)). |
| Coda | 603–84 | *Presto* | A (603–54). |
| | | *Prestissimo* | A' (655–74) Varied repetition of A (603–25). |

The arch-like ascending melody played by the horn (bars 2–3[1]) and initiated with an expansive minor ninth ($c^1$–$d\flat^2$) is based on the twelve-note set S1; the following melodic gesture in the clarinet (bar 3) is based on S2; and the cadential, tonally imbued melodic phrase in bar 4 is based on S3. The thematic phrase cadences (bar 5) with S4, followed by a large tonal segment of S3.

The Exposition consists of two extended subject groups – each having two main themes that Skalkottas calls '*Haupt-Thema*' and '*Neben-Thema*' respectively – and many other thematic ideas and subsections. The first subject group has a ternary structure. The *Haupt-Thema* 1 (*Allegro vivace*), featuring a continuous, ostinato-like dotted rhythm, is based on a series of different, consecutively presented pitch-class melodic sets that include several note repetitions; in Example 13.20 the first set is indicated as $S_{HT1}$. The thematic gestures are continuously repeated in varied forms, in the manner of a developing variation. The theme is accompanied in every

Example 13.19  Overture for large orchestra (*The Return of Ulysses*): Introduction – opening gesture (bars 1–5)

bar by several new four-note chords and other collections, which when grouped together produce twelve-note collections.

The *Neben-Thema* 1, characterized by extensive fugal writing, is structured from superimposed hexachords and trichords, distributed in four contrasting textures whose paired combinations result in twelve-note aggregates. The opening thematic gesture is based on the first hexachord of a twelve-note set ($S_{NT1}$) accompanied homorhythmically by the second hexachord (see Example 13.21). The theme introduces a new continuous triplet accompanimental figure based on

Table 13.11  Overture for large orchestra (*The Return of Ulysses*): Main themes

| | |
|---|---|
| Introductory theme | Molto Adagio |
| First theme 1 (*Haupt–Thema* 1) | Allegro molto vivace — 46 / 49 |
| Second theme 1 (*Neben–Thema* 1) | 71 |
| First theme 2 (*Haupt–Thema* 2) | 163, espress., p |
| Second theme 2 (*Neben–Thema* 2) | 214 |

Fugue 1

Fugue 2

Double fugue

Coda theme

Example 13.20   Overture for large orchestra (*The Return of Ulysses*): *Haupt-Thema* 1 – opening gesture (bars 46–9)

a new twelve-note set, which interchanges in each bar with the dotted rhythmic figure of the *Haupt-Thema*, and with short chordal episodes based on new twelve-note pitch-class collections. In bars 73–4, the predominant thematic melody, based on the first hexachord of $S_{NT1}$, is repeated as a tonal answer transposed at $T_5$; it is accompanied homorhythmically by an independent hexachord. The contrapuntal writing, featuring frequent transposition of thematic gestures, continues throughout the section.

The second subject group, also structured on ternary formal principles, consists of two themes. The first, *Sehr ruhig–espressivo* (*Haupt-Thema* 2), played first by the woodwind and then by the strings, is based on a new melodic twelve-note set ($S_{HT2}$); it is accompanied by two new '*figurations*', each based on a hexachord of a twelve-note aggregate distributed in three textural layers as pedal notes, dyads and trichordal segments. This theme has a predominant harmonic orientation towards an E♭ minor tonality, supported by an E♭ minor triad (approached by an appoggiatura-like E minor triad) played continuously in an ostinato rhythmic pattern (see Example 13.22). A long episodic section, featuring several transpositions of the second theme's opening melodic gesture, leads to the *Neben-Thema* 2, based on new sets and other pitch-class collections.

The Development, following Romantic hybridic formal prototypes, Beethovenian in particular,[13] is structured as a free, three-section fugue with two subjects (see Table 13.11). The first section consists of a seven-part fugue whose subject is a variation of the introductory theme. The second section is based on

---

[13]   Beethoven explored the integration of fugue within the context of the sonata form in several of his works, such as in the finales of the piano sonatas op.101 (in which 100 bars of fugue function as the development section), op.106 (*Hammerklavier*) and op.110, and in the finale of the cello sonata op.102 no.2. He also experimented with the integration of fugue and fugal writing in the overture *Zur Weihe des Hauses* (1821) and in several string quartets, as for example in the first movement of op.131 and the last movement of op.133 ('Grosse Fuge'); see, Rosen (1976a, 440–41); Kerman (1978, 269–302).

Example 13.21  Overture for large orchestra (*The Return of Ulysses*): *Neben-Thema* 1 – opening gesture (bars 71–4)

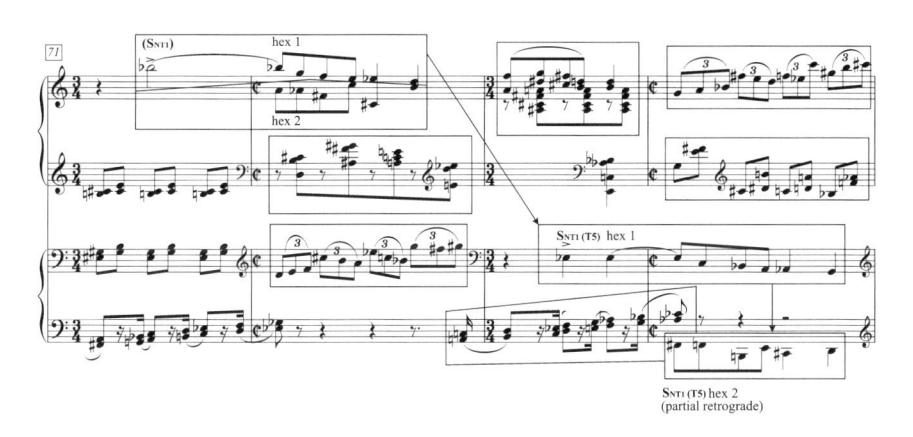

Example 13.22  Overture for large orchestra (*The Return of Ulysses*): *Haupt-Thema* 2 – opening gesture (bars 163–7)

a new, '*canon-like*' theme that derives from '*motives and characteristic short melodies*' that were developed within the Exposition, particularly the trill figure introduced in the *Neben-Thema* 1 space (bars 120–24), leading towards the varied reappearance of the *Haupt-Thema* 1. The third section is a double fugue between the introductory theme and a theme that includes predominantly semitonal intervals, which are used widely in the developmental process and herald the most prominent motivic feature of the Coda; this double fugue also shares the four-note motive D–C–B♭–A with the answer of the second fugue's theme.

In his Notes Skalkottas describes the truncated Recapitulation as 'Wiederholung', which means 'repetition', not reprise (reprise presupposes the resolution of tonal conflicts and tensions established in the Exposition). The repetition, shorter by fifty-four bars, brings back the pitch-class material of large sections of the Exposition re-orchestrated and transposed at the fifth ($T_7$) – a technique extensively employed in the large-scale concertos of the 1930s and in movements based on a large number of sets. The transposition at $T_7$ of the second *Neben-Thema* is missing, together with a fast episode with the same intervals; this is perhaps because these appear in the Coda, organized in the form of complementary tetrachords. Abruptly and briefly, within the second *Neben-Thema* space, the music returns to the original tonal level.

Example 13.23   Overture for large orchestra (*The Return of Ulysses*): Coda – opening gestures of Presto and Prestissimo sections (bars 603–5, 655–7)

The Coda, consisting of two sections (*Presto–Prestissimo*), features '*a new theme* [...] *normally found in the basses*'. This is an obsessively reiterated, *pianissimo*, ostinato, semitonal figure (c–d♭), a contracted version – a memory – of the introductory theme's opening ascending minor ninth ($c^1$–$d♭^2$). In terms of its dodecaphonic pitch-class structure, the opening of the *Presto* (bars 603–11) is built on many twelve-note pitch-class collections, each exposed within one bar, and each resulting from the superimposition of dyadic and tetrachordal segments. The pitch-class content of each bar is repeated, but reorganized, producing new motivic and harmonic formations from bar 612 onwards. The second part (*Prestissimo*) is a varied and much faster repetition of the *Presto*, which '*concludes the entire Overture with motives from the main theme and with a harmonic cadence*'. The piece ends with loud six-note chords, consisting of the superimposition of an augmented and a diminished triad (see Example 13.23).

In this Overture Skalkottas reached the apotheosis of his free dodecaphonic technique. The compositional approach explored here is based on free developmental formations of motivic and harmonic figurations, arising from the pairing and superimposition of predominantly six- and twelve-note pitch-class collections, which are distributed multidimensionally in the texture within the short space of a few beats, or a bar. In an extension to the serial technique used in the *Largo Sinfonico* (where the segmental order of a twelve-note set was reused in modified form when all the other sets had been exposed within each rotation of the superset), here, serial order is achieved by the *en bloc* varied repetition of a phrase's pitch-class collections. Coherence is ensured, however, by non-serial means such as: the motivic structure and the reiteration of certain intervals that saturate the texture, particularly the minor second; the rhythmic accompaniment, usually based on dyadic rhythmic ostinati; the exact, or progressively varied, repetition of thematic/melodic gestures; and the *en bloc* transposition of entire sections in the Recapitulation to determine the large-scale form.

# Chapter 14
# New Directions in the Last Chamber Works: Tonal Serialism

Following a period of about four years during which he predominantly composed tonal music, Skalkottas returned in 1949, the last year of his life, to dodecaphonic composition, producing a number of chamber works including *Bolero*, Largo, Serenata, Sonatina and *Tender Melody*, all for cello and piano, and the *Second Little Suite* for violin and piano. Compared with the earlier monumental orchestral works of the late 1930s and early 1940s, even the post-1945 tonal orchestral compositions, these are small-scale forays that demonstrate yet another facet of his dodecaphonic style. Although they appear deceptively simple, they combine aspects of both his strict and his free twelve-note compositional techniques, and they are all based on a tertiary harmonic foundation, with overt tonal elements permeating the texture. These works perhaps reveal that Skalkottas had reached a mature point in his compositional style, in which tonality could be meaningfully reintegrated into a dodecaphonic context. Just as he had previously tested new approaches first in small-scale works, these last chamber music pieces might have been preliminary, experimental studies in a new compositional phase that, had he lived, would have been fully developed in large-scale orchestral works.

**Serenata for Cello and Piano (1949): Large-scale use of Inversion to Determine the Form**

The Serenata for cello and piano exemplifies Skalkottas's new-found approach to twelve-note composition in that it combines the free treatment of his twelve-note technique, including the extensive use of twelve-note pitch-class aggregates and sets treated as tropes, with strict serial presentation.[1] The piece is based on eight sets (S1–S8), most of which derive from or are permutations of the source set S1, which is constantly presented as two hexachords whose aggregate gives all the notes of the chromatic scale. Furthermore, although the twelve-note operation of inversion is used only infrequently in the early Berlin works, here transposition and particularly inversion of the sets become a significant structural feature of the piece. The Serenata is modelled on traditional tonal principles, and its harmonic structure, imbued with tonal elements, outlines modulatory harmonic progressions

---

[1] Drawing on Skalkottas's own terminological understanding, I use the word 'set' to describe this material.

through twelve-note regions. As shown in Table 14.1,[2] it outlines a complicated rondo form within a large-scale ternary superstructure, with each rondo section (ABa¹cA²dA³B¹a⁴) also built as a rondo.

The eight-bar theme has a periodic structure (see Example 14.1). The antecedent (bars 1–4) is divided into two-bar phrase segments; the first (bars 1–2) is based on S1, which supports the opening thematic gesture with the first hexachord played by the cello and the second by the piano. Its continuation (the more remote motive forms) introduces new motivic and rhythmic features, and is based on sets S2 and S3, both having transpositional relationships with S1. S2 appears constantly as a pitch-class collection of two unordered hexachords whose segments are distributed freely among the cello and piano two hands. It derives from a free rearrangement of the pitch-class order within each hexachord of the $I_5$ form of S1, but although it belongs to the same set-class as $S1(I_5)$, it is distinguished from the ordered presentation of the $I_5$ form, which is also used at certain points in the piece.[3] S3, associated with the closing gesture of the first thematic phrase, derives from a permutation of the $T_4$ form of S1. In the consequent (bars 5–8), the principal idea is now based on an exact transposition of S1 at the fifth ($T_7$), establishing a tonic–dominant relationship within the opening phrase of the antecedent. Its cadence is built on S4, which derives from a reordering within each hexachord of the $I_5$ form of S3, and which has a $T_4$ transpositional relationship with the cadence of the antecedent, thus further reinforcing tonal associations within the thematic structure.

A subdominant harmonic movement is further established at the opening (bars 9–11) of the rondo section B, which is based on the $I_5$ form of S1. Its closing gesture (bar 12) is based on S5, which derives from a reordering of the $I_5$ of S2 (which itself derives from $S1(I_5)$). It is subsequently repeated transposed at the major sixth ($T_9$) in bar 13, thus initiating a modulatory movement that concludes at the end of the section (bar 16) with S4 transposed at $T_9$, and having a transpositional relationship of a major sixth with the end of the rondo section A (see Example 14.2, and Table 14.1).

A four-bar piano cadenza (bars 17–20), repeating the thematic idea of the cello transposed first at $T_3$ and then at $T_2$, is followed by a passage (bars 21–3) based on the tonal set S6 and its two transposed forms, $T_{10}$ and $T_9$; S6 consists of three tonal tetrachords: a half diminished seventh, E♭–B♭–G♭–C, a diminished seventh, F–A♭–B–D, and a dominant seventh, A–C♯–G–E. The overt tonal character of this phrase is outlined in the three textural layers, with a particularly prominent sequential modulatory movement in the cello from an A dominant seventh to

---

[2] In Table 14.1, lower case letters indicate truncated repetitions of sections and other short transitional passages.

[3] Melissa Garmon Roberts considers this form of the set $I_5$ a 'trope' (2002, 33). Although this particular presentation of the set resembles a trope, in my reading, for the sake of clarity, I avoid using this term, and consider this and other similar sets as independent sets, since they are used in this reordered, varied form at certain structural points in the piece and thus acquire their own identity.

New Directions in the Last Chamber Works 321

Example 14.1 Serenata for cello and piano: Opening thematic gesture (bars 1–8)

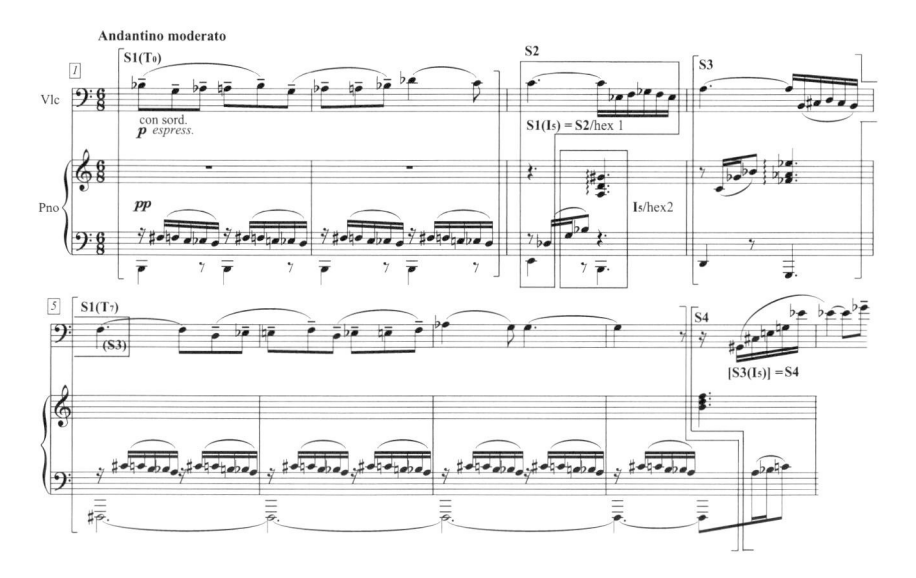

Example 14.2 Serenata for cello and piano: Rondo section B (bars 9–16)

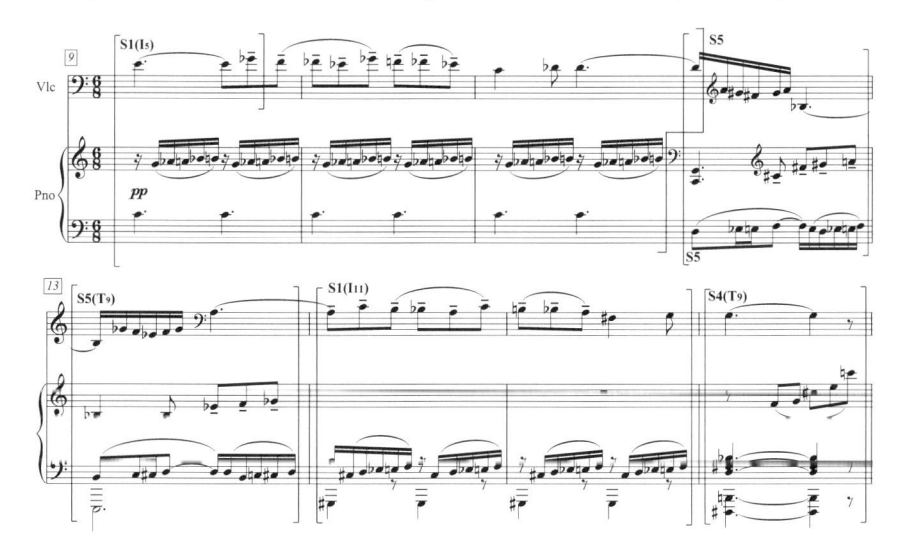

Table 14.1  Serenata for cello and piano: Formal structure and set structure

| Bars | 1–2 | 3 | 4 | 5–8³ | 8⁴–6 | 9–11 | 12 | 13 | 14–15 | 16 | 17–18 | 19–20 | 21 | 22 | 23 |
|---|---|---|---|---|---|---|---|---|---|---|---|---|---|---|---|
| Sets | S1 | S2 [S1(I₅)] | S3 [S1(T₄)] | S1(T₇) | S4 [S3(I₅)] | S1(I₅) | S5 [S2(I₅)] | S5(T₉) | S1(I₁₁) | S4(T₉) | S1(T₃) | S1(T₂) | S6 | S6(T₁₀) | S6(T₉) |
| Harmonic areas (S1) | | T₀ | | T₇ | | I₅ | | | I₁₁ | | T₃ | T₂ | | | |
| Rondo phrase segms | a | b | | a¹ | c | a² | d | | a³ | c¹ | a⁴ | a⁵ | | e | |
| Rondo phrase structure | a | | | b | | | a¹ | | b¹ | | a² | | a¹ | c | |
| Rondo sections | A | | | | | | | B | | | | | c (transition) | | |
| Large Ternary form | A | | | | | | | | | | | | | | |

| Bars | 24–5 | 26 | 27 | 28–30³ | 30² | 31–2 | 33–4 |
|---|---|---|---|---|---|---|---|
| Sets | S1(T₁) S1(T₅) | S2(T₁) S2(T₅) | S3(T₁) S3(T₅) | S1(T₈) S1(T₀) | S4(T₁) | S7 [S3(I₃)] | S8 [S1(T₁₀)] |
| Harmonic areas (S1) | | T₁ T₅ | | T₈ T₀ | | | |
| Rondo phrase segms | a⁶ | | b² | a⁷ | c² | f | g |
| Rondo phrase structure | a³ | | | b² | | | d |
| Rondo sections | A² | | | | | d (retransition) | |
| Large Ternary form | B | | | | | | |

| Bars | 35–7 | 38 | 39–40 | 41 | 42 | 43–5 | 46 | 47–8 | 49–50 | 51–2 | 53 | 54 |
|---|---|---|---|---|---|---|---|---|---|---|---|---|
| Sets | S1($T_0$) | S2($T_0$) | S3($T_0$) | S4($I_0$) | S4($I_2$) S4($T_7$) | S1($I_9$) S1($I_5$) | S5($T_4$) S5($T_0$) | S5($T_1$) S5($T_9$) | S1($I_3$) → S1($I_{11}$) → | S4($T_9$) S1($I_3$) S1($I_{11}$) | S1($T_2$) | S1($T_2$) S1($T_6$) |
| Harmonic areas (S ) | | $T_0$ | | | | $I_9$ $I_5$ | | | $I_3$ $I_{11}$ | | | $T_2$ |
| Rondo phrase segments | $a^8$ | | $b^3$ | $c^3$ | $c^4$ | $a^9$ | $d^1$ | | $a^{10}$ | $c^4$ | | $a^{11}$ |
| Rondo phrase structure | $a^4$ | | | | e | | $a^5$ | | | $b^3$ | | $a^6$ |
| Set structure and phrase structure | (35–40)=(1–4 ($T_0$)) | | | | | | | (43–5)=(9–11 (at $T_0+T_4$)) (46)=(12 at $T_0+T_4$) (47–8)=(46 at $T_3$ below) (49–50)=(14–15 at $T_0+T_4$) (51–2)=(16) | | | (53–4)=(1 ($T_2$)) | |
| Rondo sections | $A^3$ | | | | | | $B^1$ | | | | | $a^4$ |
| Large Ternary form | | | | | | | A' | | | | | |

B♭ diminished seventh via two overlapping triads, c¹–a–f♯–e♭–B♭, while the piano left hand supports it with a movement from E♭ minor to C♯ minor to C minor. The closing gesture of this section is built on two sets, S7⁴ (which derives from the I$_3$ form of S3) and S8 (which derives from the T$_{10}$ form of S1).

Overall, the large-scale rondo form is determined by the periodicity of the sets, with each set being associated with particular sections or phrases, and by the transpositional and inversional levels of the pitch-class material. Each rondo section **A** (**A, a¹, A², A³, a⁴**) is primarily built on the prime and transposed forms of the source set S1 and its derivatives S2, S3 and S4. Each rondo section **B** is predominantly (but not exclusively) built on the inverted forms of the sets. Part A of the ternary superstructure ends with a cadential passage built on a new set (S6) and functions as the modulatory transition to the contrasting, middle, ternary part B. The latter is imbued with tonal elements, and contrasts both texturally and harmonically with the more chromatic parts A that surround it. Although it elaborates the thematic material of part A, here Skalkottas's developmental process includes the superimposition of set forms with a transpositional relationship of a minor sixth (T$_1$ and T$_5$ in bars 24–7, and T$_8$ and T$_0$ in bars 28–30³), which results in consecutive minor sixths. Section **A²**, in the ternary part B, although having a minor sixth internal harmonic structure, has overall a perfect fourth, subdominant-like transpositional relationship with the opening gesture of the piece. It ends with a retransition based on sets S7 and S8, which derive from S1 and its derivative S3. These two sets are associated only with this gesture. In the ternary part A', the rondo section **A³** starts with a repetition of the opening thematic gesture at the original tonal level (T$_0$). The rondo section **B¹**, built from the superimposition of inverted and transposed forms of the sets, now resulting in minor sixths in the cello and major thirds in the piano, has the transpositional relationship of a major third with the equivalent section **B** in ternary part A (bars 9–16). This section ends with an exact repetition of the cadential bar 16 at its original transpositional level (S4(T$_9$)). Although the Serenata is thematically closed and ends with motivic elements from the opening theme, it remains harmonically unresolved; it ends with rondo section **a⁴**, which has a transpositional relationship of a major second with the opening gesture of the piece. This avoidance of harmonic closure is a typical structural feature of Skalkottas's last chamber works.

### Sonatina for Cello and Piano (1949)

*First Movement,* Allegro moderato: *Composing with Segments*

The Sonatina for cello and piano represents an advanced stage of the free compositional approach first explored in the Concertino for two pianos. Here Skalkottas composes primarily with segments, and, consciously or not, explores

---

[4] In set S7 the note F♯ is missing, while the note C is doubled.

a process based on the tetrachordal trope. All three movements are broadly built on various permutations of two closely connected and tonally imbued sets, S1 and S2,[5] which are introduced in the first movement, *Allegro moderato*. Both sets are partitioned into three tetrachords, indicated as A, B, C in Table 14.2 and in the examples.

Table 14.2    Sonatina for cello and piano, *Allegro moderato*: S1, S2 – pairing of tetrachordal segments

| Segments | A | B | C |
|---|---|---|---|
| S1 | B C♯ E B♭ | G F♯ A F | E♭ D A♭ C |
| S2 [S1($I_8$)] | C A♭ D F | B G D♯ F♯ | B♭ E C♯ A |

| Segments | A | B | C |
|---|---|---|---|
| S1 | B C♯ E B♭ | G F♯ A F | E♭ D A♭ C |
| S2 [1($I_8$)] | B♭ E C♯ A | F♯ G B D♯ | C A♭ D F |
| Segments | C | B | A |

Throughout the piece the two sets are superimposed as pairs, and their tetrachordal segments are either interpolated or presented in various combinations. The pitch-class order of the sets remains unchanged at thematic statements, whereas elsewhere both the tetrachords and their pitch-class content are reordered. This reordering produces two to three invariant pitches within tetrachordal pairs, as shown in Table 14.2. The invariance among the set segments is a significant compositional mechanism that produces specific intervallic relationships and tonal structures.[6] There are several triadic components within each set segment, and their free treatment, together with their superimposition, creates many tonal harmonies. Triads such as A♭ major (segment C of S1), B major (segment B of S2), F minor (segment A of S2) and A major (segment C of S2) assert themselves in the harmonic structure of the piece, largely through pitch-class reordering. In particular, the three chords $D^7$, $B^7$ and $C\sharp^{o7}$, created through segment reordering and/or superimposition, are used at structural points throughout the piece: $D^7$ is formed by the reordering of segment S1B (which contains F♯ and A), and S1C (which contains D and C); $B^7$ results from the superimposition of segments S1B and S2B (the B major triad appears in segment S2B, and A, which completes the seventh chord,

---

[5]    Set S2 derives from a reordering of each hexachord of the $I_8$ form of S1. Melissa Garmon Roberts considers S2 to be a trope starting on note C (2002, 122).

[6]    The first trichord of S2 (C–A♭–D) is a retrograde of the last trichord of S1, while its last tetrachord shares the diminished trichord (B♭–E–C♯) with the first tetrachord of S1. The segmental invariance between the two sets is employed extensively throughout the movement for the smooth transition between the sets, while the common dyad F♯–G in segment B of both sets is often used only once in the pairing of these segments.

in segment S1B); $C\sharp^{07}$ is formed when pitch-class G of segment S1B lies adjacent to segment S1A.

The *Allegro moderato* is in sonata form with a varied reversed Recapitulation. Table 14.3 presents schematically the formal structure and set structure of the movement. The first theme, played by the cello, in the antecedent phrase (bars 1–8) is based on S1, and is accompanied by three arpeggiated, repeated tetrachords in the piano, based on S2; in the consequent (bars 9–15) it is based on S2 (see Example 14.3). Each tetrachordal segment of S2 is played twice, in its prime and retrograde forms, each aurally and spatially associated with a forward ascending melodic contour, followed by one that descends palindromically. The cello melody is accompanied contrapuntally by a countermelody played by the piano right hand based on S1, which is melodically varied by repeating and interpolating pitch-classes of the first heptachord of the set. The left hand accompanies with reordered tetrachords of S2, equivalent to chordal inversion in traditional tonal music, resulting in a different harmonic context from that of the first presentation. The thematic gesture ends with Skalkottas's signature cadential tetrachord, set-class 4–18 (B♭–E–C♯–A), played twice by the cello over the piano left-hand chord.

Example 14.3 Sonatina for cello and piano, *Allegro moderato*: First theme (bars 1–15)

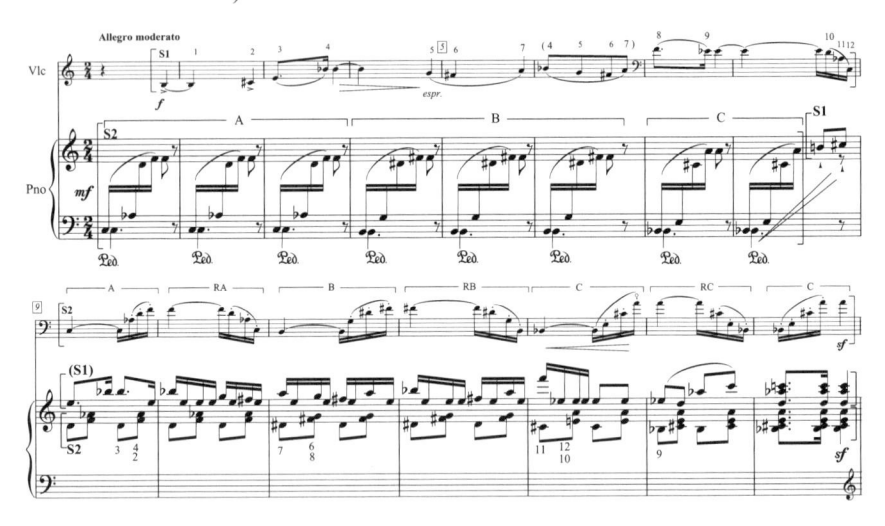

The bridge (bars 16–18) features the simultaneous linear presentation of superimposed unordered tetrachordal segments from both sets, with each tetrachord of S1 played simultaneously by the piano in prime and retrograde arrangements (Example 14.4). This segmental disposition, together with a change of metre to 3/8 and a dense semiquaver texture, is continuously associated with the bridge passages in this movement.

New Directions in the Last Chamber Works 327

Example 14.4  Sonatina for cello and piano, *Allegro moderato*: Bridge (bars 16–18)

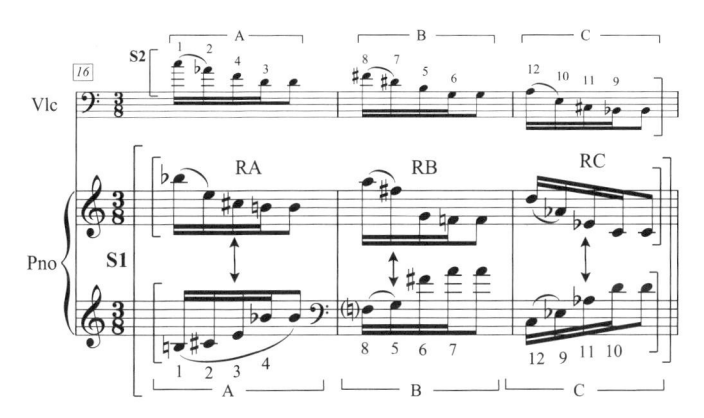

Example 14.5  Sonatina for cello and piano, *Allegro moderato*: Second theme (bars 32²–42)

Table 14.3  Sonatina for cello and piano, *Allegro moderato*: Formal structure and set structure

|  | 1–8 | 9–15 | 16–18 | 19–26¹ | 26²–32¹ | 32²–46 | 47–52 | 53–5 | 56–8 | 59–61¹ |
|---|---|---|---|---|---|---|---|---|---|---|
| vlc | S1ABC (Theme) | S2 A–RA B–RB C–RC | S2ABC | S1ABC | S1C (at 31²–32¹) | S2ABC var (Theme) | S1 (segms) | S2 (segms) | S2CBA | S2A |
| pno RH | S2ABC |  S1ABC | S1RARBRC | S2ABC (chordal) | S1AB | S1ABC (chordal) | S2ABC (Theme) | S1ABC | S1CBA (chordal) | S1A |
| pno LH |  | S2ABC | S1ABC |  | S2ABC |  | S1ABC (chordal) | S2ABC | S2CBA (chordal) | S2A |
| Phrase structure | First theme (metre 2/4) |  | Bridge (metre 3/8) | Transition (metre 2/4) |  | Second theme | Closing theme |  | Bridge-like passage (metre 3/8) | Codetta (metre 2/4) |
| Thematic structure | First subject group |  |  |  |  |  | Second subject group |  |  |  |
| Sonata form | Exposition |  |  |  |  |  |  |  |  |  |

|  | 62²–70 | 71–6 | 77–80¹ | 80–84 | 85–9 | 90–94 | 95–9 |
|---|---|---|---|---|---|---|---|
| vlc | – | S2ABC | S1ABC | S2 CBA | S1 (filler notes) | S1AB–S2C | – |
| pno RH | S1ABC–S2BC | S2BCACBA | S2ABC (chordal) | S1 CBA | S2ABCC | S2AB–S1C | S1ABB |
| pno LH | S2ABC–S2ACBA |  |  | S2C–S1BCB | S1 (segms) |  | S2ABC |
| Sonata form | Development |  |  |  |  |  |  |

|  | 100–07 | 108–13 | 114–16 | 117–24¹ | 124²–6² | 126²–36 | 136²–42 | 142²–50 | 151–8 | 159–63 | 164–73 |
|---|---|---|---|---|---|---|---|---|---|---|---|
| vlc | S2ABC (Theme) | S1ABC–RC–C | S2RA RB RC | – | – | S1ABCvar (Theme) | S2ABC | S1BC (segms) | S2C S1C S2A S1A S2B S1B S1A/B | RS1 (partial retrograde) | S1ABC |
| pno RH | S2AE[C] (Counter melody) | S1 (filler notes) | S2ABC | S2ABC | S1ABC | S2ABC (chordal) | S1ABC | S1ABCAB | S1B/S2B S1C S2ABC (chordal) | S2BCA (chordal) | S2ABC |
| pno LH | S1ABC | S1C–S2BC | S1ABC | S1ABABCA (chordal) | S2ABC |  | S2ABC | S2ABCAB | Notes G F♯ E F G |  |  |
| Phrase structure | First theme (metre 2/4) |  | Bridge (metre 3/8) | Transition (metre 2/4) |  | Second theme | Closing theme (1) | Continuation | Closing theme (2) (extension) | Bridge-like passage (metre 2/4) |  |
| Thematic structure | First subject group |  |  |  |  |  | Second subject group |  |  |  | Coda |
| Sonata form | Recapitulation |  |  |  |  |  |  |  |  |  |  |

In the second subject group, the reordering and combination of the set-segments produce new melodic gestures and harmonic accompaniment, again establishing a different harmonic region from that of the first theme. The second theme (bars $32^2$–46), played by the cello, is based on a variant of S2, which results from a reordering within each tetrachord, with pitch-class and segment repetition.[7] It is accompanied chordally by the piano, playing reordered tetrachords of S1 (Example 14.5).

The reordering within S2 not only results in a new thematic melody, starting with an arpeggiated half-diminished seventh (d–F–a♭–c), it also sounds as if it grows out of the previous melodic phrase; the cello takes over the last three-note segment of S1C (d–A♭–c), and by interpolating the note F between d and A♭ in bar 32, Skalkottas creates a variant of S1, one that is thus identical to the opening of S2. The piano remains silent at this point in order to make clear the transition from one set to the other. In bars 37–42, in particular, the piano plays the tetrachord S1C over the bass notes F and A♭, which interchange. This, together with the changing position of F and A♭ within each chord, creates two interlocking tetrachords, S1C and S2A.

Because of the continuous pitch-class variation and reordering of the tetrachordal segments, in order to demarcate the large-scale form, Skalkottas assigns thematic predominance to the rhythmic structure, with the thematic material defined by rhythm rather than by pitch-class content. The Recapitulation is initiated with the pitch-class material of the second theme, but with the exact rhythm of the first theme. That is, the cello thematic melody, having the same rhythmic structure as that of the first theme in the Exposition, is based on a troping permutation of S2, while the piano accompaniment, also recapitulating the exact accompanimental rhythm, is now based on S1. For further developmental elaboration, in bar 101 the piano right hand accompanies contrapuntally with a new melody based on S2. The reversal of harmonic, rhythmic and pitch-class set material continues for the rest of the movement. The first phrase of the second theme (bars $126^2$–36), again in an exact rhythmic recapitulation, is now based on S1; its harmonic accompaniment is based on chordal segments of S2. Similar to the motivic technique employed in the Exposition, the cello takes over the three-note segment b♭–c♯–e of S2C. Skalkottas alters the b♭ to b♮, thus creating the first tetrachord of S1 and initiating the second theme of the Recapitulation. Furthermore, by changing the order of the last tetrachordal segment to e♭–a♭–c$^1$–d$^1$, he creates a similar motivic relationship to that of the equivalent gesture in the Exposition.

---

[7] The reordering within each tetrachord of S2 results in a twelve-note set whose two hexachords (6–Z41 and 6–Z12) are different from those of the source set S2 of the first theme (6–Z29/6–Z50).

### *Tender Melody* for Cello and Piano (1949): A Study in Tonal Serialism

In *Tender Melody*, written only a few weeks before his death, Skalkottas refined his late compositional approach, which combines two compositional styles and formal openness. Stylistically, although this is a serial work, it is an example of tonal serialism, and the obvious manifestation of tonal relationships enables the listener to experience harmonic conflict and resolution – but not final closure – within a twelve-note context. Skalkottas's fascination with the fusion of traditional forms is again demonstrated through the integration of diverse formal prototypes to produce a new formal design. The piece consists of three simultaneous ostinati: melodic, in the cello; harmonic, in the piano; and rhythmic, in the form of continuous quaver rhythms, in the piano accompaniment. These underpin the entire texture and constitute the principal structural elements for unfolding the form. The harmonic ostinato consists of fourteen statements of three tetrachords, which determine the thirteen-phrase internal structure of the piece. The opening phrase (bars 1–3) outlines the first 'theme'; and each of the following twelve phrases presents either a variation of this opening material, or is a variation within a variation. These 'variations' are grouped together to determine the large-scale form, which comprises six sections and combines variation and sonata forms, as shown in Table 14.4.

Table 14.4   *Tender Melody* for cello and piano: Formal structure

| *Tender Melody* sections | Sonata form | Thematic structure |
| --- | --- | --- |
| I | Exposition | (1–10) First subject group. First theme (1–3) and its varied repetitions. |
| II |  | (11–18) Second subject group. Second theme (11–13). |
| III | Development | (19–36) Elaboration of material form the first and second subject groups. (31–6) Retransition. |
| IV | Reversed Recapitulation | (37–48) Recapitulation of the second theme. |
| V | Coda | (49–52) Recapitulation of the first theme. |
| VI |  | (53–8) Coda; establishment of F♭ minor as the tonic; final $D^{07}$ tetrachord. |

In the opening three bars, both melodic and accompanimental pitch-class material coincide. Thereafter, there is a misalignment in the melodic and accompanimental set structure. This is resolved in the Coda, where the cello and piano sets are realigned. *Tender Melody* is built on the prime forms of two independent twelve-note sets, one continuously played by the cello and the other played by the piano, as shown in Example 14.6.

Example 14.6  *Tender Melody* for cello and piano: Opening thematic gesture (bars 1–3)

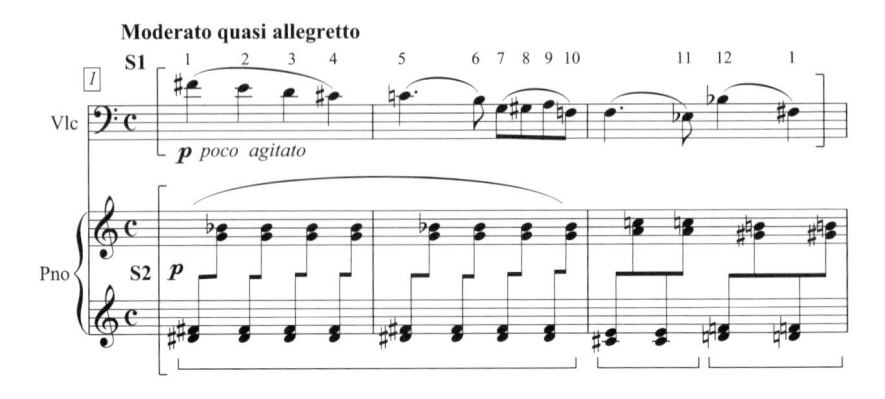

The E♭ minor context is inherent in the internal pitch-class structure of the cello set (F♯–E–D–C♯–C–B–G–G♯–A–F–E♭–B♭), with pitch-classes E♭, B♭ and F♯(G♭) grouped together within the phrase structure and frequently punctuating melodic cadences, thus producing a clear orientation towards an E♭ minor tonality. The only exception is found in the last presentation of the sets in the Coda, as will be discussed below. The piano set is presented as three tetrachords: two transpositionally equivalent ($T_6$) major–minor tetrachords, set-class 4–17 (D♯–F♯–G–B♭, C♯–E–A–C); and a diminished seventh tetrachord, set class 4–28 (D–F–G♯–B). This harmonic presentation is unchanged throughout the piece, and the minimalist, almost hypnotic, repetition of the tetrachords not only articulates but also reinforces the tonally imbued harmonic framework; it also leaves the piece open-ended. When these three tetrachords are heard in succession, they move in smooth stepwise voice-leading and produce a kind of functional harmonic progression within an E♭ major/minor harmonic area, as shown in Example 14.7.

Example 14.7  *Tender Melody* for cello and piano: Harmonic progression

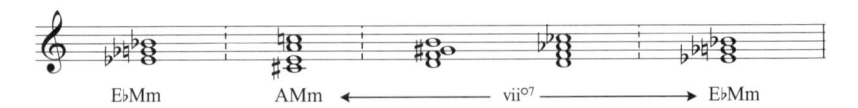

Although the A major/minor tetrachord, in the context of an E♭ tonality, can be perceived as a chromatically altered subdominant chord, it has a tritonal relationship with the E♭ and thus creates tension within the smooth voice-leading that partially subverts the implied tonal movement. Furthermore, the tetrachord set-class 4–28 can also be interpreted as a diminished seventh on G♯, thus functioning both as the leading-note chord of the A major/minor chord and as an axis within the harmonic progression. Skalkottas exploits the ambiguity of this diminished seventh chord to distinguish harmonically the first and second subject groups.

The first subject group (bars 1–10) starts with an E♭ minor chord and ends on a diminished seventh on D; the latter functions as a leading-note needing resolution to the 'tonic' E♭. The second subject group (bars 11–18) is introduced with a new lyrical theme, a new texture in the accompaniment and a different harmonic distribution of the pitch-class content of the chords, suggesting a new harmonic environment. As shown in Example 14.8, the cello melody starts with a prolonged C♯, which has a fifth, dominant–tonic-like relationship with the opening F♯ of the first theme. The textual disposition of the accompaniment now presents the third tetrachord of the progression as a G♯ diminished seventh, thus shifting the tonal predominance from the E♭ major/minor to the A major/minor chord.

Example 14.8  *Tender Melody* for cello and piano: Second theme – opening gesture (bars 10–13)

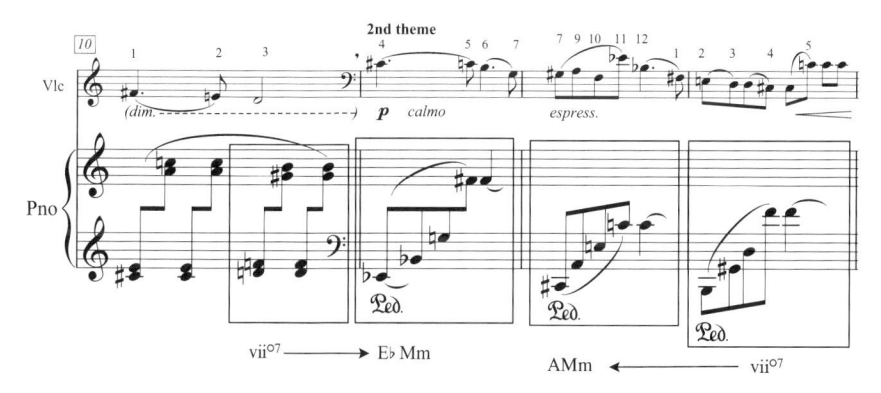

Within the Development section, bars 31–6 function as the retransition, which not only initiates a new rhythmic, modulatory-type pattern in the piano accompaniment, but also starts and closes with the diminished seventh chord on D, thus functioning as a dominant preparation in the manner of traditional sonata form, and resolving onto the E♭ major/minor tonic in the Recapitulation.

In traditional sonata form, the function of the Recapitulation is to resolve the underlying polarity and harmonic tension established in the Exposition, and to create a sense of reconciliation and closure. In the Exposition of *Tender Melody*, there is inherent tension in the modal structure of the 'tonic' E♭ major/minor chord, and an expectation of its resolution. There is also harmonic/tonal opposition between the first and second subject groups, due to the shift of harmonic emphasis from an E♭ major/minor to an A major/minor tonal centre. The reversed Recapitulation is introduced at bar 37 with the second theme, but harmonic reconciliation is evaded at this point. Although the melodic goal of E♭ is reached at bar 40, with a melodic cadence that outlines an E♭ minor arpeggio, this is supported harmonically by the A major/minor chord, reinforced throughout this passage by the presence of the G♯ diminished seventh tetrachord (see Example 14.9). Furthermore, the serial misalignment between the melodic and accompanimental pitch-class content continues throughout the Recapitulation, thus carrying over and intensifying the harmonic tension.

Example 14.9  *Tender Melody* for cello and piano: End of retransition and beginning of Recapitulation (bars 36–41)

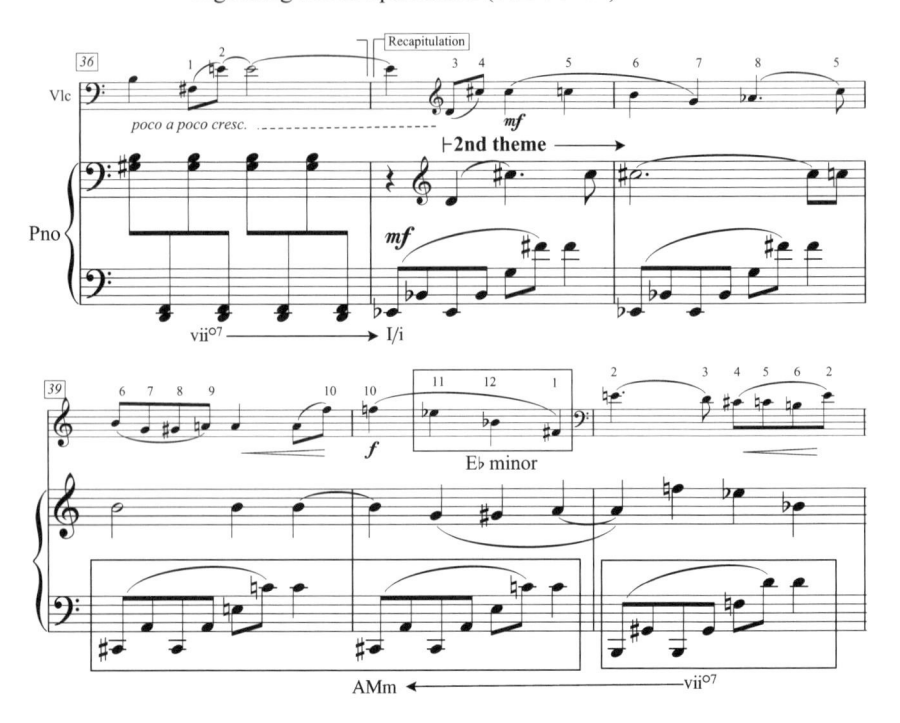

The first theme, based on a prolonged double pedal E♭–B♭, is recapitulated at the beginning of the Coda (bar 49) (see Example 14.10). Now the modal ambiguity resolves with the presentation, twice, of an E♭ minor triad (the accented G♮s in the piano right hand on the strong beats of bars 50–51 function as appoggiaturas to F♯[G♭]). But the piece does not end at that point; it ends with the initial succession of the three tetrachords, and the diminished seventh (leading-note) chord on note D as the final chord of the piece. Similarly, the final gesture of the cello melody defies structural tonal expectations and outlines the melodic interval e♭$^1$–b♭$^1$, heard as an open-ended, tonic–dominant (*I–V*) half-cadence. Thus in the Coda there is further tension and openness instead of unequivocal closure.

The work as a whole starts with a stable, albeit tonally ambiguous, chord, moves to a point of rest and resolution at the beginning of the Coda, but returns to the unstable diminished seventh chord at its final gesture. Furthermore, the cyclical, reiterative nature of the harmonic progression throughout the piece, with

Example 14.10  *Tender Melody* for cello and piano: Coda (bars 48–58)

the opening of each phrase resolving the previous one yet itself ending unresolved, undermines the sonata principle and renders the form of *Tender Melody* circular. There is the impression that the piece could continue indefinitely. Skalkottas's particular approach to the harmonic structure, which inevitably affects its large-scale form, is reminiscent of, and perhaps influenced by, Romantic attitudes towards ambiguity and open-endedness as legitimate formal principles. Or perhaps the creation of this open-ended circular form through the manipulation of the harmony was an attempt on Skalkottas's part to mirror the circular repeatability of twelve-note sets, thus expressing the essence of twelve-note composition.

Ambiguity thus becomes a structural motive of *Tender Melody*. But Skalkottas, contrary to his compositional practice in the Third Piano Concerto, for example, where he was at pains to create a large-scale, closed sonata structure, here challenges the closed principle of sonata form and its traditional tendency towards unity – both by using cyclical reiterative harmonic progression and by deferring reconciliation until the Coda, only to deny it at its final gesture. Paradoxically, therefore, the unstable diminished seventh chord can be perceived as the only possible close for this piece. Although stylistically this is a serial work, it is primarily an example of tonal serialism, and the manifestation of tonal relationships within it enables us to experience harmonic conflict and resolution within a twelve-note context, but not final closure.

# Epilogue

In his unpublished essay 'The School of Modern Composers', Skalkottas states, '*Every composer can have his own school [...] each* [school] *has its own form, carries its own name, depending on its musical elements and compositions that give us the general meaning and different direction.*' And true to his belief he created his very own, private 'school', one characterized by an unusual stylistic breadth. Throughout his career he explored and integrated several contrasting musical idioms and styles (tonality, atonality, dodecaphonism, neoclassicism and folklorism), and traditional and avant-garde elements effortlessly coexist in his works. His compositional development is not linear and diachronic, characterized by separate stylistic periods, but inclusive and synchronic, with simultaneous composition of atonal, twelve-note and tonal works. At the beginning of his career he was immersed in the European contemporary music scene for a short period, albeit rather marginally as the student of a controversial but influential figure. The later development of his twelve-note technique occurred in complete isolation from Schoenberg and the European avant-garde, and hence led to the creation of his own personal, idiosyncratic style. Furthermore, because of the hostility he faced in Greece, and in part because of his own reticence, he never really fitted into any of the prevailing Greek musical traditions.

Nevertheless, with his *36 Greek Dances*, his ballets and his hybrid dodecaphonic–folkloristic compositions, he is now seen as a central figure of what Christodoulou calls 'a new National School' (2008, 140). And yet, notwithstanding occasional pronouncements that Skalkottas is the 'forgotten genius of twelve-note composition',[1] or that he is 'internationally considered as the almost single greatest Greek composer [*sic*], a significant figure of 20th-century music [who] is for Greece what Sibelius is for Finland or Bartók for Hungary' (*ibid.*, 128), Skalkottas remains an individual, enigmatic figure in the Western art music canon. Furthermore, the inaccessibility of his manuscripts, the limited and often unreliable editions of a small number of his works, the sporadic performances of his music, and the restricted musicological research that has been undertaken on his work for much of the sixty years following his death, have all ensured that Skalkottas has been undeservedly neglected, and that his musical output has had no influence on other Greek or European composers, many of whom remain ignorant of his compositional methods. As Hans Keller prophetically observed, 'Much of Skalkottas's symphonic genius remains to be discovered: his symphonic music may have to wait as long for full recognition as

---

[1] See for example, Papaioannou (in all his articles), Demertzis (1991, 1998), Orga (1969), Keller (1994), Walker (1961).

did Schubert's, whose character and fate he seems to share in quite a few respects, productivity and lack of opportunity (or concern?) to hear his own music included' (Keller, in Wintle, 1994, 183). Nonetheless, Skalkottas's music, in all its tonal, atonal and twelve-note idioms, with its immediacy of sound, expressive power and sheer, unbridled energy, is his legacy.

His major achievement is his imaginative approach to twelve-note composition, and this, refracted through his personal, idiosyncratic style, adds another dimension to the early stages of the development of the twelve-note method. In his writings he expressed his desire to make his twelve-note music as accessible as possible to the listener, declaring: '*The twelve-note harmony is strictly connected with the development of the themes*', and '*the frequent repetition of the same harmonic material gives the listener the opportunity to grasp more easily the musical meaning of the work, both harmonic and thematic*'. Although these statements were written in the Foreword to his Notes to the First Symphonic Suite for large orchestra (1935), they may be applied to all his dodecaphonic compositions, and conveniently summarize his twelve-note compositional aesthetic. The technical devices he employed to realize this aesthetic include the use of a modified version of the twelve-note method, the establishment of an analogy between tonal regions and groups of twelve-note sets as a means of delineating form, and the reliance on continuous motivic and harmonic repetition and variation as a means of achieving coherence and comprehensibility within a movement.

Within the confines of this approach, Skalkottas conceived the individual sets (*Reihen*) in thematic terms. He did not regard them as abstract, self-sufficient interval sequences in which the pitch-class order should be strictly observed so as to retain the set's identity, but as melodic–motivic elements of a 'theme', which is then treated as a framework within which individual characteristics may be isolated and further developed. The identity of a set is determined by its constant repetition and by neighbourhood relationships between the notes of its segments. Skalkottas was more interested in preserving pitch-class relationships and harmonic formations than in retaining the pitch-class order within each set, thus displaying considerable freedom within his strict serial writing. All sets are subjected to a number of modifications, such as segmentation, reordering and the derivation of new sets. Yet, behind the apparently improvisational surface of his music lies a network of relationships that integrates every detail, with concurrent voices linked largely by the common and transpositionally or inversionally related segments shared by the different sets of the set-group. He did not avoid tonal elements in his twelve-note works, and his textures differ substantially from those based on a single basic set. Triads and other chords associated with tonal music, tonal centres and an overall allusive tonal orientation permeate his dodecaphonic textures. He extensively used an E♭ major/minor triad, his signature sound, which results either from a linear segment of a tonal set or from the superimposition and contrapuntal treatment of several sets, while the pitch-class E♭ has a prominent position in the upper line of many of his works. It is tempting to speculate that he derived this letter from the

German note-name Es, and used it as a personal signature in much the same way as it is used elsewhere by composers to represent the letter S.[2]

Unity within this diversity is established by the set-group, which functions as the generative source for a section, providing coherent pitch-class and harmonic articulations. The obsessive recurrence of the theme or fragments of it, the repetition of particular harmonic sequences, and the reiteration of common or equivalent segments embedded within the various sets, as well as the tonal elements that highlight certain structural points, all reinforce relationships and coherence, aid memorability and contribute to the immediacy of his music. This approach reflects Schoenberg's beliefs, as reported by his student (and Skalkottas's classmate) Erich Schmid, that 'There is variety through constant variation and unity through variation of the *thematic* material' (Walton, 2001, 16). Yet, although the use of more than one set as the generative source of a piece provides variety within the unity of the thematic referential material, it also creates tension between the harmonic implications that arise from the combination of these discrete sets and the ideal of all-embracing integration within a twelve-note composition. And this delicate balance between opposition and symbiosis, between what Skalkottas conceived as unity and contrast, old forms and new sounds, is a significant structural feature of his music.

Furthermore, Skalkottas appropriated traditional concepts of musical construction and adapted Classical formal prototypes to a dodecaphonic context by exploring the possibilities provided by the integration of different forms and compositional styles. His formal designs evolve largely through the presence of harmonic regions, which are established by the use of referential groups of twelve-note sets and/or their transpositions. The regional contrasts are always accompanied by thematic contrasts, in a manner analogous to traditional sonata practice, while phrase delimitation and cadential structure follow traditional models in terms of phrasing, rhythmic pattern, the movement of the melodic lines, and harmonic tension and resolution. His reinterpretation and frequent integration of two or three different forms – particularly sonata, rondo and/or variation – result in original, albeit often ambiguous, but infinitely interesting musical structures that take the tradition forward.

Much work remains to be done, and there is a great deal more to be discovered about Skalkottas's life and music. My hope is that this study precipitates a more informed and analytically thorough approach to Skalkottas's twelve-note works than has previously been undertaken, which will in turn result in a wider appreciation of the music itself, an appreciation that I believe to be long overdue.

---

[2] Similarly, Shostakovich used the notes D–E♭–C–B to represent the letters DSCH, and Berg in his *Chamber Concerto*, used the pitch-classes A–D–Es[S]–C–H–B–E–G, A–E–B–E and A–B–A–B–E–G to represent the names of Schoenberg, Webern and himself.

# Appendices

*Keep Ithaca always in your mind.
Arriving there is what you are destined for
But do not hurry the journey at all.
Better if it lasts for years,
so you are old by the time you reach the island,
wealthy with all you have gained on the way,
not expecting Ithaca to make you rich.*
(Konstantinos Kavafis, *Ithaca*)

# Appendix A
# List of Sets

**A.1 Second Sonatina for violin and piano,** *Allegro*: **Thematic set**

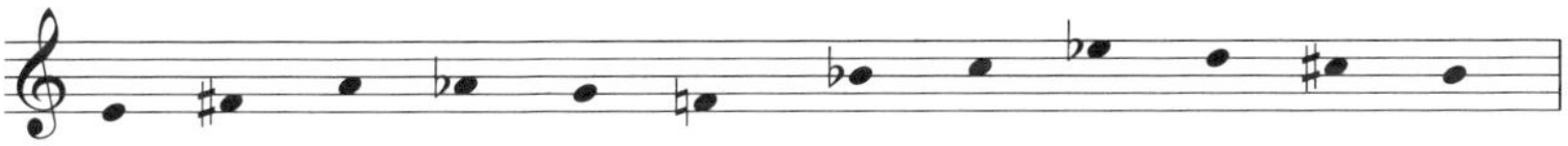

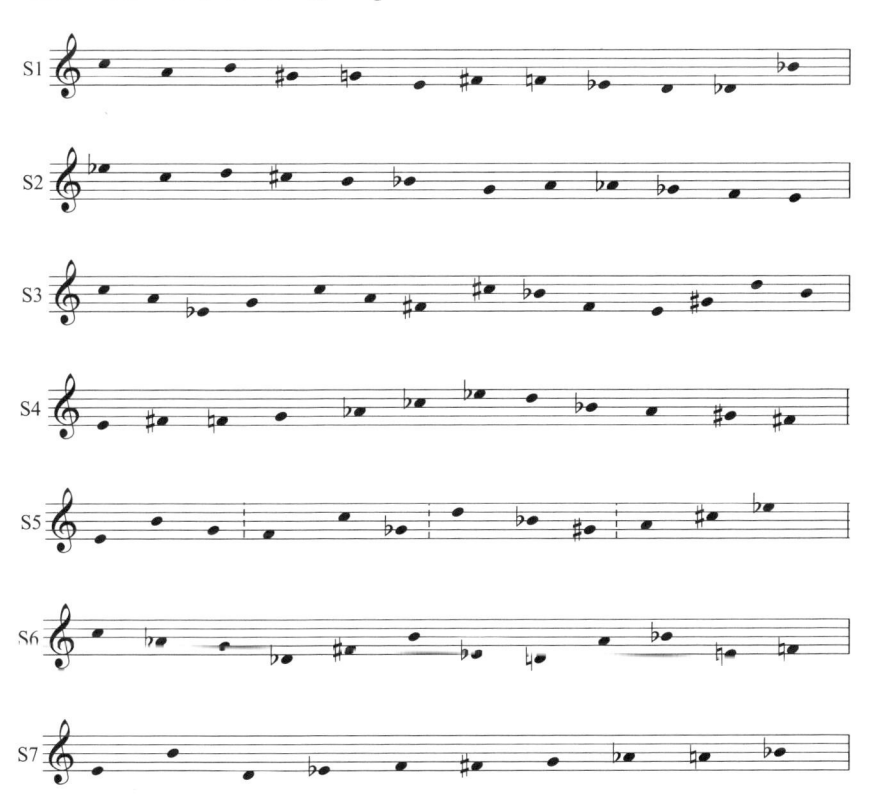

**A.2.1 First Piano Concerto,** *Allegro moderato*: **Sets**

**A.2.2 First Piano Concerto, *Andante cantabile*: Sets**

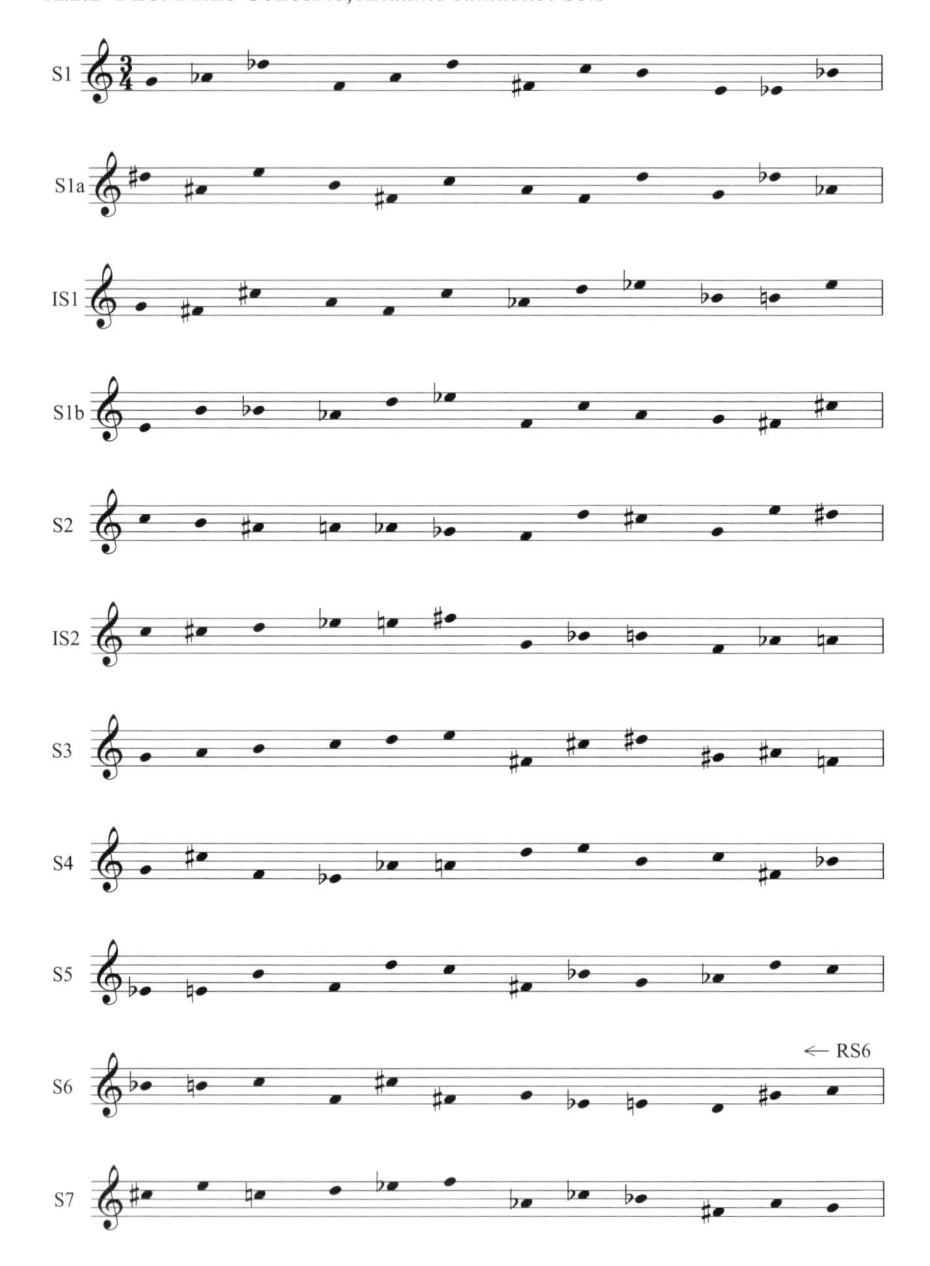

## A.2.3 First Piano Concerto, *Allegro vivace*: Sets

*continued*

**A.2.3** *concluded*

**A.3.1 Octet,** *Allegro moderato***: Sets**

### A.3.2 Octet, *Andante cantabile*: Sets

### A.3.3 Octet, *Presto*: Sets

*Appendix A: List of Sets* 349

### A.4.1 Third String Quartet, *Allegro moderato*: Sets

## A.4.2 Third String Quartet, *Andante*: Sets

### A.4.3 Third String Quartet, *Allegro vivace* (Rondo): Sets

**A.5.1 Second String Trio, *Moderato*: Sets**

## A.5.2 Second String Trio, *Andante*: Sets

## A.5.3 Second String Trio, *Presto*: Sets

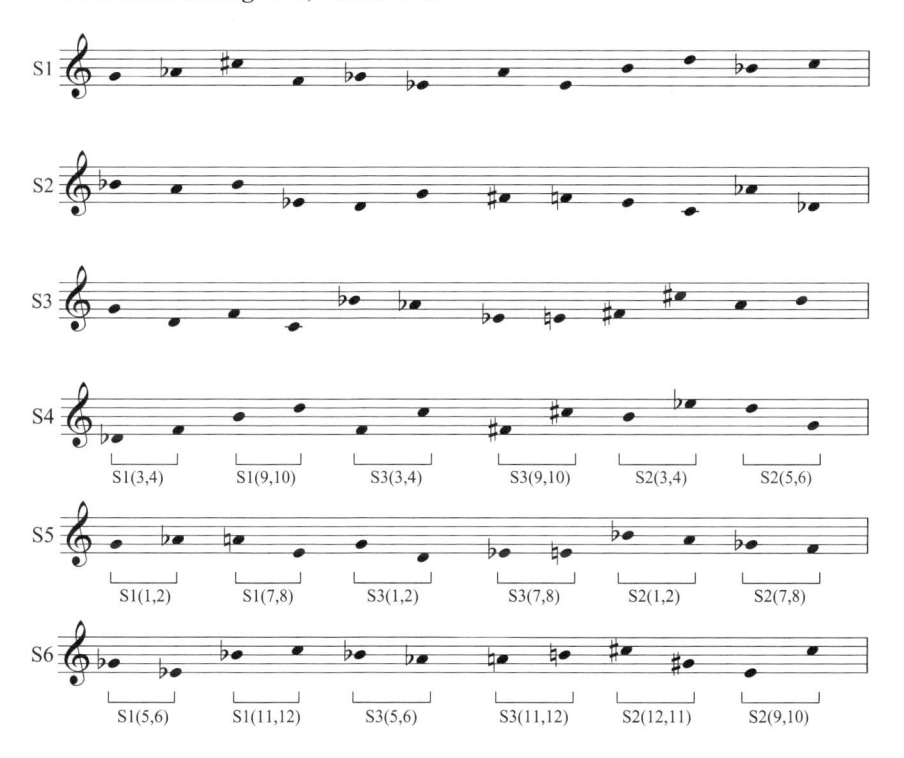

## A.6 Third Sonatina for violin and piano, *Allegro giusto* and *Andante*: Sets

## A.7 Fourth Sonatina for violin and piano: Sets

358

**A.8.1 First Symphonic Suite for large orchestra, *Ouvertüre*: Sets**

**A.8.2 First Symphonic Suite for large orchestra, *Thema con Variazioni*: Sets**

**A.8.3 First Symphonic Suite for large orchestra, *Marsch*: Sets**

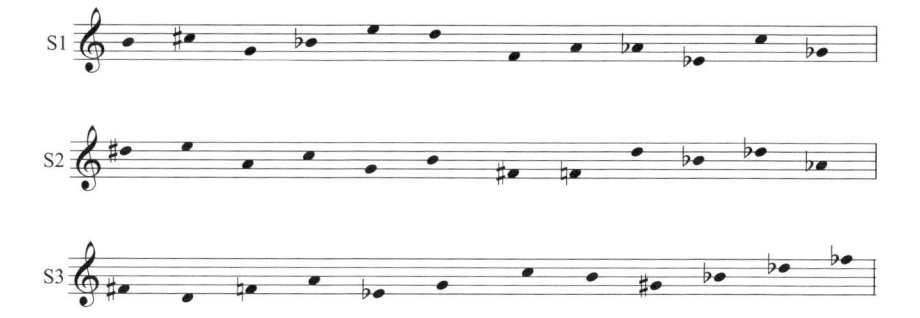

## A.8.4 First Symphonic Suite for large orchestra, *Romance*: Sets

**A.8.5a First Symphonic Suite for large orchestra, *Siciliano*: Sets**

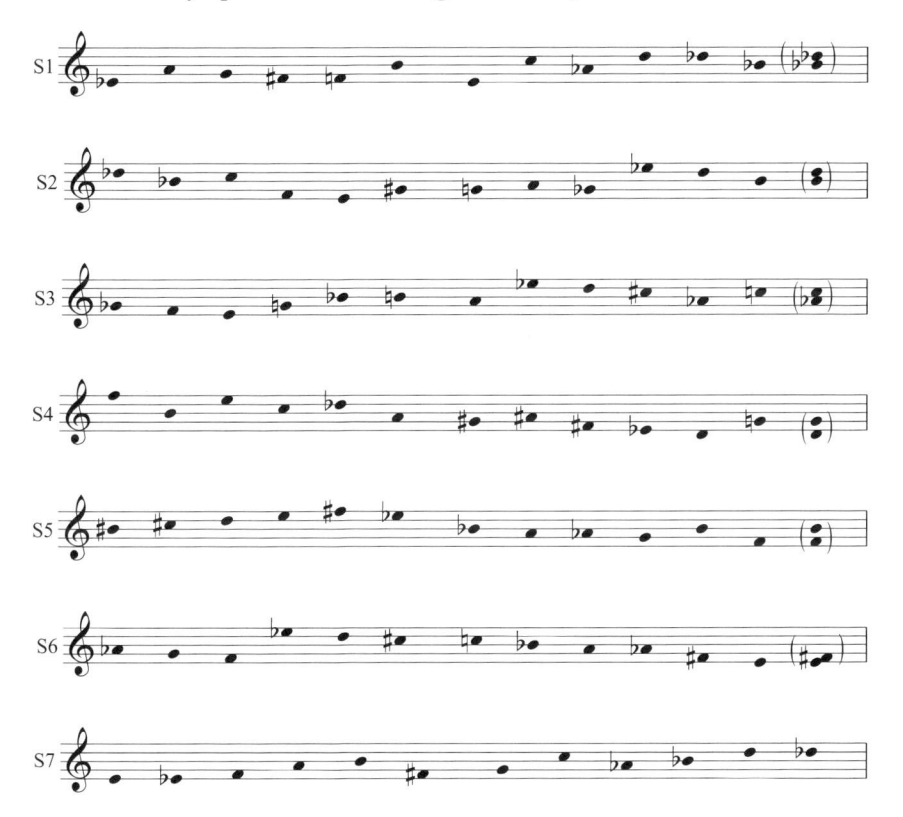

**A.8.5b First Symphonic Suite for large orchestra, *Barcarole*: Sets**

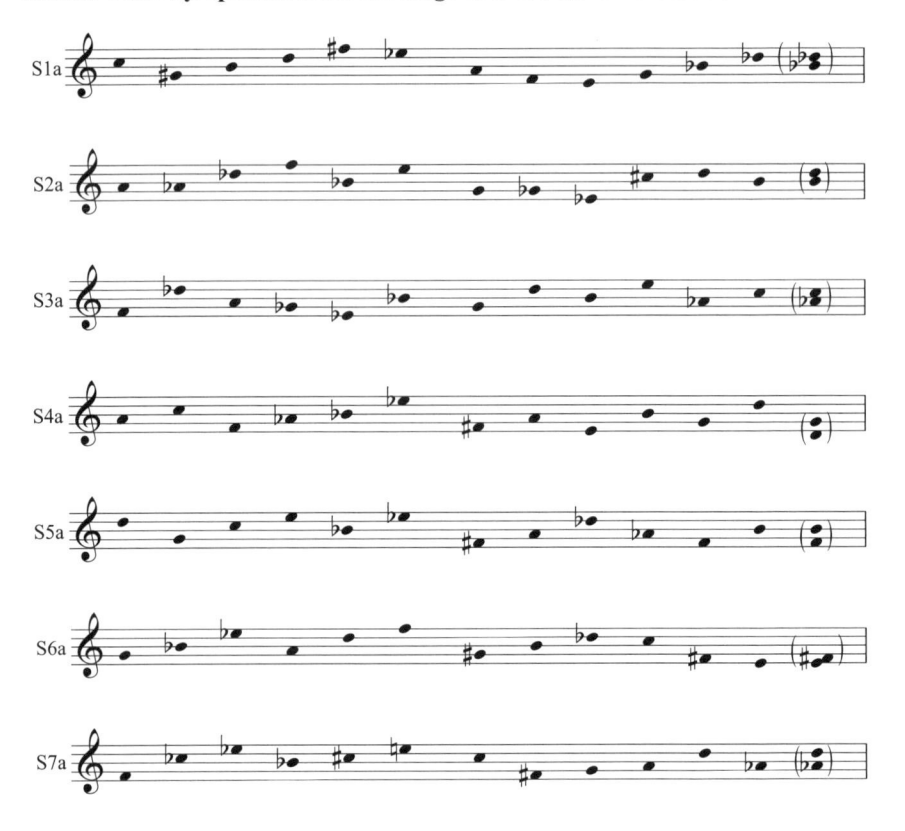

**A.8.6 First Symphonic Suite for large orchestra, *Rondo–Finale*: Sets**

364     *The Life and Twelve-Note Music of Nikos Skalkottas*

**A.9.1  Concertino for two pianos and orchestra, *Allegro*: Sets**

**A.9.2  Concertino for two pianos and orchestra, *Andante*: Sets**

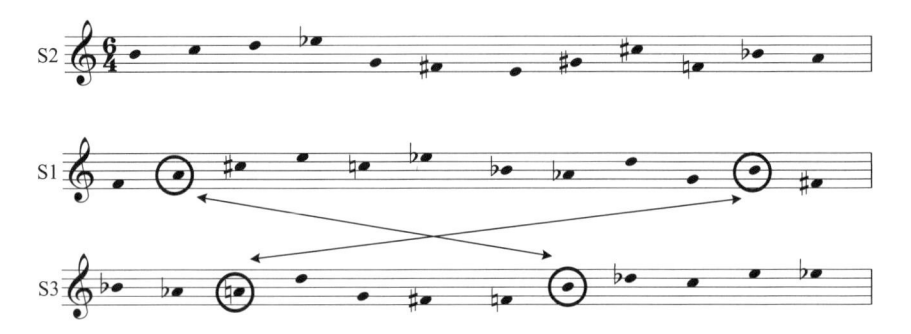

**A.9.3  Concertino for two pianos and orchestra, *Allegro giusto*: Sets**

**A.10.1 First Piano Suite, *Preludio*: Sets**

## A.10.2 First Piano Suite, *Serenade*: Sets

*Appendix A: List of Sets* 367

## A.10.3 First Piano Suite, *Menuetto*: Sets

### A.10.4 First Piano Suite, *Finale*: Sets

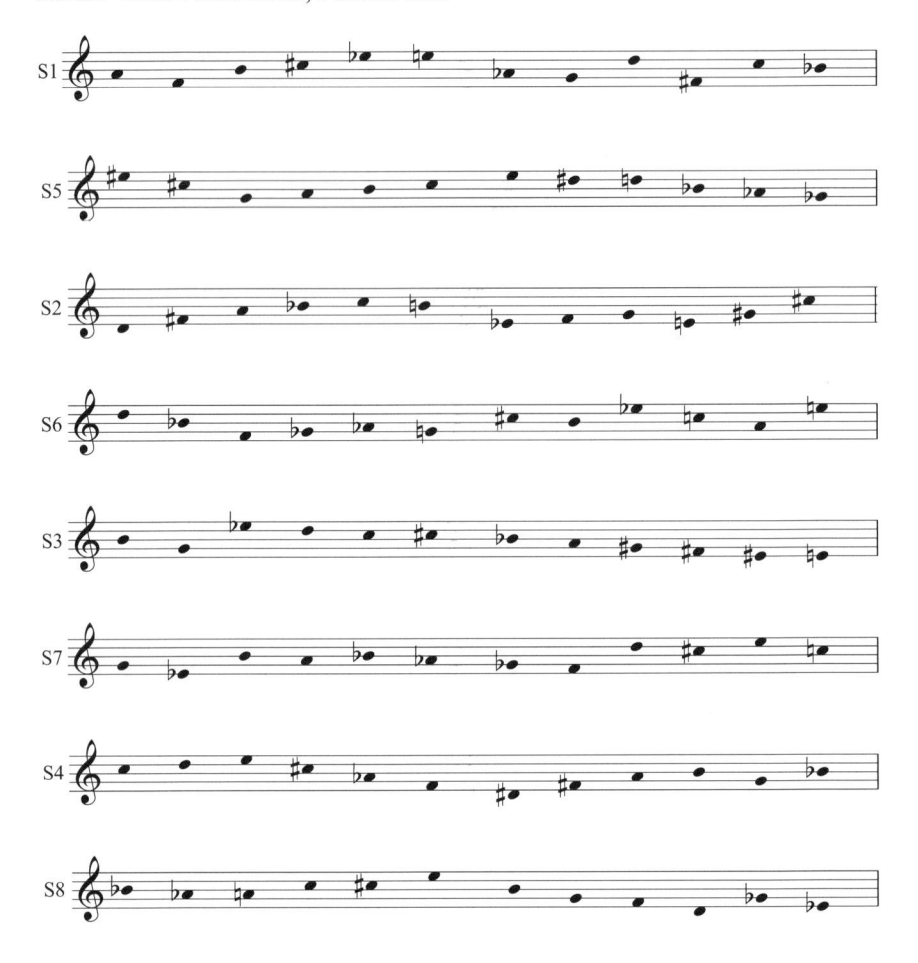

### A.11.1 Second Piano Concerto, *Allegro molto vivace*: Thematic set

### A.11.2 Second Piano Concerto, *Andantino*: Thematic set

### A.11.3 Second Piano Concerto, *Allegro moderato*: Sets

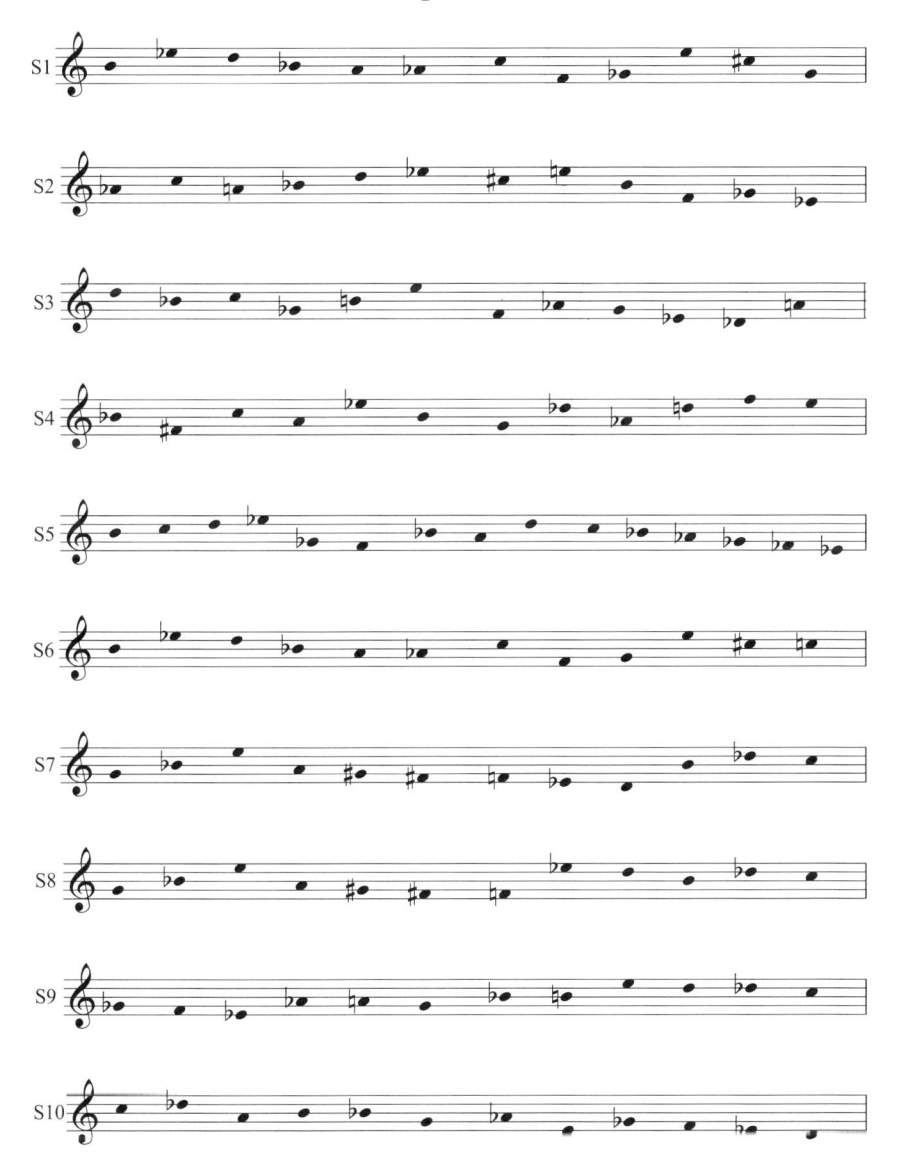

370 The Life and Twelve-Note Music of Nikos Skalkottas

**A.12 Violin Concerto and orchestra, *Molto appassionato*: Indicative sets**

*Appendix A: List of Sets* 371

### A.13 Third Piano Concerto: Thematic sets

### A.14 *Passacaglia* from *32 Piano Pieces*: Thematic set

*Appendix A: List of Sets*

## A.15 Fourth String Quartet: Indicative sets

*continued*

374　　*The Life and Twelve-Note Music of Nikos Skalkottas*

**A.15** *concluded*

**A.16** *Largo Sinfonico* **from Second Symphonic Suite: Sets**

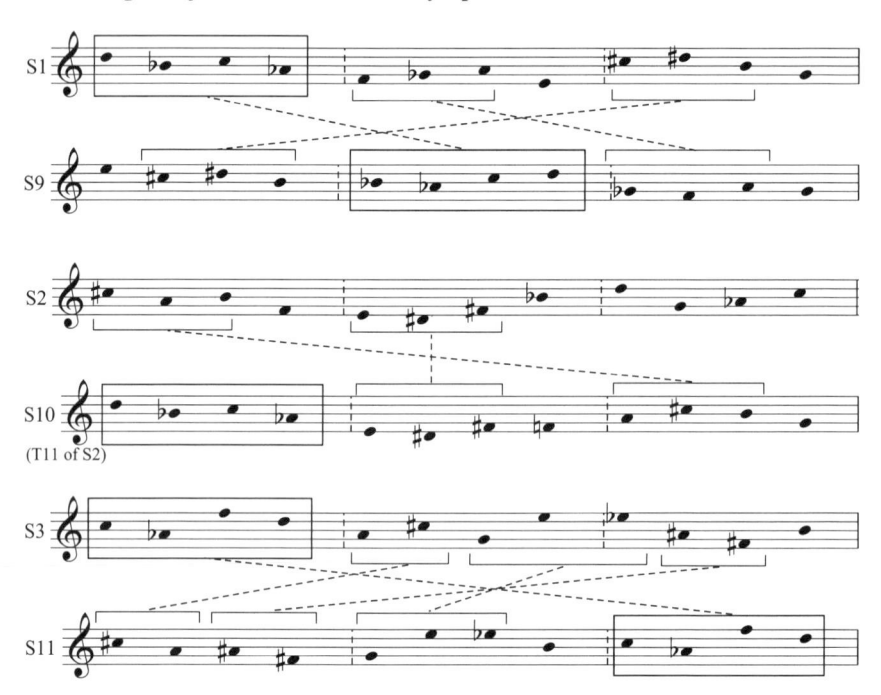

*Appendix A: List of Sets*

**A.16** *concluded*

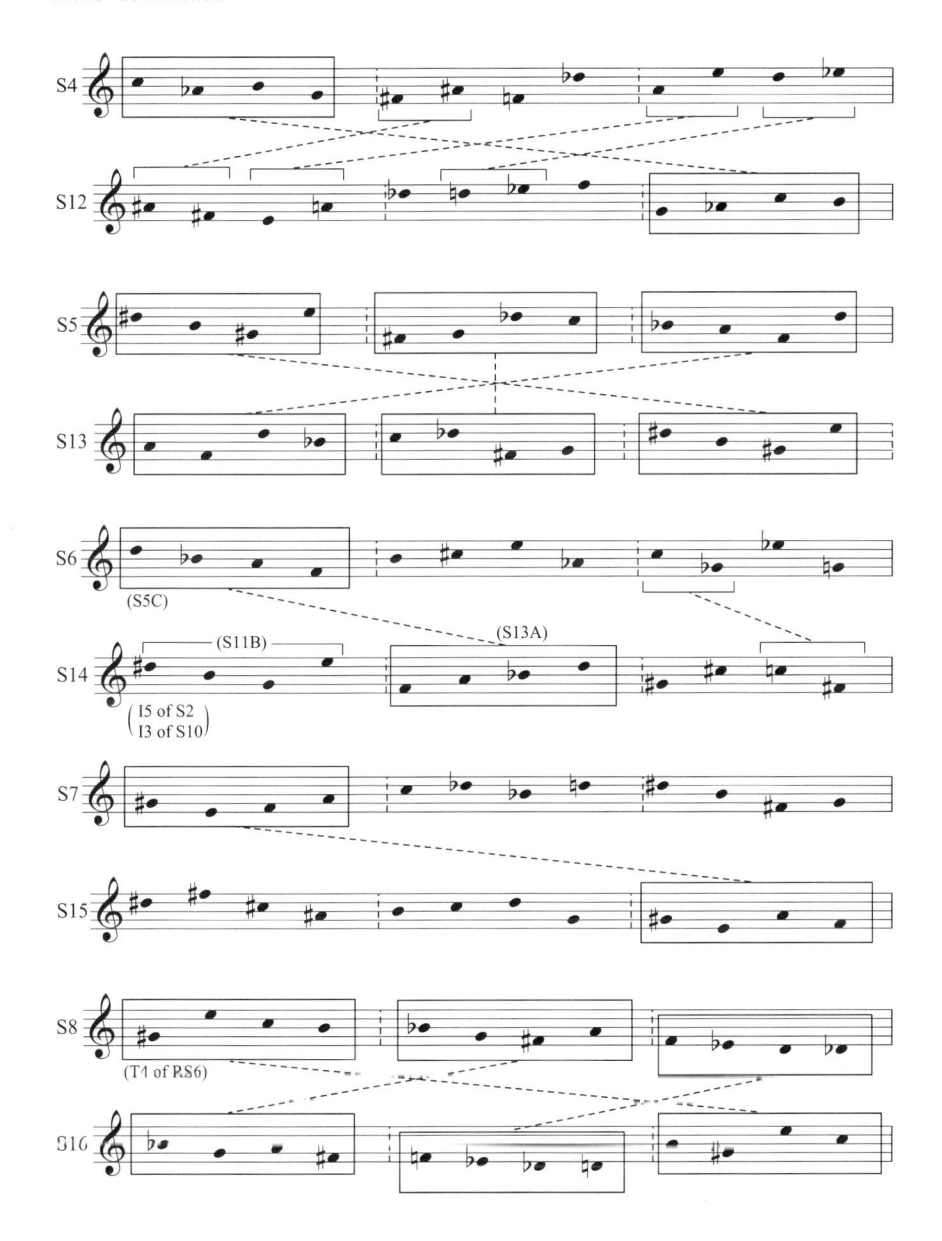

### A.17 Overture for large orchestra (*The Return of Ulysses*): Indicative thematic sets

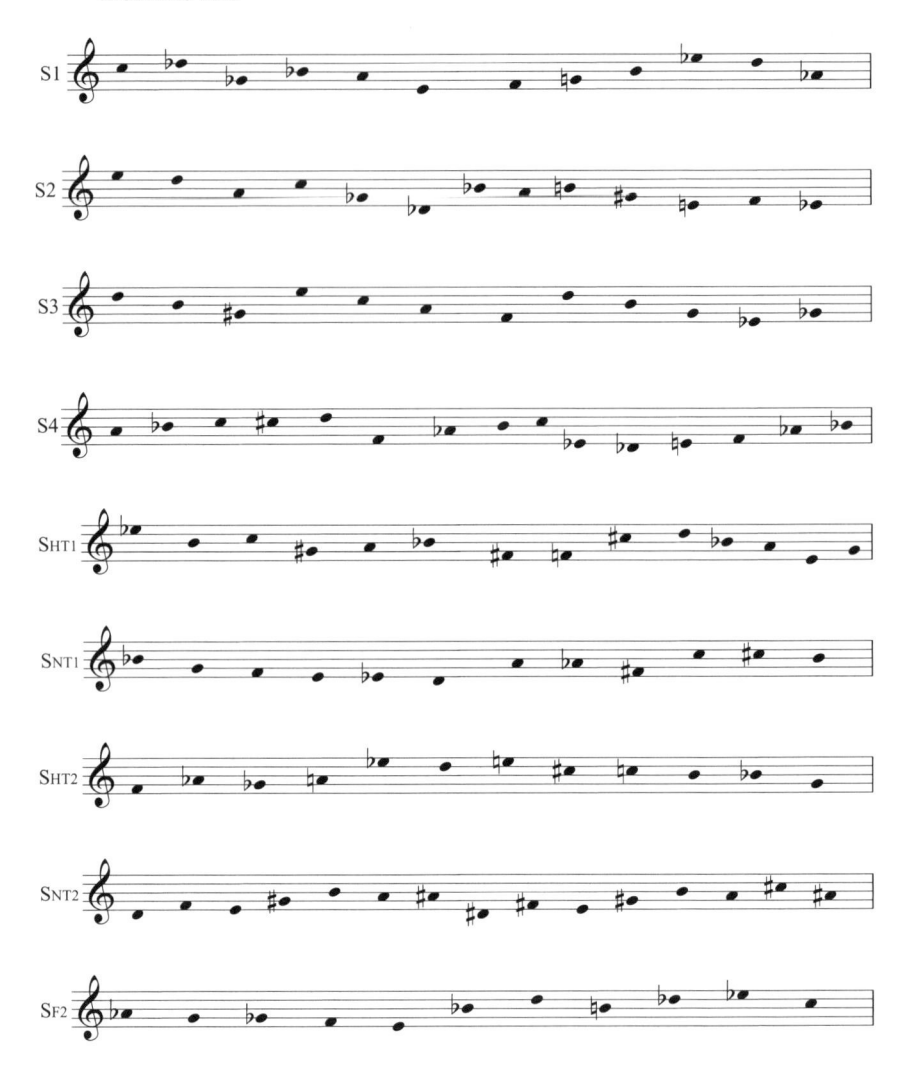

### A.18 Duo for violin and cello, *Andante molto espressivo*: Thematic set

## A.19 Serenata for cello and piano: Sets

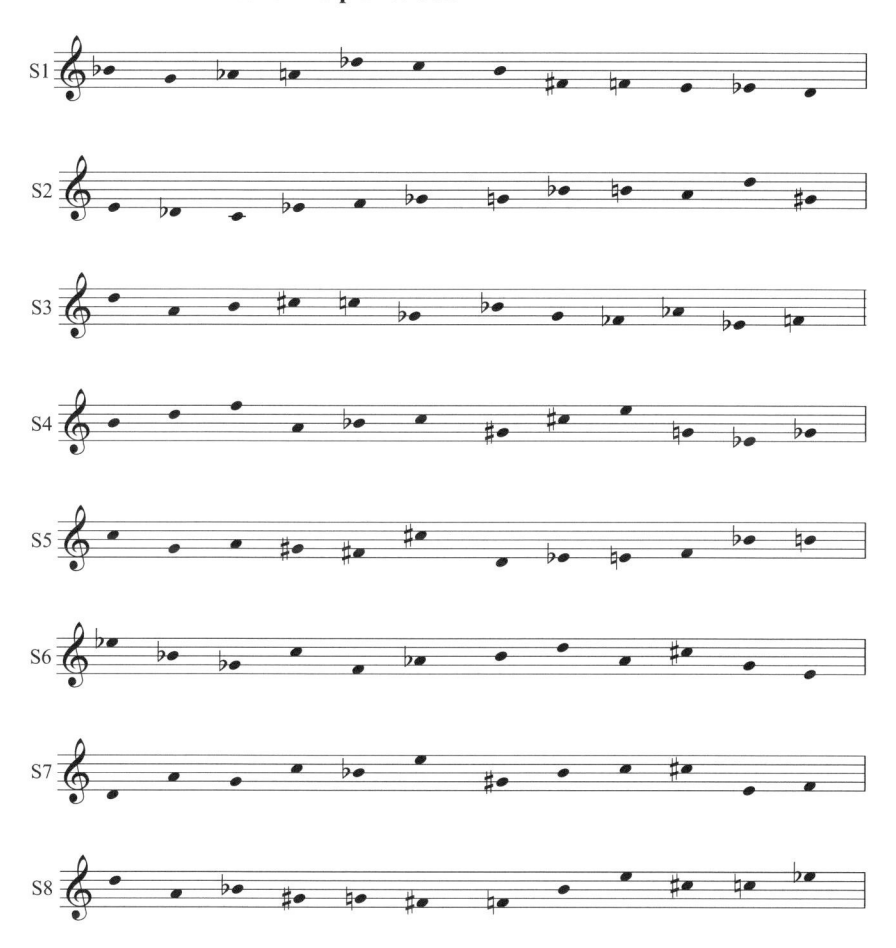

## A.20 Sonatina for cello and piano, *Allegro moderato*: Sets

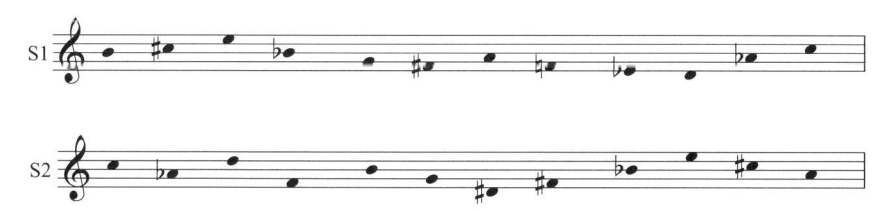

**A.21** *Tender Melody* **for cello and piano: Sets**

# Appendix B
# Chronological Worklist

Papaioannou, in his unpublished article '"The Society of Skalkottas's Friends" and the "Skalkottas Archive"' (1994), estimated that Skalkottas composed around 170 works; 70 in Berlin and 100 in Athens. From the Berlin compositions, initially all lost, eleven were found after Skalkottas's death, in friends' possessions and in second-hand shops in Berlin; today only twenty-seven works of this period can be accounted for. The majority of the Athens compositions survive; the manuscripts had been kept, and some bound, in his sister's house, where he stayed until 1945, and in his wife's house, where he lived until the end of his life. Many of the manuscripts are undated and, until recently, the only annotated catalogue of Skalkottas's works, presented in an approximate chronological order, was the 'Archive Catalogue'; this is written in Greek and is still used for reference (Papaioannou, 1969a). In recent years two other concise lists of works have appeared in English, one given by Thornley in his *Grove* article, and another provided by Margun Music. Three further lists of works have been compiled: by Demertzis (1991), Thabard (1992) and Mantzourani (1999). However, there are discrepancies among these catalogues regarding composition dates.

The chronological worklist given here is intended to be indicative only, and arises from a comparative examination of all these sources and from research in the Archive. The listing of each work is prefaced with the symbol A/K (i.e. A/K 1), which indicates the Catalogue number of each work. Dates given as 19..-19.. indicate that the piece was composed during this period; dates given as 19../19.. indicate that at the later date the piece was re-orchestrated or transcribed for a different instrumental group; dates given as (19..)*(19..) indicate that it is not certain whether the piece was composed during the first or the second date. For the titles of his compositions, and other indications within a piece, Skalkottas generally used Greek and German, but also, less frequently, French. Many of the titles are written in two or three languages; e.g. 'Quatre études pour piano', 'Vier Etüden für Klavier allein'. Here I have provided the work titles in English, although I have retained the titles of movements in their original Italian, German or French; when a title appears only in Greek and a translation has not been possible, I have presented the original Greek, but transliterated as Latin characters.

| | |
|---|---|
| (1923–24)*(1926) | **String Quartet** A/K 31a |
| | MS lost. |
| (1923–24)*(1926) | **String Trio** A/K 40b |
| | MS lost. |
| 1924 | ***Greek Suite*** **for piano solo** A/K 79a |
| | *Allegretto*; *Andantino*; *Presto* |
| 1924 | **Suite for piano solo** A/K 79b |
| | The first two pages of the first movement are missing; *Molto moderato*; *Shimmy tempo* |
| (1924)*(1925) | **Suite for two pianos** A/K 79e |
| | *Tango*; *Vivace* |
| (1924)*(1925) | **Suite for two pianos** A/K 79z |
| | *Presto*; *Fox-Trot* |
| 1925 | **Suite for violin and piano** A/K 100 [?] |
| | MS lost. |
| 1925 | **Sonata for solo violin** A/K 69 |
| | *Allegro furioso quasi presto*; *Adagietto*; *Allegro ritmato*; *Adagio* |
| 1925 | **Sonatina for piano** A/K 75a |
| 1927 | **Sonatina for piano** A/K 75b |
| | *Allegretto vivace*; *Siciliano*; the third movement has no tempo indication. |
| 1927 | ***15 Little Variations*** **for piano solo** A/K 75c |
| 1927 | **Piece for piano** A/K 75d |
| | Only the opening section survives. |
| 1928 | **First String Quartet** A/K 32 |
| | *Allegro giusto*; *Andante con variazioni*; *Allegro (ben ritmato) vivace* |
| 1929 | **First Sonata for violin and piano** A/K 49a |
| | MS lost. |
| 1929 | **First Sonatina for violin and piano** A/K 46 |
| | *Allegro giusto*; *Andantino*; *Allegro molto vivace*. Only the *Andantino* survives. |
| 1929 | **Second Sonatina for violin and piano** A/K 47 |
| | *Allegro*; *Andante*; *Allegro vivace* |
| 1929 | **Concerto for wind orchestra** A/K 6 |
| | *Allegro con brio*; *Andante cantabile*; *Allegro ben ritmato e molto vivace*: MS lost. |
| 1929 | ***Easy String Quartet*** A/K 32a |
| | MS lost. |
| 1929 | **Second String Quartet** A/K 33 |
| | MS lost. |
| 1929 | ***Little Suite*** **for violin and chamber orchestra** A/K 23 |
| | MS lost. |

Appendix B: Chronological Worklist 381

| | | |
|---|---|---|
| 1929 | **'The unknown soldier' for choir and orchestra** A/K 90 | |
| | MS lost. | |
| 1929 | **Octet for fl, cl, bsn, tpt, tbn, pno trio** | |
| | MS lost. | |
| (1929)*(1930) | *Little Suite* **for violin and small orchestra** A/K 23 | |
| | MS lost. | |
| (1929)*(1930) | **Concerto for violin, piano and chamber orchestra** A/K 21 | |
| | MS lost. | |
| (1929)*(1931) | **'I Lafina' [The Doe] for voice and piano** A/K 86 | |
| (1929)*(1931) | **'Ali Pasas' for voice and piano** A/K 87 | |
| (1929)*(1931) | **'Astrapse i Anatoli' [Lightning in the East] for voice and piano** A/K 88 | |
| 1931 | **Octet** A/K 30 | |
| | *Allegro moderato*; *Andante cantabile*; *Presto* | |
| 1931 | **First Piano Concerto** A/K 16 | |
| | *Allegro moderato*; *Andante cantabile*; *Allegro vivace* | |
| 1931–36 | *36 Greek Dances* **for orchestra** A/K 11 | |
| | Three series of twelve dances each. Reorchestrated in 1948–49. | |
| 1935 | **Third String Quartet** A/K 34 | |
| | *Allegro moderato*; *Andante*; *Allegro vivace (Rondo)* | |
| 1935 | **Second String Trio** A/K 41 | |
| | *Moderato*; *Andante*; *Presto* | |
| 1935 | **Third Sonatina for violin and piano** A/K 48 | |
| | *Allegro giusto*; *Andante*; *Maestoso–Vivace* | |
| 1935 | **Fourth Sonatina for violin and piano** A/K 49 *Moderato*; *Adagio*; *Allegro moderato* | |
| 1935 | **First Symphonic Suite for large orchestra** A/K 3a | |
| | *Ouvertüre*; *Thema con Variazioni*; *Marsch*; *Romance*; *Siciliano–Barcarole*; *Rondo–Finale* | |
| 1935 | **Concertino for two pianos and orchestra** A/K 20 | |
| | *Allegro*; *Andante*; *Allegro giusto* | |
| 1936 | **First Piano Suite [Suite No.1 for piano]** A/K 71 | |
| | *Preludio–Andante*; *Serenade–Allegretto grazioso*; *Menuetto–Moderato assai*; *Finale–Presto* | |
| 1936 | *March of the Little Soldiers* **for violin and piano** A/K 53 | |
| 1936 | **Rondo for violin and piano** A/K 54 | |
| 1936 | **Nocturne for violin and piano** A/K 55 | |
| 1936 | *Small Choral and Fugue* **for violin and piano** A/K 56 | |
| (1936)*(1939–40) | **Scherzo for quartet with piano** A/K 39 | |
| | *Allegro vivace.* | |
| 1936 | **Piano Trio** A/K 42 | |
| | *Andante*; *Thema con variazioni – Andantino*; *Molto vivace* | |

| | |
|---|---|
| 1936–37 | **Ten Canons for piano solo** A/K 79 |
| | Four two-voice canons; five three-voice; one four-voice. |
| (1937)*(1938) | **Concerto for cello and orchestra** A/K 26 |
| | MS lost. |
| 1937–38 | **Second Piano Concerto** A/K 17 |
| | *Allegro molto vivace*; *Andantino*; *Allegro moderato* |
| 1937–38 | **Suite for cello and piano** A/K 61 |
| | MS lost. |
| 1938 | **'Kapote' ['Sometime'] for voice and piano** A/K 81 |
| | On a poem by J. Stephanou, for soprano or baritone and piano. |
| 1938 | ***Eight Variations on a Greek Folk Theme*** **(Trio with piano – vln, vlc, pno)** A/K 43 |
| | *Thème populaire Grèque–Moderato assai*; Var I–*Allegro*; Var II–*Allegro vivo*; Var III–*Allegretto*; Var IV–*Moderato*; Var V–*Andante con moto*; Var VI–*Adagio*; Var VII–*Allegro ben ritmato*; Var VIII–*Allegro vivace* |
| 1938 | ***The Maiden and Death (Dance Suite)*** **for orchestra** A/K 12 |
| | *Moderato maestoso*; *Allegro*; *Andantino–Tempo di Valse (Lento)–Allegro moderato–Lento*; *Vivo*; *Allegro*; *Lament*; *Moderato assai*; *Lento–Allegro moderato–Lento* |
| 1938 | **Violin Concerto** A/K 22 |
| | *Molto appassionato*; *Andante spirito*; *Allegro vivo vivacísimo* |
| 1938/1940–47 | ***Nine Greek Dances*** **for string quartet** A/K 37 |
| | Transcription for string quartet from the orchestral version. |
| 1939 | **Third Concerto for piano, ten winds and percussion** A/K 18 |
| | *Moderato*; *Andante sostenuto*; *Allegro giocoso* |
| 1939 | **Gavotte for violin and piano** A/K 57 |
| 1939 | ***Scherzo and Menuetto cantato*** **for violin and piano** A/K 58 |
| 1939 | **Concertino for oboe and piano accompaniment** A/K 28 |
| | *Allegro giocoso*; *Pastorale – Andante tranquillo*; *Rondo–Allegro vivo* |
| 1939 | **Concertino for oboe and chamber orchestra** A/K 28a |
| 1939 | ***Ta Pagana [The Gnomes]*** A/K 15a |
| | i) Ballet for small orchestra, based predominantly on themes from Bartók: *Introduction* (Stravinsky, *The Five Fingers*, no.2); *Espressivo molto* (Skalkottas); *The Gnomes in the Underworld* (Bartók, *For Children*, vol. 1, no.29); *Carol* (Greek folk-song); *Hearth* (Early |

Appendix B: Chronological Worklist 383

music piece); *Carol* (Greek folk-song); *The Gnomes I* (Bartók, *For Children*, vol. 2, no.3); *The Gnomes II* (Bartók, *For Children*, vol. 1, no.30); *The Monster* (Bartók, *For Children*, vol. 2, no.29); *Chase* (Bartók, *For Children*, vol. 2, no.22); *Dismissal* (Skalkottas); *Chorale* (Skalkottas); *The Song of Joy* (Bartók, *For Children*, vol. 1, no.40); *Finale* (Bartók, *For Children*, vol. 2, no.2); ii) Second version A/K 110

1939–40 **Duo for violin and viola** A/K 45
*Allegro vivo*; *Andante*; *Ben ritmato*

(1939)*(1940)*(1942) **Concerto for violin, viola and wind orchestra** A/K 25
*Allegro*; *Andantino*; *Allegro vivo*

1940 **32 Piano Pieces** A/K 70
1. *Andante religioso*; 2. *Children's dance*; 3. *Short variations on a mountain theme with southern character and impressive dissonances*; 4. *Catastrophe in the jungle – film music*; 5. *Greek folkdance*; 6. *Reverie in the old style*; 7. *Reverie in the new style*; 8. *Little four-part canon*; 9. *Marcia funebra*; 10. *Sonatina*; 11. *Partita*; 12. *Little Serenade*; 13. *Intermezzo*; 14. *Tango*; 15. *Passacaglia*; 16. *Night music*; 17. *The morning serenade of the little maid*; 18. *Fox-Trot – The old policeman*; 19. *Fantastic Etude*; 20. *Lullaby*; 21. *Romance – Lied*; 22. *Gavotte*; 23. *Menuetto*; 24. *Italian Serenade*; 25. *Ragtime*; 26. *Slow Fox-Trot*; 27. *Gallop*; 28. *Blues*; 29. *Rondo Brillante*; 30. *Caprice*; 31. *Waltz*; 32. *Little peasant march*

1940 **Suite No.2 for piano** A/K 72
*Largo – con fantasia*; *Gavotte – moderato assai*; *Rapsodie – molto moderato*; *March – Allegro*

1940 **Second Sonata for violin and piano** A/K 50
*Molto allegro marcato*; *Andantino*; *Maestoso vivace (Rondo)*

(1940)*(1941–42) **'The Moon' for voice (soprano) and piano** A/K 82
1940 **Fourth String Quartet** A/K 35
*Allegro molto vivace*; *Thema con variazioni – Andante molto espressivo*; *Scherzo Presto*; *Allegro giusto*

1940 **Ten Sketches for string orchestra** A/K 8
*Sinfonia*; *Concerto*; *Passacaglia*; *Suita*; *Concertino*; *Serenata*; *Ragtime*; *Notturno*; *Capriccio*; *Rondo*

1940 **Ten Sketches for strings (suite for string quartet)** A/K 38
(1940)*(1942–43) **Concerto for double bass and orchestra** A/K 27
*Andante (Introduction) allegro*; *Andantino*; *Rondo allegro vivo et molto ritmato*

| | |
|---|---|
| 1940–43 | **Nine Greek Dances** for wind orchestra A/K 11a |
| | Transcription of nine dances from A/K 11 for wind orchestra: *Epirotikos*; *Peloponnisiakos*; *Kalamatianos*; *Mariori mou*; *Pedia ke pios to petaxe*; *Kritikos*; *Sifneikos*; *Makedonikos*; *Enas Aitos* |
| 1940–47 | **Six Greek Dances** for violin and piano A/K 59 |
| | Transcription from the A/K 11. |
| (1940)*(1941) | **Suite No.3 for piano** A/K 73 |
| | *Minuetto*; *Thema con variazioni (theme greque populaire)*; *Marcia funebra – Maestoso*; *Finale – Allegro vivace* |
| (1940)*(1941) | **Suite No.4 for piano** A/K 74 |
| | *Toccata – Vivace*; *Andantino – Con grazia*; *Polka – Tempo di polka moderato*; *Serenade – Allegro moderato* |
| 1941 | **Four Studies for piano** A/K 75 |
| | *Andante*; *Presto*; *Tempo di Valse*; *Allegro vivace* |
| 1941 | **'I told mother to get me married'** for three-voice female choir a cappella A/K 95 |
| 1941 | **'I karagouna'** for three-voice female choir a cappella A/K 96 |
| 1941 | **'Lullaby'** for choir and guitar accompaniment A/K 89z |
| | **'16 Tragoudia' (16 Songs)** for alto and piano A/K 80 (based on poems by Christos Esperas): *Ideal*; *Glimmer*; *Ad apertun libri*; *Evening*; *Revelation*; *Solitude*; *Spring*; *Fig tree*; *Chrysanthemums*; *Passage*; *The song of the loom*; *Farmer*; *The field of cane*; *In my garden*; *Tonight*; *Autumn* |
| (1941–43)*(1940–42) | **First Quartet for oboe, trumpet, bassoon and piano** A/K 40 |
| | *Moderato assai*; *Vivace* |
| 1941–43 | **Second Quartet for oboe, trumpet, bassoon and piano** A/K 40a |
| | *Tango*; *Fox-Trot*. |
| 1941–43 | **Concertino for trumpet and piano** A/K 68 |
| | *Allegro giusto* |
| 1942 | **'Mother don't beat me (The bald-headed man)'** for voice (soprano or tenor) and piano |
| | Three different versions. A/K 85, 85a, 85b. |
| 1942 | **Little Suite** for string orchestra A/K 7 |
| | *Allegro*; *Andante*; *Allegro vivo* |
| 1942–44/46/49 | **Second Symphonic Suite for large orchestra** A/K 4 |
| | *Ouvertüre Concertante*; *Toccata*; *Promenaden – Marsch*; *Largo Sinfonico*; *Thema con Variazioni*; *Perpetuum mobile (Rondo)* |
| 1942–44/49 | **Overture for large orchestra** *(The Return of Ulysses)* A/K 5 |

Appendix B: Chronological Worklist 385

| | |
|---|---|
| (1942–43)*(1946) | ***Echo*** **for piano solo (*kleine tanzstück*) A/K 77**<br>*Allegro moderato*. Other versions:<br>i) ***Echo*** **for orchestra** A/K 77a;<br>ii) ***Echo*** **for harp** (A/K 77b) |
| 1943 | ***Sonata Concertante*** **for bassoon and piano** A/K 67<br>*Allegro molto vivace*; *Andantino*; *Presto* |
| 1943/1948–49 | ***Dance Suite*** **for small orchestra** A/K 15 |
| 1943 | ***Greek Dance*** **in C minor for orchestra** A/K 11c |
| 1943 | ***Island Images***, ballet suite (for piano, in two versions) A/K15<br>*The Trawler*; *Building of Fishing Boat*; *Sea Waves*; *Launching the Fishing Boat*; *Greek Dance*; *Sunday in Church – Feast* |
| 1943–44/49 | ***Mayday Spell – A Fairy Drama*** A/K 1a<br>Incidental music for voice, recitative and piano<br>*Overture*; *Fairy Tale*; *Ballet – Dance of the Fairies*; *Love scene*; *Argyro's Song*; *Little Dance Song*; *Folk-song*; *Sort folk dance*; *Prelude*; *The mother's lament* |
| 1944–45 | **Concerto for two violins and orchestra** A/K 24<br>*Allegro giocoso*; *Variations über ein griechisches populäres Lied*; *Andante*. It survives with the piano accompaniment only. |
| 1944/48 | **'The night came on, who am I going to see?' (folk song from Roumeli) for voice and piano**<br>Transcription of the fourth *Picture* of A/K 1.<br>Several versions:<br>i) For five voices a cappella. A/K 91<br>ii) For choir with piano accompaniment A/K 92<br>iii) For orchestra and voices A/K 93<br>iv) For three female voices a cappella A/K 94. |
| 1946 | ***First Little Suite*** **for violin and piano** A/K 51<br>*Tanz preludio*; *Folk song*; *Finale (Like a village dance)* |
| 1946 | ***Five Greek Dances*** **for string orchestra** A/K 11b<br>*Epirotikos*; *Kritikos*; *Tsamikos*; *Arkadikos*; *Kleftikos* |
| 1946 | **'The music' for voice and piano** A/K 89 (based on a poem by D. Chorafas) |
| 1946 | **'The sandy beach' for voice and piano** A/K 89a (based on a poem by D. Chorafas) |
| 1946 | ***The Beauty with the Rose (Fairy-Tale)*** A/K 111<br>Ballet for orchestra based on themes from Bartók, Stravinsky, etc. |
| 1945–46 *(47) | ***Three Greek Songs*** **for violin and piano** A/K 60<br>*Griechische Volkslied*; *Olympus and Kissavos*; *My daughter go to sleep* |

| | |
|---|---|
| 1947 | **Six Greek Dances** transcription for piano A/K 76 (transcription from A/K 11)  
*Kritikos*; *Epirotikos*; *Sifneikos*; *Kleftikos*; *Thessalikos*; *Kalamatianos* |
| 1947 | **'I Karagouna' for piano solo** A/K 78  
*Moderato* |
| 1947 | **'The song of the locksmith'**  
i) Transcription for piano solo. A/K 79d;  
ii) For three voice female choir (soprano, and two mezzos) and piano. A/K 97 |
| (1947)*(1948–49) | **Dance Suite** for small orchestra A/K 15c |
| 1947 | **The old Dimos** for string quartet A/K 37a |
| 1947 | **Duo for violin and cello (Four Duetti for violin and cello)** A/K 44  
*Allegro ordinario un poco agitato*; *Andante molto espressivo*; *(Scherzo) molto vivace*; *Finale (Bauern Tanz Szenen)* |
| 1947 | **Classical Symphony in A for wind orchestra, two harps and lower strings** A/K 9  
*Small introduction in slow rhythm allegro antico*; *Andante molto espressivo*; *Allegro molto vivace*; *Fast and happy – joyful march* |
| 1947 | **Ancient Greek March** for chamber orchestra A/K 11d |
| 1948 | **Henry V** A/K 2: Incidental music for radio. MS lost. |
| 1947–48 | **The Land and the Sea of Greece**, Ballet Suite for piano  
*The Harvest*; *The Sowing*; *The Vintage*; *The Grape Stomping*; *The Trawler*; *Dance of the Waves* |
| 1948 | **Procession towards Acherondas** for piano solo A/K 79c |
| 1948 | **Ancient Greek March transcription for wind orchestra** A/K 11e |
| 1948 | **Sinfonietta (*Kleine Sinfonie*) in B♭ for orchestra** A/K 10  
*Andante sostenuto*; *Andante tristesso*; *(Scherzino) molto vivace*; *Vivacissimo (Finale)* |
| 1948 | **Little Dance Suite (*Four Images*) for orchestra** A/K 13  
*The dance of the harvest – Molto moderato*; *The dance of the sowing-time – Andante*; *The grape harvest – Allegro*; *The wine-press – Molto vivace* |
| 1948/49 | **Bolero for cello and piano** A/K 63  
*Allegro boleriano* |
| 1948–49 | **36 Greek Dances**  
Re-orchestration of A/K 11 |
| 1948–49 | **Concertino in C major for piano and orchestra** A/K 19  
*Allegro giocoso (quasi vivace)*; *Andantino*; *Molto vivace quasi presto.* |

| | |
|---|---|
| 1949 | ***Characteristic Piece*** **in C major for xylophone solo and orchestra ('*Nocturnal Amusement*') A/K 29**<br>*Molto Allegro* |
| 1949 | ***The Sea, a folk ballet*** A/K 14<br>*Overture*; *At the seashore (Son of the Sea)*; *The dance of the waves*; *The Trawl-Boat*; *The little fishes (Dance)*; *The dolphins (Dance Fantasy)*; *Nocturne – Tranquillity*; *Preparation of the mermaid*; *The dance of the mermaid*; *From the fairytale of Alexandros the Great*; *Finale – The hymn to the sea* |
| 1949 | **Overture for large Orchestra (*The Return of Ulysses*)**<br>transcription for two pianos A/K 5a |
| 1949 | ***The Mayday Spell*** **A/K 1**<br>Transcription for orchestra, singer (soprano), choir, recitative, folk dance, and ballet. MS lost. |
| 1949 | ***Second Little Suite*** **for violin and piano** A/K 52<br>*Poco lente*; *Andante*; *Allegro vivace* |
| 1949 | **Largo for cello and piano** A/K 66 |
| 1949 | **Serenata for cello and piano** A/K 64 |
| 1949 | **Sonatina for cello and piano** A/K 62<br>*Allegro moderato*; *Andante*; *Allegro molto vivace.* |
| 1949 | ***Tender Melody*** **for cello and piano** A/K 65 |

# Bibliography

*Ithaca gave you the beautiful journey.*
*Without her you would not have set out.*
*She has nothing else to give you now.*
*And if you find her poor, Ithaca hasn't deceived you.*
*Wise as you have become, with so much experience,*
*You'll have already understood by now what these Ithacas mean.*
(Konstantinos Kavafis, *Ithaca*)

## Primary Sources

*Skalkottas's Letters*

LetAsk  to Nelly Askitopoulou, 1921–28 (The letters are kept in the Skalkottas Archive).
LetGN  to George Nazos, 1 March 1923 (in the possession of Apostolos Kostios, partially published in the Greek newspaper *Kathimerini* (Sunday, 19 September 2004): 8–9, 8).
LetKon  to Yiannis Konstantinidis (in Sakalieros, 2005).
LetMB  to Manolis Benakis, 1928–33 (in Thornley, 2002a and 2002b).
LetMM  to Melpo Merlier, 16 August 1934 (in Dragoumis, 1978–79).
LetMT  to Matla Temko, 27 November 1935 (in the possession of Artemis Lindal). Letters to his wife Maria, 1947 (inaccessible at the time of writing).

*Skalkottas's Published Writings*

'Musiki Kinisis sto Verolino' ['Musical Activities in Berlin'], *Musiki Zoë*, 5 (Athens, February 1931/32): 111–13.
'Musiki Kinisis sto Verolino' ['Musical Activities in Berlin'], *Musiki Zoë*, 6 (Athens, March 1931/33): 138.
'Musiki Kinisis sto Verolino' ['Musical Activities in Berlin'], *Musiki Zoë*, 9–10 (June-July 1931/35): 113.
'Musiki Kritiki' ['Musical Criticism'], *Musiki Zoë*, 6 (Athens, March 1931/33): 124–6.

*Skalkottas's Unpublished Writings*

Accompanying Notes to the First Symphonic Suite for large orchestra (1935), in Greek and German.
Accompanying Notes to the Concertino for two pianos (1935), in Greek and German.
Accompanying Notes/Introduction to the *Thirty Two Piano Pieces* (1940), in Greek and German.
Accompanying Notes to the Overture for large orchestra (*The Return of Ulysses*) (1942–44), in German.
Accompanying Notes/Introduction to the Classical Symphony (1947), in Greek.
Accompanying Notes/Introduction to *Four Images*, and *The Sea* (1949), in Greek.
*I Techniki tis Enorhistrosis* [*Treatise on Orchestration*], in Greek, MS (undated).
Musical articles, in Greek, MS (undated): 'Orchestration'; 'New Cinema Music'; 'Folk Song'; 'Originality and Imitation'; 'Theory and Practice of the Musical Rules'; 'New Musical Literature'; 'The Musical Search'; 'Development of Musical Themes'; 'The Symphony'; 'Harmony and Counterpoint'; 'Musical Influences'; 'The School of Modern Composers'; 'Style'; 'Musical Anecdotes'; 'Collection of Thoughts'; 'How we will Write for the Theatre';

'Piano Technique'; 'Musical Accompaniments'; 'Compositional Details'; 'Dance Music'; 'Violin Technique'; 'Chamber Music for Wind Instruments and Piano'; 'The Power of Symphonic Concerts'.

*Archival Sources*

AASCV     Archiv des Arnold Schönberg Center, Vienna, Bl. 2, 4, 10, 33, 34, 35, 39, 41, 53, 57/58, 152, 161, 174, 286, T77.14, T22.13.
AHMB–1    Archiv der Hochschule für Musik Berlin, *Entwurf der Satzungen*.
AHMB–2    Archiv der Hochschule für Musik Berlin, *Jahresbericht für den Zeitraum von 1. Oktober 1921 bis zum 30. September 1924*.
AHMB-3    Archiv der Hochschule für Musik Berlin, *Akten betreffend die persönlichen Angelegenheiten der Schüler und Schülerinnen*, 159–61.
APrAKB    Archiv der Preussischen Akademie der Kunste, Berlin (Archive of the Prussian Academy of Arts, Berlin), *Frequenznachweise*, 13, 68, 76, 81, 89, 128, 1123/51.
ASOR      Athens State Orchestra Records (1943–49).
AthConsDM *Odeio Athinon: Leptomeris Ekthesis 1914–1924* [*Athens Conservatory: Detailed Minutes 1914–1924*].

*German Newspapers*

Anonymous, 'Schönberg-Schüler musizieren: Orchesterkonzert der Meisterschule für musikalische Komposition', *Berliner Dienst*, 27 May 1930.
Pringsheim Heinz, without title, *Allgemeine Musikzeitung*, 5 July 1929.
Sachse, W. 'Kunst und Wissenschaft: Konzert der Meisterschule Schönbergs', *Steglitzer Anzeiger*, 22 May 1930.
Z.V., 'Musik des Tages: Arnold Schönberg als Lehrer' *Tempo*, 22 May 1930.
Zweig, Fritz, 'Musik und Musiker: Chronik der Konzerte', *Deutsche Allgemeine Zeitung*, 21 June 1929.

*Greek Newspapers*

Anonymous, *Tachydromos*, 21 July 1921.
Anonymous, *Vradini*, 30 October 1930.
Anonymous, 'A' Laïki Sinavlia – Alfredos Corto' ['First Popular Concert – Alfred Cortot'], *Kathimerini*, 30 November 1930.
Belonis, Yiannis, 'I protes entyposeis tis kritikis' ['The first impressions of criticism'], in *Nikos Skalkottas (1904-1949)*, *Kathimerini*, 19 September 2004, 18–20.
Chamoudopoulos, Dimitris A., 'I Sinavlia tis Kratikis' ['The State Orchestra Concert'], *Eleftheria*, 2 November 1949.
Kalomiris, Manolis, 'Api tin Musikin mas Zoë – The Popular Concert' ['From our Musical Life – The Popular Concert'], *Ethnos*, 12 December 1928.

— 'Api tin Musikin mas Zoë' ['From our Musical Life'], *Ethnos*, 24 November 1930.
— 'O Thanatos tou Skalkota' ['Skalkottas's Death'], *Ethnos*, 23 September 1949.
M.K. [Manolis Kalomiris], *Ethnos*, 5 October 1936.
'Musician' (pen name of an anonymous reviewer), 'I Musiki Skini' ['The Musical Scene'], *Vradini*, 24 November 1930.
Psaroudas, Ioannis, 'I 8ⁿ Laïki Sinavlia' ['The 8th Popular Concert'], *Eleftheron Vima*, 12 December 1928.
— 'A' Laïki Sinavlia tis Orchistras tou Odeiou Athinon' ['First Popular Concert of the Athens Conservatoire Orchestra'], *Eleftheron Vima*, 24 November 1930.
— 'Alfred Cortot', *Eleftheron Vima*, 30 November 1930.
— *Eleftheron Vima*, January 1934.
— 'I Triti Simfoniki Sinavlia tou Odeiou Athinon' ['The Third Symphonic Concert of the Athens Conservatory', *Eleftheron Vima*, 9 December 1936.
— 'Sinavlies tis Simfonikis Orchistras' ['Concerts of the Symphony Orchestra'], *Proia*, 2 February 1941.
— 'Musiki Kinisis – Sinavlia Ergon N. Skalkota' ['Musical Scene – Concert with Works by N. Skalkottas'], *To Vima*, 11 April 1950.
Ramou, Lorenta, 'I Yi kai i Thalassa tis Elladas' ['The Land and the Sea of Greece'], *Kathimerini* (Sunday, 9 September), 30.
Spanoudi, Sophia, ' I "Periptosis" tou k. Skalkota' ['Mr. Skalkottas's "Case"'], *Proia*, 29 December 1930.
Vokos, Yorgos, 'I Sinavlia tis Kratikis' ['The Concert of the State [Orchestra]'], *Acropolis*, 6 May 1949.
— 'I Dio Sinavlies tis Kratikis Orchistras' ['The Two State Orchestra Concerts'], *Acropolis*, 2 November 1949.

*Greek Periodical Sources*

ME      *Musiki Epitheorisis* [*Music Review*] monthly Greek journal.
ME1     *Musiki Epitheorisis*, vol.1 (October 1921).
ME2     *Musiki Epitheorisis*, vol.2 (November 1921).
ME10    *Musiki Epitheorisis*, vol.10 (July 1922).


**Secondary Sources**

Anonymous (October 1921), 'I Kallitehnes mas en ti Xeni' ['Our Artists Abroad'], *Musiki Epitheorisis*, 1: 15.
Anonymous (December 1930), 'Musiki Kinisis Athinon' ['Musical Activities in Athens'], *Musiki Zoë*, 3: 71–2.
Adorno Theodor W. (1984), 'Zum Rundfunkkonzert from 22.1.1931', *Musikalische Schriften*, 5: 565–70.
Alsmeier, Judit (2001), *Komponieren mit Tönen: Nikos Skalkottas und Schöbergs, Komposition mit zwölf Tönen* (Saarbrücken: PFAU).

Anoyianakis, Fivos (1960), 'Musiki sti Neoteri Ellada' ['Music in Modern Greece'], in Karl Nef, *History of Music* (Athens: 'Apollon' – N. Botsis): 546–611.
Auner, Joseph (ed.) (2003), *A Schoenberg Reader: Documents of a Life* (New Haven and London: Yale University Press).
Babbitt, Milton (1955), 'Some Aspects of Twelve-Tone Composition', *The Score and IMA Magazine*, 12: 53–61.
Bailey, Kathryn (1991/1994), *The Twelve-Note Music of Anton Webern* (Cambridge University Press: Cambridge).
Baker, James M., Beach, David W. and Bernard, Jonathan W. (eds) (1997), *Music Theory in Concept and Practice* (Rochester, NY: University of Rochester Press).
Bargerstock, Nancy E. (2004), *Nikos Skalkottas (1904–1949), Greek Modernist Composer: Biography and a Critical Annotated Bibliography* (PhD dissertation: University of North Carolina at Greensboro).
Bastian, Andrea (1995), *Der Heimat-Begriff* (Tübingen: Niemeyer).
Belonis, Yiannis (2002), 'Nikos Skalkottas Under the Eyes of Manolis Kalomiris', *Polyphonia*, 1: 29–48.
— (2008), 'The Attitude of the Greek Daily and Periodical Press Towards Skalkottas During the Period 1920–1960', in Haris Vrondos (ed.), *Nikos Skalkottas: A Greek European* (Athens: Benaki Museum): 444–79.
Berger, Arthur (1968), 'Problems of Pitch Organization in Stravinsky' in B. Boretz and E.T. Cone (eds), *Perspectives on Schoenberg and Stravinsky* (Princeton, New Jersey: Princeton University Press): 123–54.
Bichsel, Michel (2008), 'The Nikos Skalkottas Archive', in Haris Vrondos (ed.), *Nikos Skalkottas: A Greek European* (Athens: Benaki Museum): 482–507.
Blickle, Peter (2004), *Heimat: A Critical Theory of the German Idea of Homeland* (Rochester, NY: Camden House).
Blumröder, Christoph von (1982), 'Schoenberg and the Concept of "New Music"', *Journal of the Arnold Schoenberg Institute*, 6/1: 96–105.
Boa, Elizabeth and Palfreyman, Rachel (2000), *Heimat: A German Dream: Regional Loyalties and National Identity in German Culture, 1890–1990* (Oxford: Oxford University Press).
Boretz, Benjamin and Cone Edward T. (eds) (1968), *Perspectives on Schoenberg and Stravinsky* (Princeton, New Jersey: Princeton University Press).
Bourlos, Thanos (1981), *Sta Dialimmata* [*During the Intervals*] (Athens: Kommydaki).
Brust, Fritz (1931), 'Aus dem Berliner Musikleben', *Allgemeine Musikerzeitung*, 58 (26 June): 519.
Bullivant, Keith (ed.) (1977), *Culture and Society in the Weimar Republic* (Manchester: Manchester University Press).
Campbell, John and Sherrard, Philip (1968), *Modern Greece* (London: Ernest Benn Limited).
Christodoulou, Nikos (2008), 'Nikos Skalkottas – A Centenary of his Birth', in Haris Vrondos (ed.), *Nikos Skalkottas: A Greek European* (Athens: Benaki Museum): 128–75.

Covach, John R. (1992), 'The Zwölftonspiel of Josef Matthias Hauer', *Journal of Music Theory*, 36/1: 149–84.
Dahlhaus, Carl (1983), *Analysis and Value Judgement*, trans. Siegmund Levarie (New York: Pendragon Press).
— (1990), *Schoenberg and the New Music*, trans. Derrick Puffet and Alfred Clayton (Cambridge: Cambridge University Press).
Dalmati, Margarita (1988–89), 'Nikos Skalkotas kai to Simadi tis Miras' ['Nikos Skalkottas and the Sign of Fate'], in *Archive of Euboean Studies*, 28 (Athens: Society of Euboean Studies): 208–13.
Delopoulos K. (ed.) (1987), *Meta Apo 120 Hronia Eleftheris Zoës, Eimetha Pali Sklavoi: To Imerologio Katohis tou Minou Dounia* [*After 120 Years of Free Life, we are Slaves Again: The Occupation Diary of Minos Dounias*] (Athens: Estia).
Demertzis, Kostis (1991), *O Nikos Skalkotas os Sinthetis Musikis gia Piano Solo* [*Nikos Skalkottas as Composer for Piano Solo*] (Chalkis: State Central Library of Chalkis).
— (1998), *I Skalkotiki Enorchistrosi* [*The Skalkottian Orchestration*] (Athens: Papazisi).
— (2004a) 'O Dimitris Mitropoulos Apo tin Plevra tou Skalkotikou Meletiti' ['Dimitris Mitropoulos from the Perspective of the Skalkottian Scholar'], *Antifonon*, 3: 20–25.
— (2004b) 'O Nikos Skalkotas tou Yiani Papaioannou: O Zografos kai to Modelo tou' ['John Papaioannou's Nikos Skalkottas: The Painter and his Model'], *Antifonon*, 7: 24–6.
Dounias, Minos (1936), 'Triti Simfoniki Sinavlia' ['Third Symphonic Concert'], *Neoellinika Grammata* [*Modern Greek Literature*] (12 December).
— (1939), 'Tris Sinavlies Musikis Domatiou' ['Three Chamber Music Concerts'], *Neoellinika Grammata* [*Modern Greek Literature*] (18 March).
— (1963), *Musikokritika* [*Musicocritica*] (Athens: Estia).
Dragoumis, M.F. (1978–79), 'Pente Sifneikes Melodies Apo ti Sillogi Melpos Merlie se Katagrafi Nikou Skalkota' ['Five Sifnos Melodies from Melpo Merlier's Collection Transcribed by Nikos Skalkottas'], *Archive of Euboean Studies*, 22: 31–8.
Drosinis, G. (1938), *G. Nazos kai to Odeio Athinon* [*G. Nazos and the Athens Conservatory*] (Athens: Estia).
Dunsby, Jonathan (1977), 'Schoenberg's *Premonition*, Op.22, No.4, In Retrospect', *Journal of the Arnold Schoenberg Institute*, 1/3. 137–49.
Epstein, David (1987), *Beyond Orpheus* (Oxford, New York: Oxford University Press).
Evangelatos, Antiohos (1949), 'Nikos Skalkottas', *Musiki Kinisis*, 11: 6.
Farneth, David (1986), 'Chronology of Weill's Life and Works', in Kim Kowalke (ed.), *A New Orpheus: Essays on Kurt Weill* (New Haven: Yale University Press): 343–57.

Fimios (pen name of an unknown writer of artistic columns) (1922), 'Ellines Musiki sto Verolino' ['Greek Artists in Berlin'], *Musiki Epitheorisis*, 10 (July): 14.

Flountzis, Antonis (1986), *Haidari: Kastro kai Vomos tis Ethnikis Antistasis* [Haidari: Castle and Altar of the National Resistance], 2nd edn. (Athens: Papazisis).

Forte, Allen (1973), *The Structure of Atonal Music* (New Haven: Yale University Press).

Fragou–Psychopaidi, Olympia (1990), *I Ethniki Scholi Musikis: Provlimata Ideologias* [*The National School of Music: Problems of Ideology*] (Athens: Foundation of Mediterranean Studies).

Frisch, Walter (1990), *Brahms and the Principle of Developing Variation* (Berkeley: University of California Press).

Garmon Roberts, Melissa (1996), *Nikos Skalkottas's Harmonic Conception as Reflected Through System 12 and System 12b* (MMus dissertation: Baylor University in Waco, Texas).

— (2002), *The Free Serial Style of Nikos Skalkottas: An Examination of the Twelve-Tone Method of his Late Serial Compositions* (PhD dissertation: University of Texas at Austin).

Gay, Peter (1981), *Weimar Culture: The Outsider as Insider* (London: Greenwood Press).

Gerhard, Roberto (1952), 'Tonality in Twelve-Tone Music', *The Score*, 6: 23–35.

— (1975), 'Schoenberg Reminiscences', *Perspectives of New Music*, 13: 57–65.

Goehr, Alexander (1974), 'The Theoretical Writings of Arnold Schoenberg', *Proceedings of the Royal Musical Association*, 100: 85–96.

— (1977), 'Schoenberg's *Gedanke* Manuscript', *Journal of Arnold Schoenberg Institute*, 2/1: 4–25.

Gradenwitz, Peter (1998), *Arnold Schönberg und seine Meisterschüler: Berlin 1925–1933* (Wien: Paul Zsolnay).

Griffiths, Paul (1979), 'English Bach Festival', *The Musical Times* 120: 589–90.

Hadjinikos, George (1966), 'Nikos Skalkottas, Greek Composer', *The Listener* (27 January): 148.

— (1974), 'Nikos Skalkotas, Ellas kai Dodekaphonia' ['Nikos Skalkottas, Hellas and Dodecaphony'], *Deltio Kritikis Discographias*, 10/13: 212–13.

— (1978–79), 'I Periptosi Skalkota' ['Skalkottas's Case'], *Archive of Euboean Studies*, 22: 21–9.

— (2006), *Nikos Skalkotas: Mia Ananeosi stin Prosegisi tis Musikis Skepsis kai Erminias* [*Nikos Skalkottas: A Renewal in the Approach of Musical Thought and Interpretation*] (Athens: Nefeli).

Haimo, Ethan (1992), *Schoenberg's Serial Odyssey: The Evolution of his Twelve-Tone Method, 1914–1928* (Oxford: Clarendon Press).

— (1997), 'Developing Variation and Schoenberg's Serial Music', *Music Analysis*, 16/3: 349–65.

Haimo, Ethan and Johnson, Paul (1984), 'Isomorphic Partitioning and Schoenberg's Fourth String Quartet', *Journal of Music Theory*, 28/1: 47–72.

— (eds) (1987), *Stravinsky Retrospectives* (Lincoln: University of Nebraska Press).
Hartog, Howard (ed.), *European Music in the 20th Century*, 3rd edn (Westport, CT: Greenwood Press).
Hauer, Josef Matthias (1962a), *Vom Melos zur Pauke* (Vienna: Universal Edition).
— (1962b), *Zwölftontechnik* (Vienna: Universal Edition).
Hinton, Stephen (1989), *The Idea of Gebrauchsmusik: A Study of Musical Aesthetics in the Weimar Republic (1919–1933) with Particular Reference to the Works of Paul Hindemith* (New York and London: Garland Publishing, Inc.).
Hogan, Clare (1982), '"Threni": Stravinsky's "Debt" to Krenek', *Tempo*, 141: 22–9.
Holtmeier, Ludwig (2008), 'Arnold Schönberg at the Prussian Arts Academy', in Haris Vrondos (ed.), *Nikos Skalkottas: A Greek European* (Athens: Benaki Museum): 256–89.
Jackson, Timothy L. (1995), 'Aspects of Sexuality and Structure in the Later Symphonies of Tchaikovsky', *Music Analysis* 14/1: 3–29.
— (1996), 'The Tragic Reversed Recapitulation in the German Classical Tradition', *Journal of Music Theory*, 40/1: 61–111.
— (1997), 'The Finale of Bruckner's Seventh Symphony and the Tragic Reversed Sonata Form', in Timothy L. Jackson and Paul Hawkshaw (eds), *Bruckner Studies* (Cambridge: Cambridge University Press): 140–208.
Jaklitsch, Nina-Maria (2003), *Manolis Kalomiris (1883–1962), Nikos Skalkottas (1904–1949): Griechische Kunstmusik zwischen Nationalschule und Moderne* (Tutzing: Hans Schneider).
Jarman, Douglas (1979), *The Music of Alban Berg* (London, Boston: Faber and Faber).
K.B. (1921), 'Musiki Kinisis Eparhion: Sinavlia Arm. Marsik en Volo' ['Musical Activities in the Provinces: Concert by Arm. Marsik in Volos'], *Musiki Epitheorisis*, 2 (November): 14.
Kalogeropoulos, Takis (1998), 'Skalkottas Nikos', *The Dictionary of Greek Music*, 5 (Athens: Giallelis): 411–17.
Kazasoglou, George B. (1978–79), 'Nikos Skalkotas: O Anthropos kai o Dimiourgos Kallitehnis' ['Nikos Skalkottas: The Man and the Creative Artist'], *Archive of Euboean Studies*, 22: 7–19.
Keller, Hans (1995), 'Schoenberg: The Future of Symphonic Thought', in Christopher Wintle (ed.), *Hans Keller: Essays on Music* (Cambridge: Cambridge University Press): 179–91.
Kerman, Joseph (1978), *The Beethoven Quartets* (Oxford: Oxford University Press).
Konstantinou, Elena (1997), *A Catastrophe?. An Investigation of Selected Piano Compositions of Nikos Skalkottas* (MMus dissertation: London College of Music, Thames Valley University).
— (2001),'Skalkottas's First Suite for Piano, First Movement (1936): From First Ideas to Realization', *British Postgraduate Musicology*, 4, http://www.bpmonline.org.uk/bpm4-index.html.
Kostios, Apostolos (1985), *Dimitris Mitropoulos* (Athens: Cultural Foundation of the National Bank).

— (1996), *Dimitris Mitropoulos: Catalogue of Works* (Athens: Orchestra of Colours – Estia).
— (1999), 'Minos Dounias (1900–1962)', *Musicologika I* (Athens: Papagrigoriou-Nakas): 143–96.
— (2008), 'Parallel paths towards opposite directions …', in Haris Vrondos (ed.), *Nikos Skalkottas: A Greek European* (Athens: Benaki Museum): 194–225.
Koutsobina, Vassiliki (1994), *Nikos Skalkottas: Two Late Works for Cello and Piano. A Historical Perspective and an Analysis* (MMus dissertation: University of Hartford, West Hartford, Connecticut).
Krenek, Ernst (1960), 'Extends and Limits of Serial Techniques', *The Musical Quarterly*, 46/1: 210–32.
— (1966), 'Some Current Terms', *Perspectives of New Music*, 4/2: 81–4.
Lambelet, George (1901), 'I Ethniki Musiki' [The National Music], *Panathinaia*, 82–90, 126–131, reproduced in Fragou–Psychopaidi, Olympia (1990), *I Ethniki Scholi Musikis: Provlimata Ideologias* [*The National School of Music: Problems of Ideology*] (Athens: Foundation of Mediterranean Studies): 217–40.
— (1928), 'New Music and Modernist Composers', *Musica Chronica*, 3: 68.
Lang, Paul Henry and Broder, Nathan (eds) (1966), *Contemporary Music in Europe: A Comprehensive Survey* (London: J.M. Dent & Sons).
Lansky, Paul and Perle, George (1980), 'Set', *The New Grove Dictionary of Music and Musicians*, 17: 197–99.
Lebrecht, Norman (1992), *The Companion to 20th Century Music* (London: Simon & Schuster).
Leotsakos, George S. (1980), 'Greece (After 1830)', *The New Grove Dictionary of Music and Musicians*, 7: 659–82.
— (1987), 'Economidis', *Pan B*, 7: 424–5.
— (2001), 'Greece III, Art Music since 1770: The Ionian Islands, 1771–1900', *The New Grove Dictionary of Music and Musicians*, 10: 349–50.
Lester, Joel (1989), *Analytic Approaches to Twentieth Century Music* (New York: W.W. Norton and Co).
Lewin, David (1962), 'A Theory of Segmental Association in Twelve-Tone Music', *Perspectives of New Music*, 1: 89–116.
Lichtenfeld, Monika (1964), *Untersuchungen zur Theorie der Zwölftontechnik bei Josef Matthias Hauer*, Kölner Beiträge zur Musikforschung, 29 (Regensburg: G. Bosse).
— (1980), 'Josef Matthias Hauer', *The New Grove Dictionary of Music and Musicians*, 8: 303–5.
Mantzourani, Eva (1991), *Skalkottas's '15 Little Variations' for Piano': An Investigation of Unity and Organic Coherence* (MMus dissertation: Goldsmiths College, University of London).
— (1999), *Nikos Skalkottas: A Biographical Study and an Investigation of his Twelve-Note Compositional Practices* (2 vols, PhD dissertation: King's College, University of London).

— (2001), 'The Disciple's Tale: The Reception and Assimilation of Schoenberg's Teachings on Grundgestalt, Coherence and Comprehensibility by his Pupil, the Composer Nikos Skalkottas', *The Journal of the Arnold Schoenberg Center*, 3: 227–38.
— (2004a), 'Tonal Influences and the Reinterpretation of Classical Forms in the Twelve-Note Works of Nikos Skalkottas', *ex-tempore*, XII/1: 47–65.
— (2004b), 'Nikos Skalkottas: Sets and Styles in the Octet', *The Musical Times*, 145: 73–86.
— (2005–06), '"All we need is geniuses"', *Annals for Aesthetics*, 43: 109–20.
— (2006), 'In the Greater Scheme of Things: Musical Form in the Twelve-Note Works of Nikos Skalkottas', in Nina-Maria Wanek (ed.), *Nikos Skalkottas (1904–1949) Zum 100. Geburtstag* (Vienna: Der Österreichischen Akademie der Wissenschaften): 71–101.
— (2008), 'An Introduction to Skalkottas's Twelve-Note Compositional Processes', in Haris Vrondos (ed.), *Nikos Skalkottas: A Greek European* (Athens: Benaki Museum): 88–125.
Matzger, Heinz-Klaus and Riehn, Rainer (eds) (2002), *Arnold Schönbergs 'Berliner Schule'*, *Musik-Konzepte*, 117/118 (Munich).
Mazower, Mark (1991), *Greece and the Inter-War Economic Crisis* (Oxford: Clarendon Press).
— (1993), *Inside Hitler's Greece: The Experience of Occupation, 1941–44* (New Haven: Yale University Press).
Mercado, Mario R. (1987), 'A Podium with a View: Recollections by Maurice Abravanel', *Kurt Weill Newsletter*, 56–8.
Merlier, Octave (1948), 'Preface', in *Four Greek Dances by Nikos Skalkottas* (Athens: French Institute).
Milstein, Silvina (1992), *Arnold Schoenberg: Notes, Sets, Forms* (Cambridge: Cambridge University Press).
Morgan, Robert (1991), *Twentieth-Century Music: A History of Musical Style in Modern Europe and America* (New York: W.W. Norton & Company).
Motsenigos, Spiros (1958), *Neohelliniki Musiki* [*Neohellenic Music*] (Athens).
Nef, Karl (1960), *History of Music*, trans. and ed. Fivos Anoyianakis (Athens: 'Apollon' – N. Botsis).
Orga, Ates (1969), 'Skalkottas: Shadowy Figure of Greek Music', *Music and Musicians*, 17/11: 36–40/46/82.
Papaioannou, John G. (1954), 'Nikos Skalkottas (1904–1949)', *Archive of Euboean Studies*, 3: 75–96 (reprinted 1955. 3–24).
— (1969a), 'I Eikosaetirida tou Nikou Skalkota' ['Nikos Skalkottas's 20th Anniversary'], *Archive of Euboean Studies*, 15: 119–40.
— (1969b), 'Skalkottas's "Ulysses"', *Musical Times*, 110: 615.
— (1974), 'A Little Dedication to Nikos Skalkottas', *Deltio Kritikis Discographias*, 10/13: 208–22.
— (1976), 'Nikos Skalkottas', in Howard Hartog (ed.), *European Music in the 20th Century*, 3rd edn (Westport, CT: Greenwood Press): 320–29.

— (1991), Liner note to *Nikos Skalkottas 36 Greek Dances*, The Urals State Philharmonic Orchestra, conductor Byron Fidetzis. CD. Lyra 0052/53.

— (1994), '"The Society of Skalkottas's Friends" and the "Skalkottas Archive"' (unpublished article): 1–26.

— (1997), *Nikos Skalkotas 1904–1949: Mia Prospathia Eisdysis ston Magiko Kosmo tis Dymiourgoas tou* [*Nikos Skalkotas 1904–1949: An Endeavour to Enter into the Magical World of his Creativity*] (2 vols, Athens: C. Papagrigoriou – H. Nakas Co.).

Perle, George (1980), *The Operas of Alban Berg. Volume One: Wozzeck* (Berkeley, Los Angeles: University of California Press).

— (1985), *The Operas of Alban Berg. Volume Two: Lulu* (Berkeley, Los Angeles: University of California Press).

— (1991), *Serial Composition and Atonality: An Introduction to the Music of Schoenberg, Berg, and Webern* (Berkeley, Los Angeles: University of California Press).

Perle, George, and Lansky, Paul (1980), 'Twelve-note Composition', *The New Grove Dictionary of Music and Musicians*, 19: 286–96.

Petropoulos, Elias (1991), *Rebetika Tragoudia* [*Rebetika: Songs from the Old Greek Underworld* (Athens: Kedros).

Ramou, Lorenta (2008), 'The Presentations of the Suite *The Land and Sea of Greece*: An Unpublished Letter by Polyxene Mathéy about her Meetings and Collaboration with Nikos Skalkottas', in Haris Vrondos (ed.), *Nikos Skalkottas: A Greek European* (Athens: Benaki Museum): 418–39.

Rauchhaupt, Ursula von (ed.) (1971), *Schoenberg, Berg, Webern: The String Quartets, A Documentary Study* (Hamburg: Polydor International).

Reich, Willi (1971), *Schoenberg: A Critical Biography*, trans. Leo Black (London: Longman).

Romanou, Kaiti (1985), 'Marios Varvoglis (1885–1967)', *Musicologia*, 2: 13–29.

— (2006), *Entehni Elliniki Musiki stous Neoterous Chronous* [*Art Greek Music in Modern Times*] (Athens: Koultoura).

Rosen, Charles (1976a), *The Classical Style* (London, Boston: Faber and Faber).

— (1976b), *Schoenberg* (London: Marion Boyars).

— (1988), *Sonata Forms* (New York, London: W.W. Norton and Co.).

Rufer, Josef (1961), *Composition with Twelve Notes*, trans. Humphrey Searle (London: Barrie and Rockliff).

Said, Edward (1994), *Representations of the Intellectual* (New York: Vintage Books).

Sakalieros, Georgios (2005), *Yiannis Konstantinidis (1903–1984) – His Life and Work: An Analytical Approach and Presentation of his Compositional Style, with Reference to his Orchestral Works* (PhD dissertation: University of Athens).

Samprovalakis, Yiannis (2006), 'Nikos Skalkottas's ballet music for piano', booklet notes to *The Land and Sea of Greece, Ballet Music by Nikos Skalkottas*, BIS–CD–1564: 4–9.

Schmid, Erich (1974), 'Ein Jahr bei Arnold Schönberg in Berlin', *Melos*, 41: 130–203.

Schoenberg, Arnold (1952/1968), 'Analysis of the Four Orchestral Songs Opus 22', trans. Claudio Spies, in Benjamin Boretz, and Edward T. Cone (eds), *Perspectives on Schoenberg and Stravinsky* (Princeton, New Jersey: Princeton University Press), 25–45.

— (1969), *Structural Functions of Harmony* (New York, London: W.W. Norton and Co.).

— (1970/1990), *Fundamentals of Musical Composition* (London: Faber and Faber).

— (1983), *Theory of Harmony*, trans. Roy Carter (London: Faber and Faber).

— (1984), *Style and Idea* (Berkeley and Los Angeles: University of California Press).

— (1994), *Zusammenhang, Kontrapunkt, Instrumentation, Formenlehre [Coherence, Counterpoint, Instrumentation, Instruction in Form]*, ed. Severine Neff, trans. Charlotte M. Cross and Severine Neff (Lincoln: University of Nebraska Press).

— (1995), *The Musical Idea and the Logic, Technique, and Art of its Presentation*, ed. and trans. Patricia Carpenter and Severine Neff (New York: Columbia University Press).

Sengstschmid, Johann (1980), *Zwischen Trope und Zwölftonspiel*, Forschungsbeiträge zur Musikwissenschaft, 28 (Regensburg: G. Bosse).

Skokos, Antonis (1950), 'Nikos Skalkottas', *Nea Estia*, 45: 598–600.

Slonimsky, Nicolas (1966), 'New Music in Greece', in Paul Henry Lang and Nathan Broder (eds), *Contemporary Music in Europe: A Comprehensive Survey* (London: J.M. Dent & Sons): 225–35.

Smith, Joan Allen (1979–80), 'Schoenberg's Way', *Perspectives of New Music*, 18/1–2: 258–85.

— (1986), *Schoenberg and his Circle: A Viennese Portrait* (New York: Schirmer Books).

S.P. (1931), 'Ai Kiriai Katefthinsis tis Sihronou Musikis' ['The Main Trends of Contemporary Music'], *Musiki Zoë*, 5: 101/120.

Spanoudi, Sophia (1928), 'Musiki' ['Music'], *Nea Estia*, 3: 376.

Spranger, Eduard (1923/1967), *Der Bildungswert der Heimatkunde* (Leipzig: Philip Reclam; Stuttgart: Reclam).

Stein, Erwin (1953), *Orpheus in New Guises* (London: Rockliff).

— (ed.) (1964), *Arnold Schoenberg Letters*, trans. E. Wilkins and E. Kaiser (London: Faber and Faber).

Straus, Joseph (1987), 'Sonata Form in Stravinsky', in Ethan Haimo and Paul Johnson (eds) *Stravinsky Retrospectives* (Lincoln: University of Nebraska Press): 141–61.

— (1990a), *Remaking the Past: Musical Modernism and the Influence of the Tonal Tradition* (Cambridge, Mass.: Harvard University Press).

— (1990b), *Introduction to Post-Tonal Theory* (New Jersey: Prentice Hall).

— (1997), 'Voice Leading in Atonal Music', in James M. Baker, David W. Beach and Jonathan W. Bernard (eds), *Music Theory in Concept and Practice* (Rochester, NY: University of Rochester Press): 237–74.

— (2001), *Stravinsky's Late Music* (Cambridge: Cambridge University Press).
Stuckenschmidt, Hans Heinz (1977), *Arnold Schoenberg: His Life, World and Work*, trans. Humphrey Searle (London: John Calder).
Symeonidou, Aleka (1995), *Dictionary of Greek Composers* (Athens: Pilippos Nakas).
Szmolyan, Walter (1965), *Josef Matthias Hauer* (Vienna: Lafite).
Taylor, Ronald (1977), 'Opera in Berlin in the 1920s: *Wozzeck* and *The Threepenny Opera*', in Keith Bullivant (ed.) *Culture and Society in the Weimar Republic* (Manchester: Manchester University Press).
— (1991), *Kurt Weill: Composer in a Divided World* (London: Simon & Schuster).
Thabard, Isabelle (1992), *Nikos Skalkottas (1904–1949) Compositeur Grec: Aspects de son Oeuvre pour Quatuor A Cordes* (MMus dissertation: Université de Paris).
Theodoropoulou, Avra (1939), 'I Musiki' ['Music'], *Nea Estia*, 25: 502–3.
— (1941), 'Sinavlies Radiofonikes – I Proti Sinavlia tis Simfonikis Orchistras' [Radio Concerts – The First Concert of the Symphony Orchestra'], *Nea Estia*, 29: 117–18.
— (1949), 'I Musiki' [Music], *Nea Estia*, 45 (15 June 1949), 799–800.
— (1961), 'O Mousourgos Skalkottas' (The Composer Skalkottas), *Angloelliniki Epitheorisi* [*English-Greek Revue*], 10, 1948, partially reprinted in *Ios*, 9 (1961), 48–49.
Thornley, John (1980), 'Skalkottas Nikolaos', *The New Grove Dictionary of Music and Musicians*, 17: 361–4.
— (2001), 'Skalkottas Nikos', *The New Grove Dictionary of Music and Musicians*, 23: 464–69.
— (2002a), '"I Beg You to Tear up my Letters …": Nikos Skalkottas's Last Years in Berlin (1928–33)', *Byzantine and Modern Greek Studies*, 26: 178–217.
— (2002b), '"… denn fortgegangen von ihm bin ich nicht": Nikos Skalkottas' Schönbergsches Berlin', in Heinz-Klaus Matzger and Rainer Riehn (eds), *Arnold Schönbergs 'Berliner Schule'*, *Musik-Konzepte*, 117/118: 103–21.
— (2004), 'Ki'an Sviso Ego, tha Yennithoun Kimata ap'ton Afro mou' ['Even if I pass away waves will be born from my foam'], *Antifonon*, 5: 18–23.
— (2008a), 'An Encounter with "Greek Artistic Reality" – Nikos Skalkottas' Return to Athens in 1933', in Haris Vrondos (ed.), *Nikos Skalkottas: A Greek European* (Athens: Benaki Museum): 334–67.
— (2008b), 'Skalkottas in Haidari', in Haris Vrondos (ed.), *Nikos Skalkottas: A Greek European* (Athens: Benaki Museum): 370–95.
Trotter, William (1995), *Priest of Music: The Life of Dimitri Mitropoulos* (Portland, Oregon: Amadeus Press).
Tsoucalas, Costas (1981), *The Greek Tragedy* (Athens: A. Livanis – 'Nea Sinora' [New Frontiers]).
Vlastou, Dora (1961), 'Mnimosinon N. Skalkota' ['Commemoration of Nikos Skalkottas'], *Ios*, 9: 51–5.
Vouvaris, Petros (2004), *Nostos and Nostalgia in Nikos Skalkottas's Second Suite for Piano* (PhD dissertation: University of Wisconsin–Madison).

Vrondos, Haris (ed.) (2008), *Nikos Skalkottas: A Greek European* (Athens: Benaki Museum).

Walker, Alan (1961), 'Nikos Skalkottas and the Secret Science', *The Listener* 65/1671: 633.

Walton, Chris (2001), '"... My Duty to Defend the Truth": Erich Schmid in Schoenberg's Berlin Composition Class', *Tempo*, 218: 15–19.

Wanek, Nina-Maria (ed.) (2006), *Nikos Skalkottas (1904–1949) Zum 100. Geburtstag* (Vienna: Der Österreichischen Akademie der Wissenschaften).

Webern, Anton von (1963), *The Path to the New Music*, ed. Willi Reich, trans. Leo Black (London: Bryn Mawr: Theodore Presser Co.).

Whittall, Arnold (2008), *Serialism* (Cambridge: Cambridge University Press).

Wintle, Christopher (ed.) (1995), *Hans Keller: Essays on Music* (Cambridge: Cambridge University Press).

Zervos, George (2001), *Nikos Skalkotas kai I Evropaïki Paradosi ton Arhon tou 20$^{ou}$ Aïona* [*Nikos Skalkottas and the European Tradition of the Beginning of the 20th Century*] (Athens: Papagrigoriou–Nakas).

— (2008), 'Musical Idioms and Aesthetic Directions in Skalkottas's Work', in Haris Vrondos (ed.), *Nikos Skalkottas: A Greek European* (Athens: Benaki Museum): 50–85.

# Index

Nikos Skalkottas is referred to as NS in the index, except for his own main entry where he appears under Skalkottas.
References to photographs and music examples are in **bold**.

Adorno, Theodor 37
Askitopoulou-Evelpidi, Nelly 2, 15, 20–32,
    34, 39, 41, 44, 59, 61, 66, 67, 68,
    76, 77
    correspondence with NS 20–32, 34, 41,
        61, 77
Athens, musical life 42–4
    Athens Conservatory 11–12, 13, 14, 15,
        22, 27, 29, 43, 44, 45, 46, 54, 55
    Hellenic Conservatory (Athens) 43, 55
    National Conservatory (Athens) 43, 55
    Orchestras
        Athens Conservatory Orchestra 12,
            14, 34, 43, 44, 45, 46, 55, 56,
            57, 64
            NS' criticism of 46
        Athens Radio Orchestra, NS
            member of 57
        Athens State Orchestra 12, 67, 73,
            297
        National Opera Orchestra (*Lyriki*
            *Skini*) 57, 68
Averof scholarship, fund 13, 14, 18, 22, 26

Bach, Johann Sebastian 25, 28, 33, 99
Bartók, Béla 65, 337, 382–3, 385
Baud-Bovy, Samuel 56
Beethoven, Ludwig van 11, 14, 33, 44, 59,
    153, 214, 217, 219, 229, 314
    Cello sonata op.102, no.2 314
    Fifth Symphony 217, 219, 229
    Grosse Fugue op.133 314
    'Pastoral' Symphony (Sixth
        Symphony) 44
    Piano sonatas op.101, op.106, op.110
        314
    Overture, *Zur Weihe des Hauses* 314
    String quartets 33
    String quartet op.131 314
    Violin Concerto 14
Benakis, Emanuel 22
Benakis, Manolis 30
    correspondence with NS 31, 34, 35, 36,
        37, 38, 39, 40, 41, 46–7, 48, 49, 50,
        51, 71, 245
    financial support 30, 39, 41–2
    *Greek Dances*, and 37, 51, 63
    photograph with **40**
    relationship 39–42, 47–8, 49, 50–51
    rift with 48, 57
Berg, Alban 1, 34, 44, 82, 83, 84, 86, 89,
    94, 99, 136, 137, 339
    Chamber Concerto 339
    *Lulu* 89, 94
    *Wozzeck* 44
Berlin
    Berlin Hochschule für Musik, 11, 17,
        18, 19, 20, 21, 22, 29, 30, 35, 39
    Berlin Krolloper 35
    Berlin Philharmonic Orchestra 36
    Berlin State Opera 35, 47
    Berlin Symphony Orchestra 36
    cultural life 17
    opera 'Unter den Linden' 22
    Prussian Academy of Arts (Academy
        of Fine Arts) 21, 32, 35, 37, 41
Bourlos, Thanos 52
Boutnikoff, Jean 12, 28
Brahms, Johannes 33, 44

Bruckner, Anton 39, 44
Busoni, Ferruccio 17, 20, 22, 32
Bustinduy, José de 12

Chamoudopoulos, Dimitris 75–6
Christodoulou, Nikos 337
Contemporary Music Research Centre, Athens 2

Debussy, Claude 43, 59
Demertzis, Kostis 2, 3, 6, 20, 21, 38, 66, 180
Dessau, Paul 17
Dounias, Minos 2, 20, 22, 57–8, 63, 64, 65, 74, 75, 76
Dvořák, Antonin 59

Economidis, Filoktitis 12, 54, 55
Efthimiopoulos, Dimitris 69
Eisler, Hans 1, 17, 34
*Eleftheri Skini* 12
Esperas, Christos, *Opos Oli* 25
Evangelatos Antiochos 22, 74
Evelpidis, Chrissos 25, 66, 68
Evelpidis, Christos, *Mayday Spell* 68

Farandatos, Spyros 22, 39, 44, 54

Gerhard, Roberto 1, 32, 33, 99
Goehr, Rudi 32, 35, 61, 64, 70, 71–2
Goehr, Walter 2, 32, 35, 71
Greece
    civil war 69–71
    economic problems 53
    fascist era 53
    language struggle 12
    German Occupation 25, 65, 66, 67, 70
    *see also* Athens
Greek composers 11, 12, 29, 43
Greek Composers' Union 54, 55
Greek National School 12, 15, 53–4, 337

Hadjinikos, George 32, 38, 52
Hannenheim, Norbert von 1, 32, 34, 36, 38
Hauer, Josef Matthias 83, 94
Haydn, Joseph 59
*Heimat* 68, 309
Hess, Willy 11, 17–18, 19, 20, 22, 30, 59
Hindemith, Paul 17, 45

Ithaca v, 9, 79, 177, 341, 389
Ionian islands 11, 65
    Ionian (Eptanisian) Music School, composers 11, 12

Jarnach, Philipp 19, 20, 21, 22, 27, 28, 32
Juon, Paul 18

Kahn, Robert 18
Kalomiris, Manolis 12, 43, 45, 54, 55, 56, 76
Katsoyani, Katy 24
Kavafis, Konstantinos v, 9, 79, 177, 341, 389
Kazasoglou, George 61, 64
Keller, Alfred 32
Keller, Hans 161–2, 337–8
Kolisch Quartet 61
Konstantinidis, Yiannis 18, 19, 20, 21, 22, 48, 49
Kopsida, Antigoni 14
Krenek, Ernst 120–21

Lambelet, George 12, 44, 54
Lavrangas, Dionysios 54, 56
Lebrecht, Norman 1
Likoudis, George 22
Lindal, Artemis 31, 32, 52, 59
Liszt, Franz, Second Piano Concerto 44

Merlier, Melpo 56, 63
    Kendro Mikrasiatikon Spoudon and 56
Merlier, Octave 13, 18, 72
    French Institute and 2, 13, 18, 72
Metaxas, Ioannis 53, 65
Milhaud, Darius 21, 35, 43
Mitropoulos, Dimitris 12, 14, 21, 22, 23, 24, 26, 27, 28, 34, 36 43, 44, 47, 53–5, 56, 64, 71
    *Cretan Feast* 21, 23, 34, 40
    relationship with NS 22, 23–4, 26, 27, 28, 36
Mozart, Wolfgang Amadeus 11, 33, 38, 245
    *The Marriage of Figaro* 38

Nazos, George 11, 13, 14, 18, 19, 55
*Noumas* 12

Orga, Ates 20, 125, 136, 203

Palamas, Kostis 12
Pangali, Maria, marriage to NS 71
Papaioannou, John G. 2, 3, 6, 13, 18, 19, 20, 21, 23, 27, 30–31, 39, 48, 49, 54, 55, 68, 74, 125, 180, 245, 309, 379
Papaioannou, Marika 36, 72
Paraskeva, Katina 22, 63
Parisis, A. 73
Paxinou, Katina 22
Perpessas, Charilaos 32
Perra, Margarita 22, 35, 37
Petridis, Petros 54, 56
Pisti, Maria 71
Politis, Nikos 21
Poniridis, Georgios 54, 56
Poulenc, Francis 21
Pratsika, Koula (Koula Pratsika Dance School) 65, 67
Pringsheim, Heinz 35, 36
Prinzhorn, Edgar 81
Psaroudas, Ioannis 45, 56, 64, 75

*rebetiko* song, 'I Magissa tis Arapias' 70
Riadis, Emilios 56
Rossini, Gioachino 11
Rousopoulou–Mathéy, Polyxeni (Mathéy, Polyxeni) 22, 36, 44, 72, 73
Rufer, Josef 32, 33, 83

Said, Edward 76–7
Schacht, Peter 32, 34, 38, 52
Schmid, Erich 32, 37, 339
Schoenberg, Arnold 1, 3–4, 8, 17, 22, 31, 43, 45, 47, 49, 52, 54, 59, 60, 61, 63, 64, 71, 73, 74
    NS studies with 32–9, 41, 81, 245
    in relation to NS's twelve-note technique 81–4, 86, 94, 99–101, 131, 136, 137, 147, 151, 153, 156, 179, 182, 190, 193, 298, 337, 339
    developing variation and 99–100
    form and 131, 152, 194
    *Grundgestalt* and 82, 83–4, 99
    works
        Eight Songs op.6 37
        *Erwartung* 35
        Fourth String Quartet 225
        *Gurrelieder* 35
        *Ode to Napoleon* 82
        Song op.22, No.4, *Vorgefühl* 246
        String Trio, op.45 82
        Suite op.29 47
        *Von Heute auf Morgen* 35
Schreker, Franz 17, 35
Schubert, Franz, Seventh Symphony 44
Schultze, Tony 13
Schumann, Robert 44
Second Viennese School 115
Shostakovich, Dmitri 339
Sibelius, Jean 337
Sikelianos, Angelos 12
Skalkottas Alexandros (Alekos, NS' father) 13, 55
Skalkottas Alekos (NS' son) 71
Skalkottas Kostas 13, 50
Skalkottas Nikos (NS' son) 74
Skalkottas, Nikos
    Archive, Skalkottas 2, 37, 66, 70, 245, 307, 379
    Archive Catalogue, (Skalkottas) 3, 21, 25, 35, 65, 67, 72, 379
    Biographical Study (NS)
        Berlin period 17–52
            Benakis affair 39–42
            early studies in Berlin 17–22
            last Berlin years 47–52
            life in Berlin, personality and relationships 22–32
            studies with Schoenberg 32–9
            1930, Athenian concerts and criticism 42–7
        early years in Greece 11–16
        Greek period 53–77
            a bitter homecoming 53–7
            last years 70–77
            Second World War and Occupation years 65–70
            working in Athens 57–65
    compositions (NS)
        'Ali Pasas' for voice and piano 35, 381
        *Ancient Greek March* 72, 386
        'Astrapse i Anatoli' ['Lightning in the East'] for voice and piano 35, 381
        *The Beauty with the Rose* 67, 385

*Bolero* 73, 319, 386
*Characteristic Piece* 73, 387
*Classical Symphony* 4, 72, 386
Concertino in C major for piano and orchestra 4, 72, 73, 386
Concertino for oboe and chamber orchestra 382
Concertino for oboe and piano 66, 180, 382
Concertino for trumpet and piano 66, 180, 384
Concertino for two pianos and orchestra 63, 94–7, 98, 111, 126, 153, 155, 282, 324, 381
 music examples **95**, **96**, **111**, **127**, **364**
 table, *Allegro* 98, 155
Concerto for cello and orchestra 382
Concerto for double bass and orchestra (Double Bass Concerto), 65, 67, 383
Concerto for two violins and orchestra 70, 385
Concerto for violin, piano and chamber orchestra 34, 36, 381
Concerto for violin, viola and wind orchestra 64, 70, 383
Concerto for wind orchestra 34, 44, 45, 380
*Cretan Feast* (Mitropoulos), orchestration 21, 23, 34, 40
*Dance Suite* for small orchestra 72, 385, 386
*Dance of the Waves* 72, 73, 386
Duo for violin and cello 130, 146–8, 386
 music examples **147**, **376**
 table, *Andante molto espressivo* 148
Duo for violin and viola 64, 383
*Easy String Quartet* 380
*Echo* for harp 385
*Echo* for orchestra 385
*Echo* for piano solo 385
*Eight Variations on a Greek Folk Theme* 4, 5, 64, 382
*15 Little Variations* for piano solo 22, 182–5, 215, 221, 252, 380

 music example **184**
 table, 183
*First Little Suite* for violin and piano 130, 385
*First of May '44* 69
First Piano Concerto 4, 5, 35, 37–8, 52, 102, 106, 118, 126, 129, 130, 153, 154–5, 188–93, 194–6 196–7, 198–9, 200, 246, 275, 381
 music examples **103**, **106**, **189**, **191**, **195**, **196**, **343–6**
 tables
 *Allegro moderato* 154–5, 192–3
 *Allegro vivace* 198–9
 *Andante cantabile* 118, 194
First Piano Suite 21, 64, 85, 86, 105, 113–14, 126, 158–9, 161, 162, 163, 164–8, 182, 185, 213, 381
 music examples **85**, **113**, **163**, **365–8**
 tables
 *Finale (Presto)* 158, 167–8
 *Menuetto-Trio* 166
 *Preludio* 86, 105, 164
 *Serenade* 165
First Quartet for oboe, trumpet, bassoon and piano 384
First Sonata for violin and piano 380
First Sonatina for violin and piano 1, 182, 380
First String Quartet 35, 185–8, 200, 246, 380
 music examples **185**, **187**
 tables
 *Allegro giusto* 186
 *Allegro (ben ritmato) vivace* 188
First Symphonic Suite 34, 63, 71, 88–91, 93–4, 125, 137, 185, 245–52, 252–5, 255–61, 261–5, 265–8, 265–73, 275, 292, 307, 338, 381
 music examples **88**, **90–91**, **92–3**, **139**, **250**, **251**, **252**,

254, 257, 258, 260, 262,
  267, 269, 272, 273, 358–63
 tables
  *Marsch* 256, 259
  *Ouvertüre* 247, 248–9
  *Romance* 263–5
  *Rondo–Finale* 270–71
  *Siciliano–Barcarole* 266, 268
  *Thema con Variazioni* 253
Four Studies for piano 65, 384
Fourth Sonatina for violin and
 piano 73, 97, 106–7, 108–9,
 126, 161, 182, 213, 238–44,
 381
 music examples **107, 108, 241,
  357**
 tables
  *Adagio* 108, 242
  *Allegro moderato* 244
  *Moderato* 239
Fourth String Quartet 65, 126,
 128–9, 158, 163, 169, 170,
 171, 172, 173, 174–5, 383
 music examples **127, 128, 169,
  170, 172, 173, 174, 373–4**
 tables
  *Allegro molto vivace* 171
  large-scale formal structure and
   set structure 175
Gavotte for violin and piano 64, 382
*Glazier* 69
*The Gnomes* 65, 382–3
*The Grape Stomping* 72, 386
*Greek Dance* in C minor for
 orchestra 385
*Greek Dances* 1, 6, 24, 37, 38, 50,
 55, 56, 57, 60, 63, 64, 71, 72,
 73, 74, 76
 *Arkadikos* 72, 385
 *Dance of Zalongo* 37
 *Epirotikos* 1, 55, 72, 384, 385,
  386
 *Five Greek Dances* for string
  orchestra 72, 385
 *Four Greek Dances* 13, 18, 55,
  60, 64, 72
 *Kleftikos* 37, 72, 385, 386

*Kritikos* 1, 37, 55, 63, 72, 384,
 385, 386
*Nine Greek Dances* for string
 quartet 382
*Nine Greek Dances* for wind
 orchestra 384
*Peloponnisiakos 1, 4, 37, 55,
 56, 72, 384*
*Six Greek Dances* transcription
 for piano 386
*Six Greek Dances* for violin
 and piano 384
*Syrtos* 37
*36 Greek Dances* 4, 23, 37, 51,
 56, 63, 73, 337, 381, 386
*Tsamikos* 1, 55, 72, 385
*Greek Suite* for piano 21, 181, 380
*Harvest* 72, 73, 386
*Henry V* 72, 386
'I karagouna'
 for piano solo 386
 for three-voice female choir 384
'I Lafina' [The Doe] for voice and
 piano 1, 35, 381
'I told mother to get me married' 384
*Island Images* 67, 385
'Kapote' ['Sometime'] for voice
 and piano 382
*Klouves* 69
*The Land and Sea of Greece* 72, 386
Largo for cello and piano 319, 387
*Little Dance Suite (Four Images)*
 4, 73, 386
*Little Suite* for string orchestra 68,
 384
*Little Suite* for violin and chamber
 orchestra 34, 36, 37, 380, 381
'Lullaby' 384
*The Maiden and Death* 5, 64, 72, 382
March of the Little Soldiers 64, 381
*Mayday Spell* 68, 69, 73, 385, 387
'The Moon' for voice and piano 383
'Mother don't beat me (The bald-
 headed man)' 63, 384
'The night came on' 385
Nocturne for violin and piano 64,
 381

Octet for fl, cl, bsn, tpt, tbn, pno
   trio, 35, 381
Octet 4, 37, 38, 47, 52, 97, 101,
   117, 118–19, 158, 197,
   200–203, 203–8, 209–11, 246,
   279, 381
   music examples **102**, **201**, **202**,
      **205**, **207**, **208**, **211**, **346–9**
   tables
   *Allegro moderato* 200, 203
   *Andante cantabile* 204–5
   *Presto* 117, 119, 210
*The old Dimos* for string quartet 386
Overture for large orchestra *see*
   *The Return of Ulysses*
*Passacaglia* for piano, from the
   *32 Piano Pieces* 138, 139–42,
   185, 383
   music examples **140**, **143**, **372**
   tables
   right-hand sets 140
   six harmonic groups 141
Piano Trio 64, 130, 158, 279, 381
Piece for piano 380
*Procession towards Acherondas*
   72, 386
*The Return of Ulysses* 5, 68, 73, 97,
   111, 158, 179, 246, 261, 307,
   308–17, 384, 387
   music examples **311**, **312–14**,
      **315**, **316**, **376**
   tables
   formal structure 310
   main themes 312–13
*Roll-call* 69
Rondo for violin and piano 381
*Scherzo and Menuetto cantato* 64,
   382
Scherzo for quartet with piano 64,
   381
*The Sea* 4, 72, 73, 387
*Second Little Suite* for violin and
   piano 73, 319, 387
Second Piano Concerto 64, 158, 159,
   275–9, 279–81, 282, 287, 382
   music examples **159**, **277**, **278**,
      **368–9**
   tables
   *Allegro moderato* 281
   *Allegro molto vivace* 276
   *Andantino* 280
Second Sonata for violin and piano
   65, 383
Second Sonatina for violin and
   piano 35, 44, 104, 117, 156–7,
   158, 182, 200, 245, 246, 380
   music examples **156**, **343**
   tables, *Allegro* 105, 117, 157
Second String Trio 63, 87–8, 109
   110, 119–20, 120–23, 132–6,
   137, 138, 161–2, 182, 213, 381
   music examples **87**, **119**, **122**,
      **138**, **353–5**
   tables
   *Andante* 134
   *Moderato* 110, 133
   *Presto* 134–5
Second Symphonic Suite 5, 69, 72,
   73, 89, 94, 111, 128, 129, 158,
   159–60, 179, 182, 185, 246,
   261, 297–308, 384
   *Largo Sinfonico* 89, 111, 129,
      261, 268, 297–308, 309,
      317, 384
   *Ouvertüre Concertante* 128,
      159–60, 297, 384
   *Perpetuum mobile (Rondo)*
      297, 384
   *Promenaden–Marsch* 297, 384
   *Thema con Variazioni* 297, 384
   *Toccata* 129, 297, 384
   music examples **128–9**, **130**,
      **302–3**, **304**, **305**, **306**, **307**,
      **374–5**
   tables
   *Largo Sinfonico* 299–301, 303
   *Ouvertüre Concertante*,
      palindromic structure 160
Serenata for cello and piano 130,
   160, 319–24, 387
   music examples **321**, **377**
   table, formal structure and set
      structure 322–3
*Sinfonietta in B flat* 4, 72, 386
*6 June* 69

16 Tragoudia [Songs] 66, 384
*Small Chorale and Fugue* 64, 381
*Sonata Concertante* 66, 180, 385
Sonata for solo violin 22, 24, 25, 182, 380
Sonatina for cello and piano 94, 324–30, 387
   music examples **326, 327, 377**
   table, *Allegro moderato* 325, 328–9
Sonatina for piano solo 22, 24, 380
'The song of the locksmith' 386
*Sowing* 72, 386
String Quartet 380
String Trio 21, 380
Suite for cello and piano 382
Suite No.2 for piano 383
Suite No.3 for piano 384
Suite No.4 for piano 384
Suite for piano solo 380
Suite for two pianos 23, 380
Suite for violin and piano 21, 25, 380
Ten Canons for piano 64, 382
*Ten Sketches* for string orchestra 4, 65, 73, 180, 383
*Tender Melody* for cello and piano 73, 319, 331–6, 387
   music examples **332, 333, 334, 335, 378**
   table, formal structure 331
'The music' for voice and piano 385
'The sandy beach' for voice and piano 385
Third Piano Concerto (Third Concerto for piano, ten winds and percussion) 64, 158, 161, 163, 173, 174, 182, 187, 280, 287–97, 382
   music example **289, 290, 291, 293, 294, 372**
   tables
   *Allegro giocoso* 295–6
   *Andante sostenuto* 292
   *Moderato* 288–9
Third Sonatina for violin and piano 115, 116, 120, 121, 126, 142, 144–6, 213, 233–8, 249, 381

   music examples **120, 121, 144, 145, 146, 233, 235, 236, 238, 356**
   table, *Allegro giusto* 116, 234–5
Third String Quartet 63, 97, 102–3, 109–11, 115–16, 117–18, 125–6, 185, 213–21, 221–5, 225–32, 238, 286, 381
   music examples **104, 110, 215, 216, 218, 219, 220, 224, 229, 350–52**
   tables
   *Allegro moderato* 118, 214
   *Allegro vivace (Rondo)* 116, 226–8, 230–31
   *Andante* 222–3, 225
*32 Piano Pieces* 4, 65, 138, 180, 185, 383
*Three Greek Songs* for violin and piano 385
*The Trawler* (*The Trawl-Boat*) 72, 73, 387
'The unknown soldier' for choir and orchestra 35, 381
*The Vintage* 72, 386
Violin Concerto (Concerto for Violin and orchestra) 64, 111, 112–13, 158, 179, 280, 282–7, 382
   music examples **112, 283, 286, 370–71**
   table, *Molto appassionato* 284–5
chronological list, 379–87
compositional development 179–336
   Berlin works 181–211
   expansion of the strict twelve-note technique 245–73
   linear serialism of mid-1930s, strict twelve-note technique 213–44
   tonal serialism 319–36
   towards a free dodecaphonic technique 275–317
compositional periods, NS
   according to Mantzourani 5–6
   according to Papaioannou 2–3
compositional styles, NS 4, 337–8

atonal music, NS compositions
    4, 5, 64, 67, 74, 76, 180, 182,
    216, 252, 287, 296, 338
atonality, and NS 4, 182, 335
bitonality, and NS 148, 181, 225
folk-song, folkloristic
    (arrangements, elements,
    material), NS 1, 4, 5, 6,
    12, 21, 37, 49, 50, 51, 55,
    56, 64, 66, 68, 73, 74, 337,
    382, 383, 385, 387, 391
tonal music, and NS 1, 4, 5,
    6, 37, 50, 72, 74, 93, 131,
    319, 338
developing variation, NS's version
    of 99, 100, 101, 125, 188, 190,
    282, 310
forms
    binary 137, 152, 159, 163, 182,
        184, 246, 254, 270, 279
    cyclical (form) 160–75, 287–97
    fugue 131, 156, 310, 313, 314,
        315
    reversed sonata 153, 156, 171,
        174, 188, 233, 234, 238,
        275, 290, 293, 296
    rondo 121, 131, 132, 158, 161,
        162, 174, 175, 188, 194,
        200, 202, 209, 211, 221,
        225–31, 235, 237, 238,
        243, 244, 268–73, 292,
        320–24, 339
    rounded binary 162, 182, 188,
        209
    sonata 7, 132, 152–3, 185,
        188, 196, 202, 203, 221,
        233, 234, 235, 237, 238,
        239, 240, 246, 270, 279,
        282, 287, 296, 297, 298,
        303, 309, 310, 314, 326,
        328–9, 331, 331, 333, 336
    ternary 131, 139, 152, 158,
        174, 187, 200, 203, 221,
        234, 236, 240, 243, 244,
        247, 248, 261, 265, 310,
        314, 320, 322–3, 324,
    variation (theme and variation,
        *Thema con Variazioni*) 70,
        88, 131, 137, 139, 140,
        142, 143, 171–2, 174, 175,
        182–5, 187, 245, 246,
        252–5, 297, 298–308, 331
Haidari concentration camp, NS in
    68–9, 70
music examples, list xv–xx
    *see also* compositions (NS)
photographs, NS **ii, 16, 23, 40, 42,
    60, 62, 75**
pitch-class collection(s) 4, 7, 139,
    140, 142, 146, 149, 163, 179,
    180, 181, 183, 185, 187, 189,
    191, 200, 266, 275, 279, 282,
    285, 291, 309, 314, 316, 317,
    320
*Reihen* 7, 83, 88, 94, 261, 338
sets, list **343–78**
signature, NS **77**
tables, list xi-xiv
    *see also* compositions (NS)
trope 83, 94, 320, 325
twelve-note technique, NS 80–86,
    87–175
    sets and set-groups 87–98
        chordal sets 83, 89–91,
            179, 213, 246, 261
        derived sets (NS) 101, 113,
            115–23, 132, 161, 162,
            166, 195, 197, 206,
            209, 225, 232, 236,
            282, 290, 309
        incomplete sets 83, 97,
            173, 201
        'iridescent' sets 190
        irregular sets 83, 97, 228
        linearly ordered sets (linear
            sets) 83, 102, 132, 190,
            246, 268
        sets defined by their
            segmental content 83,
            94–7, 105, 179
        supersets 83, 91–3, 213,
            246, 265, 268–71,
            297–8, 304, 317
        tonal sets 83, 93–4, 95,
            109, 115, 152, 232,
            320, 338

set-groups consisting of several
  discrete sets in polyphonic
  combinations 87–9
manipulation of the sets 99–114
  free manipulation of pitch-
    class content 100–101,
    111–14, 138–9, 213
  interpolation of segments
    100, 102, 106–7, 112,
    115, 118, 142, 228,
    233, 299, 309
  partitioning of sets and free
    distribution of notes in
    texture 108–9
  permutation, internal pitch-
    class order 94, 99, 100,
    101, 103–4, 142, 184
  pitch-class doubling,
    repetition (within
    single sets) 100, 101–3
  segmental rotation/
    permutation 100,
    104–6, 107, 121, 142,
    144–6, 159, 162, 233,
    234, 243, 320, 330
  simultaneous presentation
    of segments
    in polyphonic
    combinations 109–11
derivation techniques 101,
  115–23
  cyclic rotation 115,
    120–33, 161
  interchanging one pitch-
    class in each hexachord
    115, 118, 120, 126,
    236, 289
  pairing of notes and
    segment interpolation
    118–20
  through source trichords
    and tetrachords, derived
    sets 115–16, 236
  unordered hexachords of
    transposed, retrograde
    and inverted set forms
    117–18
serial transformations 125–30

inversion, set 7, 115, 117,
  118, 123, 125, 129–30,
  147, 160, 190, 191,
  194, 195, 197, 268,
  319, 320
retrograde, set 7, 88, 106,
  113, 114, 115, 117, 118,
  125, 126–9, 130, 146,
  158–9, 162, 163, 171,
  194, 195, 196, 197,
  203, 206, 221, 224,
  225, 232, 237, 243,
  268, 275, 277, 279,
  298, 305, 325, 326, 329
transposition, set 7, 115,
  117, 118, 123, 125–6,
  147, 158, 160, 190,
  191, 195, 196, 201,
  219, 221, 283, 298,
  319, 320
set structure and phrase structure
  131–49, 225, 263, 268
  harmonic areas through
    segmental rotation
    142–6
  harmonic change and
    reiteration of fixed
    harmonic formations
    137–42
  in 'free' twelve-note works
    146–8
  periodicity of twelve-note
    set-groups 132–6, 324
  tonal centres 136–7, 202,
    203, 338
set structure and large-scale
  form 151–75
  inversion, large scale 319–24
  palindromes, large-scale
    retrograde 158–60,
    162, 163, 172, 197,
    213, 275, 279, 280,
    284, 287, 291, 292
  transposition, large-scale,
    textural, *en block* 151,
    152, 153–8, 163, 173,
    181, 185, 188, 193,
    197, 200, 209–11, 213,

275, 279, 280, 282, 286, 287, 316, 317
splitting off of sets 249, 261–2
texture, twelve-note 7, 83, 84, 87, 89, 91, 95, 100, 102, 104, 108, 109, 110, 111, 113, 117–18, 126, 131, 138, 139, 146, 147, 148–9, 151, 152, 156, 157, 158, 159, 179, 180, 181, 185, 190, 191, 194, 195, 196, 199, 200, 201, 202, 203–8, 211, 214, 228, 250, 251, 252, 255–8, 266, 271, 279, 286, 287, 290, 305, 307, 317, 331
verticalization as compositional process 261–5
writings, NS 66, 391–2
*Treatise on Orchestration* 66, 308
Sklavos, George 56
Skokos, Antonis 22, 54, 63
Skouloudis, Manolis, *Cyclops*, NS orchestration of 57
Society of Skalkottas's Friends 2, 379
Spanoudi, Sofia 45
Stein, Erwin 83
Stein, Rolf 35
Straus, Johann 232
and *Die Fledermaus* operetta 232

Stravinsky, Igor 21, 43, 81, 99, 136, 255, 382, 385

Temko, Matla 30, 31, 32, 39, 41, 48, 49, 51, 52, 58, 60, 62, 63, 67, 71, 76, 245
NS, relationship 30–32, 48–9, 52
Theodoropoulou, Avra 64, 73, 74
Thornley, John 13, 20, 31, 32, 35, 36, 39, 48, 55, 57, 70, 125, 379
Tsitsanis, Vasilis 70

Varvoglis, Marios 15, 27, 54
Venizelos, Eleftherios 43, 50
Government of 53, 56
Vlastou, Dora 61, 67, 74, 76
Vokos, Yorgos 73, 76

Wagner, Richard 39, 44
Wagner tubas 308
Webern, Anton 1, 34, 82, 83, 84, 94, 115, 151, 211, 339
Weill, Kurt 17, 19, 20, 21, 22
Weimar Republic 17

Xirelis, Titos 22

Zemlinsky, Alexander von 35
Zillig, Winfried, 1, 32, 34, 37
Zweig, Fritz 35